These essays by leading theorists and researchers in sociocultural, cognitive, developmental, and educational psychology honor the memory of Sylvia Scribner, whose work is recognized by each of the author as germinal to their own thinking. The themes include the relationship between history and culture, the importance of context to thinking, the place of literacy in human activity and thought, and cognition in school and in the workplace. The volume presents applications of activity theory to fundamental issues in human behavior at work, in school, and in problem solving situations, and it analyzes historical–societal processes in science and culture. Scribner's conviction that science holds a responsibility to human welfare and understanding is carried on in these chapters.

Sociocultural psychology

Learning in doing: Social cognitive, and computational perspectives
General Editors: Roy Pea and John Seely Brown

The Construction Zone: Working for cognitive change in school
Dennis Newman, Peg Griffin, and Michael Cole

Plans and situated actions: The problem of human-machine interaction
Lucy Suchman

Situated Learning: Legitimate peripheral participation
Jean Lave and Etienne Wenger

Street Mathematics and School Mathematics
Terezinha Nunes, Analucia Dias Schliemann, David William Carraher

Distributed Cognitions: Psychological and Educational Considerations
Gavriel Salomon (editor)

Understanding Practice: Perspectives on activity and context
Seth Chaiklin and Jean Lave (editors)

Sociocultural Studies of Mind
James V. Wertsch, Pablo del Rio, Amelia Alvarez (editors)

Sociocultural Psychology: Theory and practice of doing and knowing
Laura M. W. Martin, Katherine Nelson, and Ethel Tobach (editors)

Sociocultural psychology

Theory and practice of doing and knowing

Edited by

LAURA M. W. MARTIN
Arizona Science Center

KATHERINE NELSON
City University of New York Graduate Center

ETHEL TOBACH
American Museum of Natural History

CAMBRIDGE
UNIVERSITY PRESS

Published by the Press Syndicate of the University of Cambridge
The Pitt Building, Trumpington Street, Cambridge CB2 1RP
40 West 20th Street, New York, NY 10011-4211, USA
10 Stamford Road, Oakleigh, Melbourne 3166, Australia

First published in 1995

Printed in the United State of America

Library of Congress *Cataloging-in-Publication Data*

Sociocultural psychology : theory and practice of doing and knowing /
edited by Laura M.W. Martin, Katherine Nelson, Ethel Tobach.
p.   cm. – (Learning in doing)
Includes index.
ISBN 0-521-46278-9 (hc)
1. Social psychology.   2. Culture.   I. Martin, Laura M. W., 1947–
. II. Nelson, Katherine.   III. Tobach, Ethel, 1921–   .
IV. Series.
HM251.S68715   1995
302 – dc20   95-16445
                                                            CIP

A catalog record for this book is available from the British Library

ISBN 0-521-46278-9 Hardback

Contents

Series foreword

This series for Cambridge University Press is becoming widely known as an international forum for studies of situated learning and cognition.

Innovative contributions are being made by anthropology, by cognitive, developmental, and cultural psychology, by computer science, by education, and by social theory. These contributions are providing the basis for new ways of understanding the social, historical, and contextual nature of the learning, thinking, and practice emerging from human activity. The empirical settings of these research inquiries range from the classroom, to the workplace, to the high technology office, to learning in the streets and in other communities of practice.

The situated nature of learning and remembering through activity is a central fact. It may appear obvious that human minds develop in social situations, and that they come to appropriate the tools that culture provides to support and extend their sphere of activity and communicative competencies. But cognitive theories of knowledge representation and learning alone have not provided sufficient insight into these relationships.

This series was born of the conviction that new and exciting interdisciplinary syntheses are under way, as scholars and practitioners from diverse fields seek to develop theory and empirical investigations adequate for characterizing the complex relations of social and mental life, and for understanding successful learning wherever it occurs. The series invites contributions that advance our understanding of these seminal issues.

Roy Pea
John Seely Brown

Preface

In the 1980s, as Sylvia Scribner's research shifted direction from her concern with the influence of literacy on thinking towards the modes of thinking exhibited in different activity contexts, she began planning to integrate her work in a form that would bring together different problem areas. She was looking forward to consolidating what she had learned from the past 10 years of research on learning at work into a book, or books. One idea was to synthesize her ideas in a monograph on activity and development by examining the function of each leading activity in life – play, school, and work. To prepare, she had been reading in the areas of dialectical philosophy, Soviet theory, concept development, play, work studies, and biology.

Her last years of research carried out in the Laboratory for Cognitive Studies of Work were intense, with little opportunity for reflection, and her last illness came on suddenly and lasted a few brief months. Thus, she never had the opportunity to carry out her plan.

At the time of her death in 1991, she had nearly completed two sets of empirical studies, funded by the Spencer Foundation, the National Center for Education and the Economy, and the National Center for Research on Vocational Education. These studies expanded her ideas from earlier research on workplace cognition in a dairy plant, investigating how the introduction of new technologies affected activity and thought in factory settings. Sylvia's unifying interest, of course, was studying changes in thinking as they relate to changes in work experience. This is a derivation of the fundamental question concerning the relation between culture and cognition, which motivated her work from the time that she began her career in experimental psychology in the 1960s.

Her completed work speaks for itself, and no book could substitute for what she might have produced if she had had the time. But many of those who were close to her at different times and who were influenced by her thinking wanted to put together a volume that reflected her thinking and the ways in which she influenced the thinking of others.

When Sylvia became ill early in 1991, we informed her that we wanted to produce a volume in her honor. She was pleased, especially since she felt that women scholars are too seldom given such recognition. She had a number of ideas that we have tried to incorporate, and she suggested names of people who might be willing to contribute to such a volume. Each contributor was asked to write an original chapter on a topic that had been a focus of Sylvia's own thinking at some point in her career. Each chapter reflects the point of view of the writer, as well as the interests and influences of Sylvia's thought. This is a festschrift by her colleagues; none of the contributors were her students in the usual sense, although all were her students in a deeper sense.

Sylvia's influence has been great and continues. Two books have been organized in her honor. This first volume is a collection of papers by colleagues in appreciation of her contributions to their own thinking and research. The second volume is a set of selected papers by her. The two volumes offer a fitting testament to a provocative psychologist and citizen of the world.

Laura M. W. Martin
Katherine Nelson
Ethel Tobach

Reference

Scribner, S. (1985). Vygotsky's uses of history. In J. V. Wertsch (Ed.), *Culture, communication and cognition*. New York: Cambridge University Press.

Contributors

Jerome Bruner
Department of Psychology
New York University
New York, New York

Michael Cole
Laboratory of Comparative
  Human Cognition
University of California,
  San Diego
La Jolla, California

Yrjö Engeström
Laboratory of Comparative
  Human Cognition
University of California,
  San Diego
La Jolla, California

Rachel Joffe Falmagne
Department of Psychology
Clark University
Worcester, Massachusetts

Joseph Glick
Developmental Psychology
City University of New York
Graduate Center
New York, New York

Howard E. Gruber
Teachers College
Columbia University
New York, New York

Fran Hagstrom
Department of Psychology
Clark University
Worcester, Massachusetts

Giyoo Hatano
Keio University
Tokyo, Japan

Mariane Hedegaard
Institute of Psychology
Aarhus University
Denmark

William Hirst
Department of Psychology
New School for Social Research
New York, New York

Eve Kikas
Tartu University
Tartu, Estonia

David Manier
Department of Psychology
New School for Social Research
New York, New York

Laura M. W. Martin
Arizona Science Center
Phoenix, Arizona

Tracy Masiello
University of Utah
Salt Lake City, Utah

Katherine Nelson
Developmental Psychology
City University of New York
Graduate Center
New York, New York

Barbara Radziszewska
University of Southern
  California
Los Angeles, California

Barbara Rogoff
Department of Psychology
University of California,
  Santa Cruz
Santa Cruz, California

Robert Serpell
Department of Psychology
University of Maryland,
Baltimore County
and University of Zambia

Ethel Tobach
Curator Emerita
American Museum of Natural
  History
New York, New York

James V. Wertsch
Department of Psychology
Clark University
Worcester, Massachusetts

1 Introduction

Laura M. W. Martin, Katherine Nelson, and Ethel Tobach

Scribner's historical moment in psychology, 1968–1991

The psychology that Sylvia Scribner entered from the New School for Social Research in the 1960s was a discipline newly emerging from the hegemony of learning theory and its antagonists in gestalt psychology, represented by her graduate mentor, Mary Henle. The 1960s cognitive revolution opened new doors to previously hidden landscapes; the study of mind and language were again seen as legitimate topics in psychology. Furthermore, the social and political forces of the time brought issues of schooling as a basis for educational opportunity to the forefront of national concerns. Thus Scribner's attraction to the problems of the relation of literacy, schooling, and thinking was initially in tune with the psychology of the times.

Cognitive psychology very shortly took a different turn, entering the 1970s with a fixation on the processing of information, the universal characteristics of the computational mind, and the innate basis of language and intelligence. From 1970 to 1985, concerns of cultural and contextual influences on the development of thinking skills, including issues of schooling and literacy moved to the periphery for mainstream psychologists, including developmental psychologists.

Scribner's own trajectory combined research on topics of contemporary concern to cognitive psychologists with a continuing emphasis on those issues that she viewed as most fundamental. For example, in the early 1970s she joined Michael Cole's Laboratory of Comparative Human Cognition at Rockefeller University and turned to studies of syllogistic reasoning and categorization among the Kpelle of West Africa. Her papers on these topics, which were of central interest to cognitive psychologists, became classics in the problem solving literature. Her work in this area helped to bring about recognition of contextual factors in cognitive studies. After a 20-year period of information processing dominance, cognitive psychology became more open to alternative frameworks in the mid-1980s, particularly as dissonant computer models entered the scene, challenging the monolithic symbol crunching model. At that point, different modes of thinking and representation, and of cognitive change – from novice to expert or from one conceptual model to another – both characteristic of Scribner's ongoing research concerns, became central problems within the larger field.

Although the issues are no longer viewed in terms of the dichotomies of the 1960s, the fundamental problems of modes of thinking and speaking, of literacy, of activity contexts, of cultural practices, and of education and cognitive change are now on the agenda for cognitive psychology. Scribner's contributions to these changes in the field are palpable in the works presented in this volume by many of those who found their own research enriched by her thinking, in person and in writing. The activity theory approach to cognitive psychology emerged as an alternative framework in the 1980s, incorporating many of the themes that had been the focus of Scribner's work, and it is strongly represented in the papers published here. As James Wertsch points out in his chapter, however, Scribner's work was grounded in the conviction that human thinking should be studied as a socioculturally situated activity. The general theme of "doing and knowing" is, we believe, more inclusive than any specific theory of activity, as her own thinking was not confined by any existing theory.

An outstanding characteristic of Scribner's intellectual activity was its integration of traditional dichotomies or opposites; for example, the values informing society and science, intellectual or mental and manual, "naturalistic settings" and the laboratory. She was skeptical of questions put in ways that did not explicate the assumptions underlying their formulation, and she did not accept a formulation that denied the relative nature of the possible answers to the questions. She understood that the questions and the answers reflected the situations in which they were generated, the motivations for their positing, and their theoretical history. This critical skepticism led her to the view that rather than separate factors representing an irresolvable contradiction these processes could be integrated through the recognition of their interdependence and connectedness.

In her own work, from her earliest research activities in the trade union movement, Scribner integrated the historical and societal setting of the issue that she was investigating. This integration was evident in her approach to understanding the societal significance of the treatment of "mental health" populations, and the need to see research and societal process components of such treatment as complementary and inter-related, each process moving into the other to produce changes that were necessary. This integrated approach meant that there was no separation between the societal significance of research and the search for knowl-edge.

The integrative approach was revealed in her methods, designed to ensure that the inquiry was founded on the lives of the individuals stud-ied. In Scribner's perspective, cognitive function and artifact production in manual work were never separated. The abstract and the concrete were an integrated whole, functioning together to result in the activity of the individual, the group, and society.

Organization of the book

The chapters in this book are organized in four sections, based on four themes of Sylvia Scribner's work, which came to the forefront during different periods of her career. The first section is titled "History and Culture." These papers deal with the sociohistorical and cultural processes in human development, an interest reflected in her work on the influence of schooling on thinking and in her concern with historical influences on contemporary thought. The section "Knowing and Tell-ing" concerns issues of conceptualization, problem solving, abstract thinking, and literacy, all issues that were at the forefront of her research in cognition.

The section "Doing Psychology" might in other places be called "Methodology," a major issue in Scribner's view of the discipline of psy-chology. To solve the central theoretical problems of psychology she believed that appropriate methods must be developed. She did not reject the traditional experimental method, where appropriate, but she saw it as one method among others in the science of psychology that focused on thinking in meaningful activities. Indeed, she developed a sequence of methodological approaches to study thinking in the workplace, of which experimental simulations were one part of the sequence, following eth-nographic accounts and systematic studies in the workplace itself. Her book with Michael Cole on literacy studies among the Vai people in Africa contains a fine account of developing methods "on site" as problems arose and a priori assumptions were challenged. Indeed, "Doing Psychology" was a major concern for Scribner throughout her career.

"Activity in Work and School" is the section heading we chose for the papers that relate most closely to the later phases of Scribner's research, when formal activity theory became part of her theoretical approach, and when her work concerned learning in formal and informal settings, notably in the workplace. In a sense this returned her to her roots, having spent her earlier career in a labor organization of electrical workers, during which time she gained an enduring respect for the thinking workers carry out in the course of their everyday jobs. Her studies of dairy workers filling orders preceded her last investigations of representational change in the face of automation and computer control of factory production, where she worked out her ideas about "practical" thinking. Thus this last section brings Scribner's thinking full circle. It is appropriate that it also includes one paper by a long-standing friend from her earliest days in psychology, Howard Gruber, as well as representatives of later encounters with the issues brought forth in the activity theory of the 1990s.

History and culture

The papers in this section share a significant meaning in Scribner's life and work. In her analysis of Vygotsky's use of history, and in the development of her research in community mental health, in literacy and cognition in Africa, and in education and cognition in the workplace, the integration of the sociohistorical situation in which the individual functioned and the particular personal history of the individual was the core of her outlook. This outlook extended from broad, encompassing societal history (the effects of the involvement of the United States in the Vietnam War, the significance of slave trading among the Vai) to specific experience in the workplace (individual differences in problem solving in the dairy industry). In all these situations, the developmental process of human history and individual history were serious considerations.

In Robert Serpell's paper, the sweep of colonial history and the Western history of educational practice and theory are intertwined in the particular solution of a social welfare problem by the work of training individuals. Ethel Tobach's paper offers an evolutionary history of human development. In Jerome Bruner's chapter the relationship between the historical changes in Tsarist and Communist Russia are seen as intimately interdependent with the history of Vygotsky as a theoretician and as a working scientist. In these chapters the intensive concern with individual consciousness and societal processes is clearly brought out. In the Serpell paper, the need for attention to the consciousness of the practitioner and theoretician is shown to be significant for a valid and viable sociopolitical application of psychology. In Bruner's chapter consciousness and language within the historic context are preeminent features.

Serpell addresses situation, history, and the cross-cultural approach at the societal level that engaged Scribner for most of her academic and professional life: the sociopolitical. The significance of the use of this term, rather than sociohistorical, is clear in his analysis of the introduction of Western schooling philosophy and practice into African society in Zambia. Serpell focuses on the value of understanding the sociohistorical context of theory and practice by describing how the concept of age-graded curricula was generated, how Herbartian educational policies were appropriated by different societies, such as Japan and the United States, through processes particular to each society, and how these educational activities were carried out in a colonialized society. The transfer of practice from one society to another transforms the practice in the light of the sociohistory of the receiving society. Thus, the rigid procedures derived from their educational history are adopted in Japan for different reasons than those underlying their adoption in Zambia.

He examines in detail the solution of a human welfare problem, the delivery of health care services, by the use of educational techniques derived from these histories. The results obtained can only be understood by viewing the concept of "situation" as encompassing ontogenetic and cultural processes. Taking this approach increases the likelihood that psychology can contribute constructively to development of public policies.

Tobach examines the "discontinuity" of what has been defined as uniquely human – labor and its relation to the development of mind – in the evolution of behavior from the point of view of integrative levels applied to units of analysis from activity theory. *Integrative levels* is a concept that helps organize our thinking about the processes and functions of the organism and its environment as they act on and change each other. It can bridge the distinction between biological concepts of energy exchange and cultural ones, as when an organism internalizes an aspect of its social milieu. When applied to the notion of activity, Tobach proposes, the construct of integrative levels can help elucidate the transformations that characterize different stages of phylogenetic development. It also illuminates the connection between such "higher order" activities as reflection with motivation and need states. Tobach decribes how integration of the notion of activity seen across categories of development can account for the ultimate "discontinuity" of human goal-directed activity; that is, activity that is reflective, that makes use of tools and symbols, and that is mediated.

History and culture tell the story of the mediated nature of human interaction with the world. They tell the story of how the use of signs and tools in the service of a goal-directed activity transforms the meaning of those signs and tools, and how these transformations enter into human activity systems. In tracing the history of these concepts, Tobach argues that the material basis of evolutionary theory was necessary to develop an understanding of the development of mind, as activity theory is necessary to understand the origins of the human species. Tobach calls for further work defining levels of human labor, a mission that work in Scribner's tradition could address as it searches to identify specific mediating factors contributing to intellectual functioning through work activity.

Bruner's chapter offers an approach to the questions inherent in the process by which the individual participates in society and at the same time gains consciousness about that participation, questions that attracted Scribner to Vygotsky's work, seeking answers in the material substrate from which consciousness and mind develop. Bruner seeks answers stemming from Russian literature and history, seeing literature as a guide for understanding the individual and participation in society. He offers an analysis of the particularities of Russian history from Tsarist through Communist eras. He shows how the language itself, as well as the scientific and literary activities of the individual, reflect the effects of societal history on the individual's understanding of consciousness and mind. He proposes that the special characteristics of that history and consciousness were and are derived from conflicts between an intrinsic interest in human subjectivity and an equal interest in objective knowledge. These conflicts took different forms in Tsarist times and in the Communist era, and Bruner brings the significant actors in the drama into their historical chronology: writers such as Dostoyevsky and

Chernyshevsky, as well as Akhmatova, Mandelstam, and Jakobson; scientists such as Sechenov and Pavlov; and political players such as Lenin, Trotsky, Stalin, and Krushchev.

Against this ongoing political scenario, Bruner draws a clear picture of Vygotsky as an inspiration to his students and colleagues, and as a burr under the skin of those in power. Bruner's emphasis on the "duet between language and consciousness" brings him to an optimistic proposal for the resolution of the Russian conflict: that the Russian people may now be "free to exercise the Russian genius for collective introspection and consciousness . . . that will restore the Russian strength."

The three papers in this section reveal the richness of the scholarly community in which Scribner participated. We take these papers as examples of different uses of "history," but which all speak to issues of how we understand our theories, paradigms, and the very language of psychology.

Doing psychology

This section of the book brings together four pieces which are, on the surface, about very different domains – memory, collaborative learning, informal education, and workplace cognition. The pieces, however, share questions that have to do with how psychology gets done. The chapters try, as Cole writes, "to change history through research which provide[s] deeper insight into how things had come to be the way they are and how they might be changed to serve current human ends." Hirst and Manier, for example, trace the way in which traditional cognitive psychology came to confront the limitations of its discoveries when settings outside the laboratory were examined. Rogoff, Radziszewska, and Masiello, who have been viewing cognitive development in the exchanges between mothers and children, raise questions about methods and units of analysis in the study of developmental change from a sociocultural perspective. Martin examines one application of Scribner's method of moving from naturalistic setting to laboratory and the constraints of that method on the investigator. Finally, Cole describes transformative educational work done in afterschool centers and shows how a very different "meso-genetic" reporting window is needed to capture the nature of the transformations. Each piece discusses the "cultural and historical embeddedness of the inquiry itself" (Rogoff et al., chapter 6) and each represents a call for a new kind of discourse that allows sociocultural elements to be part of the analysis.

Beginning the section, Hirst and Manier chart the conflict between limiting a study to tidy laboratory evidence and accounting for the messy, real-life factors that influence cognitive functioning. They portray the complacency among cognitive psychologists, particularly those studying memory, even as the need to address practical questions arose. Specifically, they describe the preprogrammed machine metaphors and the kinds of investigations they entailed as well as more contextual, user-driven models. They argue that the original goal of cognitive psychology to understand meaning was subverted by computational metaphors.

They review the literature of expert–novice, voluntary–involuntary memory, and "situated actions," in a continuing search for universal cognitive machinery, which may be, after all, unreachable. Models that posit distributed memory or remembering across individuals find that people may externalize rather than internalize in the process of remembering, using objects as well as other people. Hirst and Manier's research shows that the conversational roles adopted by individuals in a remembering situation affect the nature of what is remembered. They conclude that "memory grows out of social interactions," and that research questions and methods must be adopted to reflect this understanding. Hirst and Manier do not advocate discarding principles of memory but they argue for the need to integrate those generalities into culture, experience, and intention, so as to construct a scientific picture more faithful to reality, ultimately better accounting for human inventiveness, ingenuity, and diversity.

Rogoff, Radziszewska, and Masiello's chapter summarizes some assumptions of a sociocultural developmental perspective, that is, "a view of processes and individual development as they constitute and are constituted by interpersonal and cultural/historical activities and practices." Their work, as Rogoff's has in the past, contributes to the discussion of what exactly is an analysis of development according to a sociocultural (or Vygotskian) perspective. In doing so, the authors describe the concept of activity as a unit of analysis that can accommodate the multileveled, cross-individual, and cross-situational elements that enter into development and learning at levels of individual change, cultural transfer, and societal practices. Studying the process of organizing practices, specifically, is argued to capture the range of societal to individual development.

The learning process itself, in turn, can be understood as both structured by and constituting activities.

The authors then describe research on young children's acquisition of planning strategies whose results were not easy to interpret. The problem was that structuring activities that took place between children and their mothers in interaction did not relate to the children's subsequent performance on individual posttests. Rogoff and her colleagues describe the methods they used and the hypotheses they tested as well as the results, concluding that the use of the individual posttest cannot be treated as a stable measure of the outcome of a series of interactions because "from a sociocultural perspective, no situation is context-free" and therefore posttests themselves are situations with particular meaning. In fact, acquisition itself is an elusive phenomenon to capture, since application of specific skills is ever evolving as well. The authors suggest what might be examined in observations that do capture the dynamism and historical distinctness of situations, linking these to what we know about how information gets communicated and how activities get structured.

Martin's chapter discusses an attempt to understand cognitive change in manufacturing activity affected by the introduction of computer technology. Using Scribner's method of beginning with ethnographic data to develop critical task distinctions that capture cognitive development on the job, Martin and her colleagues identified constancies, schisms, and transformations of thought between manual and electronically based activity systems. Problems arose, however, in making links between hypotheses developed from the observational level and behavior in the more experimental settings. As in the other chapters in the section, difficulties of drawing a valid, sociohistorical picture while identifying causative elements in the development of thought were encountered. Martin argues that the full story of task design and subject selection should be told in order to shed light on why links appear or fail to appear between analyses in the two settings.

In searching for a way to carry out a sociocultural or sociohistorical approach to doing psychology, Cole proposes a solution to disentangle universals of human mental processes from processes that are shaped by particular cultural circumstances, or "history in the present." The dilemma of demonstrating that different streams of history influence each other and how is approached by Cole through studying activity systems within a window of change appropriately calibrated for a model system. Cole and his colleagues have been working over a period of time in after school settings, arranging social and technological encounters between children, undergraduates, and computers that could be said to broaden the children's information organizing repertoires and the youth programs' repertoires of resources for supporting children's growth. Cole recognizes that all the players are transformed in the process. What he also examines is the analysts' discovery of how events in the history of the project or planned for the future could both be traced, resulting in a new kind of analytic method: the story can be told backwards and forwards. By conducting both system analyses and analyses of individual growth and development using multiple data sources, this "mesogenetic" experimental window, in which transformations of individuals and systems are attempted in a relatively compressed time frame, yields a fuller, more organic picture of the relationship between factors that abide and those that are variable. This approach also reveals the variety of stories that can be told about a developing system, depending on the level of activity highlighted.

The papers in this section deal with issues of method, but go beyond the traditional concerns of elegant designs, control conditions, and independent and dependent variables to address the now-urgent issues of how to study cognition in all its messy real-world context and emerge with satisfying answers that hold across situations and times. The solutions are not immediately obvious, but the papers provide provocative insights into the problems.

Knowing and telling

Cognition and language have been the topics of the major portion of psychological research for the past 30 years. They have been presented primarily as static, separate, structural domains by the dominant theoretical paradigms, in contrast to the dynamic interaction implied by Vygotsky's *Thinking and Speech*. The implications of activity theory for studying cognition and language led us to reconceptualize the topic as "knowing and telling," emphasizing the situatedness in both time and space of any cognitive or linguistic activity. Further, the developmental trajectory of levels of thinking and telling demands new examination. In particular, the influence of literacy on thinking has been a key problem in this regard for many years, and was the point of departure for Sylvia Scribner's initial forays into cognitive psychology.

In this section the first two papers by Falmagne and Nelson are concerned with forms or levels of thought within the same individual or different individuals over time and situations. Falmagne's chapter characterizes different approaches to the typologies of the abstract and the concrete in the mentalist cognitive framework in comparison with dialectical logic and activity theory. These typologies are related in turn to formal and content distinctions, and to syntactic and semantic distinctions, as found in cognitive science and logical philosophical writing. Falmagne's view takes two levels of representation into account – a permanent knowledge representation that contains both syntactic and semantic relations, and an on-line problem representation that may or may not be formal. Her analysis is designed to draw out distinctions blurred in conventional accounts and to see the formal and nonformal as two parts of the same process. She introduces Barwise's situation semantics and logic as a radical reconceptualization of context as integral to process, while yet confining context to the immediate situation, and not broadening it to general knowledge structures with their historical and cultural implications. Finally, Scribner's approach is seen as integrating the activity and cognitive science views of the formal–content dichotomy in her analysis of practical and theoretical thinking. In this analysis also, context is viewed as part of the system of problem solving; theoretical thinking is, however, divorced from the concrete context, whereas practical thinking involves "mastery of the concrete." This chapter elegantly traces the tensions found in attempts to reconcile the formal abstractions of higher mental activity with the contentful situatedness of practical cognitive activity, ultimately resolved in the recognition that all thinking is situated in human activity. Modes of thinking invoke context in different ways: narrowly and broadly, abstractly and concretely.

The chapter by Nelson addresses a related question from the developmental point of view. Vygotsky's notion of the relation between spontaneous and scientific concepts is considered in the light of contemporary research on the development of children's conceptual processes. The thesis put forth is that children's initial concepts are "infiltrated" by the conventional categories displayed in the language of the community through an implicit process of deriving word meaning from social discourse. Thus exposure to the categories of language evokes a first implicit culturally mediated system of concepts, which is nonetheless individually constructed and coordinated with the prior nonlinguisitic system based on direct experience. "Scientific concepts" in Vygotsky's sense are viewed as explicit top-down systems that must be coordinated with the system derived from everyday natural language practice. Examples of the constructed mediated system are given to illustrate the process, and the proposal is contrasted with other contemporary models that view conceptual change in childhood in terms of theory change. It is related also to Scribner's ideas about the synchronic existence of different modes of thinking in individuals and change in representational systems in adults.

The next two chapters in this section are concerned in different ways with the issues of literate thinking that were raised early in Scribner's career and remained continuing concerns. Hatano's chapter reexamines issues of literacy and literate thinking developed by Scribner and Cole in their book on literacy and thought. Scribner and Cole proposed a "practice account" of the effect of literacy, noting differential effects on other cognitive tasks depending upon the specific literate practice. Hatano is concerned with the mastery of a simple form of Japanese orthography by young schoolchildren, which is accomplished easily, and the question of how and why they go on to more complex forms required for full Japanese literacy. He hypothesizes that beginning orthographic skill affects the ability to acquire knowledge from text in another communication mode, oral or written. Hatano's thesis is that children enjoy the practice of early literacy based on a simple set of characters, but that cultural pressure and practice in school is necessary to acquire more advanced orthography. The situation is complex because in addition to hirigano characters, based on a form to sound syllabary, Japanese also uses kanji characters with no relation to sound that represent semantic meanings. Whereas a beginning set of kanji characters is easy for children to use, advanced literacy requires both types, including a large set of disambiguating kanji that must be committed to memory.

Hatano's claim is that types of scripts and how they represent words are critical constituents of literacy practices, and that the skills developed through literacy participation may vary accordingly. His experiments with varying scripts and languages support his supposition, which he believes is consistent with, although different from, the specific message about practice that Scribner and Cole set forth. He speculates on many details of the proposed effects that are likely to enrich the understanding of literacy and reinvigorate the investigation of its potential implications for cognition.

Wertsch, Hagstrom, and Kikas's chapter explicates a number of the issues of literate thinking through a reexamination of Scribner's conception of the "logical" genre in the light of the theory of genre developed by the Russian literary theorist, Bakhtin. Scribner, they point out, had viewed the performance of Kpelle peoples on logical syllogism tasks in terms of a distinction between "practical" and "theoretical" thinking, where the practical was grounded in the context of everyday knowledge of people and situations. Theoretical thinking was conceived to be decontexted from everyday knowledge and was specifically invoked through school instruction, a proposition that was emphasized by Luria. She conceived of schools as instantiating a logical genre and of schooled individuals as capable of performing within such a genre, where the concept of genre was drawn from Hymes's distinctions.

Wertsch and his colleagues show how Scribner's conception fits into Bakhtin's sociohistorical system of genre and performance (a fit she would not have known of at the time, when Bakhtin's work was still undiscovered by most American scholars). Wertsch and his colleagues extend this Bakhtinian analysis to the construction of the logical genre in classroom discourse, providing an example of the kind of analysis of the relationship between speech genre and thought that was prefigured in Scribner's original work of the 1970s and that, equipped with insights from Bakhtin's work, could be used to examine the relationship of speech and thinking in other contexts.

Activity in work and school

In returning to her concern with intelligent functioning in the workplace, Scribner was not satisfied with the then current discussions of technological change, which came mostly from a naive sociological, cognitive science, or business administration point of view. Basically, texts in these fields argued that while technology could more simply and efficiently be used for training and production, workers showed decreasing motivation as they used the new technology, and that reorganizing work teams in factories was a powerful way of combating a potential (but relative) decline in production.

Such theories and the observations that supported them were, in Scribner's view, simpleminded and misleading. Working with the ideas of such scholars of workplace dynamics as David Noble and Lena Norros, Scribner addressed the commonplace ideology that was being developed by business leaders and policymakers by posing questions about the category of work as an activity, the human choices that went into the design of the new technological tools, and the socially determined routes of access to working in new environments. Scribner was not content to accept analyses that overlooked the real controlling variables of workers' motivation. She did not accept job descriptions as accurate about the actual work performed or descriptive of the kind of mental effort that people invest in their work.

The chapters in this section address issues of activities in both work and school. The relation between the individual's consciousness and social interaction or participation is demonstrated in the paper by Hedegaard. She uses the sociocultural approach and concepts from activity theory, together with an analysis of educational process to explicate the internalization of content. Within the dialectical method of "developmental teaching" the child participates in the social group, including adults as well as peers, formulates the goals of the activity, and carries them out. Further, the child's motivation and knowledge change. Through the joint process of reflection and symbolic representation of the specific content, the leap in intellectual development is realized. A new stage of social development is reached in which the child appreciates others' goals and is able to evaluate and offer criticisms of other people's work. Moreover, the relation to the school as an institution develops as well.

In this presentation the conceptualization of history as different from animal evolution and historical chronology is seen. The experience of social activity in classroom learning is reflected in the child's changing objective knowledge, social consciousness, and theoretical conceptualization.

In the second chapter of this section, Engeström studies problem solving in the workplace by analyzing an activity that offers a vital service to the community: medical care. This study can be contrasted with the application of activity theory to problems of medical care in another culture, where the societal issues are quite different, as in the first chapter of this volume by Serpell. Scribner's work on the ways in which the mental health needs of society were handled in the United States in the 1960s posed problems similar to those addressed by Engeström. He adopts the sociohistorical approach, which was elaborated by Scribner in her discussion of Vygotsky's use of history (Scribner 1985). The collective participation of the people being served, and those who serve, is a major contribution of activity theory to human welfare, as is evident in this chapter. Engeström analyzes the interactions of individuals in different settings produced by the inherent dynamics of a social system that, because of its stated goal of service, supports the activities of the individuals in the service. Opportunities for individual initiative within a socially responsible and responsive setting are developed.

Applying the same theoretical and method approach to the court system in Finland leads Engestrom to a comparative analysis of relations within a two-dimensional model of vertical hierarchies and a complementary dimension of "horizontal" systems processes, and a discussion of the relation of this analysis to Scribner's similar process analysis. The resulting integration of the two dimensions in Engestrom's model is dialectically produced by the activity of the individual and the activity of the group.

Glick's chapter concerns the development and distribution of knowledge in the workplace and in school. It focuses on how the developmental assumptions of school enter into the activity of knowing in that environment, in comparison with activities and knowledge in work environments, emphasizing the implications of these differences for our theories and metatheories of cognitive development. He argues that in school the goal is assumed to be moving away from the concrete and toward the abstract, where in work environments (specifically, production and management) theoretical (abstract) and practical (concrete) knowledge are assumed to be different domains. These assumptions are now being challenged in settings employing computer control of production, where theory begins to gain control over practice, and where the distribution of knowledge is critical. Activity (production) is transformed into the theory of activity, and the coordination of the two into a system of knowledge is accomplished.

The implication is that a new perspective on the dichotomy between the abstract and the concrete is required that is relevant to the practices of school and to our ideas about development. Glick's analysis is provocative but promissory, providing many strands to be followed or unraveled as the evolution of new automated work settings continues. This chapter is based in part on the continuing work of the Laboratory of

Cognitive Studies of Work that Scribner initiated at CUNY. Thus it is not surprising that it addresses the very issues of practical/theoretical, abstract/concrete, and transformation of knowledge systems with which she was centrally involved over the last decade of her research.

In the last chapter, Gruber conceptualizes the evolution of the meaning of work in the constantly changing human history. The technical changes that concerned Scribner are seen in their effect on human activity, resulting in the possibility of a change in the duration of engagement in various activities over a lifetime. Gruber organizes these changes within the concept of Lifespan Discretionary Time. Whereas for most of human history and for most of humanity, lives are controlled by the need to engage in alienating and demeaning work in order to survive, technical change can bring about a liberating quality of survival, offering the individual opportunities for choices of activities during one's lifetime. This may lead to a flourishing of creativity, the development of new activities that enrich the human experience.

This possibility is the basis for Gruber's analysis of the motivations for work in their historical and individual settings: intrinsic motivation, ego motivation, motivation to help others (extending not only to those in social relationships but to the planet as a whole). The need to sustain oneself is seen as a basic level in the hierarchy of motivation, but Gruber concludes from a systems approach that the concept of hierarchy of motivation does not account for the fact that more than one motivation functions simultaneously, and that no particular motivation is necessarily more significant than another. The relation between quantity and quality emerges from this analysis: the quantity of time allotted to motivated behavior not only produces difference in quality of activity, but the quality of activity organizes the quantitative character of one's lifetime. On this Gruber founds an optimistic visionary realism based on the ability of the human species to solve problems and to bring about a consonance between the need to survive and the need to engage in creative liberating activities. This chapter brings us full circle to the relation between culture, history, and the diversity of human activities in the lives of individuals with which this book is centrally concerned, emphasizing that cultural change is embedded in individual activity and in our participation in the activities of our communities. Psychology is a vital part of the community of work and benefits from the collaboration of its members in setting and solving problems.

These chapters might have been organized differently, because each of the chapters speaks to many levels of analysis. We have seen throughout the significance of historical windows on the individual and society, the importance of situations and settings, of levels of knowing and thinking, of particulars and universals, the perspective on culture and society as both agency and product. The interpenetration of theory and practice, of doing and knowing evident in these chapters was an essential characteristic of Scribner's work and activities. This interpenetration is embodied in the version of sociocultural psychology presented here. The ideas assembled in these chapters are provocative in Sylvia's tradition. We hope they will contribute to the continuing discussion and development of her ways of doing and knowing.

Part I

History and culture

2 Situated theory as a bridge between psychology, history, and educational practices[1]

Robert Serpell

The context of theoretical explanation in developmental psychology

The explanations offered in psychology for behavior and experience arise from a cultural activity. The adequacy of a theory's analytic categories is determined partly by the inherent structure of the phenomena we as theorists seek to explain – by the degree to which it succeeds in cutting the objective world "at its joints" (Boyd 1979) – and partly by the perspective that it adopts on a set of human concerns. The perspective originates from a position that is both socially defined and situationally motivated. The purpose for which we are attempting to analyze or to "cut up" the phenomena constitutes the situational motivation, and this in turn can only be understood with reference to the social relations between the author, her subject, and her audience – the context in which this purpose is formulated (Serpell 1990).

The inspiration for this chapter came from two papers by Sylvia Scribner (1976, 1985). The first is a methodological plea for distinguishing between issues of ecological validity and issues of experimental control. The second is an exploration of the role of history in explanations of cognitive development. I believe that the significance of her earlier methodological argument can only be fully appreciated if it is complemented with a sociopolitical insight implicit in her later theoretical analysis.

In the elegant paper "Situating the experiment in cross-cultural research" Scribner (1976) argues that the scientific advantages of experimental control do not carry with them a necessary implication of artificiality and lack of ecological validity. The term *situated* in the title of that paper carries two distinct but related connotations for me. On the one hand, Scribner makes a case for a particular kind of relevance of experi-

21

ments to cross-cultural research. On the other hand, the particular function that she advocates for the experiment in cross-cultural research entails designing experiments in a special way that we may call "situating" them within the range of recurrent settings structured by a given cultural system.

The key to Scribner's argument is that experiments are merely one of many types of context for cognitive behavior within a cultural system of activities. Like any other type of context, experiments have certain distinctive demand characteristics (Orne 1962). We should, therefore, no more dismiss them as intrinsically lacking in ecological validity than we should accept the classical assumption that they are content-free frameworks deriving all of their meaning from the explicit instructions specified in the experimental procedures. Rather we should seek "through an interweaving of experimental and ethnographic research" (Scribner, 1976, p. 317) to explore, for each sociohistorically specific, ecocultural niche, "how situations vary in their cognitive demands and how the particular experimental paradigm we are using fits into this spectrum" (Scribner, 1976, p. 319).

In this chapter I shall argue that, over and above culturally situating our experiments, we also need to situate our theories in the dynamic flow of cultural–historical processes. Before developing this argument, I want to acknowledge further inspiration from another paper by Sylvia Scribner that is quite different in character, devoted to a theoretical analysis and extension of "Vygotsky's uses of history." Here, Scribner (1985) argues that while Vygotsky's writing on the subject of the relationship between history and human development verges on obscurity at times, his analysis was more subtle than his critics have acknowledged, and that, in his more lucid passages, he is careful to distinguish between the character of two lines of development, one running through history, the other running through ontogenesis. Vygotsky's approach, as Scribner interprets it, was

an attempt to weave three strands of history – general history, child history, and the history of mental functions – into one explanatory account of the formation of specifically human aspects of human nature. (Scribner 1985, p. 138)

Tracing the course of development at each of these levels is an enormously complex task; analyzing the relations among them – explicating the pattern of the "weaving" – is even more complex.

Although Scribner contends that Vygotsky's position is unmistakably opposed to the parallelism and recapitulationism that have been criticized as characteristic of many developmental theories of the same era (Gould 1977; LCHC 1983), she feels that he did not "use the historical approach to the fullest" (Scribner 1985, p. 138), and she therefore proposes an expansion of the scheme that he outlined.

In Vygotsky's theory, [general] history appears as a single unidirectional course of socio-cultural change. It is a world process that informs us of the genesis of specifically human forms of behavior and their changing structures and functions in the past. For Vygotsky's model-building purposes, it might have been sufficient to look back at history and view it in this way as one stream of development.[2] But for purposes of concrete research, and for theory development in the present, such a view seems inadequate. . . . Individual societal histories are not independent of the world process, but neither are they reducible to it. To take account of this plurality, the Vygotskian framework needs to be expanded to incorporate a "fourth-level" of history – the history of individual societies. (Scribner 1985, p. 138–139)

To me the most inspiring part of Scribner's paper is precisely this last elaboration. Not only do we encounter discontinuities between individual societies as we move across the globe at a given point in time, but the sequence of events and contingencies that characterize the history of each of these societies is unique. As a result, extrapolation from the experience of one society to that of another is extraordinarily hazardous, because the criteria for evaluation of a particular innovation are necessarily grounded in the current preoccupations of those to whom it is addressed. Indeed, what is hailed as a crucial contribution to social progress in one society may be construed as diversionary or counterproductive in another.

In arguing the case for situated theory, I too will use the term *situated* in two distinct, albeit cognate, ways. First, I shall seek to show that we can better understand the challenge of practical application for developmental psychology by examining the ways in which our theory relates to preconceptions and preoccupations of politically significant groups in society. Secondly, I shall seek to show how psychological analyses can better connect with praxis if they are situated within a multidimensional array of perspectives from several complementary types of analysis. In short, psychological theory needs to be situated both with reference to the general intellectual climate of its primary audience and also with reference to other academic disciplines. To adequately situate psychology for warranted social intervention entails working out in detail the technical relevance of each concept for the particular forms of work, child rearing, hazards to mental health, etc. that prevail in the society for which the program is being designed.

I shall discuss three historical processes in the formation of psychological theory: (1) how a set of pretheoretical ideas about psychological development were formed in the context of institutional change; (2) how a set of explicit theoretical ideas about psychological development was molded and transformed in various ways by different groups of scholars in the service of their particular society's political agenda; and (3) how the sociopolitical character of transfer of technology in the late twentieth century serves to constrain what is learned in a third-world society from psychological theory developed elsewhere.

My first example will consider the historical processes that initially shaped the distinctively Western cultural institution of schooling. This general institutional form is now very widely diffused across many different contemporary societies, and is responsible for sustaining a remarkably resilient set of assumptions about the nature of child development and education. Next, I shall consider in more detail how one particular theoretical formulation within the Western educational tradition, namely the Herbartian formalization of instruction, was historically transformed in different ways in response to the demands of three different sociocultural contexts. Finally, narrowing my focus still further, I shall evaluate some more recent applications of psychological theory to educational practice in the sociopolitical context of the third-world nation of Zambia.

Historical generation of a cultural institution: The age-graded school[3]

One of the most consistent features of the contemporary school is its division of the curriculum into a series of grades through which the student is expected to pass as she or he matures. So closely are the phases of instruction linked to this age-graded progression that parents, teachers, and psychologists are not infrequently somewhat confused about their respective contributions to cognitive development. Moreover, in ` societies that lack the economic resources to provide universal access to the complete school curriculum, elementary schools find themselves in the invidious position of preparing their students for a selection process that most of them are doomed to fail. Under these conditions, elementary schools established to provide an educational service to rural communities all over Africa tend to proclaim an extractive definition of success. Instead of strengthening the capacity of the youth to contribute to the welfare of their community, the curriculum is designed to prepare them for functioning in an economically privileged, culturally alien, and often geographically remote, urban environment (Serpell 1993).

Part of the key to understanding this apparently self-defeating orientation of formal schooling for many rural African communities lies in the historical fact that the seeds of the present were more or less consciously exported by European educators during the first half of the twentieth century. Much has been written by political analysts about the motives of those pioneering teachers and their sponsors in the missionary and colonial administration concerning whether their goals were emancipatory or oppressive, humanitarian or exploitative (Rodney 1972; Snelson 1974; Serpell & Mwanalushi 1976; Tignor 1976; Ball 1983). Yet, in a longer term perspective, it may be less important to interpret the intentions of those actors than the nature of the ideas they left behind. Since the independence movement gained momentum in Africa through the 1960s and 1970s, these ideas have been appropriated by an indigenous leadership, and they have continued to evolve, while the provision of formal education has expanded far beyond the scope of what was established or indeed probably ever envisaged by its missionary and colonial pioneers.

The modern elementary or primary school is a remarkable cultural invention, designed as an instrumental approach to ecological adaptation through a specialized method of child rearing. Its origins are complex, and I will focus on one particularly salient feature in this chapter: the gradation of the curriculum into a sequence of steps each of which must be mastered before the student may embark on the next. This has now become a crucial tenet of modern educational orthodoxy. Two historical factors appear to have been critical in generating this pedagogical pattern: the formalization of didactic process and the stepwise matching of instruction with age.

Aries (1962) has documented the gradual and somewhat uneven emergence of the modern concept of the school class or grade in European schools between the sixteenth and nineteenth centuries. It is quite clear from his account (1) that schooling was institutionalized long before the gradation of students into a succession of classes was attempted, and (2) that the original function of this gradation was

to separate students according to their capacities and the difficulty of the subject matter, not to separate students according to their ages. (Aries 1962, p. 188)

The explicit formalization of a concept of didactic process became an issue of importance to educational writers within the context of a general fascination with explicit methodology that characterized the European historical epochs of the Renaissance and the Enlightenment (Berlin 1956). A supremely explicit version of the pedagogical principles that began to accumulate in the context of formal schooling during that period is the *Great Didactic* by Comenius, first published in 1657, which survived in multiple editions throughout the eighteenth century, and was acknowledged in the nineteenth century as an authoritative statement of the paradigm:

The function of pedagogy, as Comenius sees it, . . . is a mechanical operation. Comenius freely admits this and, in fact, boasts of it – 'Hitherto the method of instruction has been so uncertain that scarcely anyone would dare to say: "In so many years I will bring this youth to such and such a point; I will educate him in such and such a way . . . we must see if it be possible to place the art of instruction on such a firm basis that sure and certain progress can be made"' . . . 'a suitable environment must be provided and materials prepared, impediments must be removed, difficulties avoided and assistance given where required. Then the timing must be right and the programme must advance through the simplest steps possible, with everything necessary for success and nothing irrelevant.' (Sadler 1966, p. 202)[4]

Sadler's account of Comenius's systematic approach shows that it foreshadowed not only many of the principles of programmed machine instruction but also some of the ideas which are often associated in the twentieth century with Piaget and Froebel. But most important was his commitment to the formalization of a set of methods that could be reproduced on a massive scale through concretely specified instructional procedures, teaching aids, and above all textbooks.

Aries (1962) documents the tortuous path along which the institutional forms of European schooling evolved. The students of the first medieval universities ranged very widely in age and it was the residential arrangements of the colleges – originally conceived as boarding houses – rather than any pedagogical principles of curriculum design, that provided the initial impetus for the definition of age grades which has come to dominate educational theory and practice in modern times. It took about five centuries for a gradual consensus to emerge among the professional educators and the upper and middle classes of European society that children's minds develop along a course from vulnerable innocence to maturity that can be charted in a stepwise fashion corresponding to grades of instruction.

Whereas parents and teachers in the twelfth to fifteenth centuries apparently saw nothing wrong with mixed grouping of students ranging in age from 10 to 20 years, thereafter, especially during the seventeenth century, a doctrine arose that childish innocence requires "safeguarding against pollution by life" (Aries 1962, p. 119). This was held by those responsible for pedagogy to entail the need for adults to display "modesty" in the presence of children, avoiding the use of any behavior (including speech) with sexual connotations, segregating boys from girls, and as far as possible separating preadolescent students from adolescents. Yet it was not until the early nineteenth century that

the regularization of the annual cycle of promotions, the habit of making all the pupils go through the complete series of classes instead of only a few, and the requirements of a new system of teaching adapted to smaller, more homogeneous classes, resulted . . . in an increasingly close correspondence between age and class." (Aries, 1962, pp. 239–240)

The projection of this curricular gradation onto teachers' and parents' expectations of children at different ages has since become a Western cultural theme of great importance, influencing both the conception of education and that of child development. On the one hand, it serves to legitimate the organization of knowledge into a hierarchy of elements best taught and learned sequentially, working up from the basics to higher and advanced stages. On the other hand, it has come to inform the notion that a child's maturation is incomplete in the absence of specifiable learning experiences that follow a natural progression in the school curriculum.

The endurance of this age-by-grade matching as an integral feature of public education around the world underpins the metaphor of educational progress as climbing a staircase: a unilinear sequence of somewhat arduous movements along a predetermined path with a known set of discrete intervals and a specific, exalted destination. Several peculiar consequences have flowed historically from this conceptualization. First, "adult education, widespread in the fifteenth and sixteenth centuries disappeared in the seventeenth century and its place was taken by an education confined to children" (Aries 1962, pp. 300–301). Concomitantly, the role of "learner" became institutionalized as intrinsically suited to an immature mind. As a result, since adult education was reinvented in the nineteenth century it has had to struggle to throw off an image of education as a condescending process in which the teacher has an obligation to control and direct the student along a predetermined path. The implications of this theme of condescension include an asymmetry in the flow of information between teacher and student such that the timing of class activities is strictly controlled by the teacher and any deviation by a student from prescribed forms of behavior is subject to authoritarian correction by the teacher.

Secondly, this asymmetry has become available as a legitimating ideology for the stigmatization of whole sections of adult society, such as women, the poor, and foreigners, who for social and political reasons have not had access to the socialization institutionalized in 'our' kind of schooling. Rather than seeing these out-groups as different but equal, the equation of schooling with normal child socialization has encouraged the "products" of Western schooling to look down on them as incomplete human beings, either to be pitied for their deprivation or to be despised as not deserving this essential ingredient of becoming fully human.

This stigmatization of the unschooled as incomplete also found fertile ground in the missionaries' project of evangelization. The recipients of schooling in Africa were not only perceived by these exogenous teachers as needing "civilization," but as lost souls in danger of perdition (Snelson 1974). Schooling was conceived as an effective instrument for deliberately inducing a process of cultural change. Not only were the missionaries uncompromisingly committed to a particular religious interpretation of social and moral behavior, but they were also deeply and for the most part unquestioningly attached to the principles of contemporary Western civil life, including commerce and administration. As a result they generally saw little or no conflict between their evangelizing objectives and the imperialistic expansion of their governments' sphere of influence. In Central Africa they were thus, at best unwittingly, often instrumental in paving the way for colonial occupation.[5]

When missionaries exported the Western model of schooling to Africa, it seems that stepwise gradation of the curriculum and the assumption that the beginning student is immature were effortlessly compounded with an ethnocentric assumption of cultural superiority to justify a condescending style of pedagogy. This condescending, indeed often author-itarian, style has remained such a salient feature of schooling even in those institutions that are now run by indigenous, lay teachers employed by the government that it has acquired the appearance of a local or regional educational tradition.

Why was this particular feature of an exogenous cultural practice taken up with such commitment by African teachers? Was their appropriation of this rigidity a sign of intellectual insecurity, a protective strategy against the uncomfortable possibility that the curriculum they were administering was, in some dimly apprehended sense, fundamentally incompatible with indigenous cultural values? Or was it, rather, an acci-dental convergence between an authentic, indigenous socialization theme – the importance of respectful obedience to one's seniors – and the political overlay of colonial domination through which they encoun-tered Western education that gave rise to a conviction that only through strong discipline can a student be well raised? Stirrings of unease have been expressed by some would-be educational reformers in Africa, and the current of democratization that has swept through the domain of government in many parts of the continent in the early 1990s may create conditions more conducive to egalitarian forms of educational discourse than in the previous two decades. But the scope for innovation at the local level, whether in matters of curriculum content or in styles of instruction, is severely constrained by the prevalence of a sharply age-graded curriculum that lends itself so easily to centralized, bureaucratic control.

Transformative appropriation of theory in different societal histories

Johann Friedrich Herbart (1776–1841) is regarded as one of the founding fathers of modern, systematic education. He is also cited as an influential figure in early formulations of a *Volkerpschologie* in Germany and elsewhere on the continent, and as a progenitor of mathematical psy-chology (Cole, personal communication). A contemporary of Hegel, Fichte, and Schelling, he achieved rather limited recognition in his own time, although he published extensively in the fields of philosophy, psy-chology, and pedagogy and lectured at two German universities over a period of 40 years. It was not until the 1860s, 20 years after his death, that Herbart's ideas were taken up and promoted on a large scale as a focused educational doctrine. According to Dunkel (1969, 1970), the key proponents of the doctrine, Ziller and Rein, who promoted it under the title of *Herbartianism*, not only clarified but also drastically pruned Herbart's perspective, dropping the entire metaphysical base and relegating the ethical aspect to a sideline. Four steps of instruction were proposed by Herbart in his *General Pedagogy*: clarity (focusing the student's concentration on some single object of instruction by removing all obscurities); association (mixing the topic up with many others, relaxing concentration, and generating a felt need for order in chaos); system (introducing a tentative order, such as grammar or scientific laws, in response to the felt need to generate unity); and method (revealing the principles on which the system is based, the grounds for unity, and a test of the system's validity). The psychological rationale for this approach was that learning requires an alternation between concentration and reflection. Ziller and Rein, in addition to expanding and renaming the series of instructional steps, added two very significant dimensions to the scheme: concentration centers or topics for each year of study and a chronological sequence for these topics spread over eight years of the curriculum. This sequence reflected the notion that the child should recapitulate the intellectual history of his species and focused on a parallel sequence in German history.

Ziller apparently conceived of education as a strategic resource for societal reform; in particular, to improve the lot of the lower classes by educating them en masse. Many social reformers and intellectuals in the nineteenth century saw history as a crucial dimension for the understanding of reality in general and the human condition in particular (Dixon and Lerner 1992). Whereas Herbart toyed with the idea that certain aspects of classical literature, including Homer's epic poem the *Odyssey* and the histories of Herodotus and Tacitus, portrayed life in a naively simple way especially suitable for catching the imagination of young pupils, Ziller took a much stronger and more systematically recapitulationist approach, specifying a curricular sequence through biblical and German historical epochs as successive themes for the concentration of instruction.

Dunkel provides a thoughtful analysis of why such a scheme could become so influential on education in the United States at the turn of the nineteenth century. The felt need in the United States at the time was for "a pedagogy that was academically respectable and scientific, yet simple and practical" (Dunkel 1969, p. 245). Three young men from Illinois, DeGarmo and the McMurry brothers, traveled to Germany, a plausible source of theoretical respectability in the field of pedagogy in that epoch of American history, and found Herbartianism the dominant doctrine in both of the major German centers of pedagogical studies, Jena and Leipzig. On their return to the United States, they actively reinterpreted and promoted the doctrine for audiences of American teachers, who found it more accessible and digestible than Pestalozzianism, Hegelianism, or the incipient Child Study movement of G. S. Hall. Yet within less than 20 years the Herbartian movement had declined to the point of virtual extinction in American education, eclipsed by experimental psychology, the child-centered approach, and a focus on learning rather than on instruction.

The writings of the Herbartian school were translated into all the languages of Europe in the latter decades of the nineteenth century, and doubtless exercised considerable influence on education in several countries. One striking other context in which the doctrine was taken up was Japan. The Japanese government invited a German Herbartian scholar, Hausknecht, to teach at the University of Tokyo in 1887. Inagaki (1986, p. 79) notes that

there was . . . a major difference in the way Herbartian theory was understood and accepted in the United States and in Japan. In the United States, it was the Herbartian theory of curriculum and material construction, incorporating the concept of the methodological unit, which was adopted and developed. In Japan, however, where the government regulated curriculum and materials, the concept of formal steps, specifying the teacher's instructional procedures, was the element adopted.

One application of this concept that still continues to characterize instructional practices in Japanese elementary school science classes is described by Inagaki (1986) as follows:

Japanese teachers begin with divergent discussion, encouraging children to express their own ideas and predictions. Gradually, however, discussion focuses on major issues or questions that teachers have prepared in advance. Teachers take the leading role in the discussion, guiding students to prescribed conclusions. (p. 87)

While Inagaki expresses some misgivings about the educational value of this approach, other observers (e.g., Stigler and Perry 1988) have commended the Japanese focus on teacher-led, coherent class discussions culminating in prescribed consensus as responsible for high levels of academic achievement in the field of mathematics. Should we conclude that the particular form in which Herbartianism was incorporated in Japanese education was determined by the receptiveness of Japanese teachers to this dimension of the doctrine?

According to one Japanese theorist, "the context of reapplication of Herbartian theory was more responsible for the patterning of classroom instruction than the application itself, though the latter may have contributed" (Hatano, personal communication; cf. Serpell & Hatano, forthcoming). The question is as difficult to answer as the one raised earlier concerning the receptiveness of African teachers to the theme of teacher–learner asymmetry in the imported Western pedagogy. Inagaki himself takes the view that curricular elements of Herbartianism simply had no chance to take root in Japan at that time because the government of the day insisted on completely centralized control of all aspects of the schools' curriculum (Sayeki, personal communication). Either way, from a formal metatheoretical point of view, the lesson to be learned from this chapter of history seems to be that theoretical ideas make the transition from one society to another (be it successive generations within the same country or contemporaneous groups in distant parts of the world) through a transmission process that is governed by factors quite distinct from those that impinge on interpersonal communication among individuals.

In the case of Herbart, the situation in which the theory imported from Europe was deployed led to quite different emphases by Japanese and American interpreters of the neo-Herbartians. The latter in their turn had already selectively appropriated Herbart's ideas and developed a theory that suited their concerns. Dunkel takes a somewhat despondent view of this "educational ghost story" (1970) as illustrating "the way in which time grinds the edges off once clear-cut ideas and tosses the transformed remnants onto the general pile of educational thought" (1969, p. 132). But this verdict fails to give credit to the purposive focus with which theoretical ideas are transformed by those who appropriate them for their effective application in new social situations. As we turn in the next section to the analysis of a contemporary situation, the necessity of such purposeful choice among theoretical alternatives may become more apparent.

Application of theory to education in a contemporary society[6]

In this section, I propose to adopt a somewhat narrower focus in order to examine in detail some ways in which psychological theory can be deployed in the articulation of practical interventions in a contemporary society. I hope to show that, at this microlevel of analysis, the need to situate theory in a wider set of sociopolitical issues is just as important as it was in understanding the ways in which the broad conceptualizations of child development and education have been exported to Africa within the institution of schooling, and the ways in which the sociopolitical context transformed the focus of Herbartian theory in its various applications in different sociohistorical contexts. In order to highlight the challenge of contextual demands, I have selected for analysis an application of psychological theory to the design of an educational program that lies outside the normative assumptions of the regular school system: the training of adults for responsibility in the field of primary health care.

The sociohistorical context of this final case study is the contemporary state of Zambia in central Africa: a complex society caught up in a process of dramatic historical change, at the interface between a set of indigenous cultures based on subsistence agriculture, village settlements, and extended kinship networks, and an urban, industrial culture introduced from the West over the past century by mining prospectors, missionaries, and colonial administrators. By comparison with many other countries in Africa, Zambia in the 1980s could be characterized as a relatively modern, industrialized, and stable nation-state, including among its local resources a University Teaching Hospital where high-technology diagnostic and therapeutic techniques were in place for a number of conditions, largely operated by indigenous personnel. On the other hand, it remained true that more than 50% of the population lived in rural areas without electricity or piped water, and that preventable and/or treatable diseases such as diarrhea, measles, and malaria combined to claim many hundreds of children's lives every year. The formal sector labor force which had never exceeded 25% of the adult, working population had been shrinking steadily in both relative and absolute numbers since 1971. And the government's development planning rhetoric had shifted in the two decades since independence (following five decades of colonial occupation by Britain) from an emphasis on the expansion of free public education, health services, and infrastructural resources, such as tarred, all-weather roads, toward a much more modest set of basic needs and community self-reliance goals.

Government now acknowledged that the hospital services of the city would never cater on their own to the health care needs of the vast majority of the population, and development planners were devoting a good deal of attention to the mobilization of popular participation in the improvement of the health and welfare of people living in underserved rural areas. Inspired by the World Health Organization's (1978) Alma Ata declaration on Primary Health Care (PHC), the Zambian government launched a vigorous nationwide program to lay the foundations for such an approach to the delivery of affordable, decentralized health services with an emphasis on preventive health education. In contrast with the earlier policy principle that health services could only be disseminated to remote rural communities by training and deploying highly skilled professional personnel from the center, this new PHC program started from the premise that every community is immediately entitled to health services accessible within a radius of 15 miles from the client's home residence.

Within the framework of this initiative, several opportunities arose for educational application of psychology. One was the concept of the Community Health Worker (CHW). In order to meet the shortfall of highly trained professional personnel, the PHC program declared its intention to recruit and train local residents to provide basic primary health care. Adult education, especially when it is embedded in a service delivery system, always poses a challenge to the traditional assumptions of the pedagogy developed for use in classrooms populated by a homogeneous age group of immature children (see Levine 1982). When the services and personnel in question are situated in a sociocultural system that shares few of the standard features of an urban, industrialized society, the challenges are rendered even more stark.

Lindiwe Makubalo (forthcoming) describes the design of a Community Health Workers Handbook (Inambao & Makubalo 1986) with particular attention to its capacity to communicate ideas in the short term as a teaching resource and in the long term as a guide to intervention by a trained CHW. The motivation for this focus arose from a logistical decision to encourage the selection of middle-aged women and men as CHWs "because these tend to command more respect in their communities" than the previously favored younger products of the 1970s program of "universal and free" primary education. Also the duration of initial training "was reduced to two modules of 2 weeks each with a 4–6 month break between modules to enable CHWs to practice their skills and supervisors to observe and critically monitor their performance." In order to optimize communication with such trainees under these conditions, "the content of the course was simplified to concentrate largely on the most common disease conditions that can be treated by peripheral health workers, and preventive/promotive efforts." In addition, special efforts were made to design a picture symbol and color code system that "would guide the user to the correct page of the manual, . . . assist him/her to make a diagnosis, . . . serve to guide on drug dosage, . . . guide the CHW to the correct medicine bottle and the record book page, differentiat[ing] between age and sex." Two strands of psychological theory informed the design of this communication system: pictorial representation theory and memory coding theory.

Pictorial representation theory was originally developed to explain a set of "difficulties" encountered by "unacculturated" groups in Africa and elsewhere with the "perception" of Western-style line-drawings and photographs (Hudson 1960, 1967; Deregowski 1968; Serpell & Deregowski 1980). More recently McBean, Kaggwa, & Bugembe (1980) have shifted attention within the same set of theoretical parameters to the optimal use of pictorial conventions to represent real-life phenomena in the context of communication about issues related to economic and social development. By selectively deploying those pictorial features that are most reliably interpreted by perceivers with limited prior exposure to Western pictures and photographs, illustrators can maximize the effectiveness of their pictures in communicating "development" messages. This principle was followed by Makubalo in the design of illustrations for the Community Health Workers Handbook. For instance, the outline of key elements were printed in heavy type, and the artist avoided potentially ambiguous superimpositions and juxtapositions of figures represented as lying at different distances from the perceiver in the third dimension of "pictorial depth."

Memory coding theory was originally used successfully to predict differences in the relative perceptual salience and consequent ease of memorizing various colors and shapes depending on the accessibility of distinctive verbal categories for encoding them (Brown & Lenneberg 1954;

Carroll & Casagrande 1958). Makubalo selected a set of colors for which distinctive names exist in the local languages of Isoka District in northern Zambia, and paired each color with a particular group of illnesses for which it had a culturally plausible, iconic connotation. According to Makubalo the application of these psychological theories to the handbook was quite successful. "Having repeated and acted out these codes, the CHWs understood them quite easily and quickly memorized them. . . . (and) with constant practice and supervision the learners all got a good grasp of what was being taught." A skeptical evaluator might object that there were no control groups against which to compare the comprehension and retention of CHWs trained with this particular method. But at least these short-term observations are consistent with the hypothesis that psychological theory was applicable in this instance to the design of good educational practice and public health policy.

Two other factors, however, which received no explicit attention in the design of the intervention, may have significantly reduced the effectiveness of this application: utilization customs for written materials and community expectations of the behavior of trained health workers.

Some indication of the importance of the first of these constraints arose from pilot studies of the impact of a related program of Community Based Rehabilitation (CBR). The concept of CBR has a somewhat similar rationale to PHC, centering on the mobilization of local resources to meet basic needs. But it is both narrower in focus and more decentralized in strategy. Directed at meeting the needs of persons with serious impairments and disabilities, its guiding principle is that, whenever possible, direct, hands-on services should be provided by members of the disabled individual's family and neighborhood, within the context of the client's local home community, with professionals playing a supportive, back-up role.

During the National Campaign to Reach Disabled Children (Serpell, Nabuzoka, Ng'andu, & Sinyangwe 1988) a number of CBR Training Packages were distributed to families with a disabled child containing detailed guidance on how to train such children in self-help skills and activities of daily living. These packages were designed by a WHO team (Helander, Mendis, & Nelson 1980) along similar lines to Makubalo's Community Health Worker's Handbook, with simplified content and line drawings. At the moment of distribution, disability ascertainment personnel were briefed to explain the messages contained in the packages and to advise nonliterate family members to go over the procedures in consultation with a literate local resource person. Yet during a small sample of follow-up visits (Serpell & Nabuzoka 1985) we found that some families had carefully stored these packages away without ever using them. It seemed that they were regarded as valuable documents not to be lost, not as useful resources for the day-to-day management or education of the disabled child.

The two-week training modules for Makubalo's CHWs included much more detailed explanation than was often feasible for individual clients in the Campaign to Reach Disabled Children, and comprehension and rehearsal were reinforced through discussion, role-playing, and peer teaching. Nevertheless the evidence of different patterns of deployment of literacy skills in different cultural traditions (Scribner & Cole 1981) should serve as a warning against assuming that CHWs with only a few years of schooling would necessarily apply their training by regular reference to their manual in the prescribed manner. Indeed, short of imparting the full range of information retrieval skills associated with Western literacy, training a respected adult to rely on printed routines might tend to "cramp her style" and undermine her image as a competent practitioner.

A second constraining factor is that of community expectations. The effective value of the service provided by a Community Health Worker depends critically on the confidence she inspires in her potential clientele. The decision to limit the training of CHWs to the treatment of a small set of highly prevalent diseases and to emphasize preventive and promotional health activities appears rational from the perspective of a central planner deciding on the distribution of limited resources. But from a grass-roots perspective, the addition to a rural community of a trained health worker may seem of little value if that training does not impart some expertise beyond the existing knowledge of ordinary members of the community. This seems to have been one connotation of the rhetorical complaint raised by a local resident at an Isoka Primary Health Project seminar: "are these just doctors of pit-latrines?" (Makubalo, personal communication).

To recapitulate, the success of this application of psychological theory to the design of an adult education program in the field of primary health care could have been enhanced by situating the theory more broadly in the sociopolitical context of its application. The illustrations of the Community Health Workers Handbook are doubtless more intelligible than they would have been if they were prepared without explicit attention to pictorial perception cues. And the handbook's carefully designed coding scheme no doubt makes the information contained in it easier to retrieve and to memorize. Yet microanalysis of behavior will only deliver substantial practical benefits if it is embedded within a more macrosocial account of ways in which social relations affect the individual's deployment of his or her behavioral repertoire. In addition to the mechanisms of perception and memory we need to understand the processes of social pressure and role performance in order to predict and influence how a Community Health Worker will apply her training in the field.

The interface between cultural history and psychoeducational theory

In each of the three case studies presented above, I have attributed to historically particular circumstances the form of a project in applied educational psychology. The matching of grade with age in the modern school curriculum arose in Europe from a gradual convergence of Enlightenment philosophy with moral concerns about residential arrangements extrinsic to the pedagogical process. The various adaptations of Herbart's theoretical ideas by late nineteenth-century German, American, and Japanese educators were responsive to the constraints and challenges of each society's political conditions. And the cultural conditions of contemporary Zambia placed limitations on the effectiveness of theories of pictorial representation and memory coding for designing a training program for Community Health Workers.

Through the lens of these case studies I have explored in turn three different ways in which psychological theory may be considered culturally and historically situated: (1) How does cultural history contribute to the generation of theory in the field of educational psychology? (2) How does it influence the transfer and appropriation of such theory across generations and across societies? (3) How does it constrain the ways in which such theory is applied in practice? The focus of my analysis of the interface between cultural history and psychoeducational theory shifted as we moved from generation to appropriation to application. To argue that cultural history contributes to the generation of theory leaves open the question of whether what is generated is empowering of social progress. For Aries (1962), the regularization of age-to-grade matching was a reflection of "discovery" of a psychological reality – cutting the world at its joints. Yet, I have suggested, the resulting preoccupation with age has given rise to some socially hazardous consequences: the stigmatization of unschooled persons as incomplete and the infusion of instruction with condescension. Thus while we may not find it easy to dismiss the sense of progress achieved by this developmentally sensitized conception of schooling, acknowledging its cultural and historical situatedness may help us to acknowledge and to resist its tendency to distort certain aspects of cognition and instruction.

When contrasting the different ways in which Herbartian theory was transformed in the course of its appropriation to the felt social needs of America and Japan at the end of the nineteenth century, I raised the more explicitly relativistic possibility that historical developments that seemed natural to one society were incompatible with the sociopolitical goals of another. Yet Inagaki (1986) concludes his balanced appraisal of differences between American and Japanese schooling with the suggestion that both societies face the same underlying problem of how to reconcile the technical demands of modernization with the humanitarian ideals of child-centered education. Acknowledging the particularity of cultural strategies need not blind us to commonalities among the human problems they address.

In the last case study, by stepping into the contemporary world, my analysis shifted from the interpretation of history to the issue of how to choose among alternative policy options. Without undermining the concepts of authentic choice and moral responsibility essential to decision making, it seems to me important to retain even on the contemporary scene some of the perspectival character of the historical analyses of earlier eras. A narrow technological view of how psychology can and should contribute to the design of public policy in the field of human services typically fails because the outcomes are not socially viable. A situated theory of individual development and learning will enhance both its cultural validity and its practical utility by acknowledging not only that ontogeny is constrained and canalized by the interaction of biological with social processes, but also that theoretical conceptions of that interaction are themselves a response to particular, historically evolving, cultural concerns.

Notes

1. I am grateful to Laura Martin, Michael Cole, and Wade Boykin for their suggestions on how to revise an earlier draft of this paper.
2. Alternatively, we might suggest that this is a juncture at which Marxist–Leninist ideology led Vygotsky astray. For many interpreters of Marx, the pattern of historical change, at least in the political arena, is overwhelmingly determined by certain broad and inevitable tendencies somewhat similar to those of natural evolution.
3. This section of the paper draws on the text of chapter 3 in my book, *The significance of schooling* (Serpell 1993), where I argue in more detail that the kind of education offered in rural Zambian primary schools contains an ambitious set of promises, which in general have not been fulfilled.
4. The punctuation of this passage in Sadler's book is unclear as to which parts of this set of related propositions are translated *verbatim* from *The Great Didactic* and which are paraphrased.
5. Yet their vision was a different one from that of most colonialists in that they believed in the capacity of education to transform Africans into fully fledged persons. Here lay the seed of future conflict with European politicians who tried to use the ideology of cultural superiority to rationalize the continuation of colonial oppression even when a body of African spokesmen had emerged claiming the right to self-government in precisely the language of the Western culture that missionary schools had so successfully implanted.
6. This part of the present argument was first advanced in a paper presented at the Institute for African Studies in Lusaka, Zambia (Serpell 1989).

References

Aries, P. (1962). *Centuries of childhood*. London: Cape (transl. from the French by R. Baldick.)

Ball, S. J. (1983). Imperialism, social control and the colonial curriculum in Africa. *Journal of Curriculum Studies, 15*(3), 237–263.

Berlin, I. (1956). Introduction. In I. Berlin (Ed.), *The age of enlightenment*. New York: Mentor.

Boyd, R. (1979). Metaphor and theory change: What is "metaphor" a metaphor for? In A. Ortony (Ed.), *Metaphor and thought*, 356–408 Cambridge, UK: Cambridge University Press.

Brown R. W., & Lenneberg, E. H. (1954). A study in language and cognition. *Journal of Abnormal and Social Psychology, 49*, 454–462.

Carroll, J. B., & Casagrande, J. B. (1958). The function of language classification in behavior. In E. E. Maccoby et al. (Eds.), *Readings in social psychology* (3rd ed.), 27–31. New York: Holt, Rinehart & Winston.

Deregowski, J. B. (1968). Difficulties in pictorial depth perception in Africa. *British Journal of Psychology, 59*, 195–204 .

Dixon, R. A., & Lerner, R. M. (1992) A history of systems in developmental psychology. In M. H. Bornstein & M. E. Lamb (Eds.), *Developmental psychology: An advanced textbook*. Hillsdale, NJ: Erlbaum.

Dunkel, H. B. (1969). *Herbart and education.* New York: Random House.

Dunkel, H. B. (1970). *Herbart and Herbartianism: An educational ghost story.* Chicago: Chicago University Press.

Gould, S. J. (1977). *Ontogeny and phylogeny.* Cambridge, UK: Cambridge University Press.

Helander, E., Mendis, P., & Nelson, G. (1980). *Training disabled people in the community: A manual on community-based rehabilitation for developing countries.* Geneva: World Health Organization, DPR/80.1 Version 2.

Hudson, W. (1960). Pictorial depth perception in sub-cultural groups on Africa. *Journal of Social Psychology, 52,* 183–208.

Hudson, W. (1967). The study of the problem of pictorial perception among unacculturated groups. *International Journal of Psychology, 2,* 89–107.

Inagaki, T. (1986). School education: Its history and contemporary status. In Stevenson, Azuma & Hakuta (Eds.), 75–92. *Child development and education in Japan,* New York: Freeman.

Inambao, A. W., & Makubalo, E. L. (1986). *The community health worker's handbook.* Lusaka, Zambia: GRZ Ministry of Health/TDRC.

LCHC. (1983). Culture and cognitive development. In P. H. Mussen (Ed.), *Handbook of child psychology* Vol 1, pp. 295–356. New York: Wiley.

Levine, K. (1982). Functional literacy: Fond illusions and false economies. *Harvard Educational Review, 52*(3), 249–266.

Makubalo, L. (forthcoming). Psychological contributions to policy and practice in primary health care. In R. Serpell (Ed.), *Public policy, professional practice and the science of psychology in a third world country: Zambia.*

McBean, G., Kaggwa, N., & Bugembe, J. (Eds.). (1980). *Illustrations for development: A manual for cross-cultural communication through illustration and workshops for artists in Africa.* Nairobi, Kenya: Afrolit Society.

Orne, M. T. (1962). On the social psychology of the psychological experiment: With particular reference to demand characteristics and their implications. *American Psychologist, 17,* 776–783.

Rodney, W. (1972). *How Europe underdeveloped Africa.* Dar-es-Salaam: Tanzania Publishing House.

Sadler, J. E. (1966). *J. A. Comenius and the concept of universal education.* London: Allen & Unwin.

Scribner, S. (1976). Situating the experiment in cross-cultural research. In K. F. Riegel & J. A. Meacham (Eds.), *The developing individual in a changing world* Vol.1, pp. 310–321. Chicago: Aldine.

Scribner, S. (1985). Vygotsky's uses of history. In J. M. Wertsch (Ed.), *Culture, communication and cognition: Vygotskian perspectives.* 119–145. Cambridge, UK: Cambridge University Press.

Scribner, S., & Cole, M. (1981). *The psychology of literacy.* Cambridge, MA: Harvard University Press.

Serpell, R. (1990). Audience, culture and psychological explanation: a reformulation of the emic-etic problem in cultural psychology. *Quarterly Newsletter of the Laboratory Comparative Human Cognition, 12*(3), 99–132.

Serpell, R. (1993). *The significance of schooling: Life-journeys in an African society.* Cambridge, UK: Cambridge University Press.

Serpell, R., & Deregowski, J. B. (1980). The skill of pictorial perception: An interpretation of cross-cultural evidence. *International Journal of Psychology, 15,* 145–180.

Serpell, R., & Hatano, G. (forthcoming). Education, schooling and literacy. *Handbook of Cross-Cultural Psychology,* Vol. 2 (Basic processes and developmental psychology) J. W. Berry, P. R. Dasen, T. S. Sarawathi (Eds.), Boston: Allyn and Bacon.

Serpell, R., & Mwanalushi, M. (1976). The impact of education and the information media on racism in Zambia since independence. Unpublished report for UNESCO (mimeo).

Serpell, R., & Nabuzoka, D. (1985). Community-Based Rehabilitation for disabled children in Vulamkoko Ward: A follow-up study. Lusaka: University of Zambia, Psychology Department (mimeo).

Serpell, R., Nabuzoka, D., Ng'andu, S., & Sinyangwe, I. M. (1988). The development of a community based strategy for the habilitation of disabled children in Zambia: A case of action-oriented health systems research. *Disabilities & Impairments, 2*(2), 117–129.

Snelson, P. D. (1974). *Educational development in Northern Rhodesia, 1883–1945.* Lusaka, Zambia: NEDCOZ.

Stigler, J. W., & Perry, M. (1988). Mathematics learning in Japanese, Chinese, and American classrooms. In G. B. Saxe & M. Gearhart (Eds.), *New Directions for Child Development, No.41.* San Francisco: Jossey-Bass.

Tignor, R. L. (1976). *The colonial transformation of Kenya.* Princeton, NJ: Princeton University Press.

WHO/UNICEF. (1978). *Alma-Ata Declaration on Primary Health Care.* Geneva: WHO.

3　The uniqueness of human labor

Ethel Tobach

In applying the concept of levels of integration to cognition, or mind, Scribner (1990) projected a sociohistorical analysis based on the work of Vygotsky as a clear explication of the significance of discontinuous categories such as mind in behavioral evolution. In describing the discontinuity of human cognition, she stressed its relationship with labor, a uniquely human characteristic. (Scribner, 1990, p. 109)

"A defining characteristic of . . . human cognition . . . is that humans do not interact directly with the environment (Vygotsky 1978, 1987). Rather, they regulate their interactions with each other and with the environment through systems of 'objects'. These objects . . . 'mediate' human actions in the world. The classic case of human activity mediated by objects is labor, and Marx's (1936) description of the role of tools or instruments in this process served Vygotsky as a prototype of all human actions: 'The elementary factors of the labour-process are (1) the personal activity of man, i.e., work itself, (2) the subject of that work, and (3) its instruments. . . . An instrument of labour is a thing, or a complex of things, which the labourer interposes between himself and the subject of his labour, and which serves as the conductor of his activity.'" (Vygotsky, in Wertsch, 1981, p. 174)

This presentation by Scribner in 1989 at the T. C. Schneirla Conference on "The Evolution of Knowing" (Scribner 1990) stimulated us to plan a conference in which approaches based on activity theory and on the concept of integrative levels would be used to elucidate the evolution of labor and its uniquely human character. That conference never came to be because of Sylvia Scribner's death.

I thank Rachel Falmagne, Laura Martin, Katherine Nelson, and Erwin Marquit for their helpful comments. I am responsible for my interpretation of their questions and suggestions. I owe much to discussions with Margaret (Peggy) Cooper and to Erwin Marquit for bringing Marx's citation of the statement by Benjamin Franklin to my attention. I also thank several reviewers who wish to remain anonymous for their reactions. As always, I am grateful for the bibliographic help of Malka Grinkorn and Ruth Newman.

43

We believed this would be useful in two ways: first, to explore the relationship of the concept of integrative levels and activity theory; second, to use the concept of levels and activity theory to sharpen a comparison of nonhuman animal[1] and human manipulations of the environment. This might suggest answers to the questions implicit in Marx's essay on The Labour Process cited by Scribner previously (Marx 1936) and in Engels's essay on The Part Played by Labour in the Transition from Ape to Man (Engels 1968): that is, is labor uniquely human, and if so, what were the processes that brought that about?

To explore the relation between the integrative levels concept and activity theory, I begin with a statement of each. Both have histories, producing many elaborations of their early formulations. The term *levels* is used variously (Tobach, 1995); the concept of integrative levels as used here does not have as elaborated a history as activity theory (Cole 1976; Davydov 1991; Lektorsky 1990; Leont'ev 1978; Luria 1976, 1987; Ratner 1991; Rogoff 1990; Vygotsky 1962, 1978, 1987; Wertsch 1981). Because the research and discussion by activity theorists is extensive, I will restrict my discussion to English translations of the work of Vygotsky, Luria, and Leont'ev. My statement of activity theory is a reflection of my current stage in an ongoing study of activity theory.

This chapter is organized in four sections. First, the concept of integrative levels is presented. Second, concepts in activity theory as circumscribed previously are discussed. Third, I examine how activity theory relates to the questions posed about the uniqueness of human labor; that is, to the concepts of integrative levels, biology and culture, behavioral evolution, and to tools and labor. Fourth, an integration of the concept of integrative levels with activity theory exemplified in categories relevant to the evolution of labor, such as reflection, mediation, motivation, and activity is presented.

The concept of integrative levels

The integrative levels concept was first most extensively extrapolated from biological phenomena by Woodger (1929), then developed more generally to be applicable to all forms of matter by Needham (1936, 1937), later explicitly stated in regard to social organization by Novikoff (1945a, b) and Schneirla (1972), and has since been discussed and elaborated by others (Aronson 1984, 1987; Greenberg & Kenyon 1987; Leacock, Menashe, & Gruber 1968; Tobach, 1995).[2]

The concept reflects the actual organization of matter, which is integrated in succeeding, subsuming levels. For example, subatomic particles are subsumed in all succeeding levels, but as they become differently related to each other's changes, they may produce new integrations in a succeeding level, such as, for example, a molecular level. These may become differently integrated in succeeding levels, resulting in, for example, inanimate or animate levels. A mesolevel may be formed by the integration of its previous and succeeding levels. For example, a virus, a mesolevel, is inanimate before it becomes integrated in a cell. In the cell it can reproduce itself, a characteristic of animate matter. Thus, it is both inanimate and animate, depending on its developmental stage and the setting for its activity.

A level can only be conceptualized according to the current stage of knowledge. Before the recent formulations of genetic function, for example, one talked about the chromosomal level of heredity; today both chromosomal and the molecular levels (DNA, RNA) are cited.

Each level is qualitatively different from preceding and succeeding levels and has its own properties, requiring unique instruments and procedures for study, generating unique laws and principles as to its characteristic organization and activities. The qualitative differences among levels are produced by the ways in which the contradictions in the preceding levels are resolved (Mao Tse-Tung 1953; Marquit 1980, 1982).

Levels are subsumed in categories (Tobach 1987). A category is thus different from a level in that it is inclusive of levels and may be produced in different ways. A category may be defined by the question asked.

For example, does the question relate to the category of cosmological processes or of societal processes? The category is then described by the levels it subsumes, thus demonstrating its uniqueness so that it cannot be confused with another category. There are continuities within categories as well as discontinuities (Novikoff 1945b). If and when a level becomes integrated with a level of another category, it may itself become a category, as in the case of language. For example, language is a level in the category of interindividual stimulation. The category of interindividual stimulation subsumes the level of reciprocal stimulation (Schneirla 1946) in which two organisms exchange effective stimulation (Schneirla 1965), changing each other's behavior. Succeeding this level is the level of communication, in which effective stimulation is directed by one organism (sender) toward another in anticipation of the effect on the other organism (receiver). Language subsumes the levels of reciprocal stimulation and communication. When the levels in the categories of interindividual stimulation, social behavior, and activity are fused, a new category, language is produced.

Concepts in activity theory

The introduction by Cole & Scribner to *Mind and Society* and the afterword by John-Steiner & Souberman (Vygotsky 1978, pp. 1–14 and pp. 121–134, respectively) made it clear that Vygotsky formulated his sociohistorical theory of human activity and higher mental function (Vygotsky 1978, pp. 64–65) on the basic postulates of dialectical and historical materialism (Scribner 1985). Leont'ev's further development of Vygotsky's work continued on this basis as indicated in the following brief synopsis.

The relationship between external and internal activity was formulated by Leont'ev (1981, pp. 54–58) to achieve the goal set by Sechenov to develop theories "about the origin of mental activities" (p. 54). He pointed out that Vygotsky's ideas on this subject "came from his analysis of the features unique to human productive labor activity, which is mediated by tools" (p. 55). Human activity is social, and as a result, "internal mental activities emerge from practical activity developed in human society on the basis of labor, and are formed in the course of each person's ontogenesis in each new generation – that is, the very form of the mental reflection of reality also changes. Consciousness, or the subjects' reflection of reality also changes" (p. 56).

Three fundamental concepts are present in this synopsis: internalization of the external, mediation, and reflection. Consciousness is presented as the process of reflection, and as I discuss later, reflection is the more fundamental process in the evolution of behavior.

Internalization of the external

Vygotsky called "the internal reconstruction of an external operation" *internalization*. This reconstruction consists of several transformations of a social, developmental nature in regard to human activity. Throughout his discussion, Leont'ev was concerned only with human activity. In concluding the section on external and internal relationships, Leont'ev emphasizes that there is an "essential commonality of external and internal activity: these two types of activity mediate humans' connections with the world in which they live" (Leont'ev 1981, p. 58). "Internal activity, which has arisen out of external, practical activity, is not separate from it and does not rise above it; rather, it retains its fundamental and two-way connection with it" (p. 58).

This formulation of the relation between external and internal expresses the dialectical transformation of the two types of activity, or process.

Mediation (mediated/mediating)

In Vygotsky's formulation of the concept of mediated activity, its dialectical materialist foundation is evidenced. He cited Hegel: human reason is characterized by mediating activity "which, by causing objects to act and react on each other in accordance with their own nature, in this way, without any direct interference in the process carries out . . . intentions" (Vygotsky 1978, p. 54). Further, Vygotsky quoted Marx in reference to mediating activity: humans using "the mechanical, physical, and chemical properties of objects so as to make them act as forces that affect other objects in order to fulfill . . . personal goals" (Vygotsky 1978, p. 54). The activity that modifies the stimulus situation as a part of the process of responding to it is mediation (Cole & Scribner in Vygotsky 1978, p. 14). Mediation is indirect. As Vygotsky wrote, signs and tools are subsumed under the more general concept of indirect (mediated) activity (1978, p. 54).

In Leont'ev's terms, mediation is part of the transformation process whereby the use of objects in activity, actions, and operations produces signs and tools to achieve goals. Mediation is not the same as the internalization of the external, which involves processes other than mediation, as for example, other types of reflection. The mediation of the activity through the tool or sign transforms the significance or meaning of the tool or sign for achieving a goal.

Reflection

Leont'ev (1981) saw "[t]he development of the object content of activity . . . in the resulting development of the mental reflection that regulates activity in the object environment" (pp. 48–49). He discussed the category of objective activity within the context of the behavioral and mental evolution of animals. This suggests that reflection can be seen as a category subsuming levels that relate to evolutionary levels.

Activity theory and issues pertinent to the evolution of labor

Concept of integrative levels in activity theory

Activity theory developed from the writings of Marx and Engels who used the concept of levels of change and transformation to formulate their concept of human activity in the dialectical materialist approach. Applying dialectical materialism, Vygotsky produced many examples of a "levels" approach in his writing. In his chapter on the mastery of memory and thinking he discussed levels as stages, appropriate for developmental processes. He described the principles of transformation from one stage to another in regard to the child's development of signs and the use of tools. His elucidation of the internalization of higher psychological functions in the child is another example of the dialectical relationships among levels or developmental stages (Vygotsky 1978, pp. 56–57).

Leont'ev's formulations also demonstrated a levels approach. In his chapter on The Problem of Activity in Psychology (1981), he listed the general structure of activity. First, "[t]here can be no activity without a motive" (p. 59). Second, "the notion of a goal is connected with the notion of an action (p. 60). Third, an operation "depends directly on the conditions under which a concrete goal is attained" (p. 65). Because "an activity is a process characterized by constant transformations" an activity can be converted into an action, an action can acquire an independent energizing force and become an activity . . . an action can be transformed into a means of attaining a goal (i.e., into an operation)" (p. 65).

These three "units" are considered "levels of analysis," and each is defined by contradictions that can transform each into the other level. Further, their transformations within the category of activity occur in relation to social processes. ". . . [T]he emergence in activity of goal-directed processes or actions was historically the consequence of the transition of humans to life in society" (Leont'ev 1981, p. 60).

In discussing new work in neurophysiology, Leont'ev (1981) indicated the need for studies on more than one level of "the real relations that connect the subject's mentally mediated activity with the physiological processes of the brain" (pp. 66–67).

Concepts of biology and culture in activity theory

Marx and Engels posed biology and culture as two levels of organization, or as contradictories, a common practice in their time. This continued in the time of Vygotsky, Leont'ev, and Luria when they worked together, as it does today. This apposition is confusing: biology is the study of all living organisms. As such a category, it may be said to include the various forms of function and organization of all organisms, including human culture. As "biology" is most frequently used today, it apposes genetic processes to environmental processes, and assumes the primacy of the genetic process in all forms of function and organization of organisms, including human evolution and culture (Wilson 1975, 1978; Lumsden & Wilson 1981).

Vygotsky's use of the term *biological* could not have concerned molecular genetic processes. Beginning at the turn of the century, the use of the term *genetic* to signify "developmental" was customary. The concept of heredity was part of his contemporary scientific knowledge, and the concept of "biological" givens is clear within his theoretical framework (Vygotsky 1978, pp. 37, 39, 46).[3] Vygotsky's use of the word *biological* frequently referred to the physiological level, as for example, "tying a knot . . . extend(s) the operation of memory beyond the biological dimensions of the human nervous system" (Vygotsky 1978, p. 39).

Vygotsky made a strong distinction between the "biological" and the "cultural" (p. 46). He saw the biological givens as elementary behavior that has evolved (biological evolution) and that the higher mediated levels are culturally acquired (human history) (pp. 45–49). However, there is an implication of the existence of levels between the biological and the cultural. "Many transitional psychological systems occur. In the history of behavior these transitional systems lie between the biologically given and the culturally acquired" (Vygotsky 1978, p. 46).

Concept of behavioral evolution in activity theory

An evolutionary approach is consistent with the dialectical and historical materialism of Marx and Engels, who recognized the membership of humans in the biological world and the materialist base of Darwinian evolutionary thinking. As dialectical and historical materialism were basic to the sociohistorical concepts of Vygotsky, Leont'ev, and Luria, activity theory was central to their understanding of the origins of the human species. They were aware of evolutionary theory. Luria, however, was less convinced than Vygotsky and Leont'ev of the value of evolutionary theory.

Vygotsky used the work of comparative psychologists, such as Kohler, to demonstrate the different levels of cognitive, perceptual, and communicative function (Vygtosky 1978), and the differences in the relationship between activity and thinking in animals and in humans, particularly in comparisons with children (Vygotsky 1962, chapter 4). Vygotsky's interest had an evolutionary base: "Through an analysis of available information on phylogenesis and ontogenesis, we must attempt to identify the most useful point of departure for the resolution of the problem; we must attempt to develop a general theory of the genetic roots of thinking and speech" (Minick in Vygotsky 1987, p. 39).

In a chapter entitled "The Historical Approach to the Study of the Human Mind" Leont'ev contrasted the evolutionary or "biological" approach with the "social historical" or historical and dialectical materialist approach (Leont'ev 1964). Leont'ev was critical of reductionist biological explanations of human behavior ("Utilitarianism and pragmatism constitute an *essential* result of a mechanical transfer of biological relationships to the human level." p. 34) and of anthropomorphism ("The return to the kingdom of animals from human behavior . . . this approach in the theory of evolution supports . . . as though 'from above' . . . metaphysical, idealistic conceptions." p. 34).

In the section entitled "The Biological and Social-Historical Development of Man" Leont'ev 1964, (p. 47), he defined the relationship between the laws of biological evolution and social laws, the sociohistorical processes. The content of the problem of "man and his environment" can be seen as "general biological," but the problem is discontinuous in the formulation of "man and society." Discontinuity is the preemininent feature. He cited the comparative psychologist Roginsky in his analysis of anthropogenesis: "As is emphasized by Ya. Ya. Roginsky, we are dealing here specifically with *different* laws operating in different areas and not at all with intermediate, mixed biosocial laws" (Roginsky & Levin 1955, p. 316). For Leont'ev, the heredity of characteristics defined biological evolution; human activity characteristics were not biologically inherited and defined sociohistorical evolution.

In the afterword to Vygotsky's book, *Thinking and Speech* (Vygotsky in Luria 1987, p. 539), Luria acknowledged Vygotsky's application of animal behavior studies. He wrote that Vygotsky argued "that the development of human thinking has two independent roots, one that derives from the animal's practical action and one that derives from the animal's use of speech [vocalization] as a means of social interaction" (p. 362). Luria believed, however, that "[t]he evolutionary approach, which was quite valid for a comparative study of mental development in the animal world, found itself in something of a blind alley when it tried to study the evolution of human mental activity" (1976, p. 6). This may have been a reflection of the evolutionary theorists he cites (Haeckel and Tylor). These evolutionary theorists had "[n]otions about individual development reproducing the development of the species . . . which . . . yielded . . . superficial and reactionary conclusions that the thought processes of primitive peoples closely resemble those of children (Tylor 1874) and indicate the 'racial inferiority' of backward peoples" (p. 6). He also criticized those who "find the instincts of the individual at the bottom of all social phenomena" like McDougall (p. 4) and "ethologists who regard war as the result of innate aggressive impulses in the individual" (pp. 4–5).

Concepts of tool and labor in activity theory

In Leont'ev's (1981) discussion of the differences between the levels of actions and operations, he used the concept of the tool. The dialectical relations of these levels or "'units' of human activity" [that] "form its macrostructure" . . . [which, when analyzed] . . ."reveals the inner relations that characterize activity. . . . Objects can become energizers, goals, and tools only within the system of human activity" (p. 65). In this distinction between the levels (actions, operations), the transformations of the object and tool suggest that the objects and the tools may be levels in another category. Although Vygotsky and Leont'ev recognized that there were "transitional" phases and aspects between animals and humans, the focus was not on the transitions but understandably on human activity.

Application of the concept of integrative levels to activity theory

Any theoretical practice uses among other means knowledges which intervene as procedures: either knowledges borrowed from outside, from existing sciences, or 'knowledges' produced by the technical practice itself in pursuing its ends. (Althusser 1970, p. 171)

Applying the concept of integrative levels, another "theoretical practice" to the fundamental concepts of activity theory may elucidate the relationship between the activity of nonhuman animals and humans in regard to the uniqueness of human labor.

The categories of activity and of reflection may be seen as separate categories because each can be shown to subsume its own levels produced by distinguishably different processes. The category of activity subsumes the levels of metabolic change, work and labor, among others. The category of reflection subsumes other levels, one of them being the level of mediation. Vygotsky's concept of mediation is central to his explanation of the qualitative leap from animal to human behavior.

The categories described earlier are particularly salient because of their significance in activity theory. Another category that is salient by implication is that of social behavior. Activity theory has been primarily concerned with human activity. In integrating the concept of integrative levels with activity theory, evolutionary processes become relevant. The evolution of behavior encompasses nonhuman as well as human behavior. A consideration of the special character of the human level in the category of social behavior throughout all species is necessary to integrate the traditional human-only character of activity theory with the processes of behavioral evolution. This can explicate the significance of the categories in activity theory for both nonhuman and human behavior. The category of social behavior subsumes all levels of interactions between and among individuals of the same and different species derived from their developmental and ecological relations, that is, their evolutionary relations. The societal level in the category of social behavior is seen only on the human level; that is, it is a discontinuous level in social behavior (Tobach 1994; Tobach & Schneirla 1968). This level, the societal level, is of critical importance in the relationships of all the categories relevant to activity theory and the concept of integrative levels.

It is a critical level in that it sharpens the contradictions between the levels in the other categories relative to humans. The sharpening of the contradictions produces succeeding levels. It does this most significantly in the category of activity that subsumes the categories of work and labor. All the categories discussed are interdependent, interconnected and interpenetrating.

The category of reflection

Lenin summarized Engels's article on historical materialism: "the materialist theory, the theory of the reflection of objects by our mind, is here presented with absolute clarity: things exist outside us. Our perceptions and ideas are their images. Verification of these images . . . is given by practice" (Lenin 1943, p.173) Throughout Engels's arguments with the idealists, the activity of the individual is an interpenetrating process in the reflection of the environment ("real world") to produce the images in the brain. Reflection is not the simple mirroring of matter/energy, but the result of the interdependent processes of sensation (perception) and activity.

The category of reflection is related to Vygotsky's and Leont'ev's concept of externalizaton and internalization. The dialectic of the external and the internal has to do with the contradictions at the interface between the two, as for example, in a cell. The membrane of the cell is not a solid barrier that mechanically separates external and internal processes, but a unity of opposites: the opposites are the molecules that make up the membrane and accept or reject parts or all of the surround on both sides of the membrane. The integration or resolution of contradictions at molecular levels as well as at the level of subcellular organelles is fundamental to all processes of internalization. Such resolutions of contradictions between the internal and external are seen at all integrative levels in the organism.

Reflection is the category of the integration of organism and environment through the transformation of the external matter/energy configurations to an internal configuration that becomes a representation, which in turn can transform the external. It is an elaboration of the concept that the activity of the organism changes not only itself but its environment, and that the changes in the environment change the organism in a dialectic and developmental process.

The transformation of the external to the internal is the fundamental process in all living organisms, at all levels, beginning with the molecular interface of the membrane through the interface between the complete organism and the surround. The category of reflection applies first to animals as contrasted with plants, and second to animals with specialized structures and functions. The specialized structures are organized into different levels of integration, beginning with cells characterized by irritability (sensory), directed transmission of matter/energy (stimulating other sensory processes), and maintaining relatively stable changes (storage) (nerve cells), proceeding through later subsuming levels to cephalo–caudal neural systems of integrated specialized neurophysiological systems. These neural systems vary phyletically and developmentally.

Variations in the temporal and interconnected aspects of the process of transformation at different levels of the nervous system produce different levels of reflection. Earlier, more fundamental and pervasive levels are subsumed in later, discontinuous levels. These variations are produced in the history of the species and the individual as a function of integration with other categories.

Level 1. Internal changes of sensorimotor integration reflect "effective" changes in the surround at the interface between organism and surround. *Effective* is defined by adequacy of external change to bring about internal change. This is dependent upon the organism's state and developmental stage (Schneirla 1965). Example: reflexes.

Level 2. Stored association through temporal and spatial integration of adequate stimulation and concomitant sensorimotor changes so that the first level of reflection is modified by the association. Example: Pavlovian conditioning.

Level 3. Reflection through association of an effective stimulus configuration in the surround with the consequence of an activity with which the organism has changed the surround. Example: contingency conditioning.

Level 4. Reflection through association of an effective stimulus configuration in the surround with the consequence of an activity that is transformed qualitatively as retrievable stored representation (memory) to reflect the consequences of the activity as a goal (see discussion of need and motive following). This is the level of planning. Examples: when in a laboratory experiment, an animal, to obtain food, integrates the experience of the turns in a maze and the presence of food after one of the turns; when a primate goes to an area previously visited to obtain fruit when the fruit is ready to be eaten (Whiten, Byrne, Barton, Waterman & Heinz, 1992).

Level 5. Transformation of the association of the activity with the goal through the activity of the animal to change the effective stimulus configuration in the surround. This is the level of mediation, in which the reflection of the activity and consequent changes in the animal's relation to the surround result in an object as a producer of change in the surround. Example: a chimpanzee uses a rock and an anvil to crack nuts that cannot be opened by biting (Boesch & Boesch, 1981).

When the level of mediation is integrated with different levels in other categories, such as the societal level in social behavior, the qualitative leap between human and nonhuman organisms takes place. But the societal level of social behavior is at the same time the product of the qualitative changes that take place in the level of mediation stemming from the characteristics of the preceding level in the category of reflection; that is, the level of planning, in fusion with the earlier levels of social behavior, featuring such processes as social facilitation (Aisner & Terkel 1992; Zohar & Terkel 1991; Sherry & Galef 1984, 1990) in problem solving. As a result of these relations with preceding levels and with levels in other categories, the mediation level becomes a category, subsuming levels of mediated/mediating objects (see "Category of mediation").

Level 6. The psychological level may be seen as the level of higher mental function discussed by Leont'ev. The neurophysiology of the internalization process in human activity (higher mental function) (Leont'ev 1964), is in another level of structure/function in the category of reflection. The activity of the organism makes the interface more or less available to transformation of the external to the internal. This brings about the integration of the neurophysiological and other physiological systems (motor, endocrine) which in integration with the societal level and the tool level produces the psychological level; that is, psychological reflection.

Category of mediation

The category of mediation is produced by the fusion of levels in various categories as described previously. The category of mediation does not include action of the animal with its body or parts of its body, with its conspecifics or products of metabolic activity. It is the activity of the entire organism in the movement of some heterospecific biotic or abiotic object(s) in the environment. The production of mediated/mediating objects is a result of this activity. Each level in the category of mediation has within itself the possibility of changes that could produce the next level in which it is subsumed.

Level 1. Moves soil or other types of substrate by body action (burrowing).

Level 2. Changes location of discrete objects in the environment (rocks, vegetation).

Level 3. Uses object (utensil) to obtain some part of the surround.

Level 4. Uses object (tool) to change a utensil to produce something that was not there before. Here the processes bringing about the societal level are dialectically transforming the utensil level as the changes from utensil to tool dialectically transform the social to the societal level.

As Marx noted, Franklin said that animals cannot make tools; only humans do (Marx 1936, p. 173).[4] I suggest that this fourth level of mediation helps us to distinguish the activity of animals and humans by using the words *utensil* and *tool* discriminatingly.[5]

The terms *utensil* and *tool* are seen as different levels of objects related to different levels in the category of mediation. The etymological history and the dictionary definition of the two words are informative of their differences in English. The English word *tool* reveals its inherent meaning in human activity. Etymologically it is derived from old English and German roots for preparing, making, currying, and dressing raw materials, as in conversion of skins into leather (*Oxford Dictionary of English Etymology* [ODEE] 1983; Skeat 1968). The dictionary defines *tool* as any implement, instrument or utensil held in the hand and used for cutting, hitting, digging, rubbing, etc. (*Webster's New World Dictionary* [WNWD] 1988). Animals use objects as "implements, utensils, or tools" according to this definition.

An examination of the etymological history of "utensil" indicates its dependence on the concept of "use" (ODEE 1983; Skeat 1968), although the derivation is related to "domestic" use as an implement or vessel. I am suggesting, however, that we arbitrarily assign the word *utensil* to animal behavior, as a reflection of the known use of objects by animals, and *tool* for human behavior. The differences between them may reflect human experience as indicated in the linguistic history of the two terms.

The category of motivation (goal directed behavior)

The concept of integrative levels suggests the following processes in the category of motivation. When the energy processes (metabolic, physiological) of the entire organism or specific physiological systems change so that the external contradictions becomes secondary or subordinate to the internal contradictions (deficit or excess of some biochemical, protein, water, enzyme, nutriment), the activity of the organism as a whole is increased or decreased. Depending on the energy characteristics of the surround, the phyletic level, the developmental stage, and the level of social behavior (dependence on or independence of conspecifics) the change in activity will be related to some change in the surround (moving toward a source of chemical stimulation that changes the membrane interface between the external and the internal) so that food is ingested, as in the amoeba. This change in the amoeba's state as a result of its activity is transitory, ephemeral, and subject to further metabolic change so that it does not store the relation between activity and result. Its experience plays only a temporary role in its behavior.

In the case of a mammal, such as a neonatal rat pup, moving toward a source of higher temperature leads to tactile stimulation by the fur of the lactating adult. This experience is internalized as the activity of the animal makes for a change in its relation with the environment. It results in the increased probability that the next time the internal change becomes dominant the result of the previous activity will lead to a change in the organism, which once again brings it into a relation with an object in the environment, the lactating adult. This internalized experience, in which the activity of the individual, functioning through neural and physiological processes, changes the biochemical level to a new level. The deficit is transformed into a need for a particular object or activity, changing its external relation to the environment. Until this transformation takes place, it was not a need because there was no object or activity connected with the internal state. Once the need has been developed, the organism, depending again on its phyletic and ontogenetic status, can develop a goal because the organism has internalized the mediating activity and mediated object (indirect change in relation to the environment), and has transformed the activity dialectically in relation to the result, to produce the activity called *motivation*.

The category of activity

Introducing the category of activity changes the entire conceptual framework of psychology. (Leont'ev 1978, p. 46)

I believe that it can change the entire conceptual framework of behavioral evolution.

Although Leont'ev was addressing the problem of the development of the human mind, the category of activity is relevant to all living organisms, including plants and the mesolevels between plants and animals, for example, blue-green algae. "The process of living is the aggregate, or, more precisely, the system of activities that succeed one another" (Leont'ev 1978, p. 46).

The number of systems involved in the activity of organisms is defined by the evolutionary (species) and developmental (stage and state) history of the organism. Structure (morphology, from subcellular to total organismic structure) is viewed as interconnected, interrelated, and interdependent with function (physiology). In all levels, the activity of the organism changes it internally, changes its effective surround, and changes its relation to the effective surround, in turn changing the organism internally. The dialectical process of internalization/externalization/internalization is present in all activity levels. Each of these levels subsumes the preceding level.

Level 1. Metabolism The changes in which external matter/energy is transformed into internal energy/matter forms, producing a shorter or longer lasting effective internal change. Example: oxygen is changed in the organism and in the air surrounding it.

Level 2. Approach/withdrawal movement (Schneirla 1965): The organism moves to or away from the source of effective stimulation. Example: amoeba moving away from a strong concentration of acid in the environment.

Level 3. Object action: The organism changes the location or position of movable, biotic (not conspecific) or abiotic parts of the surround. Examples: an ant carries particles to the colony location; a bird moves grass or similar objects to a location in the fork of a tree and manipulates the objects; a beaver cuts down young trees and lays them in a body of water. The similarity between this level in the category of activity and the second level in the category of mediation exemplifies the interdependence and interpenetration of activity and mediation. Here the distinction that Leont'ev makes between "action" ("operation") and "activity" also distinguishes the category of mediation and activity (Leont'ev 1981).

Level 4. Mediated object activity: The organism modifies a biotic or abiotic part of the surround to carry out another activity. Example: a woodpecker enlarges a cleft in a tree and inserts a pine cone from which it removes and eats the seeds (Krushinksy, 1990).

Level 5. Work: Activity with a mediated/mediating object (utensil). The organism modifies a movable biotic or abiotic object in the surround to carry out another activity that qualitatively changes the essence of the object. Example: a chimpanzee strips leaves from a branch producing a mediated/mediating object that is now a probe for insertion into an opening (Brewer and McGrew, 1990).

Level 6. Labor: Activity in which an object in the surround is used to modify another object that becomes a mediated/mediating object (tool) in order to carry out another activity in relation to the societal level. The essence of the object that is worked on is changed through the activity with a utensil so that it becomes a tool. Example: a hominid sharpens a stone with another stone in order to scrape meat off a bone (Leakey, 1971).

Labor is a level that subsumes the level of work; the level of tool subsumes the level of utensil. Each of these levels, that is, work and utensil, produce the succeeding levels of labor and tool. Because these levels have resulted from fusion with levels in other categories (particularly the societal level in the category of social behavior), they themselves become categories.

An examination of the linguistic English history of the two words *work* and *labor* also suggests significant differences and possible usage. The etymological history of the word *work* probably begins with the Indogermanic root "werg" which may also be related to the Greek root "erg" signifying energy, activity, and work (Skeat 1968). The action expressive of energy becomes synonymous with its product, so that one works and at the same time produces a work (ODEE 1983; WNWD 1988).

Labor, derived from the Latin, has a rather simple history in the English language. It is thought to be related to the toil or work associated with plowing, the work of oxen, or the cultivation of crops (ODEE

1983). The synonym *toil* has a varied history, relating it to negative aspects of activity, such as soiling, struggle, being torn and spoilt, with some possible ties to machines for bruising (as with a mallet) or beating, or tilling or manuring of lands. The sources of toil are not clearly related to work, except, interestingly enough, that activities characteristic of agriculture also are included.

Engels (1940, p. 76) discusses the differences between the English "work" and "labor" and the German "Werk" and "Arbeit." Despite the limitations of the knowledge of physics of his time, he distinguishes between the use of the terms in relation to *work* as a physical concept and *labor* as an economic concept.

The category of work

The level of work in the category of activity may be seen as a category as well. The brief consideration of the concept of work given previously contrasts animal work with work as a mechanical process in inanimate matter: work as the product of force times distance. The earliest level of work as an animate process is the matter/energy action and production that takes place continually and continuously in the living organism (metabolic work). There are several forms of potential energy for work: chemical, mechanical, thermal, electrical, and radiant. The integration of these forms of energy on many levels in many categories is the activity of the organism. Thus, the category of activity subsumes levels of work in the physical material processes described earlier as well as the level of labor. Integration with other categories (neurophysiology, social behavior, reflection, and activity) produces a qualitative change in behavior that results in a significant discontinuity: the integration of goal-directed activity. The development of this behavior results, in the sense of the etymological root of the word, in the identity of the work and the product (Leont'ev 1978).

The work of apes and the labor of humans

Because of the evolutionary closeness of apes and humans, the tool using activity of apes has been extensively studied (Kohts 1959; Greenfield 1991; McGrew 1992; Stiner 1993; van Lawick-Goodall 1970) as this might provide clues to the relation between the work of apes and the labor of humans, thus explicating the origin of the human species. As indicated previously, apes and humans use utensils but only humans make tools, for example, the use of one stone (hammer) to produce stones with different shapes (Leakey 1971).

Activity theory as elaborated by Vygotsky and Leont'ev and the concept of integrative levels suggest the continuity and discontinuity in the processes that produced this difference in the activity of apes and humans.

There are many examples of the behavioral continuity in the work of using utensils for obtaining food. The use of modified sticks by apes was probably only one of many behavioral patterns of animals (Beck 1980) that were part of the experience of the early hominids (Stiner 1993). Other patterns were the regularity of the behavior of animals as they hunted and scavenged, thus leading the hominids to the source of food; or the pattern in which animals went to different plants when all or parts of the plants become edible at different times of the year (Milton 1981; Whiten et al. 1992). Another example of behavioral continuity is the work of using utensils as when apes use stones as hammers and rocks as anvils to crack nuts (Sugiyama & Koman 1979). All these activities resulted in the object mediation that was the basis for planning of feeding behavior.

Other regular changes in the surround such as sprouting of seeds as a result of deposition of food in caves, seed scattering during feeding and undigested seeds developing in feces (Jansen 1988) and the seasonal cycle of plant development (MacNeish 1991; Marshack 1972; Cohen 1977; McCorriston & Hole 1991;) produced significant objects for actions and operations leading to new activity, new tools.

There is a continuity of object use to obtain food (utensils in work), as the early hominids probably obtained food in similar fashion (Stiner 1993). The repeated and continual association of the results of such activity with the activity that made the changes in the surround produced the qualitative change, the discontinuity of making tools for labor.

In the production of the societal level, the critical discontinuity in the category of social behavior, the category of feeding, that is, the category subsuming all activities relating to nutritional sustenance, may be most important, and is probably more significant than the category of organismic reproduction. The differences in the significance of the two categories, that is, feeding and organismic reproduction, in the production of the societal level may be important for understanding the uniqueness of human labor.

Final word

My father died when he was 29 years old. A tree with a broken limb is carved on his gravestone, a symbol of an untimely and early death according to my family's folklore. Sylvia Scribner was somewhat older, but intellectually she was a strong tree with a broken limb . . . an untimely death.

In the plans that Scribner and I made for the conference, it was appropriate that Scribner would be responsible for investigating the usefulness of the concept of integrative levels for the analysis of human labor. The levels in the category of human labor remain for her students to develop. A good beginning for that project is the study of Scribner's 1985 paper on Vygotsky and his use of history.

Notes

1. For brevity's sake, *animal* will be used henceforth.
2. For various approaches to the concept, see the T. C. Schneirla Conferences Series, edited by Gary Greenberg and Ethel Tobach (Volumes 1–4, [1984–1990] Hillsdale, NJ: LEA; Volume 5, 1995, Garland Press, Inc.).
3. See also John-Steiner and Souberman, p. 124, and their footnote (p. 139) in which they interpret "Vygotsky's use of 'natural' as 'biologically given features, such as reflexes present at birth.'" (Cole, Scribner, John-Steiner & Souberman 1978). See also Scribner 1985.
4. I am indebted to Erwin Marquit who reminded me of this citation by Marx, and to Ruth Newman who found the source in Boswell's Life of Johnson.
5. Space does not permit a thorough review of the many discussions of the definition "tool" (Gruber 1969; Binford 1977, 1979; Beck 1980; Toth & Schick 1986; Wynn & McGrew 1989; Andrews & Martin 1991; Schick & Toth 1993). Most of the discussions reflect concern with criteria for distinguishing between humans and animals. Some clearly use toolmaking as the discriminating activity (Gruber 1969), and some use other aspects of the differences in human and ape activity, such as using objects expediently and immediately or at another location and at a later time (curational) as in Binford's distinction between expedient and curated tools (1977). Thus, Toth (1985) states that apes use expedient tools, while hominids used curated tools, and Wynn and McGrew (1989) point out that there are two behavior patterns seen in hominids that are not seen in modern apes: "carrying tools or food for thousands of metres and competing with large carnivores for animal prey. (p. 383). Others reject any consideration of a difference between humans and animals as necessary in defining tool and tool use (Beck 1980). It should be noted that in all the discussion of tool and tool use, the concept of work is not discussed, but the term "use" is ubiquitous. The concept of work is related to energetics of food intake and foraging and ingestion (e.g., papers in Whiten & Widdowson 1992). The issue of distinguishing the

activity of animals in using "tools" to obtain food for individual survival and the societal activity of humans in producing food is not in evidence, although there is some consideration of social feeding and the possibility of food sharing in animals.

References

Aisner, R., & Terkel, J. (1992). Ontogeny of pine cone opening behaviour in the black rat, *Rattus rattus*. *Animal Behaviour, 44*, 327–336.

Althusser, L. (1970). *For Marx*. New York: Vintage Books.

Andrews, Peter & Martin, Lawrence. (1991). Hominoid dietary evolution. In A. Whiten & E. H. Widowson (Eds.) *Foraging strategies and natural diet of monkeys, apes and humans*, pp. 199–209. Oxford: Clarendon Press.

Aronson, L. R. (1984). Levels of integration and organization: a reevaluation of the evolutionary scale. In G. Greenberg & E. Tobach (Eds.) *Behavioral evolution and Integrative Levels*, pp. 57–81. Hillsdale, NJ: LEA.

Aronson, L. R. (1987). Some remarks on integrative levels. In G. Greenberg & E. Tobach (Eds.). *Cognition, language and consciousness: Integrative levels*, pp. 269–286. Hillsdale, NJ: LEA.

Beck, B. B. (1980). *Animal tool behavior: The use and manufacture of tools by animals*. New York: Garland STPM Press.

Binford, Lewis R. (1977). Forty-seven trips: A case study in the character of archaeological formation processes. In R. V. S. Wright (Ed.) *Stone tools as cultural markers: Change, evolution and complexity*, pp. 24–36. Canberra: Australian Institute of Aboriginal Studies.

Binford, Lewis R. (1979). Organization and formation processes: looking at curated technologies. *Journal of Anthropological Research, 35*, 255–273.

Boesch, Christophe, & Boesch, Hedwige. (1990). Tool use and tool making in wild chimpanzees. *Folia Primatologica, 54*, 86–99.

Brewer, Stella M., & McGrew, W. C. (1990). Chimpanzee use of a tool-set to get honey. *Folia Primatologica, 54*, 100–104.

Cohen, Mark Nathan. (1977). *The food crisis in prehistory*. New Haven: Yale University Press.

Cole, Michael. (1976) Foreword. In A. R. Luria, 1976, *Cognitive development: Its cultural and social foundations*, pp. xi–xvi. Cambridge, MA: Harvard University Press.

Cole, M., & Scribner, S. (1978). Introduction. In L. S. Vygotsky, *Mind in society*. M. Cole, V. John-Steiner, S. Scribner, & E. Souberman (Eds.) pp. 1–14. Cambridge, MA: Harvard University Press.

Davydov, V. V. (1991). The content and unsolved problems of activity theory. *Multidisciplinary Newsletter for Activity Theory, 7/8*, 30–35.

Engels, Frederick. (1940). *Dialectics of nature*. New York: International Publishers.

Greenberg, G., & Kenyon, G. Y. (1987). Issues for continuing discussion of integrative levels. In G. Greenberg & E. Tobach (Eds.). *Cognition, language and consciousness: Integrative levels*, pp. 277–288. Hillsdale, NJ: LEA.

Greenfield, Patricia M. (199).1 Language, tools and brain: the ontogeny and phylogeny of hierarchically organized sequential behavior. *Behavioral and Brain Sciences.* *14*, 531–595.

Jansen, Daniel H. (1988). Costa Rican anachronisms: Where did the Guanacaste tree come from? In Abelardo Brenes (Ed.). *The comparative psychology of natural resource management. Advances in comparative psychology* Vol. 1, pp. 13–27. Napoli, Italy: University of Calabria.

John-Steiner, V., & Souberman, E. (1978). Afterword. In L. S. Vygotsky, *Mind in society.* M. Cole, V. John-Steiner, S. Scribner, & E. Souberman (Eds.) pp. 121–134. Cambridge, MA: Harvard University Press.

Kohts, Nadjejeta. (1959). The handling of objects by primates (apes and monkeys in the light of anthropogenesis. *Proceedings of the XV International Congress of Zoology*, London.

Krushinsky, L. V. (1990). *Experimental studies of elementary reasoning.* New Delhi, Amerind Publishing Co.

Leacock, Eleanor, Menashe, Louis, and Gruber, Helmut. (1968). *Unity, diversity, and levels of integration.* Brooklyn, NY: Polytechnic Institute of Brooklyn, Department of Social Sciences.

Leakey, Mary D. (1971). *Olduvai Gorge. Vol.3: Excavations in beds I and II, 1961–1963.* Cambridge, UK: Cambridge University Press.

Lektorsky, V. A., & Engeström, Yrjö (1990). *Activity: Theories, methodology and problems.* Orlando, FL: Paul M. Deutsch Press, Inc.

Lenin, V. I. (1943). *Materialism and empirio-criticism* (Vol. 11). In *Selected works.* New York: International Publishers Co., Inc.

Leont'ev, A. N. (1964). Problems of mental development. Washington, D.C.: Office of Technical Services, U.S. Department of Commerce (transl.).

Leont'ev, A. N. (1978). *Activity, consciousness and personality.* Englewood Cliffs, NJ: Prentice-Hall, Inc.

Leont'ev, A. N. (1981). The problem of activity in psychology. In J. V. Wertsch (Ed.). *The concept of activity in Soviet psychology*, pp. 37–71. Armonk, NY: M. E. Sharpe, Inc.

Lumsden, C. J., & Wilson, E. O. (1981). *Genes, mind and culture: The coevolutionary process.* Cambridge, MA.: Harvard University Press.

Luria, A. R. (1976). *Cognitive development.* Cambridge, MA: Harvard University Press.

Luria, A. R. (1987). Afterword. In R. W. Rieber & A. S. Carton (Eds.).*The collected works of L. S. Vygotsky* (Vol. 1, pp. 359–373). New York: Plenum Press.

MacNeish, Richard S. (1991). *The origins of agriculture and settled life.* Norman, OK: The University of Oklahoma Press.

Mao Tse-Tung. (1953) *On contradiction.* New York: International Publishers.

Marquit, Erwin. (1980). Physical systems, structures and properties. *Science and Society*, *44*, 155–176.

Marquit, Erwin. (1982). Contradictions in dialectics and formal logic. In Erwin Marquit, Philip Moran, & Willis H. Truitt (Eds.). pp. 67–83. Minneapolis: Marxist Educational Press.

Marshack, Alexander. (1972). Upper Paleolithic notation and symbol. *Science. 178*, 817–828.

Marx, Karl. (1936). *Capital: A critique of political economy*. New York: The Modern Library.

McCorriston, Joy, & Hole, Frank. (1991). The ecology of seasonal stress and the origins of agriculture in the Near East. *American Anthropologist. 93*, 46–69.

McGrew, W. C. (1992). *Chimpanzee material culture*. Cambridge, UK: Cambridge University Press.

Milton, K. (1981). Distribution pattern of tropical plant foods as an evolutionary stimulus to primate mental development. *American Anthropologist. 83*, 534–548.

Needham, Joseph. (1936). *Order and life*. New Haven, CT: Yale University Press. Reprinted MIT Press, 1968.

Needham, Joseph. (1937). Integrative levels: A revaluation of the idea of progress. Oxford: Clarendon Press.

Novikoff, A. B. (1945a). The concept of integrative levels and biology. *Science. 101*, 209–215.

Novikoff, A. B. (1945b). Continuity and discontinuity. *Science. 102*, 405–406.

Oxford dictionary of English entymology. 1983. C. T. Onions (Ed.). Oxford: Clarendon Press.

Ratner, Carl. (1991). *Vygotsky's sociohistorical psychology and its contemporary applications*. New York: Plenum Press.

Rogoff, Barbara. (1990). *Apprenticeship in thinking*. New York: Oxford University Press.

Schick, Kathy D., & Toth, Nicholas. (1993). *Making silent stones speak*. New York: Simon & Schuster.

Schneirla, T. C. (1946). Problems in the biopsychology of social organization. L. R. Aronson, Ethel Tobach, Jay S. Rosenblatt, & Daniel S. Lehrman (Eds.). *Selected writings of T. C. Schneirla*, pp. 417–439. San Francisco: W. H. Freeman & Co.

Schneirla, T. C. (1965). Aspects of stimulation and organization in approach-withdrawal processes underlying vertebrate behavioral development. In, *Selected writings of T. C. Schneirla*, L. R. Aronson, Ethel Tobach, Jay S. Rosenblatt, and Daniel S. Lehrman (Eds.). pp. 344–412. San Francisco: W. H. Freeman & Co.

Schneirla, T. C. (1972). *Selected writings*. L. R. Aronson, Ethel Tobach, Jay S. Rosenblatt, & Daniel S. Lehrman (Eds.). San Francisco: W. H. Freeman & Co.

Scribner, Sylvia. (1985). Vygotsky's uses of history. In *Culture, communication and cognition*. New York: Cambridge University Press.

Scribner, Sylvia. (1990). A sociocultural approach to the study of mind. In Gary Greenberg & Ethel Tobach (Eds.). *Theories in the evolution of knowing*, pp. 107–120. Hillsdale, NJ: LEA.

Sherry, David F., & Galef, B. G., Jr. (1984). Cultural transmission without imitation: Milk bottle opening by birds. *Animal Behaviour, 32*, 937–938.

Sherry, David F., & Galef, B. G., Jr. (1990). Social learning without imitation: More about milk bottle opening by birds. *Animal Behaviour, 40*, 987–989.

Skeat, Walter W. (1968). *Etymological dictionary of the English language.* Oxford: Clarendon Press.

Stiner, Mary C. (1993). Modern human origins – faunal perspectives. *Annual Review of Anthropology, 22*, 55–82.

Sugiyama, Y., Koman, J. (1979). Tool-using and -making behavior in wild chimpanzees at Bossou, Guinea in 1979–1980. *Primates, 22*, 435–444.

Tobach, Ethel. (1987). Integrative levels in the comparative psychology of cognition, language and consciousness. In G. Greenberg & E. Tobach (Eds.). *Cognition, language and consciousness*, pp. 239–267. Hillsdale, NJ: LEA.

Tobach, Ethel. (1994). Personal is political. *Journal of Social Issues, 50*, 221–244.

Tobach, Ethel. (1995). One view of the concept of integrative levels. In *Development of behavior and the approach-withdrawal concept*, pp. 399–414. Springfield, Ill: Garland Press, Inc.

Tobach, E., & Schneirla, T. C. (1968). The biopsychology of social behavior in animals. In R. E. Cooke (Ed.). *The biologic basis of pediatric practice*, pp. 68–82. New York: McGraw-Hill.

Toth, Nicholas. (1985). The Oldowan reassessed: A close look at early stone artifacts. *J. Archaeological Science*, 12–120.

Toth, Nicholas, & Schick, Kathy D. (1986). The first million years: The archaeology of protohuman culture. *Advances in Archaeological Method and Theory, 9*, 1–96.

van Lawick-Goodall, Jane. (1970). Tool-using in primates and other vertebrates. In D. S. Lehrman, Robert Hinde, & Evelyn Shaw (Eds.). *Advances in the study of behavior*, (Vol. 3, pp. 195–249). New York: Academic Press.

Vygotsky, L. S. (1962). *Thought and language.* E. Hanfmann & G. Vakar (Eds. and transl.). Cambridge, MA.: MIT Press.

Vygotsky, L. S. (1978). *Mind in society.* Cambridge, MA.: Harvard University Press.

Vygotsky, L. S. (1987). *Problems of general psychology.* Norris Minick (transl.). R. W. Rieber & A. S. Carton (Eds.). New York: Plenum Press.

Webster's New World Dictionary. (1988). Victoria Neukfeldt (Ed.). New York: Webster's New World.

Wertsch, James V. (1981). *The concept of activity in Soviet psychology.* Armonk, NY: M. E. Sharpe, Inc.

Whiten, A., Byrne, R. W., Barton, R. A., Waterman, P. G., & Heinz, S. P. (1990). Dietary and foraging strategies of baboons. In Whiten & Widdowso (Eds.). *Foraging strategies and natural diet of monkeys, apes and humans.* pp. 189–197. Oxford: Clarendon Press.

Wilson, E. O. (1975). Sociobiology: The new synthesis. Cambridge, MA.: Belknap Press of Harvard University Press.

Wilson, E. O. (1978). *On human nature.* Cambridge, MA.: Harvard University Press.

Woodger, J. H. (1929). *Biological principles.* London: Keegan Paul.

Wynn, T., & McGrew, W. C. (1989). An ape's view of the Oldowan. *Man, 24*, 383–398.

Zohar, O., & Terkel, J. (1991). Acquisition of pine cone stripping behavior in black rats (*Rattus rattus*). *International Journal of Comparative Psychology, 5*, 1–8.

4 Reflecting on Russian consciousness

Jerome Bruner

I have often thought about the curious contradiction that has existed in Russian intellectual culture – how a country with such a long and chilling record of despotically suppressing ideas, even consciousness, could at the same time breed such searchingly conscious literature. Indeed, the contradiction, so evident in Czarist Russia, even survived the revolution of 1917. It even manifested itself within the microcosm of Russian psychology, torn as it has been for over a century between the gross and reductionist reflexologies of Sechenov and Pavlov, on the one side, and the psychological and cultural subtleties of Vygotsky and Luria on the other. Here is a culture of unquestionable social and intellectual power that seems forever torn between the conflicting ideals of unreflective and mindless obedience backed by force and deeply subjective, conscious reflection. Even as I write, the Russian nation is being subjected to two such crazily divergent scenarios as the bombardment of its Parliament building, its "White House," accompanied by a request to reflect on a new Constitution – both on the orders of the same leader, its "President."

I want particularly to set down my reflections on this puzzling issue in this volume dedicated to the memory of Sylvia Scribner. For she was one of two people with whom I ever discussed this matter seriously – the only psychologist – the other being Sir Isaiah Berlin who was the president of my college at Oxford and my good friend during a decade of teaching at that great university. I do not have a resolution to offer; far from it. Rather, I want to use this occasion and this tormented topic better to understand the place of "psychology" in a society and in a culture. Russia provides an opportune case study. I would have liked to consider the matter in more general terms – or even more particularly in terms of the American case. But as for the general case, I simply do not have a deep enough grasp of the issues to know how to begin. And as for America and American psychology's place in our culture, I know all too well that the fish may be the last to discover water.

II

It is usually taken as a truism that notions about what mind "is" or how it "works" have deep cultural and ideological roots. Such notions, in any case, have deep ideological consequences, whether intended or not. A view about what mind "is" or how it "works" – or what reflective consciousness accomplishes, these are said to be stances that affect our notions of what people can be held responsible for. Or what education they deserve to be given. We psychologists, so driven by a quest for the "real" nature of mind, are usually insensitive to such matters, and perhaps we should be. But certainly those concerned with the authority of the state are concerned, *must* be concerned. That is surely the claim, and it seems a reasonable one.

Indeed, most great political revolutions have been accompanied by counterpart revolutions in conceptions about the nature of mind. The Renaissance was both inspired and legitimized by the new humanism in which reason was put on an equal footing with revelation (Gilson 1938). And the labors of the Encyclopaedists, offering the promise of openly available knowledge, is said to have fueled the French Revolution, just as the elaboration of empiricism by John Locke is believed, once and for all, to have toppled the conception of the monarch's divine rights (Brinton 1957; Laslett 1956). The bold psychological premise that all men, king and commoner alike, are originally "in a state of nature," subject alike to the natural laws of reason and experience, while originally intended as a skirmish in the battle against Charles II, eventually found its way into the United States Constitution.

Characteristically, to return to the Russian case, Czar Alexander II simply abolished both psychology and philosophy as topics for study when the serfs were emancipated in 1861. His censors thought it better to suppress all discussion of such sensitive subjects during that transition. An extreme solution, yes, but was it out of character? How different were later Soviet aspirations to build a socialist state on "scientific principles"? Were these principles to include notions about what should occupy the Soviet citizen's mind? Was Ivan Petrovich Pavlov, Russia's own Nobel laureate, to provide these guiding principles, to operate side by side with Karl Marx's historical–economic ones? But most puzzling of all, are these the right questions to ask in an inquiry into how a state or society is created or how it operates?

I rather think not, for I believe matters of state are much less "top down" than such questions suggest. Yet, I'm led to pursue them by a recent reading of David Joravsky's remarkable book, *Russian Psychology: A Critical History* (1989). It purports to deal with how the Russians themselves have gone about conceiving of mind and consciousness in the century or so since the freeing of the serfs. Along with Raymond Bauer's classic on the "New Soviet Man," it provides interesting hints about that "Russian contradiction" with which we started (Bauer 1952). Neither book resolves our dark question, but perhaps they help frame it better.

III

Best begin with a characteristic twist of history. At the start of the Russian century that started with the freeing of the serfs, Western "modernism" was the envy of Russian intellectuals. They yearned to emulate it, even to surpass it. For them, backwardness and superstition in the Russian peasant, buttressed by the church, was the major obstacle to achieving modernism at home. It was this sense of being thwarted that attracted them particularly to "scientific modernism," and particularly to its antiillusionist stance toward the human condition. The materialist, objectivist, antisuperstitious sound of the new theories of "reflexology" appealed particularly as antidote to the Russian Orthodox Church. They liked the hard-nosed, biological sound of it all. So here it begins at mid-century: Russian intellectuals, worshipful of the justly famous and conspicuously "conscious" novels, plays, and poems of the Russian literary giants, but also enamored of the antiillusionary reflexology imported from abroad as a weapon in the war against backwardness.

But not all of them could live easily with that schizoid division. And certainly not the restless Dostoyevski. He expressed his acute disquiet in *Notes from the Underground*. When it appeared in 1864, it was promptly banned by the censors for its "nihilism." For in that haunted book, man is portrayed as so reduced, so stripped of humanity, so limited in consciousness as to be aware of his own fate yet unable to affect it. What provoked Dostoyevsky to write *Notes* in 1864? Here the bizarre story begins to reveal the depth and tangled density of that Russian contradiction, the ambivalence about consciousness. For, in fact, Dostoyevsky wrote *Notes* in angry reaction to a novel by Chernyshevsky entitled *What Is to Be*

Done? That novel's thoroughly "modern" hero is, yes, one of those young reflexologists, big with belief about the ability of the new science to demystify man and his mind. But Chernyshevsky's hero was not quite a fictional figure. He was "real," or in any case the fictional figure was about to create a "real" one soon enough. Art was about to imitate life which was about to imitate art – the archetypal dilemma of Russian literariness.

Enter Sechenov. Anyone who knows anything about Russian science will have encountered I. M. Sechenov, always, then and now, and by whomever quoted, "the father of Russian physiology." He was the model for Chernyshevsky's hero. But a closer reading suggests that Sechenov might equally as well have been inspired by Chernyshevsky's hero. Fiction rather than life may have turned the real Sechenov into the idealized progressive of progressive Russian intellectuals. He turns out to be as much a fiction as a product of real life.

The flesh-and-blood Sechenov, the soon-to-be "father of Russian physiology," got into this half-fiction, half-real plight step by step, as in a dream. In the early 1860s the real-life Sechenov wrote an essay entitled "Reflexes of the Brain" and sent it to Chernyshevsky's widely read review, *The Contemporary*. It was accepted and then promptly banned by the Czar's censors: too materialistic in its view of human nature. The censors insisted it be altered and then, hoping it would disappear, decreed its revision be published in a technical medical journal. But given the power of word of mouth among the Moscow intelligentsia, everybody found it in the obscure medical journal, its renown instantly inflated by its banishment. The essay was all about how the human mind could be reduced to brain functions, a point of view hardly appreciated by the Russian Orthodox Church.

Chernyshevsky, the editor of *The Contemporary* whose eventual novel was soon to anger Dostoyevsky into despair and to inspire his *Notes from the Underground*, had been packed off to prison shortly before Sechenov's piece was suppressed – though on charges having nothing to do with this matter. Chernyshevsky, in prison, was of course enraged by the banning, and swiftly wrote *What Is To Be Done?*, the novel whose engaging and radical physiologist hero might as well have been Sechenov. The fictional hero even has a "free love" affair, like one in which Sechenov was said to be involved. The fictional hero became the immediate darling of the radical intelligentsia.

Flesh-and-blood Sechenov did not linger far behind. He soon became the champion of reflexes of the brain alone as the source of man's highest self-gratification: service to mankind. But in fact, as far as we can tell, Sechenov was scarcely a political radical (he admired Herbert Spencer's scientific "progressivism" and his own chief contribution to physiology was a theory of neural inhibition). Indeed, he even recanted on his fervent materialism and became a dualist. Despite himself, he always retained the aura of radicalism. David Joravsky has an interesting observation to make about this persistent aura: "The 'sons' of the 1860s would not be feckless romantic dreamers, like the 'fathers' of the 1840s, easily repressed when the autocrat inclined that way. The 'new men' (and women) of the 1860s were determined to awake from idle dreams and see the world in its actual condition, however repellant. Hence a passion for science as the destroyer of illusory values . . ." (1989, p. 55).

But history has more than a single voice. For though Sechenov's views about the liberating value of the new materialism were widely admired, interest in the critical power of searching "consciousness" remained undiminished – rather like yang to the yin of materialist antiillusionism. Indeed, after the enthusiasm about "political reflexology" occasioned by Chernyshevsky's book, Sechenov's article, and Dostoyevski's *Notes*, interest waned. By the 1870s and 1880s it was mostly latent. Sechenov's radical aura dwindled apace. Indeed, he became "respectable," and as an established and honored professor, his stock grew ever-more gilt-edged – particularly when gracious tributes from the "progressive" West began arriving, like a fulsome one from Sir Charles Sherrington, the undisputed world doyen of reflexology. The erstwhile romantic hero soon became the emblem of Russia's new "world class" science.

Successful science breeds professionalism, not romanticism. And by 1904 Russia won its first Nobel Prize. This time, enter Pavlov. This "first" Nobel laureate got the prize for his work on the digestive system. But he too soon grew bigger than life. Before long he spread his wings beyond digestion to those very same "reflexes of the brain," advocacy of which had initially made Sechenov an ideological hero. I do not propose now to psychoanalyze the historical Pavlov, nor is it necessary. There was obviously a niche in Russian culture waiting to be filled by Pavlov – the same antiillusionist, antibackwardness niche that had been there all along, probably since Peter the Great.

Deep down, one suspects on the basis of the record that Pavlov was no more flamingly progressive than Sechenov had been. The son of an Orthodox priest destined from childhood for the priesthood, he is said to have hated the dogmatism of the seminary, escaping into medicine and physiology. He eventually married a religious woman and settled into the cozy but iron routine of the *gelehrter* "working scientist." Who knows what his initial impulse may have been, but his theory was as conventionally cut and dried as any nineteenth-century reductionism could be. He confessed never to have been the least interested in the "poetry" of his doctrines. The conditioned stimulus simply substitutes for a natural one, a bell serving in place of the sight or smell of food in evoking salivation and gastric secretion. All behavior, he claimed, no matter how complicated, reduced to this formula. His theory, he kept urging, was simply required by the facts. He was a flat-out empiricist, yet tolerant enough about what strangers chose to study – so long as their methods were empirical. He even sent a letter of congratulations to the founders of the first, quite un-Pavlovian Institute of Psychology in Moscow in the mid-1920s.

From about the turn of the century until 1917, over the years when Pavlov was surely becoming the best known Russian in the world, he scarcely gave a thought to politics. It is said that he lost faith in the Czar when the Russian fleet was destroyed off Korea in 1905, and with it went his interest in politics. And be it noted that on their side, the aspiring Marxist political–intellectual Left that grew up in Russia between 1905 and the revolution never so much as mentioned Pavlov's name in its journals. Which is hardly to say that the budding Marxists were not interested in mind, consciousness, and their uses.

IV

In that decade before the revolution, indeed, Marxist intellectuals were passionately engaged in debating just such matters. But neither Pavlov nor academic psychology figured in their discussions. The role of consciousness in "revolutionary" activity became so fevered a topic on the Left that it literally split the movement down the middle. It began in the fateful year of defeat, 1905, when Mensheviks and Bolsheviks fell out bitterly over whether the revolutionary task ahead was to be accomplished by raising the consciousness of the proletariat or by releasing revolutionary indignation into direct action under the leadership of trained cadres. Was revolution to be fueled by indignant action or by proletarian consciousness of possibilities?

Again, the "Russian contradiction," this time embodied by Lenin himself. Like the Chernyshevsky–Sechenov–Dostoyevsky story, this one is full of ambivalence, second thoughts, recriminations. It erupted when Lenin changed his mind. He had originally taken a position he claimed to have derived from A. A. Bogdanov, a professed disciple of the great Ernst Mach. Mach had argued in his famous *Analysis of Sensations* (1897) that all knowledge of the world originated in human conscious experience, in the physical senses. Physics and psychology were simply two different ways of construing the testimony of the senses (Mach 1897). Human action, in Bogdanov's view, depended on consciousness as its guide. Therefore, if consciousness is instilled in the masses, mentored by disciplined cadres, true revolution was inevitable.

But with the 1905 fiasco, Lenin had second thoughts about consciousness inspiring revolutionary action. He condemned poor Bogdanov for his "Machism," and had him summarily thrown out of the Party. Why this flip-flop from "consciousness-raising" to "upsurge-of-indignation" theory of revolution? Some argue (including Joravsky) that the volte-face was Lenin's reaction to the humiliation of 1905. I think it is deeper. I think it was Lenin's typically Russian ambivalence about the roles of consciousness/reflection and impulse/action in life generally and in politics particularly. I say "typically Russian" because, as I shall try to argue, it bedeviled official Russian thinking right into and through the years of Soviet Communism, just as it had before. For the Bolsheviks, as for their nineteenth-century forebears, it seemed always to be a matter of binary opposition: one or the other, not a mix of the two.

Typically, the matter never stayed settled in Lenin's mind. Thanks to Joravsky's diligent documentary research, we know that during his enforced leisure in Switzerland during the war years, when Lenin was reading philosophy, he made this entry in his journals: "The consciousness of man not only reflects the objective world but also creates it" (Lenin 1941–1967). So one part of Lenin was constructivist or Machian, at least during his enforced idleness in Switzerland. But once returned to the arena of revolutionary action in Russia, he lurched back to a theory of direct action, with little patience for issues of consciousness raising. By 1908, even Karl Kautsky, then chief of the orthodox German Marxists, deplored this antiintellectual extremism in his Russian comrade, and

Rosa Luxemburg remarked that "Tartar Marxism grates on the nerves" (Joravsky 1989, p. 195).

But the story is hardly begun!

V

For once the Revolution seemed to have been secured, consciousness got another short inning, this time occasioned by the debate over the "New Soviet Man" at the time of the New Economic Policy in the early 1920s.[1] By then a new generation of intellectuals had come on the scene, pining (it would seem) for a return to critical consciousness, reflection, and self-awareness as part of the revolutionary ideal. In the end, their leaders were all either killed or forced to flee abroad – Akhmitova, Bakhtin, Mandelstam, Jakobson, Khlebnikov, Shklovsky, and indeed even Lenin's star-struck Commisar of Public Education, Anatoly Lunacharsky, who believed that emerging Soviet art could produce the "critical consciousness" for the new age.[2] Lev Vygotsky, who now comes into our story, was on the fringe of this gifted group. The distinguished linguist, Ivanov, writing many years later, characterized these apostles of the New Consciousness as Russia's "visitors from the future" (Ivanov 1983). Though they never succeeded in restoring reflective consciousness to the approved toolkit of the New Soviet Man, they struck a nerve among Russian intellectuals – one that existed before the revolution, persisted after, and remains still today.

It was just as talk about the New Soviet Man was fading that the Soviet establishment made its first official approach to Pavlov, its big play to "co-opt" him to the side of the Soviet system. Was he to be a bulwark against renewed interest in critical consciousness? Did the Party think that his ideas of conditioning would help get collectivization working? Or were the ideologues interested in wrapping themselves in the "correct" flag of materialism? Well, maybe all these interpretations are true. But I take a somewhat cooler view of the matter. Surely the Party felt they needed Pavlov's fame and legitimacy to prop up prestige at home and abroad after the disorganization of the New Economic Policy. And surely they liked his materialism. But there was more to it than that, as we shall see.

The actual wooing of Pavlov is most puzzling. Joravsky recounts it in his book with ironic grace. Pavlov, it seems, made his first public speech in praise of the revolution at his institute in the early 1920s. It was surely never cleared with anybody. In the course of it he took it upon himself to explain the revolution in terms of conditioned reflexes. Some dogs, he told his lecture audience, had a "reflex of slavery" and showed no signs of resistance when put into the conditioning harness. But others, a minority, had a "reflex of freedom" and resisted the harness. And so it was with the revolution where the reflex of freedom had at last prevailed: "How often and in what varied forms has the reflex of slavery appeared on Russian soil, and how useful it is to become conscious of it!" Joravsky quotes Pavlov as saying (1989, p. 78).

This was hardly the Party line. Indeed, it was a technical rehash of a jaundiced bourgeois view about Russian peasants. A lesser lecturer might have been called to account for such heresy. But so exalted was Pavlov's reputation that three major bigwigs, Zinoviev, Trotsky, and Bukharin (the chief Party ideologist), politely set out to correct in published articles what Pavlov had allegedly said in his lecture. Pavlov's unpublished lecture was, of course, known only by word of mouth. The published articles by the bigwigs clucked correctively, yet managed to praise Pavlov's materialism. He was disciplined in no way.[3] Indeed, he was never disciplined. On the rare occasions when he expressed displeasure with the regime (always privately), he was simply cajoled or exhorted (once even by the revered Maxim Gorky). Once he was even given some extra funding to smooth his ruffled feathers about an academic appointment going to the wrong candidate.

So why the leniency? What did the bigwigs get in return? It is hard to find any occasion on which Soviet ideologists used the corpus of Pavlov's theoretical works explicitly or derivationally to generate or justify a policy. I realize, of course, that this runs against the usual mythology. But I would want to make the case that Pavlov was used principally for two things. The first was to get some light to shine on the regime: you can't have your most famous scientist in residence, perhaps the best known Russian in the world, and not have him on your side. But far more important, I think, is the symbol of Pavlov as antiillusionist, as a "modern" in the struggle against backwardness, like official atheism, say. I can't resist the conclusion that the Party leadership was using Pavlov much as the "men of 1860" had used Chernyshevsky's hero and Sechenov himself in the struggle against that Russian bugaboo, backwardness.

When Stalin took power in 1925, Congresses were called to bring things into line with Marxist doctrine, including one to bring psychology and the brain sciences into line with Marxism generally and "Pavlov" particularly. I put his name in quotes, because it is difficult to find concretely what Pavlov was supposed to stand for. Pavlovian doctrine had by then become banal through popularization: anything could serve as a conditioned stimulus (even quite symbolic events), and virtually anything (including emotions) as a conditioned response. With that degree of permissiveness, Pavlovian theory becomes just a way or style of talking about anything. And that is what the psychological Congress turned into: how to talk about what you wanted to study. It was the progressive authority of Pavlov that the regime was invoking, not the substance.

Let me say a word about that Congress for it brings on stage the next major actor in our drama of conflict. A young, rather unknown psychologist (or rather, intensely well known but only to a small circle of colleagues and students) was assigned to give one of the major speeches on, of all things, "consciousness" (*soznanie*, the thinking, feeling mind). His audience of psychologists and neurologists had their own interests and were prepared to bend a ritual knee to Pavlov in order to be left alone to follow them. The Congress, by the way, took place just as Bukharin's reply to Pavlov's "reflex of freedom" came out, in which the Party's chief ideologist scolds Pavlov while celebrating the conditioned reflex as a "weapon from the iron arsenal of materialism." As for Vygotsky's topic, his "fellow psychologists were an enthusiastic audience, for they shared his conviction that subjectivity and consciousness are central to the science of the mind," Joravsky reports (1989, p. 259).

Vygotsky's was apparently a superb performance. He mentioned Pavlov sparsely, only as needed, and always with deference. When he questioned Pavlov's views, he invoked the sacrosanct Sechenov – for example, to the effect that thinking involved not reflex activity but an interruption or inhibition of it. Or he contrasted Pavlov's switchboard model of a brain to the highly structured "funneling" proposed by Sherrington, who in turn had hailed Sechenov. To protect his ideological flank, he even fell back on Bukharin's favorite sausage metaphor, but with a twist: "A human being is not at all a skin sack filled with reflexes, and the brain is not a hotel for a series of conditioned reflexes accidentally stopping in" (Joravsky 1989, p. 260). As a conclusion, he proposed the "historical–cultural method" by which one related human development (ontogenetic and phylogenetic alike) to the emerging patterns of human societies, with the Marxist state as its highest form. And he gave pride of place to language as the hub of the wheel of mind – language as both a biological given in human evolution and, more important in a Marxist perspective, as a carrier of cultural and historical meaning. Psychology was to be "the science of the new man," in his phrase, a science without which Marxism would be incomplete: it had not yet emerged but it would eventually do so if Marxist psychology would only adhere to the cultural–historical method. His proposal was at once empirical and theoretical, and above all it was plausible: it showed his audience of psychologists how, in effect, to justify their concern with consciousness while being good Marxists and good psychologists (that is, empirical), both of which they wanted very much to be.

In effect, to use street slang, Vygotsky had thrown the whole ball of wax – all of the suppressed elements in the deep Russian conflict. Amazingly, a glowing if cautious report of young Vygotsky's address appeared some weeks later in *Red Virgin Soil*. As for the local reverberations, Vygotsky became the darling of the less "Party disciplined" younger psychologists. And there were some unexpected twists as well. Eventually, even the haughty and pampered Pavlov gave his version of what had been Vygotsky's major theme – the appeal to the centrality of language. He did so by proposing a "Second Signal System" through which physical stimuli impinging on human beings are converted into linguistic form and operate according to their meanings, while in the First Signal System they remain governed only by laws of the natural world. The world of the Second Signal System is the world of language and culture. Vygotsky was given no credit at all, not even mentioned. Perhaps it was all Pavlov's idea anyway.

My own view is that Pavlov, by now full of years, had finally found a "Russian peace" somewhere between strict antiillusionist reductionism on the one side and soft literary subjectivity on the other. It was his way of resolving the persistent Russian contradiction. While Pavlov never really developed the "Second System" in any detail, his nod of approval toward the "transformation of stimuli into language" in humans bestowed a renewed respectability to dualism – to a distinction between nature subserved by the First Signal System and culture and consciousness by a second. It is hard to know why Party ideologists didn't come down on his head for this Pavlovian excursion into "bourgeois idealism."

Perhaps they weren't paying attention, perhaps they didn't care – both of which seem highly unlikely in the light of what remains to be recounted. Or perhaps they liked it "unconsciously" as a way of reconciling their own "Russian contradiction." Interestingly, there has never been the least murmur of official disapproval of Pavlov's new dualism. Not even so assiduous a digger in the Russian ideological literature as David Joravsky can find one.[4] As for professional psychologists, I suspect they too greeted the new development as a welcome relief from that same contradiction.

Meanwhile – the most ironic twist of all – the new Second Signal System provided Vygotsky's followers in the latter 1930s (principally Luria, Leont'ev, Sokholov, and Zinchenko; Vygotsky having died of tuberculosis in 1934) with just the ideological umbrella they needed to bring the cultural–historical method in out of the rain. This was the time of "the battle of consciousness" in the late 1940s and 1950s, as everybody in Moscow psychology often later called it.[5] Vygotsky's disciples did not win the battle, but at least they were given posts, grants, and pulpits. Now when presenting their research on the influence of language on thought they could respectfully cite Pavlov chapter and verse. By the time I first visited the Institute of Psychology in Moscow in the early 1960s, it was standard, almost ritual practice for researchers to begin their seminar reports on the role of language in this or that form of "higher mental function" with a pious curtsey to Pavlov's Second Signal System – particularly directing their gaze toward the American visitor when doing so. And when, in those years, I lectured on similar issues in Moscow, I too was snugged in under its shelter by whomever was introducing me.

But we've skipped over Vygotsky as mythic figure, how he vaulted from a virtual unknown at that "let's-get-it-in-line" Congress in the mid-1920s to a real hero figure by the time of his death little more than a decade later. I think it has to do not just with his genius but with the niche he filled in Russian culture. For while he was obviously a man of genius, he fit a recognizable template in Russian literary culture. And he also helped nourish a real aspiration among the young to make Marxism psychologically real. From the start Vygotsky, newly arrived in Moscow, himself fresh out of literary studies, was plainly and evidently in search of a genuine, humane, and principled Marxist psychology. He was searching for a psychology that resonated with the consciousness-centered notion of human mentality that animated the Russian literary tradition from which he had sprung. It was a tradition all about understanding and awareness and about language as their medium. For in Russian culture (as in French) there is a deep conviction that language, especially poetic language, is the vehicle of deep thought.

There have been heroes in Russian literary history who embodied this ideal – gifted, intense, morally engaged, philosophically obsessed, driven to search out the links between language and life. For them, by legend, death comes early – from exhaustion. During their short lives, they have an electrifying effect on their contemporaries, as if somehow (as Isaiah Berlin has suggested) there is a prepared place in Russian intellectual life that requires their luminous and short-lived presence. As Berlin remarks, "No society demanded more of its authors than Russia, then or now" (Berlin 1978, p. 272). But their heroic presence is forever endangered by the savagely vindictive authority with which Russia has been ruled from the Czars to the advent of *glasnost*. In the latter nineteenth century, the critic–moralist Vissarion Belinsky, near whose grave the exiled Ivan Turgenev instructed that he should be buried, was one such. Eventually Turgenev was buried nearby when his remains were returned from Paris in 1883. The towering linguist Baudoin de Courtenay, who intuitively grasped the idea of the phoneme as the building block of language based on meaning rather than physiology, was another – at least for Jakobson, Troubetskoy, and a generation of brilliant young linguists (Jakobson 1978).

Vygotsky was perpetually on the edge of trouble with the Party. My own opinion is that his ideas were too close to the raw nerve of the great Russian contradiction.[6] He even had to vacate Moscow for Kharkhov to keep out of harm's way. Finally, like the classic "heroes of consciousness" before him, he was dead of exhaustion (tuberculosis) by 1934 before the age of 40. Had he lived into the darker days of the Stalinist purges, it might have gone even worse for him: too intense to compromise, too involved in the generative powers of historical consciousness to be safe in an era of *partiinost* (party discipline), and a Jew besides. Though his work was banned for many years after his death, its underground existence as *samizdat* attracted some of the best minds of the next generation of psychologists. It would not have come as a surprise to me if one of his distinguished disciples, say Alexander Romanovich Luria, had asked to be buried close to Vygotsky's grave – like Turgenev in reverence to Vissarion Belinsky.

Let it be said that such heroes also had their appeal in the West – much as Russian novels do and always have had. A decade ago, Stephen Toulmin characterized Vygotsky as "the Mozart of psychology" (Toulmin 1978). Nearly two decades before that I hailed the English translation of his now renowned *Thought and Language* as transcending "the ideological rifts that divide our world so deeply today" (Bruner 1962, p. x). For years after Vygotsky's death, his former student, A. R. Luria, enjoyed a vast reputation abroad as the voice of Vygotsky's inspiration. Even during his own lifetime, we learn from contemporaries, his lectures at the Institute of Psychology (now finally published) were the talk of the town.[7] Perhaps Western ears found in Vygotsky a viewpoint that made the Russian contradiction seem less threatening, more amenable to compromise.

Why, one wonders, didn't the Russian Party establishment simply adopt Vygotsky as they had Pavlov? Surely a better Marxist case could have been made for his theories than for Pavlov's. Was Rosa Luxemburg right about "Tartar Marxism"? Does the answer lie buried in Russian ambivalence, caught between obedience/despotism/reflexology and sensibility/freedom/consciousness? There has never been a moment's respite between them, neither under the Czars nor the Communist Party. Under despotism, consciousness could only be taken as an instrument of dissent. As for that early high-flown rhetoric about shaping the consciousness of the New Soviet Man, it evaporated as soon as power had to be consolidated after the failure of the New Economic Policy. "In an attempt to explain the Russian Revolution to Lady Ottoline Morrell, Bertrand Russell once remarked that, appalling though Bolshevik despotism was, it seemed the right sort of government for Russia: 'If you ask yourself how Dostoevsky's characters should be governed, you will understand'" (Kelly 1978, p. xiii).[8]

Surely Stalin never wanted a principled doctrine of "cultural consciousness" as the centerpiece of his state policies. I would argue that that cynical and opportunistic genius had no real interest in basing policies on any psychological doctrine – certainly not Pavlovian reflexology, and probably not even Marxism. If Stalin had been interested in a reflexology with a political cast (in place of Pavlov's blandly apolitical version of conditioning), he could always have turned to V. M. Bekhterev, Pavlov's younger contemporary. For Bekhterev was the classically gung-ho ideological reflexologist deriving Marxist–Leninist principles from the principles of reflexology themselves. He was even into collective reflexology, and had all the proper emulate-the-West credentials – a degree in neurology from Berlin, studies with Wundt at Leipzig, and with Charcot in Paris. He had even spoken out against capitalism in 1905 and made a show of appointing "progressives" to his Psychoneuorological Institute in St. Petersburg, where he also daringly set up a department of sociology.

All to no avail. Instead of power he got endless cossetting with minor honors for his zeal. Indeed, aside from that short period of concern for the New Soviet Man, psychology never figured as a foundational source for a theory of Russian socialism. And even during that New Economic Policy period, it was not "conditioned reflexes" that interested the authorities but (as Raymond Bauer vividly points out), the idea of *nost*, or "alertness of consciousness" that was given center stage.[9] And then quickly shooed off again!

VI

I need to do proper justice to the place of language as a source of consciousness in Russian thought. I've politicized it too much to make Vygotsky's appeal plausible. The duet of language and consciousness has always been a major theme in Russian linguistics, particularly in poetics and literary theory. Its theme is that language creates consciousness, and such creation is the domain of the literary. It was a Russian, the towering Roman Jakobson (who fled to Prague shortly after the revolution) who first proclaimed that the principal function of language was to establish the distinction between the marked and the unmarked – that which is worthy of consciousness, and that which can be left in the background to be dealt with automatically (Jakobson 1982). Successful literature, Jakobson urged, keeps thought and consciousness from becoming banal and automatic, produces *literaturnost*. In Viktor Shklovsky's (1990) words, it "makes things strange again," brings the world freshly into consciousness.[10] This theme is as alive today in the writings of Joseph Brodsky as it was at the turn of the century.[11]

Jakobson was my companion on a flight from Boston to Moscow in 1967, his first return to Russia since he'd fled. I recall his saying as we flew the last leg from Berlin to Moscow that it was almost impossible to "think Pavlov" in Russian, a language so rich in a syntax and lexicon dedicated to making nuanced distinctions about state of mind. He found Pavlov's very language "cramping" and "artificial" and "unRussian." I recall wondering at the time whether this was a literary man speaking, with the usual distaste for the lexicon of psychology, or whether Jakobson might not be speaking as a prototypical Russian intellectual. Now again, Jakobson's remark leads me to wonder whether, perhaps, the Stalinist embrace of Pavlov – even if it "bought" some vague kind of scientific sponsorship for the regime – didn't signal some early and deep alienation from the professed ideals of Russian sensibility. Perhaps it was this alienation, with its attendant self-hatred, that made Vygotsky such a threat, such a reminder of the renounced. For Vygotsky had captured the high ground of both Russian consciousness worship and Marxist historicism while, in Jakobson's phrase, one couldn't even "think Pavlov" while thinking in Russian. Vygotsky was forever preoccupied with the troubling question that had occupied the restless and brilliant Lenin, idled in wartime Switzerland, reading treatises on philosophy – how "a cultural process . . . creates the human mind even as it is created by it" (Lenin 1941–1967). It is a question that Russian intellectuals find hard to put aside.

Perhaps if it had genuinely interested Stalin, it might have changed history. But then again, when glasnost finally came, it turned everything on its head. Stalin, in his mad genius, probably knew that releasing all that energy in open discussion would have dangerous side effects. I draw that conclusion not entirely out of the blue. When the Red Army was most beleaguered in the dark days of the Battle of Stalingrad, it is said that Stalin himself ordered the removal of political commissars from the front. The late Henry Dicks, one of the great scholars of Russian mentality in the past generation, who interviewed many participants in that bloody battle, told me that on their departure, Russian soldiers stayed up through the night talking, free at last of surveillance, free to exercise the Russian genius for collective introspection and consciousness. Did Stalin believe, finally, that this would restore their Russian strength? I confess that I certainly do.

VII

I suppose finally I should reach some deep conclusion after this excursion through the troubled Russian past. Certainly one shallow conclusion might be that Pavlov was a deeply compromising investment for the Russian regime. But not really. I think they got good value for their ruble – just the value they wanted. Pavlov, after all, made them seem somehow sensible when Lysenko might have made Stalin's little Kremlin gang seem like baseless fools. Besides, he brought honors and honored guests to Russia's door, particularly from America: Pavlov as guest of honor at the Yale International Congress of Psychology in 1929, Walter Bradford Cannon on virtually a state visit to Pavlov from Harvard in the 1930s, among others. If anything, the watered down Pavlov of Russian ideology probably gave the Party a freer hand for opportunistic maneuverings.

And as for the other side, whether critical consciousness might have played a more powerful role in the forging of the state, I suspect that some around Stalin would have loved to have had a Potemkin village that honored that ideal – if they could have kept it under control, kept it as just a Potemkin village. I recall a brilliant young Latvian graduate student at the Institute of Psychology in Moscow in the early 1960s, an ex-dancer and literary to the fingertips, telling me (with the enthusiastic assent of a half-dozen fellow graduate students gathered at the "dorm" in Lenin Hills) that in her view, Vygotsky was the only thing that could save Soviet Marxism. But what a view of Marxism she had! We had all gathered for a party after an evening at the Moscow Circus and were discussing the thinly veiled antibureaucratic skits of the great clown Popov. The little group had been emboldened by the newly come-to-power Nikhita Khrushchev's breezier style. What they had in mind for Russia was no Potemkin village: it was openness, consciousness, even irony!

But from Krushchev on, things took another route. There was to be a new psychology of efficiency that, so to speak, would make the trains run on time, or as one of the new leaders in Russian psychology told me on that same visit, "We want a psychology that will keep empty lorries from being sent past each other in opposite directions on the road between Moscow and Leningrad." The new line was to be information theory and cybernetics. After all, I was told, that is what makes America efficient!

So I am still wrapt in thought about how notions about mind and consciousness affect the destinies of states. That is why I dedicate this essay to Sylvia Scribner's memory. For so was she.

Notes

1. For a particularly vivid and engaging picture of this era, see Clark & Holquist (1985). Bauer (1952) gives a perceptive account of the sharp rise of early postrevolutionary interest in a more active conception of man.
2. See Hughes (1981, p. 87) for an account of Lunacharsky and the ambivalent support he received from Lenin.
3. What Trotsky said in rejoinder to the infamous "freedom reflex" lecture was that Pavlov's theory of conditioned reflexes, unlike Freud's views, avoided the "turbid" and "arbitrary" and went "to the bottom and [then] rises experimentally to the top" (Joravsky 1989, p. 211). And Bukharin was even more forgiving, praising the Pavlovian doctrine as "a weapon from the arsenal of materialism," then adding the assertion that Pavlov gave lie to the vulgar belief that man was little more than a sausage stuffed with whatever he encountered – which, indeed, most critics then believed and still believe is the very rock on which conditioning theory finally founded.
4. So far as I know, there has been no systematic research in the newly available state archives for mentions of Pavlov or of documents about him.
5. I was unable to find a direct use of this expression in the printed works of Luria, Leont'ev, or the others in the Vygotsky circle. I consulted Michael Cole to inquire whether his memory conformed to mine about the currency of the expression "battle of consciousness" in Moscow conversations. His memory matched mine.
6. I am aware of Vygotsky's first encounter with the authorities in his study of "peasant mentality," which for a variety of reasons was an off-limits topic. But I think the real aftereffect of that episode was to bring him to the attention of the authorities as a troublemaker whose ideas were profoundly dangerous and at odds with the party line.
7. At least one volume of these lectures has been published as Vygotsky (1987). For an overview of his views in those lectures and his other publications, see my "Prologue" to the Plenum volume.
8. In fact, Dr. Kelly goes on to argue that Lord Russell's remark revealed a certain lack of understanding of the conflicted stance that many Russians took toward their nation's future.
9. Bauer (1952) discusses the early arguments presented for the role of consciousness in human learning, arguments that even distinguish problem solving in chimpanzees from humans, by virtue of the habit-boundedness among the former in contrast to the consciousness among the latter. See particularly p. 163ff.
10. A brilliant commentary on this work is to be found in Mukarovsky (1977, p. 134–142).

11. See particularly in Brodsky (1986) his remarks on the effectiveness of Anna Akhmatova as poet in "The keening muse" (p. 34ff.).

References

Bauer, R. (1952). *The new man in Soviet psychology*. Cambridge, MA: Harvard University Press.

Berlin, I. (1978). *Russian thinkers*. London: Hogarth Press.

Brinton, C. (1957). *The anatomy of revolution*. New York: Vintage Books.

Brodsky, J. (1986). *Less than one: Selected essays*. New York: Farrar, Straus, & Giroux.

Bruner, J. (1962). Introduction. In L. S. Vygotsky, *Thought and language*, pp. v–x. Cambridge, MA: MIT Press.

Clark, K., & Holquist, M. (1985). *Mikhail Bakhtin*. Cambridge, MA: Harvard University Press.

Gilson, E. (1938). *Reason and revelation in the Middle Ages*. New York: Scribner.

Hughes, R. (1981). *The shock of the new*. New York: Knopf.

Ivanov, V. V. (1983). Roman Jakobson: The future. In R. Jakobson, *A tribute to Roman Jakobson, 1896–1982*. Amsterdam: Mouton deRuyter.

Jakobson, R. (1982). The marked and the unmarked. *Collected papers* (Vol. 1). Amsterdam: Mouton deRuyter.

Jakobson, R. (1978). *Six lectures on sound and meanings*. Cambridge, MA: MIT Press.

Joravsky, D. (1989). *Russian psychology: A critical history*. New York: Basil Blackwell.

Kelly, A. (1978). *Introduction: A complex vision*. In I. Berlin *Russian thinkers*, pp. xiii–xxiv. London: Hogarth Press.

Laslett, P. (1956). The English revolution and Locke's two treatises of government. *Cambridge Historical Journal, 12*, pp. 40–55.

Lenin, V. I. (1941–1967). *Sochineniia, xxxviii*, p. 204.

Mach, E. (1897). *The analysis of sensations*. LaSalle, IL: Open Court.

Mukarovsky, J. (1977). *The word and verbal art*. New Haven: Yale University Press.

Shkovsky, V. (1990). *Theory of Prose*. (B. Sher, trans.). Elmwood Park, IL: Dalkney Archive Press.

Toulmin, S. (1978). The Mozart of psychology. *New York Review of Books*, 28 September, *25*(14), 51–57.

Vygotsky, L. S. (1987). *The collected works of L. S. Vygotsky*. New York: Plenum.

Part II

Doing psychology

5 Opening vistas for cognitive psychology

William Hirst and David Manier

Sometimes we can be too smart in seeking the solution to a problem, outwitting ourselves with our own cleverness. Prompted by the light of our reasoning, we find our way as if to a smartly appointed room. Here we become surprisingly comfortable, and the artificial brightness of the internal logic we have pursued nearly convinces us the room is illuminated by the problem we set out after. As often as not, our journey ends here. Yet in reality we have been led astray: Ours is a stuffy, windowless room, shut off from the "real world" – a reclusive chamber of our own construction. Over the last few years, the authors of this essay, like several other scholars (e.g., Neisser 1992; Scribner 1984; Bruner 1990), have reluctantly come to the conclusion that the branch of psychology in which we have labored, the one responsible for the study of cognition, may have cleverly constructed and be happily residing in just such an artificial enclave, cut off from the still unresolved problems that originally inspired it. In short, we have concluded that cognitive psychology now confronts an impasse. This chapter will outline the dimensions of this impasse and suggest ways to surmount it.

As cognitive psychologists, we hesitantly come to this conclusion in part out of frustration at our inability to offer satisfactory responses to the persistent queries of friends and relatives. Our area of expertise is memory, and friends and relatives often ask us why they have such poor memories, or why they have trouble remembering names, facts, appointments, or the details of their children's school lives.

These questions spring naturally from even a desultory reflection on memory. They are troublesome, yet fascinating, and people reasonably expect someone who studies memory to have insight into these issues. A

We would like to acknowledge the support of NIMH Grant #42064 and a grant from the McDonnell-Pew Program in Cognitive Neuroscience, and to express our gratitude for helpful comments from Jerome Bruner, Mayumi Kuribayashi, Silvia Léon, Joan Lucariello, Edward Manier, and especially, Katherine Nelson.

89

large industry has sprung up to accommodate the pressing demand for means to ameliorate the perceived fragility of memory (e.g., Robinson 1961; Lorayne & Lucas 1974). Cognitive psychologists, however, have had little input into this effort. Instead, we have tended to look at it disparagingly (see Hirst 1988). We have produced general theories, as well as a host of laboratory findings, and have often treated attempts to link theory to real-world problems and concerns as an uninteresting sideshow. It is little wonder, then, that we have no appropriate responses for our friends and relatives – only vague statements noting, for example, that meaningful things are memorable. Outside the cloisters we create for ourselves as cognitive psychologists, in the real world of lay friends and relatives, we feel much as Neisser (1978; see also Neisser 1976) did when he surveyed the field of memory. As he averred, if a question about memory is of interest to the so-called man on the street, cognitive psychology has had little if anything of interest to say about it.

There are, of course, good reasons why cognitive psychologists have concentrated on general theories supported by carefully designed laboratory experiments. We have traditionally ferreted out generalities of human cognition. Endeavoring to dig beneath the surface of behavior, we have hoped to uncover the common underground source of superficially distinct particularities. Wilhelm Wundt (1900), the father of the experimental study of cognition, was skeptical about whether generalities could be found for the full range of mental phenomena. More specifically, he was dubious about the prospects for a "scientific" study of memory. However, the field of experimental psychology, including its most recent variation, cognitive psychology, has paid little heed to Wundt's skepticism.

Cognitive psychology has hotly pursued elusive generalities, wishfully emulating physics. In the area of memory, Ebbinghaus (1964) dislodged whatever reservations Wundt held about a psychology of memory by introducing the "nonsense syllable," a purportedly "meaningless" consonant-vowel-consonant trigram, hundreds of which Ebbinghaus himself endeavored to memorize. Ebbinghaus used this device to mine beneath the surface of memory – littered as it is with meaning, associations, and the effects of person history – seeking what one British reviewer of his classic monograph called "the raw material of memory" (Jacobs 1885).

The nonsense syllable has not proven to be the golden tool Ebbinghaus thought it. Whereas Ebbinghaus maintained that the "nonsensical" quality of his innovation would allow him to strip away idiosyncratic effects of meaning, associations, and personal history, other investigators soon discovered that people refuse to treat the nonsense syllable as meaningless (Müller & Schumann 1889). Doing what comes naturally to humans, people imposed meaning where none was intended. For example, the meaningless trigram B-E-W, reweaved by human meaning-making propensities, becomes the mirror-image of "web," or the beginning of "bewilder." Although nonsense syllables no longer hold the appeal they initially did, most psychological students of memory have nevertheless unswervingly followed the path Ebbinghaus charted, keeping their sights firmly on the need for generalities and away from the snares and tangles of the admittedly interesting, but scientifically irksome, particularities of behavior.

Twenty-five years ago Neisser (1967), whose views have since changed dramatically, articulated the level of generality cognitive psychologists hoped to achieve when he advocated tracing the flow of information in the mind from input to output. Conceiving the study of cognition in these terms, Neisser pointedly adopted an information processing or computational approach. Tracing the path information processing takes as it transforms stimuli into actions, cognitive psychologists, in Neisser's erstwhile conception, chart a topography that constrains mental processing. This topography can sometimes be so limiting that only one path is possible, i.e., there may be only one way that a human could possibly process information of a given kind (Fodor 1983). In other cases, an individual can take myriad routes, with culture, personal history, and situational variables determining the actual path. Whether tightly restricted or broadly constrained, the charted mental topography was said to offer a general description of the cognitive world onto which all particularities of behavior can be mapped.

Challenges

The information processing paradigm has been and continues to be fruitful, and it does suggest a means of going from the general to the particular. Yet certain psychologists (e.g., Bruner, Neisser, Shweder, Scribner, Cole, Gergen, and Moscovici) have voiced skeptical protests. Even the most ardent theoretical scientist wants general science to apply to particularities. The physicist may model an idealized, frictionless world, but the problems tackled, and the ones students are quizzed on, involve real-world events, such as plotting the trajectory of projectiles, supporting moving weights, and calculating the aerodynamics of a moving wing. Should not psychologists be able to tackle, and their students be quizzed on, the application of cognitive theory to real-world situations? Although the information processing paradigm provides a potential framework for mapping theory onto real-world problems, our experience is that, while both our colleagues and our students may know much about specific experiments and models, when it comes to applications the results are often tenuous, vague, and broadly unsatisfactory. The kind of real-world problems that routinely appear on physics examinations do not have a parallel in the standard cognitive psychology exam.

Cognitive psychologists can say much about the purported mental topography of memory – the way people represent information in memory, the means by which they encode and retrieve it, the dynamics of proactive and retroactive interference, and so on – but these discoveries offer only vague answers to those interested in how these mechanisms work in specific contexts, e.g., in their own behavior or that of friends and relatives. Some applications do exist, of course, but ones that rely strictly on cognitive theory remain few. (For some examples of such applications, see Bruer 1993.)

To be sure, psychologists offer precise, elegant answers to questions generated within the information processing paradigm, answers designed to further understanding of human mental topography. In this sense they may be said to have secured for themselves a most comfortable dwelling. But for the skeptics, with whom we have begun to feel, however reluctantly, much sympathy, the artificially bright illumination of the received paradigm outshines and overwhelms the natural light emanating from concrete problems of daily cognitive activity. For a discipline that trades on science's claims for precision, cognitive psychology offers only imprecise and unspecific observations on the psychological nature of everyday life. It can do little more than fecklessly waive its hands when people insist that it discuss not general mental topography but particular real-world applications of this topography.

Frustration with cognitive psychology's inability to provide compelling responses to the problems of everyday mental life has inspired psychological skeptics to intensify their protests. The resulting rebellion against now-established Cognitive Science marches under many banners: a call for consideration of distributed and situated cognition (Pea & Kurland 1984; Lave 1991, 1993; Greeno 1989; Brown, Collins, & Duguid 1990; Perkins 1990; Suchman 1990); a return to the investigation of "acts of meaning" (Bruner 1990); the study of "social representations" (Moscovici 1983); a demand for ecologically valid experimentation (Neisser 1978; Neisser & Winograd 1988); a battle cry for cultural psychology (Stigler, Shweder, & Herdt 1990; Shweder 1991); and an introduction of activity theory to the United States (Scribner & Cole 1977, 1981; Vygotsky 1978; Leont'ev 1981; Wertsch 1981; Scribner 1984, 1985).

These scientific insurgencies have in common that they call for a new unit of analysis for cognitive psychology. Specifically, they want to direct cognitive psychology's attention away from the characterization of cognitive "machinery" in the abstract and toward the uses people make of this machinery. To this aim they examine cognitive acts in everyday life, investigating the ways people marshal their cognitive abilities to meet real-world challenges. They begin with the particular, rather than following the traditional route going from the general to the particular. In this they follow a method that has by now become mainstream in developmental psychology, where certain scholars inspired by Vygotsky (1978) have for many years concerned themselves with issues of how children learn to master the cognitive tasks set for them by their social environment (Meacham 1977; Ratner 1980, 1984, 1986; Paris, Newman, & Jacobs 1985; Nelson 1986, 1990, 1993; Fivush & Hudson 1990). But, partly as a result of their commitment to studying naturalistic phenomena viewed within a particular social contest, those who adopt a contextualist approach in developmental psychology have become somewhat marginalized from the dominant orthodoxy in cognitive psychology. The textured and compelling findings of these developmental psychologists are often viewed by cognitive psychologists as having relevance only to the dynamics of development and the way children interact with educators and care givers, but not as providing fundamental insights into the nature of the adult mind. In this chapter we will not review in any detail the developmental literature – rather, our primary aim will be to take up the methodological issues raised by both developmentalists and the "psychological skeptics," and consider the implications these issues have for revitalizing the psychological study of adult cognition, with particular reference to adult memory.

Machinery and its use

Miller, Galater, & Pribram (1979) in their groundbreaking book *Plans and the Structure of Behavior* lamented that psychologists know a lot about the information that impinges upon the sensorium and about the resulting behavior, but little about how people get from one to the other. In response, traditional cognitive psychologists have struggled to uncover the universal principles of human action. Seeking generalities about cognitive machinery (see Lachman, Lachman, & Butterfield 1979; Posner 1989), they follow the cynosure of a powerful metaphor.

The computer has served as the dominant guiding metaphor for cognitive psychologists since midcentury. In computers there exists a clear distinction between the fixed, general characteristics of the machine and the ways in which this machinery is used. Computers have characteristics independent of application, characteristics that hold despite variations in the content of the processed material or its use. But computers also utilize programs and applications that essentially govern the use of the machinery. To the extent that cognitive psychologists have successfully mapped this distinction onto their information processing paradigm, they mainly have focused their efforts on understanding the fixed, general characteristics of the human information processing system – the cognitive "machinery" – rather than on the way people use the system.

First, cognitive psychologists from the information processing tradition seek to characterize the properties of the machinery. Cognitive psychologists studying adult memory are interested in such issues as the capacity of short-term memory, the rate at which information is forgotten, the relation between stimulus similarity and interference, the format of information stored in short-term and long-term memory, the form of mental representations, whether it is analog or propositional, the subcomponents of the memory system – implicit, explicit, episodic, semantic – and so on. That is, they want to discover the general properties of the cognitive "mechanisms" governing human memory (see Klatzky 1975; Crowder 1976). This scientific enterprise follows the precedent set by Ebbinghaus when he searched for the "raw material of memory."

Second, these same cognitive psychologists want to know how the machinery functions when its actions involve genetically programmed automatic processes, processes that can be conceived of as "data-driven" actions as opposed to more variable "user-driven" actions. Fodor (1983) had such data-driven actions in mind when he developed the notion of "module" and insisted that cognitive psychology confine its science to studying how these modules function. Modules can be likened to the "hardwired" programming of a computer. This hardwiring prescribes fundamental actions of encoding, storage, retrieval, and computation that no "software" program can circumvent. The software can only utilize these preestablished hardwired programs. Fodor's (1983) lexical recognition module, the concept of spreading activation elaborated by Anderson (1984) and others, and interference theorists' (see Baddeley 1976) mechanism of response competition are examples of data-driven processes. Data-driven processes are rarely open to introspection and generally require rigorous experimentation to be explicated.

Mainstream cognitive psychologists have given far less attention to what might be considered the articulation of the strategies and skills people employ to guide the machinery's use. These strategies and skills are usually, if not always, learned – for this reason, those favoring a contextualist approach in developmental psychology have devoted considerable research to this topic (Ratner 1980, 1984, 1986; Dowd 1990; Fivush & Hudson 1990; Nelson 1990, 1991, 1992, 1993). Unfortunately, the implications of this developmental research have not been fully recognized by scholars concerning themselves with the cognitive psychology of the adult mind. People organize, image, associate, elaborate, and undertake a host of other sophisticated actions to help them memorize and remember (see Bower 1970). As some developmental psychologists have emphasized, the exact way people memorize and remember will depend on many factors, including developmental and cultural ones (Kagan, Klein, Finley, Rogoff, & Nolan 1979; Rogoff & Waddell 1982; Rogoff & Mistry 1990; Rogoff 1990; Harkness 1992). When given a list of categorizable words to remember, Western-educated college students spontaneously put the words into semantic categories, whereas Western children and members of the Kpelle tribe in West Africa adopt other strategies (Cole & Scribner 1974; Scribner 1974). The Kpelle, for instance, prefer to make a story out of the words. Human cleverness makes almost boundless the different ways people can memorize and remember.

Any cognitive psychologist who undertakes the study of how people remember must sedulously trudge through a morass of bewildering complexity and particularity. Psychologists with a scientific bent naturally fear they may bog down in this particularity. Rather than ending with a few concise, general statements – the ideal that physics offers – they may find themselves making seemingly endless lists of what people may do in this situation or that culture, with this background or that motivation. Faced with this possibility, they may heed Jerry Fodor's advice and confine themselves to statements about the general characteristics of mental machinery and data-driven processing.

This delimited vision does not, of course, preclude cognitive psychologists from examining what people do with short-term memory or how they extend their short-term memory capacity. Cognitive psychologists study such matter, however, mainly to collect data from which generalized statements can be made about the properties of the machinery and the processing within a genetically programmed, data-driven module. The study of mnemonic strategies and skills, then, is interesting to many psychologists not because of what it says about the different ways people can memorize and remember, but because it specifies which kinds of mnemonic representations lead to more efficient retrieval, or because it supplies insight into the relation between storage and retrieval (cf. Bower 1970). Only a few cognitive psychologists interested in memory explore such matters as how people remember appointments, what variables affect people's memory for real-life events, how people preserve memories that are important to them, how people narrate their lives and how this narration impacts on self-concept, how traditions and stories are passed on from one generation to the next, or what is remembered and what is forgotten from early childhood (cf. Neisser 1982; Harris & Morris 1984; Gruneberg, Morris, & Sykes 1988; Neisser & Winograd 1988; Rubin 1988a; Usher & Neisser 1993). For those interested in the ways people use memory in everyday life, these problems and others like them are among those most worth studying. Traditional cognitive psychologists meagerly investigate these problems because they believe that few generalities are likely to emerge (cf. Banaji & Crowder 1989, and several responses, e.g., Loftus 1991).

Some would argue that cognitive psychology's focus on information processing machinery represents a deviation from the motives that led to its inception. For example, Jerome Bruner (1990), in his book *Acts of Meaning*, reflects deeply on cognitive psychologists' desire for generalities and the resulting limitation on the range of studied phenomena. In what some may take to be revisionist history, Bruner criticizes cognitive psychologists for losing their way, a revolution if not betrayed at least gone astray. For Bruner, the initial impetus for breaking away from the stranglehold of behaviorism was the need to understand a specific cognitive act, how people give meaning to their lives and the world. According to Bruner, the initial drive to understand acts of meaning was subverted by a quest to understand the computational principles of mind: Psychologists began to mistake their tools, and the heuristic language they provided, for the thing they wanted to study. For Bruner, the promising initiative of cognitive psychology eventuated in a sterile science, one that, as we have already suggested, fails to make contact with the phenomena of interest – in Bruner's case, "acts of meaning." Bruner urges psychologists to study what they want eventually to explain – how people give meaning to their lives. If we are to achieve this goal, psychologists must study not only the general principles of cognitive machinery, but also how people use this machinery, and the meaning they give to its use.

Content and context

Cognitive psychologists have largely avoided studying how people actually use their memories in daily life, fearing that by becoming mired in the quicksand of particularity they would not be able to achieve desired levels of general and scientific rigor. Such fears might be justifiable if it turned out that progress made in understanding the fixed, general characteristics of the mind was swift and in turn helped us to understand how people use their mental machinery. But progress has had to confront at least one major obstacle. Specifically, the computer metaphor makes it appear as if fixed, general characteristics of the mind can be easily divorced from the use of the machinery. All one need do is separate mechanism from the influence of content, context, culture, social structure, or more generally, use. As Ebbinghaus's disciples learned to their dismay, this divorce is difficult if not impossible to achieve. Psychologists confront this troubling conclusion repeatedly.

Consider the issue of memory capacity – the assumption that some people have better memories than others. When memory is thought of as a faculty, a mechanism independent from what one does with it or what one memorizes or remembers, then it is natural to attribute differences in the mnemonic ability of individuals to "biological endowment."

Chase & Simon (1973) showed, however, that one could not meaningfully discuss memory capacity without considering the what and how of encoding, retrieval, and storage. In their study, a novice chess player and a chess master studied a legitimate chess position for five seconds. After a delay, the two subjects reproduced the position. The novice correctly placed only six or seven pieces whereas the master usually reproduced the entire position accurately.

It would be wrong, however, to attribute to the master, despite his prowess, a larger memory capacity or biological endowment than that of the novice. The master's spectacular performance depended on what he had to remember, on content. When shown an illegitimate position, with pieces arranged randomly, the master's reproduction was no better than that of the novice. It follows that his memory was not uniformly better. In a series of ingenious experiments, Chase & Simon traced the master's apparently "better" memory to the use he made of his superior knowledge of chess to "chunk" (Miller 1956) the pieces on the chess board. The chess master organized the pieces in his head, perceiving familiar configurations – such as patterns of attack and defense, casting positions, and so on – thereby forming a representation that could be easily retrieved. The novice saw and encoded only random pieces, forming a disorganized, easily forgotten trace.

This study, with a host of others on expertise, established that capacity cannot be measured by a single test, or even discussed as a general attribute of a person's memory. The same person who can remember little in school might know everything about baseball; Chinese chefs can remember Chinese recipes, but not French ones; Serbo-Croatian folk singers can remember poems hours long, but otherwise evidence average memories (cf. Lord 1960). There is no single measure of mnemonic ability. It is content specific. Test performance depends on the content of what must be remembered, the strategies used to remember, and what one knows about the to-be-remembered material. One cannot discover the capacity of Ebbinghaus's raw material of memory, revealing this characteristic independent of content, strategy, related knowledge, and use. These "complicating" factors cannot be eliminated or factored out – they are essential to the phenomenon of remembering, and without understanding their role one cannot properly be said to understand memory.

The same point can be made in another setting. Activity theorists like Istomina (1975; see also Scribner & Cole 1977; Kail 1990; Rogoff 1990) have focused on how memory is embedded in the various activities people perform. Whereas information processing psychologists focus on the computational cognitive *process* as the primary unit of analysis, activity theorists take into consideration the *activity* broadly understood. They define an activity as encompassing a set of actions directed toward accomplishing a particular goal. They maintain that human cognition can only be fully understood when psychologists view cognitive processes in the larger context of activity.

With this point in mind, Istomina explored the difference between "voluntary memory," in which one intentionally sets out to remember something, and "involuntary memory," in which remembering is incidental to the primary purpose of what one is doing. Deliberate rote memorization is an example of voluntary memory, whereas remembering a movie watched for the sake of enjoyment is an example of involuntary memory.

Istomina examined the memory of two groups of children for a list of grocery items. In a voluntary memory condition, Istomina asked children to memorize and later to recall the list of items. In an involuntary memory condition, she asked other children to go to a grocery store down the hallway and get a number of items to provide lunch supplies for the group, the same items she had listed for the children in the first condition. The memory demands and the content of what had to be remembered were formally the same in both conditions. What differed was the *activity* in which the memory act occurred and the *goal* sought by the activity. In the voluntary condition, the task explicitly involved memorizing and remembering; in the involuntary condition, the memory task was embedded in the common activity of grocery shopping and obtaining lunch supplies.

The activity in which the memory task was embedded made a measurable difference. Children in the involuntary memory condition remembered more items than those in the voluntary memory condition. As Chase & Simon found that content mattered to memory, so too here it was impossible to separate the "mechanisms" of memory from the larger goals the children had in mind. The children in the involuntary memory condition apparently did well because they had the skills to function effectively in the context of grocery shopping. However, children obviously cannot easily transfer these skills to situations where they simply have to "remember" the list. Subsequent studies have modified Istomina's conclusions somewhat (see Weissberg & Paris 1986; Schneider & Brun 1987). Nevertheless, this study and others like it effectively demonstrate that children's use of memory skills depends on their goals, the enveloping activity, and the broader context (cf. Scribner & Cole 1981; Ratner 1986; Rogoff 1990; Rogoff & Mistry 1990).

These experiments underline a more general point made by several psychologists emphasizing "situated cognition" (Pea & Kurland 1984; Lave 1988, 1991, 1993; Greeno 1989; Brown, Collins, & Duguid 1990; Perkins 1990; Suchman 1990). These psychologists argue that the situation, the context in which a cognitive act occurs, shapes and gives substance to the cognitive act. They maintain that one cannot abstract away from the situation to talk about cognitive acts in a general way. Rather, any discussion of cognition must be grounded in the situation itself.

Suchman's (1990) *Plans and Situated Actions* may offer the most cogent articulation of the philosophy underlying situated cognition. In the cognitive psychological framework elaborated in Miller, Galanter, & Pribram's (1979) *Plans and the Structure of Behavior*, people develop plans of action, which they then execute. Plans, in this framework, reduce to a set of instructions to be followed. The action itself derives from the plan. Suchman notes, however, the people's intended actions, their plans, may never be realized. A statement of intent often says little about the action that follows. For example, a canoeist may devise a detailed plan to navigate a sequence of hair-raising rapids – deciding to head toward the left bank until getting to the white pine, then to turn right, and so on – yet may find this plan cannot be translated into action. The situation takes over, as previously unobserved rocks appear, currents change, and tree limbs loom. The canoeists' expert skills guide the actions in response to the ever-changing situation. A study of action, then, should reach far beyond the investigation of plans people devise, the domain of most cognitive psychology research. It should focus on skilled individuals confronting and navigating through situations.

Cognitive psychologists account for findings such as those of Chase & Simon and Istomina, as well as the concerns of scholars such as Suchman, with two conceptual tools central to any computational model, *representation* and *process* (cf. Atkinson & Shiffrin 1968). The argument basically is as follows. Mnemonic performance depends both on how something is stored (representation) and on the strategies (processes) used to encode and retrieve this material. Certain representations – in particular, well-organized ones – allow people to retrieve more easily a desired memory than do other representations, just as a well-organized storage system allows library users to find a desired book more easily than does a disorganized system. Encoding strategies, or processes, affect how well-organized, and hence how mnemonically effective, a representation will be; retrieval strategies either take advantage of the organization of the representation, and thereby aid remembering, or work counter to it.

The argument of these cognitive psychologists is that content, context, and activity influence memory capacity by affecting the strategies one uses to memorize and remember as well as the representations one forms. Chess masters thus could be said to adopt different strategies for encoding a legitimate chess position than do novices, forming a more organized representation and permitting more effective retrieval strategies. For material other than legitimate chess positions, for example, randomly placed chess pieces, chess masters do not differ from novices in their encoding and retrieval strategies. Likewise, context could be said to matter in Istomina's experiment because embedding remembering in the activity of grocery shopping leads to enhanced retrieval. A similar argument could be advanced to account for the ever-changing plans of Suchman's canoeist. The canoeist's initial plan may never be realized because it is revised on-line, changing internal representations to reflect the present context. The argument, then, is that the encoding and retrieval strategies people use to adjust to content and context transform internal representations, replacing them with new representations that are more organized, mnemonically effective, and situationally appropriate (cf. Lachman, Lachman, & Butterfield 1979).

This line of argument suggests a general move for mapping particular uses of cognitive machinery onto general characterizations of the machinery. Specifically, the information processing paradigm suggests that psychologists should determine how people internally represent "in the head" the outside world and what processes they use to manipulate these internal representations. People specify the particularity of the world by translating it into specific mental language, a language ideally suited for manipulation by fixed, universal machinery. People employ this language to express in what could be called "mentalese" their knowledge of the world and the structure they see in it. The chess master sees an organized board and captures this organization internally in a mental language that his cognitive machinery can act upon. The exact information he represents may be particular to him, but the format of the language and the way the machinery interacts with the elements of this language are both fixed and universal.

Most models of memory adopt this line of argument. For example, Anderson (1984) developed a propositional language that he claimed captured the way people represent both visual and verbal material. He also posited retrieval processes, such as spreading activation, that interact with this representation in a fixed, universal manner. In his model, the effectiveness of any act of memorizing or remembering will depend on how the to-be-remembered material is represented and what encoding and retrieval strategies a person uses.

By trying to explain content and context effects merely in terms of internal representations and mnemonic strategies, cognitive psychologists are implicitly accepting that somewhere, deep below the surface, they can find a quantifiable mnemonic capacity independent of content and context. As general intelligence has been quantified with "I.Q. numbers," so mnemonic capacity might be measured, as Ebbinghaus's reviewer suggested, in terms of "British Association Units" (Jacobs 1885). Models based on this approach assume a fixed, universal representational language and fixed, universal cognitive machinery that manipulates this language. Like any machine, the fixed, universal component presumably has a specific capacity. If only they could spy directly into this machinery rather than indirectly through the machinery's manipulation of the representation, these cognitive psychologists believe they could specify an organism's general mnemonic capacity.

But as the Chase & Simon, Istomina, and other examples demonstrated, it is impossible to see directly into human "internal machinery." At least for memory capacity, a biological endowment hidden deep beneath the surface of behavior may exist, but it is and will remain elusive. This point can be illustrated by again turning to the example of the computer. Could anyone determine the memory capacity of a computer simply by observing its behavior? A computer, after all, is no better than the programs running on it. Clever programming can expand its memory capacity greatly, even though the hardware may remain the same. One might try to ascertain a computer's memory capacity by measuring its reaction times, the noises it makes, its rate of output. But these and all other externally observable aspects of a computer's "behavior" could simply reflect idiosyncrasies of the computer's programming, and give no clear indication of underlying memory capacity. Even observing when the computer breaks down provides no definite indication of capacity (unless of course the computer displays a preprogrammed error message indicating in what way its capacity has been exceeded).

Similarly, can anyone determine in precise terms the capacity of human memory simply by observing human behavior? People are not only clever at finding ways around their limitations, but their performance is never independent of what they do with their memory. The "cognitive impenetrability" (Pylyshyn 1980) of the workings of the machinery of memory makes the desire to discover Ebbinghaus's "raw material of memory" like pursuing the proverbial will-o'-the-wisp: It is an endless chase after an ever-elusive phantom, leading one farther and farther from one's original goal – in this case, understanding memorizing and remembering in everyday life.

We are not here rejecting the progress fostered by the Cognitive Revolution. The information processing metaphor has advanced the understanding of many aspects of cognition. In the study of human memory, cognitive psychologists have made strides toward distinguishing different kinds of memory (Johnson & Hirst 1991), have clarified the effectiveness of various strategies for memorizing and remembering (for a review see Hirst 1988), and have begun to understand the dynamics by which people determine the origin of a memory (what is called "reality monitoring" – Johnson & Raye 1981; for a recent review see Johnson, Hashtroudi, & Lindsay 1993). More importantly, cognitive psychology has given us a vocabulary that permits detailed task analysis. Notwithstanding these advances, we want to emphasize the futility of any quest to define the limits and characteristics of mnemonic capacity independent of content, context, and particular use.

Capacity is not the only putative property of the fixed machinery of memory from which it is impossible to divorce mechanism from its content or context. It is extremely difficult to find any mental phenomenon that is not affected to some degree by content and context. For example, the size of short-term memory can vary widely with content, context, and practice, with a subject in one experiment expanding his digit span from an "normal" 7 to nearly 80 after several weeks of practice (Ericsson, Chase, & Faloon 1980). The parameters of retrieval processes such as spreading activation may also depend on content and context (Smith, Adams, & Schorr 1978). Outside the field of memory research, it has been demonstrated that contextual variable affect even something as putatively fundamental as the perception of gestalt form (Mack, Tang, Tuma, Kahn, & Rock 1992; Rock, Linnett, Graut, & Mack 1992).

Distributed memories

The effort to translate what is "out in the world" into representations "in the head" assumes that our so-called internal mental machinery controls our actions. However, we find the boundary between "inner" and "outer" fuzzy at best, with many acts of memorizing and remembering shaped and guided by factors independent of our internal mental machinery.

Much of what people remember they encode, store, and retrieve not in the head, but in the world, that is, they "externalize" the memory. Both collectively and individually people structure the environment so as to distribute memories across individuals, as well as between individuals in the world. Consider the fact that experienced bartenders can remember orders much better than novices (Beach 1988). This superior memory does not reflect a greater memory capacity or even, as in the case of Chase & Simon's chess players, superior skills at internally encoding the orders. Rather, experienced bartenders structure the world so that it does the memorizing for them. As customers order drinks, experienced bartenders place the appropriate glasses on the bar. Inasmuch as different drinks require differently shaped glasses, the use of glasses to "externalize" a memory should be and is effective. When experienced bartenders are deprived of this external memory aid, and are made to use uniformly shaped glasses, their "superior memory" vanishes.

Similarly, society structures the world so that the mnemonic burden is shared between individuals and the world outside them. In addition to a host of external memory aids, from libraries to computer retrieval systems, there are other more subtle ways people distribute and externalize the act of memorizing and remembering. An external memory may not actually store the memory but rather provide access to it. For instance, society builds monuments to memorialize or commemorate past events and the dead (Radley 1990). These monuments serve as reminders, stimulants for our memory. The monument can be designed to evoke memories of a particular historic event, as does the Iwo Jima Monument, or may be configured to serve merely as a memorial stage for a wider range of mnemonic reflection – for example, the Vietnam Veterans Memorial (Sturken 1991). In either case, the world has been structured so that human memory is facilitated by it and in turn becomes dependent on it (cf. Connerton 1991).

The human proclivity to distribute and externalize mnemonic burdens is pervasive. We design cities to be memorable (Lynch 1960). We also communicate myths conveying important messages in mnemonically coherent forms, preserving them with a host of external devices, from artwork, advertising, and propaganda to storytelling, mass media, and childhood indoctrination (Lord 1960; Yates 1966; Passerini 1987; Billig 1990). Families, married couples, friends, bosses and secretaries will all carefully develop strategies for sharing and thereby externalizing their mnemonic burdens (Wegener 1986; Wegener, Erber, & Raymond 1991). Societies, especially oral cultures, will usually assign highly valued roles to those responsible for the preservation of collective knowledge (Havelock 1963; Ong 1967). In every case, objects or people are assigned specific kinds of knowledge to remember and specific roles to play in both memorizing and remembering.

The deliberate, conscious ways people make use of things in the world to aid their memories is only part of the story. In the course of daily life we all engage in any number of additional actions or behaviors that serve the unstated, often unplanned, yet no less effect function of preserving traditions, commemorating important occurrences, and bringing to mind forgotten events. David Reiss (1981), analyzing what he terms the information processing functions served by the family, points out that family rituals often serve implicitly commemorative functions. Reiss notes that members of a family, in their interaction with each other and with the world outside the family, develop a distinct "family paradigm," which is a "deep-seated and persistent attitude or set of assumptions about the family's social and physical world" (Reiss 1981, p. 226). Such paradigms are conserved through interaction behaviors that serve "to modulate and retain information as well as to objectify that information as a basis for action in the external world" (Reiss 1981, p. 228). Family paradigms are conserved with great effectiveness by family rituals, which are interaction behaviors that are extremely organized, conspicuous, and stable over time, for example, the ways family members interact and behave on holiday occasions.

One might, of course, try to separate the machinery of individual memory from the use this machinery makes of the external world, asserting that psychology should focus on the internal machinery. Such a maneuver echoes the efforts described earlier to divorce content and context from the machinery of memory. But just as it proved impossible to divorce content and context from the machinery of cognition, so also is it impossible to divorce memory "in the head" from the diverse ways people share their memory burdens with others and with the "external world" generally. Any act of cognition occurs in the world, and in the course of life people customarily use the external world to buttress their memory. The experimentalist can endeavor to free the experiment from confounding variables, but even in a white-walled, windowless laboratory there are vast possibilities. The words to be remembered in a verbal learning experiment must, after all, appear on a presentation device, which in turn must rest on a supporting structure, which itself occupies a particular place in the room. These spatial locations provide hooks that people can and do employ as they attempt to memorize words in a "sterile, controlled environment" (see Johnson & Hasher 1987; Manier, Hirst, Greenstein, & Piers 1992).

Psychologists do not agree about the extent to which people and societies distribute memories. We suspect that distributed memories are the norm rather than the exception – to a considerable degree, human memory capacity rests on our cleverness in distributing our memories. An explanation of human mnemonic performance based solely on the innovative means by which we organize our internal representations is insufficient. Human memory capacity depends not only on the characteristics of the machinery in the head, but also on what happens in the outside world. To provide yet another example, people may "remember" their way around a city because various large structures, such as the Empire State Building in New York, serve to anchor their memories (Lynch 1960). If these landmarks were suddenly destroyed, or if one's view of them were obstructed, people might find that they could no longer effectively navigate the city. Coming out of the same subway stop from which I have exited for the past 10 years, now unable to see the Empire State Building, I no longer know which way to turn. My memory for how to navigate in the city would be "lost," not because of the decay of anything in the head, but because the removal of guideposts I had formerly used to orient myself. Destroying or obstructing landmarks would not simply destroy the fit between what is in the head and what is in the environment; rather, it would destroy the memory that is constituted by the interaction of mind and environment. Much of this interaction may occur outside of conscious awareness: I do not deliberately use the Empire State Building to aid in the construction of my memory, but once my view of it is obstructed I suddenly find myself disoriented and unable to find my way around.

Similarly, old people who are mildly demented often can function normally until they are taken from their familiar surroundings and moved to a new location (Csikszentmihalyi & Rochberg-Halton 1981). They may have had no trouble remembering what to do over the course of a day when they lived in their old house. The house essentially did the remembering for them. Rather than following an internal script – "get up, bathe, make breakfast," etc. – they followed well-worn paths taken daily – from the bedroom, to the bathroom, to the kitchen, etc. Once the external memory aids, the familiar "paths," are removed, they no longer remember their daily routine. Not passing the bathroom when they rise in the morning, they no longer remember to bathe. What is in the head remains the same, but the memory is nevertheless lost. Again, this is because the interaction of mind and environment has been altered so as to destroy the living, "externalized" memory of the daily routine they have for so long taken for granted.

The psychological theory of "scripts," as developed by Schank & Abelson (1977), has proven fruitful for analyzing many types of situations, but the scripts metaphor could lead to some misleading conclusions if applied to the cases we are discussing here. If we think of a script in its ordinary usage as a text memorized by an actor, then changing a script should be relatively straightforward: I no longer turn left when I see the Empire State Building but rather when I see the new skyscraper obstructing my previous view. The old person remembers to bathe, not when he passes the bathroom along the well-trodden path, but after he passes his grandchild's bedroom in his new home. But the matter is not so simple: I may not be able to substitute the new skyscraper, the old person may not be able to follow a new path. Forming a new memory is not as easy as revising a script – rather, remembering in a changing world means adapting to alterations in the relation between mind and environment. In this sense, it is wrong of psychologists to conceive of memory as merely what is internally encoded, stored in the brain. We have stressed the point repeatedly: Memory unavoidably entails an interaction between mind and environment. Often our memories are externalized in a world familiar to us: People navigate cities and follow daily routines often using skills of which they are not fully aware and which, partly as a result, are intractable to change. In such case, memory is a (not entirely conscious) pattern of interaction with the environment.

Thus, it is incorrect to argue that changing the environment of an old person or city dweller does not change that person's memory. Memories are not simply representations "in the head." Rather representations in the head, although they can be said to exist (in terms of particular neurological configurations), are known to others, and even to ourselves, only in the context of some sort of interaction with the environment. Memory is best conceived of in verb form, as memorizing and remembering. Pure, context-free mnemonic representations are like Kant's *ding an sich* – they are unknowable "in themselves" and are known to us only through the act of remembering. A memory does not simply rest in the head waiting to be retrieved. Neisser (1967) dubbed this the "reappearance hypothesis" and, following Bartlett's lead, argued strenuously against it. Rather, a memory arises out of an act of remembering, and as such is inseparable from content, context, environment, and social setting. Change a person's environment and you will change how they remember.

Again assume the Empire State Building is destroyed. In the minds of New Yorkers, some representation of this skyscraper will presumably continue to exist, although in a highly variable and inconstant form. But unveiling the nature of this representation as it exists in the head of any given New Yorker will be highly problematic: New Yorkers will think and talk about this destroyed icon quite differently depending on whether they are in an expensive restaurant, a neighborhood bar, an architecture class, their own home, or . . . a psychologist's cognitive science laboratory. On the other hand, what will be readily observable, we argue, is that many New Yorkers will suddenly show diminished skills at navigating the city. In this sense, their memory of how to get around the city – which inevitably consists of an interaction between mind and environment – will be impaired.

It should be clear then why the language of information processing psychology may not be sufficient to explain actions in everyday life. An adequate explanation of memory must include not only what is in the head, but also what is in the world. Otherwise, psychologists will be unable to predict mnemonic performance, especially as the tasks they study become more directly related to people's actual experiences. Psychologists need to develop a representational language that captures how memories are realized through the interaction between the internal and external worlds, between mind and environment. In developing this language, they may well find that the separation between internal and external representation is artificial, even misleading. They also may debate whether the current information processing language, developed to discuss internal representation, can be extended to the external component or whether a new language must be developed. Whatever the outcome of this exploration, the discipline of cognitive psychology, and what it defines as a psychological problem, will be revitalized by vistas expanded to include the ways people share their memory burdens with others and with the world around them.

The influence of social factors on remembering

If cognitive psychology is to meet Neisser's (1978) challenge and achieve greater ecological validity, it must not only consider the ways a structured world distributes mnemonic burdens, but must also confront the fact that remembering is inescapably a social act. This point has been the focus of studies of what can be called "social remembering." By this we do not have in mind the active field of social cognition, which seeks to understand in information processing terms such social acts as attribution. Rather we are referring her to work that searches for the way culture and social structures shape cognitive acts such as problem solving and remembering (cf. Middleton & Edwards 1990). Much of this work is in the tradition of French sociologist Emil Durkheim (1984; see also Dowd 1990), who maintained that the "major part of our states of consciousness would not have been produced among isolated beings and would have been produced otherwise among beings grouped in some other manner."

Maurice Halbwachs (1980), a student of Durkheim, exploring what he termed "collective memory," made the radical claim that purely individual memory simply does not exist. No act of memory can be said to be innocent of social influence: "our most personal feelings and thoughts originate in definite social milieus and circumstances" (Halbwachs 1980, p. 33). Memory acts are shaped by their social environment. As with content and context, if you try to strip away social factors – an impossible task, but seductive nevertheless – you will have nothing. Halbwachs analyzes infant memory in search of an instance of individual, not social memory, but even here he finds memory rich in social structure. The uniqueness of an individual's memory, for Halbwachs, comes from the intersection of different social memories reflecting the different groups or "societies" people belong to, which will not be precisely the same for any two individuals. Halbwachs does not posit a "group memory" in some abstract or superstitious sense, but rather remembering and memorizing constituted and derived from social interaction.

Part of what Halbwachs discussed can be captured in the language of *schema* (cf. Bartlett 1932). Societies, or more generally the demands of a particular environment, provide individuals with schemas and strategies that crucially affect both how and what they remember. Herdsmen of Swaziland can remember that price and description of cattle sold at auction many years back because cattle are central to their livelihood and form the basis of the economy of their culture (Bartlett 1932). Australian aboriginal children, who have been raised to detect slight nuances in relatively undifferentiated environments such as the desert Outback, evidence superior visual memory (Drinkwater 1976). As mentioned previously, people from certain non-Western cultures, such as the Kpelle, adopt different remembering strategies than Western students: for example, they tell stories to remember word lists rather than using semantic categorization (Cole & Scribner 1974; Scribner 1974). In each instance, society, culture, and environment guide both what is remembered and how it is remembered.

Halbwach's contribution is not limited to his emphasis on how the social environment provides schemas and strategies to guide an individual's memorizing and remembering. He also urges us to consider how remembering and memorizing occur in social occasions. Much of our remembering does not occur in isolation, but in groups. Remembering is affected by the size of the group: Reminiscence taking place in conversation between 2 people will differ from memories shared between 200 people gathered together at a memorial service (cf. Clark & Stephenson 1989). Remembering is also affected by the social and cultural character of the group: People remember differently in the intimate context of the family than they do among their friends, and in another manner again in more formal contexts of the workplace or in the schoolroom (cf. Mercer 1981; Scribner 1985; Edwards & Mercer 1987; Edwards & Middleton 1988).

Remembering in a group – be it large or small, intimate or impersonal – cannot be reduced to the sum of each individual's memory. It cannot be thought of as equivalent to an individual sitting alone in a laboratory multiplied by 5, 20, or 40, depending on the size of the group. A small group working together, for instance, generally seems to remember more than any one group member remembering singly yet less than the sum of the memories of each single member (cf. Clark & Stephenson 1989; Benjamin 1992). An entire set of social factors must be included to account fully for why certain memories expressed outside the group do not surface in the group, and for how individuals interact to elicit the memories that do emerge.

To the extent that memorizing and remembering are group activities, they will reflect not only the mnemonically relevant "programs" in the heads of individuals, nor even the simple sum of the internalized programs provided by a group, society, culture, or the environment generally, but a complex social dynamic emerging from a wide range of interaction behaviors. For instance, as suggested previously, different families probably remember their past differently as a consequence of their interaction behaviors, the means by which they communicate with each other and with the outside world (Reiss 1981). Family memories grow out of the interaction between members of the group rather than from the head of an individual or the simple sum of individual memories. Part of this process is described in the rapidly expanding developmental literature exploring how children are "inducted into the process of remembering experiences" through interaction with their parents and the social mediation of adults generally (cf. Nelson 1990, 1992, 1993; Rogoff 1990, Ratner 1984). The contribution this complexity of social factors, including the patterns of interaction, makes to any act of remembering cannot be easily reduced to effects on representation and processing. Simply studying individual strategies for encoding, storage, and retrieval will not be enough, even if one includes the representation of social and cultural beliefs.

Small group remembering can be thought of as a matter of communication and interaction, in which social roles play an important part. Presumably, diverse factors, ranging from expertise to personality to culturally defined positions of power, will impact on the degree to which an individual dominates the discourse (cf. Gumperz & Hymes 1972; Lakoff 1975; Leet-Pelligrini 1980; Tannen 1990). We would predict that the question of who dominates the discourse will shape the final group recollection as expressed in conversation, as well as subsequent rememberings. Just as Istomina pointed out certain unintended benefits to memory from one's engagement in a familiar activity, like grocery shopping, so here the conversational role one adopts – whether dominant and active or passive and reactive – may have incidental (or involuntary) effects on subsequent recall.

In a recent study, we tested these hypotheses by examining the conversational roles taken on by members of a family as they recalled some recent events in their lives (Hirst & Manier, in press; Manier & Hirst, in press). We asked four members of a family to recall both individually and collectively several shared episodes, such as the preceding Christmas and a recent family outing to Coney Island. In a careful analysis of transcripts of family remembering, we detected three different roles: Narrators – who assume the primary function of telling the story; Monitors – who listen to Narrators and give them feedback on whether their recollections are accurate; and Mentors – who prompt Narrators to tell a complete story by providing retrieval cues, narrative directions, and facilitating remarks. In the family we studied, the 15-year-old daughter functioned as Narrator, the father as Mentor, and the mother and 17-year-old son as Monitors. The family members adhered to these roles consistently throughout the group remembering.

Interestingly, the roles adopted had consequences for what was remembered. Whereas most cognitive psychological studies of memory stress the accuracy of recall, acts of recall in everyday life rarely put a rigid and overriding emphasis on accuracy. Although people in their interactions with one another routinely attempt to recall past episodes, it is rare for explicit guidelines to be specified regarding how much should be recalled, what details should be stressed, and what themes should be developed. These matters are determined – at least in family rememberings such as those we studied – by patterns of group interaction, and especially by the conversational roles assumed by group members. The importance of conversational roles in remembering – especially relating to "mentoring" and "scaffolding" – has been stressed in the developmental literature (cf. Bruner 1983; Eisenberg 1985; Fivush & Fromhoff 1988; Lucariello & Nelson 1987; Hudson 1990; Nelson 1993). Our research fits in with these findings, but does not limit its focus to the "apprenticeship in thinking" (Rogoff 1990) of young children. Rather, we examine the impact of conversational roles – including monitoring and narrating, as well as mentoring – in a family with adolescent children. In fact, our method could be extended with only slight modifications to groups consisting entirely of adults.

Our study identified several consequences of the conversational roles family members took on. The main consequences related to effects of who played the role of Narrator – in this case the daughter. The daughter, as Narrator, was particularly effective at introducing into the group recollection details that only she had remembered when family members were interview singly, prior to the group recollection. Even if two or more family members mentioned the same details when interviewed singly, this did not impart any special advantage in their later introducing these details into the group recollection. The daughter's role as Narrator was decisive in determining whether a detail mentioned in the individual interviews made it into the group recollection, not the number of participants who had separately recalled that detail.

We also discovered interesting findings about the group recollections as compared to the individual interview, or "pregroup recollections." Close to half the details mentioned in the group recollections did not occur in any of the pregroup recollections. The group recollection was more detailed than any single pregroup recollection, but did not include as many details as the sum total of all the pregroup recollections. These findings mean that the story told collectively by this family was substantially different from that told by the family members individually. The group dynamics and social interaction processes at play in the group recollections presumably were responsible for this difference (see Manier & Hirst, in press).

Other unpublished work done in our laboratory (done in collaboration with Elizabeth Pinner) suggests that what people say during group recollection affects what they subsequently remember individually. One cannot understand human memories without considering the social settings in which the memory is initially formed and subsequently retrieved. Discourse structure, conversational styles, and the dynamics of social interaction affect memory within groups, whether large or small. Cognitive psychologists might accept all this, yet attempt to treat these social factors as variable to be added onto individual memory factors. This reflects the traditional strategy of cognitive psychology, one that we have encountered several times: Start with the universal characteristics of the human mind discovered through well-controlled laboratory experiments that strip away complicating factors, and later add on the effects of context, content, external factors, group membership, social processes, and cultural traditions and influences. From this perspective, group remembering might be reduced to the effects of cueing and social factors, such as the bystander effect.

This maneuver will fail as surely as did the attempts to create a sterile experimental environment that eliminates the effects of content, context, situations, and the external world. Psychologists may be "institutionally incapable of remembering that humans are social beings," as Mary Douglas (1986) laments, but they must resist this bias. The interpretation of every utterance in a group must inevitably be social and will depend on group dynamics: It is impossible to find a nonsocial utterance onto which social factors can simply be added. Even a seemingly straightforward cue like "I met her at the beach – what's her name?" cannot be divorced from the social dynamics of the group. The usefulness of this cue will depend on who said it, and his relation to the other members of the group will be crucial. If he is generally disliked, distrusted, and ignored, then the cue itself might be ignored, or even used in a perverse way: He said "beach," which must mean it was at the mountains. Besides, the point in the discussion at which the probe appears makes a difference. If a conflict is at hand, the probe may be viewed as a means of avoiding or evoking a conflict, rather than a "valid" cue (cf. Levinson 1983). Discussants may even recognize the probe as a cue, but if the normal social conventions of conversation are observed, the flow of the conversation may be too brisk to allow time for the cue to be effective. Everything uttered during group remembering is saturated with social meaning.

Even if we acknowledge that individual remembering cannot be divorced from social remembering when remembering occurs within a group, one could still insist that there exist individual memories independent of social context onto which social factors can be added. People do sit in small rooms, alone, and manage to remember quite a bit. Yet, although a "subject" in a cognitive science laboratory may be physically alone, he still carries with him a social context. He still hears the inner voice of the experimentalist, for instance, and presumably carries on a mental dialogue with her about what is expected of him. He also may internally converse in his imagination with other authorities, such as teachers or parents, and reflect on their recommendations for effective memorizing and remembering. Many scholars have recognized this when they refer to the "dialogical" nature of mind, that is, when they emphasize that internal dialogue plays a prominent role in human thought (see Bakhtin 1981; Wertsch 1991).

Cognitive psychologists who treat these social factors as "noise" that they hope will be controlled through averaging are mistaken. Just as they must realize that they cannot sensibly discuss memory as separate from the content of what is learned and who is doing the learning, they also must make sure not to separate memory artificially (and ineffectively) from it social environment. Memory grows out of social interactions. Research on memorizing and remembering must both acknowledge this fact and investigate it.

What of traditional cognitive psychology?

In the beginning of this pater, we advanced several questions for cognitive psychology – questions concerned with cognitive acts in the real world as opposed to the characteristics of cognitive machinery. We suggested considering an alternative approach because we were frustrated at cognitive psychology's inability to offer straightforward translations of its theories of cognitive machinery to real-world situations.

The reason for these difficulties should now be apparent. Over and over again, we have come up against a fundamental fact: Human cognitive machinery cannot be separated from its use. Rather, any cognitive act grows out of the complex interactions of content, intentions, context, the external world, social processes, and cultural influences, as well as biological constraints. Mnemonic performance is affected by the content of the material, the intentions of an individual, the context in which the memorizing and remembering occurs, the structure of the world, cultural dynamics, and social interactions. One cannot unveil the raw material of memory by stripping each of these factors away. Everything that is remembered has content; everyone who memorizes or remembers has intentions; every act of memory occurs in a specific context, in a world structured by a particular manner, in a cultural and social environment; and every act of memorizing and remembering grows out of social interaction, even if it is only the internal dialogue of a solitary person's recollections. The direct probe Ebbinghaus sought, and his descendants still yearn for, simply does not exist, nor can it ever.

It is no wonder then that cognitive psychology has had difficulty applying its general models to particular, real-world settings. It has striven to analyze general machinery, yet this machinery never occurs in pristine form in any cognitive act. A cognitive act is enmeshed in content, intentions, context, the external world, and social and cultural milieus. Cognition arises out of the complex interactions of these variables and out of an individual's navigation through them. How could cognitive psychologists possibly be expected to understand cognitive acts in a real-world setting if they know little if anything about these interactions and the navigational strategies of individuals?

It is tempting to reduce content, intentions, context, and social and cultural milieus to information in the head that shapes behavior. But these variables do not reduce simply to internal representations and internal programs. This move will not account for how people distribute memories and the consequent dependence of any act of memory on external as well as internal factors. Nor will it account for the manner in which memories grow out of social interactions. Psychology must reach beyond the confines of the skin, beyond what is in the head, and begin to discuss the generation of mental acts in the world if it is ever to understand memorizing and remembering as they occur in an environmentally, socially and culturally complex environment. Future research must acknowledge this aspect of human cognition and study it as central to a full understanding of memory, not merely as an afterthought.

In arguing for a broader conception of psychology, we do not mean to reject wholesale the significant advances that have been made by cognitive psychology. Whereas we believe that the almost single-minded search for fixed, universal characteristics of cognitive machinery has blinded psychologists to the important task of understanding how people use this machinery, we also accept that the human mind has certain biological endowments. Its memory clearly differs from that of a rat as well as from that of a computer. Cognitive neuroscience has in recent years made significant advances in understanding the cognitive implications of the structure and function of the human brain (Gazzaniga 1994; see also Manier, in press). In fact, we argue elsewhere that the study of neurobiology may even provide unanticipated insights into such apparently unrelated topics as autobiographical narrative telling (Manier & Hirst, in press).

The human mind also possesses certain characteristics that are immutable across cultural context. For instance, people are much better at memorizing something if they can make the material meaningful. Such a "principle of memory" may not seem surprising when it comes to humans, but a memory device need not have this property. Computer memories, for instance, do not. Psychologists undeniably have the task of discovering these properties.

Such generalizations may be few, and those that exist serve at most to constrain behavior. Cognitive acts, acts of memorizing and remembering, do not simply grow out of such principles of memory and generalizations, but they do confront boundaries such principles impose. To this extent the discovery of such principles can help us understand cognitive acts.

Yet human ingenuity – and the fact that memorizing and remembering are inextricably intertwined with content, context, intentions, the external world, and cultural and social milieus – essentially make such principles only a preface to the broader psychological story. Humans are remarkably clever in overcoming and utilizing to best advantage the limitations and boundaries presented by our common biology. As Bruner (1990, p. 21) notes, reflecting on the implications of memory being represented as culturally meaningful "chunks" (Miller 1956) of information rather than artificially discrete bits, "we have broken through the original bounds set by the so-called biology of memory. Biology constrains, but not forevermore."

The "broader story," that is, the prospect for a revitalized and enriched psychology of memory, seeks to describe how people in various cultures and differing social context – within their families, among their friends, in their classrooms, and at their workplaces – use the gift of memory to make their lives meaningful and enjoyable, achieve the goals they set for themselves, and increase their knowledge of themselves, each other, and the world around them. The result may be a science with less of the purity and precision associated with physics. But perhaps cognitive science has been too hasty in its drive to emulate physics by formulating abstract general theories about the universal characteristics of the human mind, theories based on and confirmed in artificially contrived and well-controlled laboratory settings. For all their elegance and precision, the general theories have not proven to admit of straightforward application to real-world situations. Perhaps now is the time for taking a step back from formulating and confirming general theories. The wealth of information waiting to be discovered about how people actually go about remembering – at home, at school, at work, among friends – may lead to a transformed science, one more resembling the richly descriptive accounts of ethology and ethnography (cf. Cole & Scribner 1975; Scribner & Cole 1981; Scribner 1984, 1985; Martin & Scribner 1991).

But this broader story can only be told if cognitive psychologists rethink their pursuit of a sterile content-free science, taking a step beyond the windowless cloisters to which they have unwittingly confined themselves. It can only be told from the vantage of psychological vistas that encompass the boundless complexities of human culture through which people navigate using sophisticated strategies and adaptations – vistas that permit careful, systematic observation of the astonishingly diverse remembering activities people perform throughout their lives.

References

Anderson, J. (1984). Spreading activation. In J. Anderson & S. Kosslyn (Eds.), *Tutorials in learning and memory: Essays in honor of Gordon Bower*. San Francisco: W.H. Freeman.

Atkinson, R., and Shiffrin, R. (1968). Human memory: A proposed system and its control processes. In K. W. Spence & J. T. Spence (Eds.), *The psychology of learning and motivation: Advances in research and theory*, Vol. 2, pp. 89–195. New York: Academic Press.

Baddeley, A. (1976). *The psychology of memory*. New York: Basic Books, Inc.

Bakhtin, M. M. (1981). *The dialogical imagination: Four essays by M. M. Bakhtin*. M. Holquist (Ed.), C. Emerson & M. Holquist (Transl.). Austin: University of Texas Press.

Banaji, M., & Crowder, R. (1989). The bankruptcy of everyday memory research. *American Psychologist*, *44*(9), 1185–1193.

Bartlett, F. (1932). *Remembering: A study in experimental and social psychology*. Cambridge, UK: Cambridge University Press.

Beach, K. (1988). The role of external mnemonic symbols in acquiring an occupation. In M. Gruneberg, P. Morris, & R. Sykes (Eds.), *Practical aspects of memory: Current research and issues*, Vol. 1, pp. 342–346. New York: John Wiley & Sons.

Benjamin, K. (1992). *Group versus individual memory for dynamic and static stimuli*. Ph.D. dissertation, Graduate Faculty for Political and Social Science, New School for Social Research, May 1992.

Billig, M. (1990). Collective memory, ideology and the British royal family. In D. Middleton & D. Edwards (Eds.), *Collective remembering*, pp. 60–80. London: Sage Publications.

Bower, G. (1970). Organizational factors in memory. *Cognitive Psychology*, *1*, 18–46.

Brown, J., Collins, A., & Duguid, P. (1990). Situated cognition and the culture of learning. *Educational Researcher*, *18*, 32–42.

Bruer, J. (1993). *Schools for thought*. Cambridge, MA: MIT Press.

Bruner, J. (1990). *Acts of meaning*. Cambridge, MA: Harvard University Press.

Bruner, J. (1983). *Child's talk: Learning to use language*. New York: W.W. Norton.

Chase, W., & Simon, H. (1973). The mind's eye in chess. In W. Chase (Ed.), *Visual information processing*, pp. 215–281. New York: Academic Press.

Clark, N. K., & Stephenson, G. M. (1989). Group remembering. In P. B. Paulus (Ed.), *Psychology of group influence*, pp. 357–391. Hillsdale, NJ: Lawrence Erlbaum.

Cole, M., & Scribner, S. (1975). Theorizing about socialization of cognition. *Ethos*, *3*(2), 249–268.

Cole, M., & Scribner, S. (1974). *Culture and thought: A psychological introduction*. New York: Wiley.

Connerton, P. (1991). *How societies remember*. New York: Cambridge University Press.

Crowder, R. G. (1976). *Principles of learning and memory*. Hillsdale, NJ: Lawrence Erlbaum.

Csikszentmihalyi, M., & Rochberg-Halton, E. (1981). *The meaning of things: Domestic symbols and the self*. Cambridge, UK: Cambridge University Press.

Douglas, M. (1986). *How institutions think*. London: Routledge & Kegan Paul.

Dowd, J. J. (1990). Ever since Durkheim: The socialization of human development. *Human Development*, *33*(2–3), 138–159.

Drinkwater, B. (1976). Verbal thinking and learning skills of Australian aboriginal children. *Topics in Cultural Learning*, *4*, 10–12.

Durkheim, E. (1984). *The division of labor in society*. New York: Free Press.

Ebbinghaus, H. (1964). *Memory: A contribution to experimental psychology*. New York: Dover Publications, Inc.

Edwards, D., & Mercer, N. (1987). *Common knowledge: The development of understanding in the classroom*. London: Methuen.

Edwards, D., & Middleton, D. (1988). Conversational remembering and family relationships: How children learn to remember. *Journal of Social and Personal Relationships*, *5*, 3–25.

Eisenberg, A. R. (1985). Learning to describe past experiences in conversation. *Discourse Processes*, *8*, 177–204.

Ericsson, K. A., Chase, W. G., & Galcon, S. (1980). Acquisition of a memory skill. *Science*, *208*, 1181–1182.

Fivush, R., & Fromhoff, F. A. (1988). Style and structure in mother-child conversations about the past. *Discourse Processes*, *11*, 337–355.

Fivush, R., & Hudson, J. A., (Eds.). (1990). *Knowing and remembering in young children*. New York: Cambridge University Press.

Fodor, J. (1983). *The modularity of mind: An essay on faculty psychology*. Cambridge, MA: MIT Press.

Gazzaniga, M. S. (Ed.). (1994). *The cognitive neurosciences*. Cambridge, MA: MIT Press.

Greeno, J. (1989). A perspective on thinking. *American Psychologist, 44*, 134–141.

Gruneberg, M., Morris, P., & Sykes, R., (Eds.). (1988). *Practical aspects of memory: Current research and issues*, 2 vols. New York: John Wiley & Sons.

Gumperz, J. J., & Hymes, D. (Eds.). (1972). *Directions in sociolinguistics: The ethnography of communication*. New York: Holt, Rinehart and Winston, Inc.

Halbwachs, M. (1980). *Collective memory*. New York: Harper & Row.

Harkness, S. (1992). Cross-cultural research in child development: A sample of the state of the art. *Developmental Psychology, 28*(4), 622–625.

Harris, J. E., & Morris, P. E., (Eds.). (1984). *Everyday memory, actions and absent-mindedness*. New York: Academic Press.

Havelock, E. A. (1963). *Preface to Plato*. Cambridge, MA: Harvard University Press.

Hirst, W. (1988). Improving memory. In M. Gazzaniga (Ed.), *Perspectives in memory research*, pp. 219–244. Cambridge, MA: MIT Press.

Hirst, W., & Manier, D. (In press). When a family remembers. In D. Rubin (Ed.), *Autobiographical memory, Vol. 2*. New York: Cambridge University Press.

Hudson, J. A. (1990). The emergence of autobiographic memory in mother-child conversation. In R. Fivush & J. A. Hudson (Eds.), *Knowing and remembering in young children*. New York: Cambridge University Press.

Hyman, I., & Rubin, D. (1990). Memorabeatlia: A naturalistic study of long-term memory. *Memory & Cognition, 18*(2), 205–214.

Istomina, Z. M. (1975). The development of voluntary memory in preschool-age children. *Soviet Psychology, 13*, 5–64.

Jacobs, J. (1885). [Critical Notice.] Ueber das Gedchtnis. Von H. Ebbinghaus. *Mind, 10*, 454.

Johnson, M. K., & Hasher, L. (1987). Human learning and memory. *Annual Review of Psychology, 38*, 631–668.

Johnson, M. K., Hashtroudi, S., & Lindsay, D. S. (1993). Source monitoring. *Psychological Bulletin, 114*, 3–28.

Johnson, M. K., & Hirst, W. (1991). Processing subsystems of memory. In R.G. Lister & H.J. Weingertner (Eds.), *Perspectives on cognitive neuroscience*, pp. 197–217. New York: Oxford University Press.

Johnson, M. K., & Rate, C. (1981). Reality monitoring. *Psychological Review, 88*, 67–85.

Kagan, J., Klein, R. E., Finley, G. E., Rogoff, B., & Nolan, E. (1979). A cross-cultural study of cognitive development. *Monographs of the Society for Research in Child Development. 44*(5, Serial No. 180).

Kail, R. (1990). *The development of memory in children (3rd ed.)*. New York: W.H. Freeman.

Klatzky, R. (1975). *Human memory: Structures and processes*. San Francisco: W.F. Freeman.

Lachman, R., Lachman, J., & Butterfield, E. (1979). *Cognitive psychology and information processing: An introduction*. Hillsdale, NJ: Lawrence Erlbaum.

Lakoff, R. (1975). *Language and woman's place*. New York: Harper & Row.

Lave, J. (1988). *Cognition and practice*. New York: Cambridge University Press.

Lave, J. (1991). *Situated learning*. New York: Cambridge University Press.

Lave, J. (1993). *Understanding practice*. New York: Cambridge University Press.

Leet-Pellegrini, H. M. (1980). Conversational dominance as a function of gender and expertise. In H. Giles, W. P. Robinson, & P. M. Smith (Eds.), *Language: Social psychologial perspectives*, pp. 97–104. Oxford, UK: Pergamon Press.

Leont'ev, A. N. (1981). *Problems of the development of the mind*. Moscow: Progress Publishers.

Levinson, S. (1983). *Pragmatics*. New York: Cambridge University Press.

Linton, M. (1986). Ways of searching and the contents of memory. In D. Rubin (Ed.), *Autobiographical memory*, pp. 50–70. New York: Cambridge University Press.

Loftus, E. (1991). The glitter of everyday memory . . . and the gold. *American Psychologist*, *46*(1), 16–18.

Lorayne, H., & Lucas, J. (1974). *The memory book*. New York: Stein & Day.

Lord, A. (1960). *The singer of tales*. Cambridge, MA: Harvard University Press.

Lucariello, J., & Nelson, K. (1987). Remembering and planning talk between mothers and children. *Discourse Processes*, *10*(3), 219–235.

Lynch, K. (1960). *The image of the city*. Cambridge, MA: MIT Press.

Mack, A., Tang, B., Tuma, R., Kahn, S., & Rock, I. (1992). Perceptual organization and attention. *Cognitive Psychology*, *24*(4), 475–501.

Manier, D., & Hirst, W. (In press). The brain doesn't tell the whole story. In E. Manier (Ed.), *Neurobiology and Narrative*. Notre Dame, IN: University of Notre Dame Press.

Manier, D., Hirst, W., Greenstein, M., & Piers, C. (1992). Implicit knowledge of spatial location contributes to false recognitions. *International Journal of Psychology*, *27*(3–4), 111.

Manier, E. (Ed.). (In press). *Neurobiology and narrative*. Notre Dame, IN: University of Notre Dame Press.

Martin, L., & Scribner, S. (1991). Laboratory for cognitive studies of work: A case study of the intellectual applications of a new technology. *Teachers College Record*, *92*(4), 582–602.

Meacham, J. A. (1977). Soviet investigations of memory development. In R. V. Kail, Jr., & J. W. Hagen (Eds.), *Perspectives on the development of memory and cognition*, pp. 273–296. Hillsdale, NJ: Lawrence Erlbaum.

Mercer, N. (Ed.). (1981). *Language in school and community*. London: Edward Arnold Ltd.

Middleton, D., & Edwards, D. (1990). Conversational remembering: a social psychological approach. In D. Middleton & D. Edwards (Eds.), *Collective remembering*, pp. 23–45. London: Sage Publications.

Miller, G. (1956). The magical number seven, plus or minus two: Some limits on our capacity for processing information. *Psychological Review*, *63*, 81–97.

Miller, G., Galanter, E., & Pribram, K. (1979). *Plans and the structure of behavior*. New York: Adams, Bannister, Cox.

Moscovici, S. (1983). The phenomenon of social representations. In R. Farr & S. Moscovici (Eds.), *Social representations*. Cambridge, UK: Cambridge University Press.

Müller, G. E., & Schumann, F. (1889). Über die psychologischen grundlagen der vergleichung gehobener gewichte. *Pflügers Archiv für Physiologie, 45*, 37.

Neisser, U. (Ed.). (1967). *Cognitive psychology.* New York: Meredith Publishing Company.

Neisser, U. (Ed.). (1976). *Cognition and reality.* San Francisco: W. H. Freeman.

Neisser, U. (Ed.). (1978). Memory: What are the important questions. In M. M. Gruneberg, P. E. Morris, and R. N. Sykes (Eds.), *Practical aspects of memory.* London: Academic Press

Neisser, U. (Ed.). (1982). *Memory observed: Remembering in natural contexts.* San Francisco: W. H. Freeman.

Neisser, U., & Winograd, E. (Eds.). (1988). *Remembering reconsidered: Ecological and traditional approaches to the study of memory.* New York: Cambridge University Press.

Nelson, K. (1986). *Event knowledge: Structure and function in development.* Hillsdale, NJ: Lawrence Erlbaum.

Nelson, K. (1990). Remembering, forgetting, and childhood amnesia. In R. Fivush & J. A. Hudson (Eds.), *Knowing and remembering in young children.* New York: Cambridge University Press.

Nelson, K. (1991). Cognitive structure: A component of cognitive context. *Psychological Inquiry, 2*(2), 199–201.

Nelson, K. (1992). Emergence of autobiographical memory at age four. *Human Development, 35*(3), 172–177.

Nelson, K. (1993). The psychological and social origins of autobiographical memory. *Psychological Science, 4*(1), 7–14.

Ong, W. (1967). *The Presence of the Word.* New Haven: Yale University Press.

Paris, S. G., Newman, D. R., & Jacobs, J. E. (1985). Social contexts and functions of children's remembering. In C. J. Brainerd & M. Pressley (Eds.), *Cognitive learning and memory in children.* New York: Springer-Verlag.

Passerini, L. (1987). *Fascism in popular memory: The cultural experience of the Turin working class.* R. Lumley & J. Bloomfield (Transl.). Cambridge, UK: Cambridge University Press.

Pea, R., & Kurland, D. (1984). On the cognitive effects of learning computer programming. *New Ideas in Psychology, 2*, 137–168.

Perkins, D. (1990). *Person plus: A distributed view of thinking and learning.* Paper delivered in Boston at the Symposium on Distributed Learning at the annual meeting of the A.E.R.A.

Posner, M. (Ed.). (1989). *Foundations of cognitive science.* Cambridge, MA: MIT Press.

Pylyshyn, Z. (1980). Computation and cognition: Issues in the foundation of cognitive science. *Behavioral and Brain Sciences, 3*, 111–132.

Radley, A. (1990). Artifacts, memory and a sense of the past. In D. Middleton & D. Edwards (Eds.), *Collective remembering,* pp. 46–59.

Ratner, H. H. (1980). The role of social context in memory development. In M. Perlmutter (Ed.), *Children's memory: New directions for child development, Vol. 10,* pp. 49–68. San Francisco: Jossey-Bass.

Ratner, H. H. (1984). Memory demands and the development of young children's memory. *Child Development, 55*(6), 2173–2191.

Ratner, H. H. (1986). Development of memory for events. *Journal of Experimental Child Psychology, 41*(3), 411–428.

Reiss, D. (1981). *The family's construction of reality.* Cambridge, MA: Harvard University Press.

Robinson, F. (1961). *Effective study.* New York: Harper & Row.

Rock, I., Linnett, C., Graut, P., & Mack, A. (1992). Perception without attention: Results of a new method. *Cognitive Psychology, 24*(4), 502–534.

Rogoff, B. (1990). *Apprenticeship in thinking: Cognitive development in social context.* New York: Oxford University Press.

Rogoff, B., & Mistry, J. (1985). Memory development in cultural context. In C. J. Brainerd & M. Pressley (Eds.), *Cognitive learning and memory in children.* New York: Springer-Verlag.

Rogoff, B., & Mistry, J. (1990). The social and functional context of children's remembering. In R. Fivush & J. A. Hudson (Eds.), *Knowing and remembering in young children.* New York: Cambridge University Press.

Rogoff, B., & Waddell, K. J. (1982). Memory for information organized in a scene from two cultures. *Child Development, 53,* 1224–1228.

Rubin, D. (Ed.). (1977). Very long-term memory for prose and verse. *Journal of Learning and Verbal Behavior, 16,* 611–621.

Rubin, D. (Ed.). (1988a). *Autobiographical memory.* New York: Cambridge University Press.

Rubin, D. (Ed.). (1988b). Learning poetic language. In F. Kessel (Ed.), *The development of language and language researchers: Essays in honor of Roger Brown.* Hillsdale, NJ: Lawrence Erlbaum.

Schank, R. C., & Abelson, R. P. (1977). *Scripts, plans, goals, and understanding.* Hillsdale, NJ: Lawrence Erlbaum.

Schneider, W., & Brun, H. (1987). The role of context in young children's memory performance: Istomina revisted. *British Journal of Developmental Psychology, 5*(3), 333–341.

Scribner, S. (1974). Developmental aspects of categorized recall in a West African society. *Cognitive Psychology, 6*(4), 475–494.

Scribner, S. (1984). The practice of literacy: Where mind and society meet. *Annals of the New York Academy of Sciences, 433,* 5–19.

Scribner, S. (1985). Knowledge at work. *Anthropology & Education Quarterly,* 16(3), 199–206.

Scribner, S., & Cole, M. (1977). Cross-cultural studies of memory and cognition. In R. V. Kail, Jr., & J. W. Hagen (Eds.), *Perspectives on the development of memory and cognition,* pp. 239–272. Hillsdale, NJ: Lawrence Erlbaum.

Scribner, S., & Cole, M. (1981). *The psychology of literacy.* Cambridge, MA: Harvard University Press.

Shweder, R. (1991). *Thinking through cultures: Expeditions in cultural psychology.* Cambridge, MA: Harvard University Press.

Smith, E., Adams, N., & Schorr, D. (1978). Fact retrieval and the paradox of interference. *Cognitive Psychology, 10*(4), 438–464.

Stigler, J., Shweder, R., & Herdt, G. (Eds.). (1990). *Cultural psychology: Essays on comparative human development.* New York: Cambridge University Press.

Sturken, M. (1991). The wall, the screen, and the image: The Vietnam veterans memorial. *Representation, 35,* 118–142.

Suchman, L. (1990). *Plans and situated actions: The problem of human-machine communication.* New York: Cambridge University Press.

Tannen, D. (1990). *You just don't understand: Women and men in conversation.* New York: William Morrow & Company.

Usher, J., & Neisser, U. (1993). Childhood amnesia and the beginnings of memory for four early life events. *Journal of Experimental Psychology: General, 122*(2), 155–165.

Vygotsky, L. S. (1978). *Mind in society:* Cambridge, MA: Harvard University Press.

Wegener, D. (1986). Transactive memory: A contemporary analysis of the group mind. In B. Mullen & G. Goethals (Eds.), *Theories of group behavior,* pp. 185–208. New York: Spinger-Verlag.

Wegener, D., Erber, R., and Raymond, P. (1991). Transactive memory in close relationships. *Journal of Personality and Social Psychology, 61*(6), 923–929.

Weissberg, J. A., & Paris, S. G. (1986). Young children's remembering in different contexts: A replication and reinterpretation of Istomina's study. *Child Development, 57,* 1123–1129.

Wertsch, J. (Ed.). (1991). *Voices of the mind: A sociocultural approach to mediated action.* Cambridge, MA: Harvard University Press.

Wertsch, J. (Ed.). (1981). *The concept of activity in Soviet psychology.* Armonk, NY: M. E. Sharpe.

Wundt, W. (1900). *Völkerpsychologie.* Leipzig: Engelmann.

Yates, F. (1966). *The art of memory.* Chicago: University of Chicago Press.

6   Analysis of developmental processes in sociocultural activity

Barbara Rogoff, Barbara Radziszewska, and Tracy Masiello

This chapter discusses conceptual commonalities underlying emerging sociocultural approaches that examine how developmental processes at individual, social, and cultural levels constitute each other, and considers implications for the conduct of research on developmental processes in sociocultural activity. It focuses on how we conceive of developmental change, of the relation between the individual and others, and of activity as a unit of analysis. It examines issues of how to observe learning, reinterpreting some methods that have traditionally attempted to isolate individual learning and proposing alternative approaches that are more consistent with a sociocultural approach.

We begin with a general discussion of sociocultural theory and then concentrate on implications for the conduct and interpretation of research on children's learning, employing a series of studies we carried out on children solving mazes with or without their mothers' assistance, to examine transformations in how learning can be observed from a sociocultural perspective.

Sociocultural approaches

A complex of related but heterogeneous proposals for sociocultural theory are emerging from discourse across disciplines and cultural and historical communities. The various proposals represent a general

We greatly appreciate comments and discussion with Nancy Bell, Eugene Matusov, Mary Gauvain, and Artin Göncü. We are grateful to the children and mothers who participated in the studies reported, and appreciate the facilitation provided by the Jewish Community Center Preschool and the Garden Park Ward. The assistance of Amy Urbanek, Christine Mosier, Sharon Akimoto, and Cindy White was very important to the research, which was supported by the National Institute of Child Health and Human Development (HD 16973). Correspondence concerning this article should be addressed to Barbara Rogoff, Psychology Department, Kerr Hall, University of California, Santa Cruz, CA 95064.

125

agreement revolving around a view of processes of individual development as they constitute and are constituted by interpersonal and cultural/historical activities and practices. The stance of sociocultural approaches to child development is that the development of children occurs as they participate in sociocultural activities. In this section, we provide an overview of what we see as key common ground in a variety of emerging sociocultural approaches.

Sociocultural perspectives assert that individual developmental processes are inherently involved with the actual activities in which children engage with others in cultural practices and institutions, and that variation is inherent to human functioning. Children discern the relations {'transfer'} between genres of activity across contexts as children with others constitute those activities. Units of analysis focus on processes rather than on characteristics of individuals. Generalities are sought in terms of the nature of the processes as people participate in and constitute activities, rather than simply assuming context-free generality or seeking it in separated characteristics of the person or the task. The person is conceived as a participant in activities, constituting the activities with others through their developing roles.

Traditional approaches to understanding individual and sociocultural processes dissected them and settled them within the boundaries of disciplines, making it difficult to address questions of sociocultural and individual development in an integrated manner. For psychology, the awareness that individual functioning had something to do with culture led to studies adding cultural factors as influences (in the form of independent variables) on what was assumed to be basic individual functioning (often examined with tests yielding dependent variables). For anthropology and sociology, there has been a surprisingly small effort devoted to understanding child development in sociocultural institutions and practices. Currently, scholars in psychology, anthropology, sociology, and linguistics are seeking ways to overcome the limitations of concepts derived from the dichotomy between the individual and society.

The sociocultural approach inspired by Vygotsky and Leont'ev provides many sociocultural scholars with a common language and perspective, particularly in the concept of "activity" and the emphasis on integrating levels of analysis. In addition, there are a number of other converging perspectives that enter the discourse to form the conceptual basis of sociocultural research. The works of G. H. Mead and of Dewey, for example, contribute to the sociocultural approach, as do more recent writings from sociolinguistics, sociology, psychology, and anthropology. The concept of activity has developed in work in sociocultural psychology, pragmatics, ethnography of speaking, practice theory, and other theoretical enterprises.

There are several central assumptions that are held in common across sociocultural approaches to child development deriving from the different disciplines. They have to do with the use of activity or event as the unit of analysis to examine human functioning in endeavors with sociocultural organization, the roles of variation and similarity, the importance of analysis of process and of development, the integrated analysis of individual, interpersonal, and community processes, and the cultural and historical embeddedness of the inquiry itself. We discuss each of these in turn, and then describe transitions in our own thinking in a series of studies on children's learning.

Unit of analysis

The activity or event provides a unit of analysis that focuses on people engaged in sociocultural endeavors with other people, working with and extending cultural tools and practices inherited from previous generations. As individuals and groups of people develop through their shared involvement, they also contribute to transforming the cultural tools, practices, and institutions of the activities in which they engage. The concept of activity focuses attention on sociocultural events as the unit of analysis, seeking a unit of analysis that preserves the inner workings of events of interest, rather than separating an event into elements that no longer function as does the living unit (Leont'ev 1981; Cole 1985; Wertsch 1985; Zinchenko 1985). For example, in the maze studies reported later, the practice sessions and the posttests would be viewed as events involving children, their mothers, and the experimenter in attempting to accomplish particular goals with the material at hand in the context of the structured nature of laboratory experiments in a U.S. university of the 1980s.

Variation and similarity

Variation in the direction and course of individual development in differing communities must be understood in order to understand development, because there is no generic development independent of actual communities and their practices. The challenge for understanding development is to see how people make connections across activities with practices that are related under some circumstances, rather than to assume that the processes are inherently general or automatically general within domains. The sociocultural approach does not assume generality, but seeks to understand both similarities and variation according to the processes involved as people participate in cultural practices. For example, in the maze studies to be reported, children's planning may well be unrelated to how they would plan a birthday party or a route through their neighborhood; it may, however, relate to their planning of mazes in puzzle books or at preschool. The question of how peoples' efforts in one activity relate to those in another is an empirical question that requires examination of the nature of the activities (in terms of the individual, social, and cultural aspects of the activity). Likewise, the findings cannot be assumed to generalize (or to be specific either) to children of another cultural community than that observed.

Process and development

To understand the purpose and structure of human phenomena, it is essential to examine their development and the processes by which humans organize their efforts and practices. Hence, analyses of process become the focus, replacing the examination of products separated from their development (see Rogoff, Baker-Sennett, & Matusov 1994). This approach questions distinctions between process and product (or content), between competence and performance, and between culture and biology.

Analysis of sociocultural activities involves examination of the active and dynamically transforming contributions from individuals, their social partners, and historical traditions and materials as people engage in shared endeavors. As Scribner (1985) pointed out, Vygotsky's emphasis on the interrelated roles of the individual and the social world in microgenetic, ontogenetic, sociocultural, and phylogenetic development includes individual and environment together in successively broader time frames. Development over the life course takes place within developmental processes occurring over the course of cultural history, on the one hand, and phylogenetic history, on the other. These levels of analysis of development are inseparable: the efforts of individuals constitute cultural practices that further organize individuals' development, and similarly, human biological development cannot be separated from the cultural institutions and practices that characterize humanity. Rogoff (1992) proposed that sociocultural approaches involve observation of developmental processes in different planes of analysis (personal, interpersonal, and community) depending on the question at hand, but with each plane of analysis only making sense in the context of the whole, and none seen as more fundamental than the others.

Relation of individual and social and cultural levels of organization

Inherent to sociocultural approaches is a premise that individual, social, and cultural analyses are inseparable. This notion differs from approaches that seek the impact of culture on the individual in which each is conceived as separate (termed "interactional" approaches by Rogoff (1982), and contrasted with "contextual event" approaches). Within sociocultural approaches, the aim is to understand the developmental processes involved in activities, at the level of individual, interpersonal, and community (or cultural) processes.

The relation between "activities" and learning can be conceived in several ways. Ochs (personal communication, 1989) distinguished between two views. In the first, learning is seen as *structured by* activity, and research involves examining the emergent structure of activities that relate to local economic, political, and other ideological systems that link one social activity to another and thus organize learning and cognition across activity contexts. That is, children extract sociocultural knowledge by discerning variations and commonalities across activities as they attend to the ordinary, repeated practices of care givers that are systematically linked to economic and political practices. In the second, learning *constitutes* activities. Cognitive efforts not only underlie and are constrained by local activities and ideological systems, such work builds these activities and systems. In this perspective, members socialize children into the cognitive tools to construct social contexts (i.e., society).

Similarly, Rogoff (1995) stressed the idea that individuals develop as they participate (either face to face or distally) with others in shared endeavors that both constitute and are derived from community traditions. Rogoff suggested that the examination of individual, interpersonal, and community developmental processes involves differing planes of observation, with any one plane being the topic of focus but with the others necessarily observed in the background. For example, in solving mazes, the contributions of either the children or the mothers can be described in a sociocultural approach, but each must be described as they relate to the other rather than as "independent" entitities. And each person's efforts both constitute and are constituted by the sociocultural activity of solving mazes in an experiment.

Cultural–historical nature of the research endeavor

As noted by many scholars, the sociocultural activities of researchers, as well as of children, are changing rapidly with changes all around the world in politics, communication, and historical events. The questions and methods of understanding developmental processes are themselves culturally and historically situated. Researchers can gain an understanding of the research endeavor and of the phenomena studied by examining their own roles in the inquiry and those of the institutions in which the inquiry occurs. This is made easier by discourse across disciplines, nations, and historical time periods that is inherent to the sociocultural approach, and by the aims of this line of work to understand individual functioning as it is constituted by and constitutes social and cultural processes. The observations we make of others' endeavors in their cultural institutions facilitate our awareness of how our own endeavors, including experiments in academic laboratories, build on and within the traditions and goals of the institutions involved.

In the next section, we examine how a sociocultural approach led us to rethink assumptions that we had been using in a series of studies attempting to examine processes of individual development. It happens that the results of these studies did not fit with our preconceptions, and so challenged us to think more deeply. The studies do not prove or disprove the arguments of this paper, but merely provide a concrete illustration to ground the discussion. We offer this analysis as both a reflection on a developmental transition for ourselves as researchers and as the basis for a discussion of how a sociocultural approach could transform interpretations of and methods for observing developmental change in the people whom we observe in research.

A transition in observation of developmental change

About a decade ago, Jamie Germond and Barbara Rogoff carried out a study attempting to determine the "effects" of maternal assistance on preschool-age children's facility in solving mazes, which surprised us by showing no difference in posttest performance between children who had or had not previously solved mazes with their mothers' assistance. We followed that study up with two more studies varying the procedure to see if the results of the first study had been caused by procedural shortcomings, but the second and third studies yielded the same results as the first.

Since beginning these studies, we broadened our perspective from that with which the work began. First, we began to devote more attention to trying to understand the circumstances under which one might expect social interaction to aid children's learning. This led to several hypotheses having to do with the nature of maternal assistance, which we explored.

However, we also gave further thought to our assumptions regarding how one could assess whether individual development had occurred and whether social events had anything to do with such development. Attempts to locate learning solely in the head of the learner and to separately examine the effects of social experience often employ a treatment-posttest design such as we used. Our central point in discussing this series of studies is that there are complications in attempting to localize learning in terms of whether or not (or to what extent) an individual has "attained" a concept or "acquired" a skill. The problem has to do with separating social "influence" from "individual" learning.

Studies of the influence of social interaction on cognitive development (including our own) – like investigations of children's solitary cognitive efforts – often assume that it is possible to design a situation that allows evaluation of children's competence, independent of the dynamic nature of the activity and of the sociocultural nature of all events. However, in a sociocultural perspective, learning and development are regarded as processes of changing participation in cultural activity; no activity is purely individual. Thus a posttest cannot be interpreted as revealing purely individual performance, in that posttests occur in interaction with experimenters in activities that are staged in particular cultural practices (e.g., tests). The common assumption that a posttest provides access to an individual's state of knowledge *separable from the circumstances* is called into question.

If we regard thinking as a process occurring as people participate in sociocultural activities, the question becomes how people's participation changes as an activity develops, rather than whether individuals have or have not yet "acquired" information or skills. The idea of thinking as being the acquisition of skills or knowledge is inconsistent, in our view, with a sociocultural emphasis on process. Rogoff, Baker-Sennett, and Matusov (1994) argued that attempts to assess competence require the assumption that children possess (or do not possess) mental capacities or skills, conceived as objects that can be acquired. The competence/performance distinction is linked to the question of whether people do or do not yet have some skill, and leads to methodological manipulations to clear away situational artifacts that "get in the way" of evaluating children's possessions of skills or concepts.

Ours is basically an argument that thinking is more parsimoniously regarded as a process than as the storage and retrieval of mental objects, and that developmental and cognitive processes that have been regarded as mysterious can be observed when thinking and developmental processes are the focus of study (see Guba & Lincoln 1982; Rogoff et al. 1994). The metaphor of cranial file boxes for the storage of knowledge or skills may get in the way of advancing the understanding of thinking from a sociocultural perspective. In our perspective, what individuals do and how they think is the focus, rather than efforts to determine what they *can* do or think; variation and similarities in their participation in varying activities become central rather than nuisances to clear away in the attempt to observe "pure" competence.

We argue that it is problematic to interpret posttests as being in a priveleged position of assessment of the state of an individual's understanding.[1] From a sociocultural perspective, the "treatment" is at least as interesting a situation in which to understand children's learning as is the posttest. Neither the treatment phase nor the posttest would provide a window on "pure" thinking. Our stance is that all situations are social and cultural; a person's efforts in any activity provide some, but limited, information allowing inferences regarding what kind of support a person might need or responsibility they might be able to manage in related circumstances.

Evaluation would involve attention to the person's participation in actual events, not attempts to infer context-free knowledge or skill. If posttests are interpreted as sociocultural activity of a particular social and cultural construction, there is no reason to question their use. However, if any situation – including a posttest – is accorded a particular status that is regarded as "purer" than other activities, we argue that such interpretation is inconsistent with a sociocultural approach.

The fact that we found no posttest differences in our series of studies may have impelled us to think more deeply about what individual posttest performance means. However, the assumptions that we discuss are as relevant to studies that show differences as to studies that do not. What was problematic in our studies was not their outcome (no difference on the posttests) but the theoretical assumption of separation of individual and social processes as products. We provide an account of our series of studies in hopes that this example will allow consideration of the assumptions involved in research on social "influence" on "individual" development (and especially the treatment–posttest design) in a more concrete way.

Children's solution of mazes after having had or not had maternal assistance

At the time this project began we were concerned that initial enthusiasm over social influences on children's cognitive development often assumed that there was social influence without actually testing whether the presence of assistance benefitted children's later performance (Steward & Steward 1974; Childs & Greenfield 1980; Rogoff & Gardner 1984; Rogoff, Malkin, & Gilbride 1984; Saxe, Gearhart, & Guberman 1984; DeLoache & Plaetzer 1985). Our series of studies attempted to relate the presence or absence of maternal assistance to children's subsequent success in solving mazes and the extent to which they planned ahead. We expected that maternal assistance would allow middle-class 3- to 4-year-old children to solve more mazes and to plan ahead more frequently than they would otherwise.

This prediction is consistent with investigations with middle-class 9- to 10-year-olds planning imaginary errands, in which interaction with skilled adult partners led to a greater likelihood of efficient later planning of routes than did interaction with child partners less skilled in the task and/or in involving child partners in decision making (Radziszewska & Rogoff 1988, 1991). However, in work with younger children, results have been less clearcut, with Kontos (1983) finding no advantage of working with adults in young children's skill with puzzles, and Gauvain and Rogoff (1989) finding no overall differences in posttest planning of routes through a model grocery store between 5-year-old children who had or had not previously worked with an adult or peer partner.

It was clear that the assumption of necessarily beneficial results of working with more-skilled partners needed qualification. For example, there is evidence that merely being in the presence of another person does not confer advantages, but that making decisions jointly with another person sometimes leads to improved performance on a later occasion (Glachan & Light 1982; Gauvain & Rogoff 1989; Blaye, Light, Joiner, & Sheldon 1991). There is also evidence that it is not the amount of interaction that matters but the contingency of a skilled partner's support to the child's task success, the initiative allowed to the child, the explicitness of strategic or rule statements, and the provision of challenging questions that encourage children to distance themselves from the immediate task (Sigel & Cocking 1977; Wood, Wood, & Middleton 1978; Zimmerman & Blom 1983; Ellis & Rogoff 1986; Wood 1986; Radziszewska & Rogoff 1988, 1991).

There are doubtless other factors that could be taken into account in understanding whether an interaction would lead to learning, such as the nature of the task itself (such as whether it is easy to share) and the characteristics of the child and the partner (such as the child's age, the partner's expertise, and their comfort with each other). We will consider these in our interpretation of the studies.

However, as our thinking on the topic has changed over the course of the project, our primary purpose now is to go beyond the attempt to relate specific background variables such as the nature of the task or of the child or the partner or their previous interaction, to question the assumption that one observation be regarded as learning and another be regarded as influence on learning. Our initial plan to examine the impact of social interaction on individual cognitive development was based on the assumption that it was possible and desirable to characterize somewhat enduring and self-contained individual levels of skill. But now we question the possibility of attributing levels of skill to individuals apart from their participation in actual activities, as we view thinking as inherently a dynamic sociocultural activity from which individual cognitive efforts can neither be truly extracted nor assumed to characterize the individual in an enduring fashion.

We describe the first study and its results, then summarize the second and third studies and their results more briefly, to give an idea of the

Figure 6.1. Four-year-old planning a maze route with her mother's assistance. Reprinted from Rogoff 1990.

kinds of social and task adjustments we attempted in order to study the effects of maternal assistance.

Study 1. Fifty-eight middle-class children (in groups of average age 3.17 and 4.5 years) were randomly assigned to either work with their mothers during practice or to work alone. The children were presented with four mazes for a pretest, eight new mazes for a practice (in which children worked with or without their mothers' assistance), and eight new mazes for a posttest. The mazes were drawn on 20-inch square sheets of safety glass with raised lines of bathtub putty forming low walls to separate the alleyways of the maze. The children drew with an erasable marking pen, starting from a "lost" baby duck sticker in the center of the maze to a "waiting" mother duck sticker placed at the maze exit. The mazes were fastened to a lectern concealing a video camera aimed through the glass to the participants' faces and hands as they worked on the maze (see Figure 6.1).

The pretest began with orientation to the rules by the experimenter as the child was shown a sample maze:

Here we have a lost little baby duck who wants to find her mother. (Experimenter points to the sticker of the baby and mother duck.) But this baby duck is too little to jump or fly over these walls. (Experimenter points to the raised putty walls and asks the child to touch them to see that they really are solid walls.) So the baby duck needs to find her way out to her mother by walking through open doors. (Experimenter points out the first open door.) And the baby duck doesn't want to get trapped in any of the dead ends because then she has to turn around and it takes longer to find her mother. (Experimenter draws into the dead end with her finger and exaggerates bumping into the dead-end wall.)

Then the experimenter asked the child to draw the route for the baby duck to follow to find her mama. If the child hesitated, the experimenter encouraged the child and asked her/him to follow the experimenter's finger with the marking pen as she drew out to the mama duck. Then each child received three more mazes to solve without assistance (or less if the child failed to solve two consecutive mazes). Immediately following the pretest, children began the practice phase. Mothers who did not assist their children sat in a position in which they could not see the mazes but could encourage their children. Mothers who were asked to assist their children were asked to sit with the child on their lap and help the child learn how to solve the mazes more efficiently. The posttest followed the practice phase, with each child starting with a simple maze and continuing until they either successfully solved the last maze or failed to solve two mazes.

A research assistant coded the videotapes for each child's number of mazes solved and strategies used to plan ahead in the practice phase and the posttest. The number of mazes solved was the number of mazes that the child completed without making more than three errors (dead-end entries) on the simplest mazes of the set or more than five errors on the more complex mazes. The planning strategy score for each child was the mean of the score for each maze the child solved, which was coded globally on a rating scale ranging from 1 to 5:

1. Random planning: the child did not look ahead or consider the route, went into the same dead end repeatedly, or often got stuck and did not try to find an alternate route.
2. Mostly random planning: most of the child's moves were random, but the child looked ahead in order to move out of dead ends.

3. Low-prevention planning: the child used some planning to avoid get-ting stuck, looking ahead briefly when starting to draw or pausing fleetingly at a choice point.
4. High-prevention planning: the child planned entire route segments in advance.
5. Advance planning: the child appeared to plan most or all the route in advance, tracing the route with a finger or visually before starting to draw with the pen.

There were no differences in the number of mazes solved or in the extent of advance planning in the posttest between children who had worked with their mothers' assistance and those who had worked with-out their mothers' assistance during the practice phase (F values were 0.3 and 0.5).[2] Our surprise at this result led us to reanalyze the data in an embarrassing number of alternative ways (e.g., separately examining results for children who were already performing near ceiling, and experimenting with different criteria for "failing" a maze). Nothing changed the basic finding of no difference between groups with or with-out maternal assistance. We also tried various ways of examining what the mothers were doing during the practice phase to see if children who received more help of various kinds did better subsequently, but none of these efforts produced interesting findings.

Studies 2 and 3. To investigate whether something about our procedure in Study 1 had made it difficult to find an effect of maternal assistance, we carried out two further studies varying the procedure, in the follow-ing ways:

-   The pretest phase was eliminated to reduce the amount of practice before the treatment phase to increase the appropriateness as well as the salience of maternal intervention and to decrease the likelihood of a ceiling effect.
-   The range of mazes presented to the children added more difficult mazes in order to eliminate the possibility of a ceiling effect.
-   Study 3 employed mazes that differed in terms of whether their dead ends could be discerned with only a short search or required more extensive checking down paths, with the idea that mothers might help children to distinguish mazes that were most effectively solved with advance planning from mazes that could be solved with less advance planning. The mothers who were asked to help their children them-

selves practiced on the two kinds of mazes before beginning to assist their child, but the specific nature of the mazes was not pointed out.

- The range of ages of children was reduced to less than a year to reduce variability due to age differences. Study 2 involved 30 middle-class children from 4.0 to 4.5 years, and Study 3 involved 32 middle-class children from 4.0 to 4.92 years.
- The instruction by the experimenter in orienting the children to the rules for solving mazes was reduced (e.g., eliminating the story of a lost baby duck, replacing the three-dimensional putty maze walls with flat lines) to make sure there would be something for the mothers to contribute.
- Mothers were asked more explicitly to prepare children for a posttest and to help them learn to plan ahead.

We developed coding schemes for analyzing the contingent nature of maternal assistance to the child's success in the task and the frequency of maternal reference to the strategies of looking ahead and avoiding dead ends. The maternal contingency measure was a percentage of all the episodes in which maternal help was contingent, based on Wood et al.'s (1978, p. 133) contingency rule: "If the child succeeds, when next intervening offer less help. If the child fails, when next intervening take over more control." We judged the mothers' assistance to be contingent if she refrained from directing or taking over on episodes in which the child was just beginning or pausing or progressing on the right track (not giving specific directions for the next move or physically taking over the task) OR if she provided assistance when the child was going into a dead end or on an incorrect route (stating strategies useful for solving the mazes, such as looking ahead to determine where to go next, avoiding dead ends, and working backward from the exit to the starting point).

As in Study 1, children who worked with versus without their mothers' assistance did not differ in the number of mazes they solved or in the extent of their advance planning in the posttests of Studies 2 and 3 (*t* values ranged from 0.5 to 1.6). Given our zealous attempts to examine the data for any possible differences and the replication of the findings in Studies 2 and 3 in which we made great efforts to adjust the procedure to maximize the chance of differences, we consider the findings of no difference between preschool children's maze planning following practice with or without maternal assistance to be quite robust. Of course, the null effects are specific to the tasks, the ages, and the social class group that we observed; however, the same would be true of studies in which differences are observed.

We explored the lack of benefit provided by having practiced with maternal assistance by examining differences among the mothers in the extent to which their aid to the children was contingent on the children's success in solving the mazes, and the extent to which they suggested strategies to the children.

An average of approximately 60 to 65% of maternal responses to children's actions were contingent, with mothers providing strategic assistance when children got stuck and refraining from being directive or taking over when children were not having difficulty.[3] To examine whether variation between mothers in contingency might be influential in the extent to which their children benefited from their assistance, we combined the results from Studies 2 and 3 (to increase sample size). Maternal contingency during the practice phase did not relate to the number of mazes that children solved in the posttest, but did correlate with the extent of advance planning used by children when later planning without their mothers' assistance, $r(29) = .48, p < .01$.

Consistent with the finding that children's advance planning related more strongly to previous maternal assistance than did the number of mazes solved is the finding that mothers emphasized the strategy of looking ahead. The mothers expressed the need to look ahead on average approximately 2.5 times during the practice sessions of both Studies 2 and 3. In Study 2, but not in Study 3, children whose mothers more frequently stated the "look ahead" strategy planned ahead in the posttest to a greater extent, $r(13) = .56, p < .05$.

Another maternal strategy was to tell children to avoid dead ends, which mothers did approximately 0.5 to 1.5 times during the practice session. However, the expression of this strategy correlated *negatively* with the number of mazes that the children solved during the posttest, $r(29) = -.38, p < .05$, and marginally negatively with the children's advance planning during the posttest, $r(29) = -.31, p = .08$. We assume that these findings reflect the greater likelihood of reminding children who had difficulty with the mazes to avoid dead ends.

Discussion. The three studies consistently found no posttest differences between children who had or had not received their mothers' assistance in the number of mazes solved or in planning in advance. They also provided some plausible ideas regarding aspects of maternal assistance (e.g., contingency of maternal response) that could relate to the finding of no difference.

However, we do not want our account to end with a sigh of relief that we did find something significant with which to explain our results. In fact, we believe that the most important aspect of our data is the finding of no difference between conditions and the questions that this prompted us to raise about our assumptions regarding the relation between an interactional practice session and a subsequent "solo" performance (posttest). Before we examine our assumptions about the nature of cognition and of social interaction, we consider several possible immediate explanations for the finding of no difference between children who worked with the assistance of their mothers or without it.

Children's age. A Piagetian account might focus on the youth of the children, to argue that children who are this young are still egocentric and thus have difficulty benefiting from the ideas of other people. This is an inviting idea, but can be easily discarded because of evidence that still younger children benefit from social interaction in learning language (Hoff-Ginsberg & Shatz 1982; John-Steiner & Tatter 1983; Nelson, Denninger, Bonvillian, Kaplan, & Baker 1984; Snow 1984; Papousek, Papousek, & Bornstein 1985; Hoff-Ginsberg 1986; Tomasello & Farrar 1986; Valdez-Menchaca 1987), and evidence that young children benefit from working with skilled partners in construction and memory tasks (Wood et al. 1978; Mistry & Rogoff 1987; Pacifici & Bearison 1991; Göncü & Rogoff 1994).

Task × age characteristics. An alternative is to focus on the task or the interaction of task and the characteristics of the participants. Perhaps there is something idiosyncratic about this task that makes it difficult for children to benefit from interaction. Interpretations that we considered – and dismissed after informal exploratory examination of the interactions – were

1. that with their mothers instructed to assist them, these young children relinquished the problem solving to their mothers (but they did not seem to) or else focused on trying to negotiate whose job it was to solve the mazes when working with their mothers rather than focusing on the task itself (very rare), or

2. that the mothers were surprised that their young children could do any mazes at all (which they often were, though the children did mazes well) so they just watched with amazement rather than attempting to assist (which they did not).

Perhaps a planning task like this requires participants to be able to communicate about phenomena that are not present to point at (i.e., future courses of action) and would tax the communication skills of such young children more than would sharing decision making in a task in which the phenomena are present to point at and discuss (such as learning to recite the names of objects or to classify things). It may be more difficult to share decision making or understanding of a problem that deals with imagined or future events than to achieve intersubjectivity in dealing with concrete, present referents. Perhaps it is easier for young children to work with others on memory and construction tasks, learning information that is physically presented without the need for complicated interpersonal understanding, than it is on planning tasks, which require discussion of future possibilities and strategies for dealing with the efficient coordination of several possible actions.

This idea is supported by findings that 5-year-olds who actually shared decision making with their partners in another route planning task performed better in subsequent unassisted planning than did children who worked with a partner but without shared decision making (Gauvain & Rogoff 1989). There were no overall differences in posttest planning between children who had or had not previously worked with a partner, as in the present study. But children who shared decision making with their partners rather than working independently or dividing the task into independent turns performed better than the children who had had no partner or who had had a partner with whom they had not worked jointly.

Features of maternal assistance. An explanation that receives some support in the data is that assisting children in learning is a complicated skill, with sufficient variation between individuals that one should not expect advantages from just anyone teaching. In Wood et al. (1978), the experimenter who was trained in contingent instruction still only followed the contingency rule 85% of the time. It is not surprising that the untrained mothers in this study used a contingent approach only about 60 to 65% of the time. With such young children, contingency may be both more important and more difficult to achieve than with older children (with whom research results more consistently show advantages of working with mothers). The idea that variation in the mothers' contingency of responding to their children's problem solving might relate to the children's later performance is supported by our correlation between the extent of maternal contingency in the assistance phase and the extent of children's planning in advance in solving mazes later.

However, there are some problems in accepting this relationship as conclusive, not the least of which is the problem that correlation does not indicate causation. Recall that maternal contingency correlated positively with later performance and strategy statements warning children to avoid dead ends correlated *negatively* with later performance. One might too easily assume that effective instruction should involve more contingency and the avoidance of avoid–dead-end strategy statements. But the negative correlation could have resulted from the mothers' need to state strategies for children who were doing poorly: For a child who is impulsively entering many dead ends, a mother might caution to avoid dead ends, a strategy statement occasioned by the child's behavior. This is merely a demonstration that the direction of effect from a correlational finding cannot be assumed; a warning that is as old as the hills though often overlooked.

Problems of assumptions regarding what is cognitive and what is social

The deeper problem that we wish to raise is that seeking the influence of social interaction on individual development may be incompatible with a sociocultural approach at least in this form.[4] The training/posttest design is borrowed from many years of tradition that attempted to examine the effects of one or another kind of training on an individual's learning. It refers to the phase when two people are observed as a training phase, with the phenomenon of interest being the trainer's actions on the relatively passive subject, and casts the phase when the subject is asked to carry out a related task without the support of the trainer as a measure of independent learning or development of ability or acquisition of skill.

However, this design often carries problematic assumptions having to do with what is regarded as social and with characterizations of skills as enduring individual possessions. (See also Perret-Clermont, Perret, & Bell (1991) for a discussion of concerns with the posttest design.) Both the training phase and the posttest involve social interaction – with an active but ignored subject in the training phase, who might direct the actions of the trainer rather than just soaking up the training, and a subject trying to communicate in one way or another with an experimenter in the posttest, rather than simply revealing their current state of knowledge or their changed level of ability.

The child who is regarded as working independently in the posttest is in fact working within the constraints and supports provided by the experimenter and by the research tradition and scholarly institutions that encompass *The Posttest*. The subject is indeed *subject* to a communicative contract that delineates the appropriate form of communication and resources available in responding to the problems posed by the experimenter.

Such a communicative contract is one that is tied to the discourse patterns of schooling and testing, with a knowledgeable person asking a less knowledgeable person questions to which the knowledgeable person already knows the answers but will not help the less knowledgable person – a rare situation in discourse outside of schools and tests. (Cultural differences in communication with toddlers suggest that the discourse pattern of schooling is also used between middle-class parents and their preschool-age children but not between parents and children in some other groups [Heath 1983; Ochs & Schieffelin 1984; Rogoff et al. 1993].) To regard the posttest as being independent of social interaction and social tradition is to ignore a sociocultural context that is problematic for individuals with less experience of schooling, including young children and people in communities that do not stress formal schooling (Rogoff 1981, 1990; Heath 1983; Bell, Grossen, & Perret-Clermont 1985).

The division of the two phases into an intervention and an assessment often involves the assumption that the posttest taps into some rather stable outcome such as the acquisition of a skill or the attainment of knowledge. The posttest may be regarded as a context-free window on the intellectual possessions (whether general or domain-specific) of the subject. However, from a sociocultural perspective, no situation is context-free. The training and the posttest phase are simply two different social situations, both social and both involving processes of learning and communication.

Thus neither phase would be privileged as revealing what an individual *can* do and think. The focus instead is on what people *do* do and think, without the assumption that performance is merely a clouded window on competence. The assumption of abilities or skills as stable possessions of individuals, definable without regard to the context of action, we argue should be dropped in the sociocultural approach in order to examine the contributions of individuals as they occur in dynamically, socially, and culturally defined and constituted activities. The individual cannot be dissected from the activity (including the involvement of other people, the constraints and resources provided by cultural tools such as language and maps, and institutional traditions such as ways of behaving when told to demonstrate knowledge).

A sociocultural approach demands closer attention to the ongoing dynamic development of social interaction and of problem solving by people participating in sociocultural activity – whether the activity is a teaching/learning situation in school or in learning a trade, or whether the activity is demonstrating knowledge on demand for a researcher in a laboratory posttest. It focuses on evaluation of the process and individuals' participation in and contributions to the ongoing activity rather than on "outcome" and individuals' possessions of concepts and skills.[5]

It is often difficult to detach the training/posttest design from the assumption system focusing on individual characteristics and influences so as to interpret the design within the assumption system of sociocultural theory. Readers and reviewers in psychology tend to reinterpret findings in terms of the usual assumptions of "pure" individual characteristics and social influence rather than individual participation in sociocultural process.

However, if interpreted from a sociocultural perspective, the design could provide interesting information consistent with the approach as a way of examining what happens next under particular circumstances. If the two phases are interpreted as being simply two related events that each give a window on social and cognitive processes, then there would be nothing inherently more or less interesting about adopting the constraints of the training/posttest design over observing any other two related events (such as a child working first with one partner and then with another on related problems). Attention would be given in either case to the social and cultural features of the participants' interactions and problem solving. Neither would be regarded as revealing an individual's "true inner state;" rather, both would be interesting for understanding the dynamic sociocultural processes in which individuals with others engage in setting and solving problems. And the connection between the two similar events would be of great interest for understanding how people's contributions to both are related – a recast of the question of transfer of training.

Sociocultural observations would emphasize how the children, mothers, and experimenter arranged their relative contributions to planning the maze routes and to managing each other in both the practice and posttest events, and would examine how the contributions of each related to the prior and subsequent event and to the larger sociocultural system (involving experiments, psychology, and academia) which these events constituted and were constituted by. We would examine how the children, mothers, and experimenter collaborated and avoided collaborating in the practice and posttest sessions (according to the rules of the experiment, which would also be an object of study), and how each person's role transformed and was transformed by those of the others. The maze planning itself would be viewed as a function of the contributions of the participants in the sociocultural activity, and the similarities across the two events would be revealing in terms of the nature of the responsibility taken by the different contributors.

For the purpose of aiding children or others in learning more, the flux of social interaction can provide information on what aspects of problem solving a child or other person handles with what types of support. As Brown and French (1979) have suggested, it may be more informative for the fostering of cognitive development to understand what children do *with* other people than to try to understand what they do when other people simply constrain performance (as in traditional testing).

The dynamic processes of interaction and arrangements between people in both supportive and constraining situations require analysis within the cultural tradition and institutions in which they function in order to understand both what children do as they plan and how others can assist (or derail) them in managing more sophisticated problems. Our definitions of sophisticated problem solving and of social support and constraint inherently reflect the values and traditions of our institutions, especially schools and laboratories. We suggest that it will help progress in research to pay greater attention to the assumption systems of our research methods and questions. Consistent with a sociocultural approach, we argue that research observations are not separable from the traditions of the institutions and communities in which they occur, and at the same time that researchers constantly constitute such cultural traditions as we carry out such practices, transforming them as we do.

Notes

1. Such an interpretation of posttests is not inevitable, but appears common.
2. There were also no effects of assistance or interactions with age when the age range was divided into younger and older children.
3. This was also the average level of contingency that we found when we returned to the data of Study 1 and applied the same analyses.
4. Thanks to Jean Lave for discussions on this whole topic.
5. See Skager (1975) for a critique of educational evaluation for ignoring processes in the illusory effort to assess output.

References

Bell, N., Grossen, M., & Perret-Clermont, A. N. (1985). Socio-cognitive conflict and intellectual growth. In M. Berkowitz (Ed.), *Cognitive-developmental approaches to conflict resolution*, pp. 41–54. San Francisco: Jossey-Bass.

Blaye, A., Light, P., Joiner, R., & Sheldon, S. (1991). Collaboration as a facilitator of planning and problem solving on a computer-based task. *British Journal of Developmental Psychology*, *9*, 471–483.

Brown, A. L., & French, L. A. (1979). The zone of potential development: Implications for intelligence testing in the year 2000. *Intelligence*, *3*, 255–273.

Childs, C. P., & Greenfield, P. M. (1980). Informal modes of learning and teaching: The case of Zinacanteco weaving. In N. Warren (Ed.), *Studies in cross-cultural psychology* (Vol. 2, pp. 269–316). London: Academic Press.

Cole, M. (1985). The zone of proximal development: Where culture and cognition create each other. In J. V. Wertsch (Ed.), *Culture, communication, and cognition: Vygotskian perspectives*, pp. 146–161. Cambridge, UK: Cambridge University Press.

DeLoache, J. S., & Plaetzer, B. (1985). Tea for two: Joint mother-child symbolic play. Paper presented at the conference of the Society for Research in Child Development, Toronto, Ontario, Canada.

Ellis, S., & Rogoff, B. (1986). Problem solving in children's management of instruction. In E. Mueller & C. Cooper (Eds.), *Process and outcome in peer relationships*, pp. 301–325. New York: Academic Press.

Gauvain, M., & Rogoff, B. (1989). Collaborative problem solving and children's planning skills. *Developmental Psychology*, *25*, 139–151.

Glachan, M., & Light, P. (1982). Peer interaction and learning: Can two wrongs make a right? In G. Butterworth & P. Light (Eds.), *Social cognition: Studies of the development of understanding*, pp. 238–262. Brighton, UK: Harvester Press.

Göncü, A., & Rogoff, B. (1994). *Children's categorization with varying adult support.* Manuscript in preparation.

Guba, E. G., & Lincoln, Y. S. (1982). Epistemological and methodological bases of naturalistic inquiry. *Educational Communication and Technology Journal, 30,* 233–252.

Heath, S. B. (1983). *Ways with words: Language, life, and work in communities and classrooms.* Cambridge, UK: Cambridge University Press.

Hoff-Ginsberg, E. (1986). Function and structure in maternal speech: Their relation to the child's development of syntax. *Developmental Psychology, 22,* 155–163.

Hoff-Ginsberg, E., & Shatz, M. (1982). Linguistic input and the child's acquisition of language. *Psychological Bulletin, 92,* 3–26.

John-Steiner, V., & Tatter, P. (1983). An interactionist model of language development. In B. Bain (Ed.), *The sociogenesis of language and human conduct,* pp. 79–97. New York: Plenum.

Kontos, S. (1983). Adult-child interaction and the origins of metacognition. *Journal of Educational Research, 77,* 43–54.

Leont'ev, A. N. (1981). The problem of activity in psychology. In J. V. Wertsch (Ed.), *The concept of activity in Soviet psychology,* pp. 37–71. Armonk, NY: Sharpe.

Mistry, J. J., & Rogoff, B. (1987). Influence of purpose and strategic assistance on preschool children's remembering. Paper presented at the meetings of the Society for Research in Child Development, Baltimore, MD.

Nelson, K. E., Denninger, M. S., Bonvillian, J. D., Kaplan, B. J., & Baker, N. D. (1984). Maternal input adjustments and non-adjustments as related to children's linguistic advances and to language acquisition theories. In A. D. Pelligrini & T. D. Yawkey (Eds.), *The development of oral and written language in social contexts,* pp. 31–56. Norwood, NJ: Ablex.

Ochs, E., & Schieffelin, B. B. (1984). Language acquisition and socialization: Three developmental stories and their implications. In R. Schweder & R. LeVine (Eds.), *Culture theory: Essay on mind, self, and emotion,* pp. 276–320. Cambridge, UK: Cambridge University Press.

Pacifici, C., & Bearison, D. J. (1991). Development of children's self-regulations in idealized and mother-child interactions. *Cognitive Development, 6,* 261–277.

Papousek, M., Papousek, H., & Bornstein, M. H. (1985). The naturalistic vocal environment of young infants. In T. M. Field & N. Fox (Eds.), *Social perception in infants,* pp. 269–298. Norwood, NJ: Ablex.

Perret-Clermont, A. N., Perret, J. F., & Bell, N. (1991). The social construction of meaning and cognitive activity in elementary school children. In J. M. Levine, L. B. Resnick, & S. Behrend (Eds.), *Socially shared cognition,* pp. 41–62. New York: APA Press.

Radziszewska, B., & Rogoff, B. (1988). Influence of adult and peer collaborators on the development of children's planning skills. *Developmental Psychology, 24,* 840–848.

Radziszewska, B., & Rogoff, B. (1991). Children's guided participation in planning imaginary errands with skilled adult or peer partners. *Developmental Psychology, 27,* 381–389.

Rogoff, B. (1981). Schooling and the development of cognitive skills. In H. C. Triandis & A. Heron (Eds.), *Handbook of cross-cultural psychology* (Vol. 4, pp. 233–294). Rockleigh, NJ: Allyn & Bacon.

Rogoff, B. (1982). Integrating context and cognitive development. In M. E. Lamb & A. L. Brown (Eds.), *Advances in developmental psychology* (Vol. 2, pp. 125–170). Hillsdale, NJ: Erlbaum.

Rogoff, B. (1990). *Apprenticeship in thinking: Cognitive development in social context*. New York: Oxford University Press.

Rogoff, B. (1995). Observing sociocultural activity on three planes: Participatory appropriation, guided participation, apprenticeship. In A. Alvarez, P. del Rio, & J. V. Wertsch (Eds.), *Perspectives on sociocultural research*. Cambridge, UK: Cambridge University Press.

Rogoff, B., Baker-Sennett, J., & Matusov, E. (1994). Considering the concept of planning. In M. Haith, J. Benson, R. Roberts, & B. Pennington (Eds.), *The development of future-oriented processes*. Chicago: University of Chicago Press.

Rogoff, B., & Gardner, W. P. (1984). Developing cognitive skills in social interaction. In B. Rogoff & J. Lave (Eds.), *Everyday cognition: Its development in social context*, pp. 95–116. Cambridge, MA: Harvard University Press.

Rogoff, B., Malkin, C., & Gilbride, K. (1984). Interaction with babies as guidance in development. In B. Rogoff & J. V. Wertsch (Eds.), *Children's learning in the "zone of proximal development,"* pp. 31–44. San Francisco: Jossey-Bass.

Rogoff, B., Mistry, J., Göncü, A., & Mosier, C. (1993). Guided participation in cultural activity by toddlers and caregivers. *Monographs of the Society for Research in Child Development, 58* (7, Serial no. 236).

Saxe, G. B., Gearhart, M., & Guberman, S. R. (1984). The social organization of early number development. In B. Rogoff & J. V. Wertsch (Eds.), *Children's learning in the "zone of proximal development,"* pp. 19–30. San Francisco: Jossey-Bass.

Scribner, S. (1985). Vygotsky's uses of history. In J. V. Wertsch (Ed.), *Culture, communication, and cognition: Vygotskian perspectives*, pp. 119–145. Cambridge, UK: Cambridge University Press.

Sigel, I. E., & Cocking, R. R. (1977). Cognition and communication: A dialectic paradigm for development. In M. Lewis & L. A. Rosenblum (Eds.), *Interaction, conversation, and the development of language: The origins of behavior* (Vol. 5, pp. 207–226). New York: Wiley.

Skager, R. (1975). Evaluating educational alternatives. In J. I. Goodlad, G. D. Fenstermacher, T. J. LaBelle, V. D. Rust, R. Skager, & C. Weinberg (Eds.), *The conventional and the alternative in education*, pp. 99–122. Berkeley, CA: McCutchan Publishing Corp.

Snow, C. E. (1984). Parent-child interaction and the development of communicative ability. In R. Schiefelbusch & J. Pickar (Eds.), *The acquisition of communicative competence* (pp. 69–107). Baltimore, MD: University Park Press.

Steward, M., & Steward, D. (1974). Parents and siblings as teachers. In E. J. Mash, L. C. Handy, & L. A. Hamerlynck (Eds.), *Behavior modification approaches to parenting*, pp. 193–206. New York: Brunner/Mazel.

Tomasello, M., & Farrar, M. J. (1986). Joint attention and early language. *Child Development, 57*, 1454–1463.

Valdez-Menchaca, M. C. (1987). The effects of incidental teaching on vocabulary acquisition by young children. Paper presented at the meetings of the Society for Research in Child Development, Baltimore, MD.

Wertsch, J. V. (1985). *Vygotsky and the social formation of mind*. Cambridge, MA: Harvard University Press.

Wood, D. (1986). Aspects of teaching and learning. In M. Richards & P. Light (Eds.), *Children of social worlds*, pp. 191–212. Cambridge, MA: Polity Press.

Wood, D. J., Wood, H., & Middleton, D. (1978). An evaluation of four face-to-face teaching strategies. *International Journal of Behavioral Development, 2*, 131–147.

Zimmerman, B. J., & Blom, D. E. (1983). Toward an empirical test of the role of cognitive conflict in learning. *Developmental Review, 3*, 18–38.

Zinchenko, V. P. (1985). Vygotsky's ideas about units for the analysis of mind. In J. V. Wertsch (Ed.), *Culture, communication, and cognition: Vygotskian perspectives*, pp. 94–118. Cambridge, UK: Cambridge University Press.

7   Linking thought and setting in the study of workplace learning

Laura M. W. Martin

Introduction

One of the last projects that Sylvia Scribner supervised at the Laboratory for Cognitive Studies of Work was a project called Technical and Symbolic Knowledge in CNC Machining. Computer Numerical Control (CNC) is an electronic technology that affects the traditional organization and definition of jobs in the industrial workplace. Specifically, it introduces machines in which manual setup operations are replaced by setup dependent on electronic commands executed through a computer program. Over the three years of its existence, the CNC project looked at how machinists learn to use computer-based machine tools and sought to address several key questions about adult learning.

First, the research looked at changes in activity when electronic technology is introduced and at the nature of the relation between someone's existing technical knowledge and newly acquired symbol system based on programming code. It asked whether the new system is additive to the old, whether the new displaces the old, or whether it transforms the old system in some way. The study also asked about the forms adult learning might take and whether the formal or informal origins of the knowledge affect the application of particular concepts. What were the differences, we asked, between knowledge that is acquired through practical, hands-on activity and that which is based on abstract representation (such as computer code) learned in the classroom? In addition to questions about technical knowledge, we asked about the relation between machinists' educational backgrounds and their problem solving strategies, as well as about their images of themselves as workers.

The analysis of the studies described in this chapter were developed in collaboration with King Beach. The author wishes to thank Michael Cole, Katherine Nelson, and Ethel Tobach for their very helpful comments on the piece.

150

The goals of our work were to understand the machinists' workplace, traditions, and activities; to characterize the relation between their work settings, actions, and cognitive processes; and to demonstrate what we discovered and make responsible recommendations for training programs.

In framing the research agenda and developing experimental approaches to achieve our goals we worked with research methods developed by Scribner (1984). These seek to understand the action-based origins of knowledge by focusing inquiry on the activity setting broadly and then on individuals specifically. In the process of carrying out the work this way, the project staff confronted a series of methodological issues that had implications for the objectives of our inquiry. By trying to describe and pinpoint intellectual change in the machine shop, we were engaged in the theoretical and material activity of constructing scientific truth: our own activity as investigators of machine shop learning – for which there was little precedent – would determine the story of what we found.

There were two essential questions: First, could the method result in an empirically verifiable study of contextualized cognition? Second, could this method be described in a way that supports its validity? I hope to contribute to the discourse of studying workplace learning by describing some of the challenges we encountered during the research process in a way that will make the experiences useful to the scientific community. Specifically, I would like to address the relation between cognitive activity as seen in different complex settings and the nature of investigating that activity. First, I'll describe our theoretical framework and what the method we used attempts to accomplish. Then, I'll describe some findings of the project and the issues they raised for the general research enterprise, in a kind of case study of a study. I will also discuss the implications of our work on what we can understand about practical knowledge and on what methods we can meaningfully employ to study it.

The theoretical framework

The theoretical framework of the CNC project had its origin in activity theory, based on the work of L. S. Vygotsky (1978; 1987), V. V. Zinchenko (Zinchenko & Gordon 1985), and others. This approach views cognitive processes as embedded in and arising from activity structures whose goals they serve. Activities themselves involve tools and symbol systems that mediate the way in which intellectual tasks are accomplished. The theory holds that people's understandings of operating tools as, for example, a mechanical system develop from a complex of physical and social elements whose images, goals, and expressions are internalized and reconstituted as psychological functions by individuals (Davydov 1988).

Within this framework, new tools would be expected to change the way in which activity is accomplished and thus change intellectual aspects of the activity. The theory, however, is not a technologically deterministic one. We have argued elsewhere that "the unit of analysis for cognitive studies of new technologies cannot be restricted to a study of the technology itself, nor to isolated tasks removed from the context of their performance" (Martin & Scribner 1992, p. 585). This is to say that new intellectual demands cannot be derived from an analysis of the structure of the tools themselves. Rather, it is in understanding how tools are utilized – for what purposes and by which people in the workplace – that we can begin to understand their cognitive demands. Furthermore, to understand the cognitive *consequences* of the new technologies, it is necessary to know how tools are integrated into ongoing activity.

Getting from the setting to thought

An assumption of the CNC project and of Scribner's work in general is that while cognition is constructed and reinforced in carrying out practical tasks it is at the same time a mental process, a process in the head. The link between doing in the world and cognition in the head is seen to be activity.

Recent work in the area of cognition and learning strongly argues that cognition can only be understood through its application, that is, in context. Studies of everyday cognition (Ceci & Liker 1986; Rogoff & Lave 1984) and studies of "situated" learning (Brown, Collins & Deguid 1990; Suchman 1990), for example, as well as studies of other collaborative learning situations (Wertsch & Hickmann 1987; Rogoff, in press) attempt to capture naturalistic elements, including social interactions, that mediate or otherwise impact upon what a learner derives from an event. At the same time, recent work by a number of psychologists (for example, Carroll 1992; Simon 1992) reject what we thought we had learned in the past two decades about cognition in context and the meaning of activity, and renew justifications for standardized testing of abilities and for analyzing structures in the mind through "mental tasks undertaken as 'ends in themselves'" (Scribner 1984, p. 2), that is, apart from functioning in everyday circumstances (see Falmagne, this volume). In short, the dialectic of setting and mind is at a point where methodological developments in experimental cognitive science and neuroscience on the one hand and in psychological anthropology and cultural psychology on the other are emphasizing anew polarities within the field of psychology.

Scribner's work stands in between. She supported reciprocity between experimental and observational methods, between the multiple case study and the single subject design. She avoided the term "context" in her writing and dissociated her work from "situated cognition" because she emphasized activity as the defining event for practical intellectual activity, an integrated function of thought and setting. She did this because separating out the elements of thought and setting implies an environmentally deterministic structure, or, mental functions arising from nonsocial origins. At the same time, Scribner held that general mental schemas of understanding and patterns of executive cognitive control arise in and from everyday activity. She argued that these can be measured in somewhat rarified settings, namely, the laboratorylike experimental task setting. Scribner did not believe the laboratory was a neutral setting, because she held that all situations are culturally located, but she did believe that, given tasks that tapped the "germ" of a concept, the experimental interview could capture some essential understandings of cognitive functioning developed in the process of activity across groups of study participants. The method she developed to study workplace cognition made use of such dislocated tasks to identify cognitive processes and to create refined descriptions of those processes (Scribner 1984). Scribner also included broader conversation with study participants as part of her information gathering. How workers viewed their activity and experiences yielded data relevant to how setting influences thought.

In our work with machinists, the application of Scribner's method depended on explicating how to get from our in situ observational studies to the "lab," that is, it depended on our theory of the characteristics of the tasks in the two settings. The relation between these analyses, or levels, was not always clear. Although Scribner's methodology allowed us leverage for capturing cognitive change, highlighting the link between levels of analysis in the method necessitated making some significant choices among descriptions. Scribner's method accomodates the corollary in activity theory that cognition is both input and outcome in one individual as she or he carries out daily work activities. To analyze this in different settings and find the relation between the settings in defining the corollary is tricky. Equally important, Scribner, in her reports, tried to include discussion of methodological choices (see Scribner & Sachs 1990) in order to clarify other aspects of the particular relations between settings in a domain. In the next section I will describe some aspects of the CNC project that presented us with choice points for creating links between levels of analysis.

Phases of the study

The observational phase

The first task we undertook toward understanding the implications of CNC technology for learning was an analysis of other technological changes in manufacturing and in the machining industry more specifically (Martin & Scribner 1992). Here I tell a story about how we began the second phase in the CNC project – observing machinists at work in a factory – and what our investigation allowed us to say and do.

The fact that we began the empirical investigation with a case study is a statement about the relation between theory, method, and data. It says that theories of cognition in context are not immediately amenable to explanatory demonstration because of what experimenters need to understand, and because of participants' individual histories, variation of controlling variables in natural circumstances, and people's subjectivity. Moreover, it says that interactivity, that is, the chance to interact, talk, ask questions, socialize, is one of the defining characteristics of non-laboratory settings and is necessary for getting at cognitive phenomena at a certain level.

To begin our study in the field, I visited a factory at frequent intervals (sometimes several times a week, sometimes once a month) over a year-and-a-half period. The first phase of visits allowed me to learn about the machinist's job, to get to know machinists, to ask a lot of questions and develop my own hypotheses, and to become familiar with factory routines. At the same time, I read technical magazines, talked with instructors of machining, union representatives, and engineers, and completed a week-long CNC programming course. In discussion with colleagues at the Laboratory for Cognitive Studies of Work, we reviewed notes and documents from the field and formulated a data collection plan for our taped observations.

The plan was that after I became familiar with the machinists' work I would videotape a skilled machinist working at specific tasks alone, with a peer, and with a less-skilled colleague. I would also tape the novice working on his own at these tasks. These different social configurations were commonly occurring ones. The tasks were ones that emerged as critical in the machining sequence and involved three phases of the process: planning, programming, and troubleshooting. The plan was that when the machinists worked in pairs we would analyze their talk. When they worked alone we would encourage a think-aloud procedure to give us material to analyze.

As I spent time in the factory getting to know the machinists, getting them to explain their work, and videotaping them, it became clear that it was not possible to set up systematically varied interactive conditions to examine cognition in this context. Our observations had shown us the variation inherent in the setting; there was little that could be called constant about the work. Machining activity is simply not systematic on certain key dimensions, for example, whom you do it with, what unknowns are part of the machining problem, and how long it takes to do things, especially when observed by outsiders. Circumstances intruded. For example, the factory supervisors would not let us tape the novice during his first sessions working on CNC programming: they wanted him to be up to speed before we conducted our observations. This meant that we could not collect a complete longitudinal record as we had planned, but needed to rely more on cross-sectional examples, which lessened our ability to follow transformations of thought in an individual. Other cases of intrusions included worker absence, an emergency job or a lull, a schedule change such that the task to be taped was completed before the observer arrived, all throwing our plans off track. The well-known problem of observer effect also occurred: in our case, we suspected that the problem solving talk we recorded was more explicitly didactic than it would have been had a researcher not been a witness. Nonetheless, from our tapes, we culled many interesting individual "cases" of the ways that workers shared and constructed knowledge.

Although these general procedures and constraints are not particularly new when we think of the many accounts by social scientists studying complex events, they do become significant in view of Scribner's method for verifying claims about fairly close-grained and evolving cognitive phenomena. They give us a lot of latitude in how we talk about the patterns in the data and therefore how we create analytic terms to get us to lablike situations validly. Essentially the process demands that we guess at controlling variables, make decisions about what would constitute error variance, and design experimental tasks that either include setting factors, as in the case of simulation tasks, or not, as in the case of transfer tasks.

To arrive at a picture of what was transpiring in the factory, we analyzed protocols for evidence of cognitive processing. This presented interesting challenges. Because the transcripts were of different lengths, involved different specific tasks, and so on, we tried to find ways to create a baseline percentage of talk, and to compare and count events. A second step was to try to attribute to individuals evidence of cognitive processing derived from interactive situations, such as peers or differently skilled machinists working together. A third step was deciding what constituted integrated physical and mental activity contributing to the development of thought. Each of these were key in formulating hypotheses about the nature of the relation between old and new knowledge systems.

Looking for evidence of old and new knowledge systems, we found an embarrassment of higher psychological riches. In our tapes of experts working together we identified a wide range of elements they consider as they work: mechanics, physics, mathematics, safety, economics, social issues, production schedules, and more. Their programming talk was so seamless that we could not always identify when programming of one operation left off and another began. We found that the machinists worked with some inefficiency at times – as when they took 20 minutes to solve a problem using trigonometry that could have been solved more quickly using geometry. Still, these experienced machinists checked to see where they were in their calculations, whether the strategy they were applying at the moment was proving useful, and whether their results were reasonable; a phenomenon observed among expert math problem solvers (Schoenfeld 1985). They used programming code as meaningful semantic units ("I was going to G50 it for the groove"). They used a variety of symbol systems (e.g., blueprints, layout sheets, programs), each for a variety of functions such as getting information, checking answers, and guiding sequence. They seemed to be visualizing a lot as they planned and programmed.

When we observed a novice working alone, we noticed differences in his descriptions of the machining sequences compared to the expert. The expert's talk was more like programming in its step-by-step linearity, while, the novice anticipated later operations and referred to previous operations as he explained a machining sequence. We noticed his dramatic but decreasing use of literal gesture over time, suggesting that an interesting internalization process was taking place (Butterworth & Beattie 1978; Sasaki, 1991). We also noticed where his errors differed from the experts' (more programming and machining errors) and where they were the same (the range of problems).

The ultimate aim of our observations was to trace the activity into a single person's head. To do so, we tried to control for topic by taping examples across interactive conditions that were formally analogous, that is, during planning, programming, and troubleshooting phases. However, since the examples we collected to analyze involved different specific parts being made, the cognitive tasks varied in some senses. Because of this, we worried that we had too few examples and too few participants to tell what was personal style, for example, in the use of gesture and language, and what was likely to be true for most machinists in that situation. Because our funding only permitted us a limited amount of time for data collection, we couldn't collect as many examples of what we wanted and, indeed, the number of examples we wanted probably would have been impractical to collect. Thus, we had an abundance of material, more so than was expected for this phase of the research, but as yet no close evidence of the how thought was transformed in this setting.

From our observations, however, we felt we could hypothesize that the three task phases – planning, programming, and troubleshooting – are psychologically distinct, placing different cognitive demands on machinists. We also believed we could hypothesize that the most important phenomena to look at related to the restructuring of knowledge were the visualization processes machinists use to solve three-dimensional problems, verbal and gestural changes related to the development of concepts, and linearity of talk as a reflection of thought that was becoming more programlike. We were particularly eager to validate these observations and to see how engineers, in comparison with machinists, would perform on a series of tasks involving these processes. We also wanted to see how CNC machinists would compare with traditional machinists, because education and experience are two of the main factors of interest according to activity theory.

The experimental phase

Experimental analysis. It was not practical to test all our hypotheses so we chose to develop tasks that probed some of the more important cognitive processes we perceived to be at work and some of the specific ways in which workers of different backgrounds organize their knowledge. As it turned out, the activity of discovering and creating the tasks gave us understandings of the constituents of machinists' and engineers' knowledge, while the results of the task interviews yielded findings about the parameters of their thinking.

Following Scribner, several of the tasks we tried to include simulated shop floor activities, such as planning and programming a job from a blueprint. Others tried to tap whether intellectual activity involved in programming generalizes to other tasks beyond those with factory-based goals. Our first set of difficulties came in developing the latter kinds of tasks. An example of one set of tasks involving visualization illustrates these difficulties.

The development of visualization was felt to be a critical cognitive function to trace. It was described by our machinist informants as an important mental activity they engage in while programming: they envision the tool position in space in relation to the raw stock in order to write commands to the machine. Visualization was also cited in the sparse literature on learning machining as one of the skills that changes with experience. It has also been cited in other problem solving research as related to point of view, a diagnostic of problem representation (Hutchins & Levin 1981; Miyake 1986).

To look at changes and differences in visualization patterns, we first tried to replicate a task that had been used in a study of student machinists (Lebahar 1987): programming of a functionally familiar part that the subject had never programmed before, in this case a wood screw and an engine piston. Following published experimental procedures (Lebahar 1987), workers were asked to imagine they were on the tool point as it machined these parts and to describe what they saw as the tool moved. In contrast to student machinists interviewed by Lebahar, many of our participants had difficulty taking the tool perspective. When they were able to do so, they were unable to describe the specifics of the part with any useful detail. Finally, they used very general language, unlike the student machinists who adopted and moved between three distinct types of perspectives verbally. After many attempts to reword our instructions and alter the task, we decided to discard it.

Another task we had to discard also attempted to tap visualization skills that may develop with programming experience. We asked machinists to describe the path a tool would have to make in machining a doorknob – a very difficult part to plan on conventional machines because of its spherical shape, but relatively easy to describe with a CNC program. Again, all our informants answered so generally as to suggest that the task tapped nothing at all about machining experience.

The significance of a related skill, specifying movement through space symbolically, emerged when CNC trainers told us that getting machinists to understand a Cartesian coordinate system (used to locate the tool point in space) was one of the biggest hurdles for machinists in learning to program. To tap this skill, we developed numerous versions of a pencil and paper maze, which asked our pilot subjects to plot a course, in some cases identical to a tool path, laid out according to coordinates and landmarks. None of these evoked the application of CNC-related skills; rather, from their talk we surmised that machinists were consistently applying map reading and navigation skills.

Other tasks were rejected for practical reasons; for example, one asking people to modify a program was too time consuming. In our final experimental procedure we audiotaped and videotaped over 90 hours of interview material in addition to taking structured and unstructured notes, but many rich aspects of the performance remain unanalyzed (for example, language and gesture use) because of the time constraints on the study.

These were three examples of goal-directed but nonfactory-based tasks we developed to tap some of the critical cognitive phenomena we observed but which had to be discarded from our experimental phase of testing. In the end, the tasks that remained in the final protocol were tasks that could be said to be simulation tasks rather than generalization or transfer tasks. They included planning a part from a blueprint, writing directions to the machine tool, and completing some problem solving scenarios. The one task that was included that was not a simulation of what workers actually do on the shop floor was a chunking task for programmers: they were asked to draw lines on pages of code to show which sets of commands went together. This task was very hard for participants to grasp and yielded no differences between the groups of participants.

Scribner viewed job simulation tasks as possible "middle links" between observations in the field and experiments in a controlled setting, which are less directly configured as work activities (Scribner 1984, p. 4). In this case, our experimenting with a variety of tasks led us to question that there was a systematic way to construct decontexted experimental tasks.

Recruiting participants. Another challenge of the experimental phase of the CNC project also related directly to the nature of our questions and to the nature of acceptable professional discourse. This challenge came about in trying to find participants, particularly in finding participants who fit into clear categories of experience and training.

The process of recruitment for experiments (as opposed to that of describing population characteristics) is often taken for granted, but I believe that is because experimental work usually deals with college students, schoolchildren, or clinic populations as subjects, and individuals from these institutional groups are relatively easy to assemble. In recruiting a large sample of workers for an experimental procedure, however, we faced important practical and demographic obstacles because a greater variety of critical experience is found among constituents of a workplace.

In our situation, the practical problems became apparent first. Although many professional organizations were cooperative and encouraging and interested in our work, it was hard to find groups of willing participants among machinists at the shop level. They had to be recruited one by one. Individual machinists and machine operators are not usually tied into professional networks nor were the ones we contacted particularly interested in the research work. Newspapers would not put recruitment ads in their Help Wanted sections but only in the Personal sections, which we did not feel would be useful for us. A large mailing, conducted with the help of a statewide professional association, yielded a handful of responses. These did lead us to some machinists, who led us to others. Engineers were equally unresponsive on the whole, although they were more easily contacted through professional networks. Ultimately most of our engineers were recruited from a nearby technical university and therefore yielded a skewed sample of younger individuals.

In our attempts to control the testing setting, we also discovered that individuals would not travel to our lab or to a space that was offered by a manufacturer's association for the 2-hour interview. Consequently we had to go to each workplace (often hours away from *our* workplace) and set up our apparatus and materials under a wide variety of conditions.

Central to our investigation were possible differences between those individuals with traditional hands-on experience (non-CNC machinists), those with hands-on and programming experience (CNC machinists), and those who program but have no hands-on experience (industrial engineers). As we tried to recruit study participants, the subject categories kept multiplying because we could not find enough people who fit into a category, but mostly because people's experiences were much more diverse than we had expected. For example, we met machine operators who didn't know how to "set up" a machine and some who did, and each had knowledge of very different sorts of machines. Operators might have studied programming in a class even though they didn't program on the job. Programmers, even experienced programmers, often had less hands-on experience than traditional machinists and so we couldn't necessarily equate backgrounds across those two groups. By the time our experimental phase began, engineers without hands-on experience who programmed were becoming a rarity: the new technologies necessitated changes in plants such that engineers were now spending time on the shop floor and machinists were in offices designing programs. In addition, and very importantly for our ultimate recommendations about training, most of our study participants had had continued classroom training after beginning work, albeit to varying degrees, which further complicated our ability to test the formal versus practical origins of concepts.

Our interviews pointed to the fact that a good deal of the difference between people's views of themselves, their views of how they fit into the changing industry, and their levels of commitment to the field hinged on opportunities they had for learning. Hence, workers' backgrounds and identities become as integral to understanding their learning as were their traditional or technology-oriented thinking patterns.

That our experimental results depended on differences in training histories was a central assumption of our work. Those histories were, in reality, messy. They forced us to qualify our findings and also permitted us to examine the findings at different levels of specificity than we had expected. Interestingly, the attempt to control background and test its effects by working with large numbers of participants invited variance to enter into the analysis that the experimental method was attempting to suppress.

Activity theory allowed us to look at these differences and locate them historically in a particular field. It allowed us to see how macro- and microanalyses are related and with what cognitive consequences. Specifically, we saw that symbol systems are learned on the job, and that those with more formal training (engineers) are acquiring more hands-on experience than before. Furthermore, the idea of the self as a learner in this climate is critical to learning; the main barriers to mental transformation are social and economic, not cognitive.

Conclusions

There are three sets of conclusions we can make about our exploration into changes in thinking resulting from new machining technologies. The first has to do with what we were able to discern about mental activity in machining itself. Though not the focus of this chapter, it bears mentioning that our work allowed us to make several claims about the relation between old and new forms of knowledge (Martin & Beach 1992, Martin & Beach 1993).

First, in relation to practical thinking, our findings suggested that CNC programming is integrated into machining so that it becomes machining activity and does not stand apart from it: machinists are solving machining problems on the CNC machines not CNC problems. This means that the knowledge and the skills that are necessary to plan and execute a programmed machining sequence become subordinated in the service of a practical goal, namely, as a means to machining in general as the skill is mastered. At the same time, machining becomes a different job than in the past because it involves new mediators of machining activity. The concrete information on which traditional knowledge rests is represented in new symbolic ways in CNC. The traditional foundation is important for manipulating the symbolic system, or code; thus, programming can be learned on the job fairly efficiently, given a solid machining knowledge base. Formal training in programming alone is inadequate, though it probably can partially compensate for the dimunition of sensory feedback experience.

Our investigations of practical thinking per se told us that the different mental steps and processes learned through activity with the new technology can be continuous (e.g., reading blueprints), discontinuous (e.g., programming), or transforming (e.g., into linear thinking) of old knowledge systems simultaneously: there is no single integrative rule. Finally, the new technologies are breaking down some of the traditional social and functional distinctions in the factory as information is redistributed among machinists and engineers, precisely because the technical and symbolic are so integrated.

We would claim that the findings support the idea that action and the development of thought are a unit that is first understood by looking at practical activity and that that activity is tied to its function within the larger social unit of the manufacturing plant. In the present case, the shop floor cognition we observed was not easily extricable to another setting. Only some characteristics of cognitive processing, like the linearity of verbal accounts of machining sequences, seemed to be mentally portable, and these only insofar as the planning task was portable. Other mental functions based on practical activity involving the use of gesture and visualization in programming, for example, seemed to emerge exclusively under the exigencies and goal settings of actual shop floor conditions. At the same time, some essentially abstract and school-learned processes, such as mathematical thinking, were relatively easily applied in practical settings, as were concepts of practical origin.

Designing experimental tasks that probe knowledge of a purely abstract sense (i.e., that which can be applied to problem analogues) was a difficult pursuit because, without goal analogues, there was no generative rule for formulating the tasks. The variations needed to make such tasks comprehensible and discriminative (through the addition of contextual clues) turned them into simulations rather than analogues by involving activity goals common to shop floor experiences.

A second set of conclusions has to do with the question of the method and its implications. In seeking to verify contextualized cognition, Scribner developed a method of first observing practical activity to identify domains and patterns of cognitive functioning, followed by presenting simulative and experimental tasks to individual subjects. This process could be iterative (Scribner 1984), and enabled Scribner to test hypotheses about the contours of the variables and mental mechanisms of interest. The method clearly implies that cognitive mechanisms are internalized and are carried by the subject to new situations outside the work setting.

In the study described here, we encountered difficulties in moving from the practical level of cognitive analysis to the experimental. Again, despite an assumption that the testing situation was a culturally determined context, only simulation tasks, that is, tasks that were based on simulated activity goals, were ultimately useful in the "lab" setting to tap the phenomenon of interest. "Transfer" tasks were not. Thus, to answer our earlier question, the method resulted in an empirically verifiable study of contextualized cognition but not of decontexted cognition.

Study participants who fit into our conceptual categories of experiences were not easy to identify. In this domain we didn't know what kind of variance would be introduced by clustering individuals into experimental groups. Difficulties in task design and subject selection that influence the shape of a study are not always possible to report as part of the scientific investigation process because professional reviewers tend not to accept these kinds of discussions for publication and because such discussion brings the choices of the investigator into the results. Adhering to conventions of reporting may create a false contrast between cognition in context and "portable" cognition, particularly in the case of work studies, because discussion of the process of getting from one observation setting to another is limited. So we must say in answer to the second question raised in the Introduction that the method can be described in a way that supports its validity but not necessarily within the traditional structure of reporting.

For the same reason that cognitive events in formal and informal settings are hard to compare, the commonalities of thinking in the two settings of workplace and "lab" are not easily understood at a very fine-grained level because there are other factors than task design and goal structure at work. One clue is that, for engineers, we had less difficulty creating transfer tasks, a possible indication that exposure to schooling, once again, can be seen to influence a person's ability to respond to abstract features of tasks taken out of their goal setting. Because most of our informants did not have as much formal education as the engineers, we had to be particularly careful about comparisons between machinists' and engineers' performances on tasks in the different problem solving situations.

What are the methodological solutions to acknowledging a dichotomy between observational settings through reporting conventions or task design? Do we maintain parallel universes among settings? Do we narrow our discussion of the problems? The answers have implications for the theory that has guided our investigation, a third area to which the CNC study contributes.

In the process of carrying out the work, it became clear that we had to speak about the contradictions we encountered and about the need to construct language around them that explicates how the science gets done and at the same time confronts the data in new ways. As we all begin to look more and more directly at populations from walks of life that are not those upon which psychology and psychological methods were originally developed, we will have further need to confront our experimental difficulties and the underlying assumptions of our methods for studying thought in society.

What I have tried to do is describe the theory that lead us to examine workplace cognition and lead us to a claim that cognition is internalized through activity. Our empirical findings, extracted in the way they were, support an activity theory interpretation in that we saw new mental processes develop and become integrated with old ones as we studied the course or results of everyday practices. Furthermore, for this particular domain, thought is linked to setting, as far as we could measure. The theory, in fact, helps us to see that such practical activity is the defining event for intellectual development in the workplace.

I next tried to outline approaches to how one would verify this internalization process, citing Scribner's approach as a useful reconciliation between scientific paradigms that can possibly get us from one setting (the workplace) to another (the "lab"), where internalized cognition can be studied in a more precise way. Developing our task interviews gave us evidence that some cognitive elements based on the introduction of new technology can be said to be portable. At the same time, these elements were inextricable from workplace tasks; so to the extent that the tasks traveled, the thinking traveled. Once we developed experimental tasks that many machinists and engineers could respond to, we could generally identify differences based on activity history (schooling and job experience).

Scribner's method necessitates a unique kind of scientific articulation process in terms of experimental task development and consideration of variance in order to understand how getting from one setting to another can demonstrate the internalization of activity as thought. The articulation, in turn, helps us clarify our theory about how similar tasks may function in different settings. It reveals much of the relationship between the categories of activity, thought, and setting, and also highlights the fact that the investigators' words and actions contribute integrally to the construction of the understanding.

References

Brown, J., Collins, A., & Deguid, P. (1990). Situated cognition and the culture of learning. *Educational Researcher, 18*, 32–42.

Butterworth, B., & Beattie, G. (1978). Gesture and silence as indicators of planning in speech. In R. N.Campbell & P. T. Smith (Eds.), *Recent advances in the psychology of language*. New York: Plenum.

Carroll, J. B. (1992). Cognitive abilities: The state of the art. *Psychological Science, 3*(5), 266–270.

Ceci, S., & Liker, S. (1986). Some lifelong everyday forms of intelligent behavior: Organizing and reorganizing. In R. Sternberg (Ed.), *Practical intelligence*. New York: Cambridge University Press.

Davydov, V.V. (1988). Problems of developmental teaching: The experience of theoretical and experimental psychological research. *Soviet Education, 30*, [whole issue].

Hutchins, E. L., & Levin, J. V. (1981). *Point of view in problem solving*. Unpublished paper, Laboratory of Comparative Human Cognition, University of California, San Diego.

Lebahar, J. -C. (1987). L'influence de l'apprentissage des machines-outils à commandes numériques sur la représentation de l'usinage et ses niveaux de formalisation,. *Le Travail Humain, 50*(8), 237–249.

Leont'ev, A. N. (1981). *Problems of the development of mind*. Moscow: Progress Publishers.

Martin, L. M. W., & Beach, K. (1992). *Technical and symbolic knowledge in CNC machining: A study of technical workers of different backgrounds*. Technical Report. National Center for Research in Vocational Education, University of California, Berkeley.

Martin, L. M. W., & Beach, K. (1993). *Technical and symbolic knowledge in CNC machining*. Paper presented at the biennial meeting of the International Society for the Study of Behavioral Development, Recife, Brazil.

Martin, L. M. W., & Scribner, S. (1992). Laboratory for cognitive studies work: A case study of the intellectual implications of a new technology. *Teachers College Record*, *92*(4), 582–602.

Miyake, N. (1986). Constructive interaction and the iterative process of understanding. *Cognitive Science*, *10*, 151–177.

Rogoff, B. (In press). Observing sociocultural activity on three planes: Participatory appropriation, guided participation, apprenticeship. In A. Alverez, P. del Rio, & J. V. Wertsch (Eds.), *Perspectives in sociocultural research*. Cambridge, UK: Cambridge University Press.

Rogoff, B., & Lave, J. (Eds.). (1984). *Everyday cognition: Its development in social context*. Cambridge, MA: Harvard University Press.

Sasaki, M. (1991). *Verbal gestification as inner speech*. Unpublished manuscript. Waseda, Japan: Waseda University.

Scribner, S. (Ed.). (1984). Cognitive studies of work. *The Quarterly Newsletter of the Laboratory of Comparative Human Cognition*, *6*(1–2), [whole issue].

Scribner, S., & Sachs, P. (1990). *A study of on-the-job learning*. Technical Paper No. 13. New York: National Center for Education and the Economy, Teachers College.

Schoenfeld, A. H. (1985). Metacognitive and epistemological issues in mathematical understanding. In E. Silver (Ed.), *Teaching and learning mathematical problem solving: Multiple research perspectives*. Hillside, NJ: Erlbaum.

Simon, H. (1992). What is an "explanation" of behavior? *Psychological Science*, *3*(3), 150–161.

Suchman, L. (1990). *Plans and situated actions: The problem of human-machine communication*. New York: Cambridge University Press.

Vygotsky, L. S. (1978). *Mind in society*. Cambridge, MA: Harvard University Press.

Vygotsky, L. S. (1987). *Thinking and speech*. R. W. Rieber & A. S. Carton (Eds.), *The collected works of L.S.Vygotsky, Volume I: Problems of general psychology*. New York: Plenum.

Wertsch, J. V., & Hickmann, M. (1987). Problem solving in social interaction: A microgenetic analysis. In M. Hickmann (Ed.), *Social and functional approaches to learning and thought*. San Diego: Academic Press.

Zinchenko, V. P., & Gordon, V. M. (1985). Methodological problems in the psychological analysis of activity. In J. V. Wertsch (Ed.), *The concept of activity in Soviet psychology*. Armonk, NY: Sharpe.

8   Cultural–historical psychology:
A meso-genetic approach

Michael Cole

. . . we can view the past, and achieve our understanding of the past, only through the eyes of the present. – E. H. Carr 1961, p. 28.

> . . . all experience is an arch wherethrough
> Gleams that untravelled world whose margin
> fades
> Forever and forever when I move. – Tennyson 1842

In the course of the two decades during which Sylvia Scribner and I interacted around questions of culture and cognition, the problem of how to implement the historical aspect of a cultural-historical approach to human mental functioning was a recurrent theme of our discussions. This theme was present, for example, in our joint explorations of cultural variations in thinking, where the history of people's cultural practices, as well as the current intellectual consequences of these practices, occupied our attention (Scribner & Cole 1981). It was present in a different way in the many cases when we worked with people of different ages and conducted learning experiments that permitted us to observe ontogenetic and "microgenetic" changes in the organization of behavior (Scribner & Cole 1972; Cole & Scribner 1977; Mandler, Scribner, Cole, & DeForest 1980). However, while Sylvia wrote explicitly about the concept of history in psychological research (Scribner 1985), historical questions were more often the subject of our informal discussion than the focus of our joint research.

As a means of continuing Sylvia's efforts to focus attention on the historical aspects of cultural-historical psychology, I will devote the bulk of

At various times the work upon which this chapter is based has been supported by the Spencer Foundation, the Mellon Foundation, and the University of California at San Diego. I wish to acknowledge the seminal contributions of Peg Griffin and Ageliki Nicolopolou to the ideas expressed here.

this essay to describing a line of research that began in the mid-1980s, several years after our direct collaboration had come to an end and our interactions were restricted to aperiodic phone calls and discussions at meetings in which we traded notes about the progress (or lack thereof!) of our separate pursuits of common intellectual goals. The particulars of the research I will describe are quite different from those that character-ized our joint research in the 1970s or those that occupied Sylvia in the last decade of her life. However, I believe that this work is relevant to Sylvia's general interest in the historical dimension of human activity and human thought.

Kinds of history

An appropriate starting point for my comments is Sylvia's 1985 article, "Vygotsky's uses of history" which was first presented at a con-ference in 1980.[1] Her goal in that paper was to explain how Vygotsky attempted to weave general history, ontogeny, and the history of mental functions into a single framework for interpreting human nature.[2] A spe-cial virtue of Vygotsky's approach, in her opinion, was his assumption that different levels of history take place concurrently and mutually influence each other. But, she wrote, neither Vygotsky nor contemporary researchers had made sufficient progress in finding ways to study these mutual influences. As she noted,

It is customary for investigators concerned with culture and thought to single out for emphasis one or another level of changes as seems suitable for the inquiry at hand. Psy-chologists, for example, tend to conceive of the individual as a dynamic system while assuming in their research designs that history on the societal level is static; anthropolo-gists often make the reverse assumption. (S. Scribner 1985, p. 140)

One strategy for overcoming this shortcoming in studies of culture and cognition is to examine historical circumstances of rapid cultural change where, in principle, one can observe the mutual influence of cul-tural and ontogenetic change on each other. Sylvia mentioned in this regard the work of Geoffrey Saxe (1982) on the development of arith-metical thinking among the Oksapmin of New Guinea, where children and adults were encountering and acquiring a base-10 number system in addition to their indigenous system based on 23 body parts. He showed that the ontogenetic development of arithmetical concepts depended upon their exposure to schooling and intrusion of money-based eco-nomic exchanges into their daily activities. Saxe's more recent work on the development of arithmetic thinking among Brazilian child street vendors under conditions of rapid inflation and Patricia Greenfield's studies of changes in the ontogeny of pattern generating ability among weavers associated with a rapid conversion to a money economy in Zinacantan provide other excellent examples of such as strategy (Saxe 1991; Greenfield 1992).

My own recent efforts to address this set of problems have taken a very different route. Instead of turning to third-world countries undergoing a period of rapid change, my colleagues and I have been creating small model activity systems with their own collections of artifacts, norms, and "designs for living" (e.g., their own distinct cultures) which we embed in various preexisting social institutions. We then trace over a number of years the development of these systems and the children who participated in them.

I refer to the study of the development of these model systems as "meso-genetic" to highlight the "in-betweeness" of the time scale involved. The "meso-temporal" character of these systems is especially relevant to the question of the dynamic relations between different levels of genetic analysis because cultural change within them is rapid relative to the ordinary pace of cultural change in their institutional settings, in the society as a whole, and in the children who inhabit them and give them life. Because of the cycles of activity in the institutions that house these systems, it is also possible to observe several cycles of cultural change in a variety of institutional ecologies, unlike the cross-cultural situation, where the changes of interest are generally a one-shot affair (e.g., once a base 10 counting system has been introduced among the Oksapmin, the "experiment of nature" cannot be repeated). Our meso-genetic methodology also allows us to examine a basic dilemma associated with historical analysis – the fact that, in E.H. Carr's words, we can gain an understanding of the past only from the perspective of the present.

Creating model activity systems

Our research at LCHC using a model systems methodology began in the early 1980s in connection with attempts to create diagnostic/remedial reading environments for elementary schoolchildren who were experiencing difficulties in learning to read (LCHC 1982; Griffin & Cole 1987). In response to the difficult problem of inducing children who have been failing in school to participate in afterschool reading activities, we divided the children's time between specially designed small group reading activities and a melange of computer-based activities involving computer games and telecommunication. These computer-based activities eventually evolved into a system that we dubbed "The Fifth Dimension" (hereafter, 5thDimension) in which children played games within a loosely structured adventure world framework that appropriated the games to the goals of promoting reading, writing, problem solving, and knowledge of computer-based communication (Cole 1992; Griffin & Cole 1987). I'll have more to say about this particular model system presently.

By our reckoning, both the reading activities and the 5thDimension were successful model systems (Griffin, King, Diaz, & Cole 1989; King 1988). Children came voluntarily to participate in them. These children benefitted from the experience according not only to our criteria, but to those of the school personnel and parents. We also found that the systems offered productive ways to investigate basic theoretical questions about the relation between learning and development. However, in one respect, they clearly failed: no sooner did the period of external support for the research expire than the activity systems came to an end. In this respect, they shared the fate of most educational innovations, even those deemed a success. Such systems are generally not sustained once the external funding that supported them as innovations dried up (See Cole, Griffin, & LCHC [1987] for further discussion).

Distressed by the failure of our model system to survive, despite its demonstrable virtue, we decided to focus on the issue of sustainability. For this purpose, we concentrated directly on the possibilities of using computers and computer-based telecommunications as elements from which to construct activity systems. It seemed to us, on the basis of our limited experience with the 5thDimension, that it should be possible to create activities that would be both attractive to elementary-age school children and effective from the perspective of adults. We decided to create several such systems, each to be located in a different institutional context. We framed our goals in terms of the sustainability of the innovations we introduced: could we conduct our research in such a way that the systems would survive and perhaps even multiply once the project was officially "over." We did not specify the precise content of these systems ahead of time. We simply imagined that they would involve children and undergraduates who engaged in some sort of joint activity using computers and telecommunications networks as primary artifacts.

We focused our efforts on institutions that are open to children during after school hours. This focus was motivated by our belief in the potential of such institutions to enrich children's educational experience and to allow a good deal of freedom and flexibility in the design of activities.

We planned for the project to last for 4 years, after which, if any of its model systems survived, they would have to continue to exist on their own. Year 1 would be devoted to goal formation – each institution, in collaboration with the project staff, would investigate a broad range of potential computer-mediated activities for children they thought suitable to their site. Years 2 and 3 would be devoted to creating the system and running it. Year 4 would be the "uptake year" during which each institution would work with the project staff to make the adjustments needed to continue the project once the special funding with which we began had been terminated. That was the plan.

The institutions

Initially we worked with four institutions in a suburban town north of San Diego, California. Each institution deals with elementary-age children: the school system, the library, a Children's Center, and the local Community Youth Club.

The school

The small school district in the town where we worked had two elementary schools, each of which exposed children to computers on a systematic, if not intensive basis. The school made its facilities available to local programs for children during the afterschool hours. A particularly attractive alternative was a special computer room in one of the schools with a number of Apple computers.

The Children's Center

The Children's Center is a community child-care center supported partly by government funds and partly by private funds (mainly tuition). Bureaucratically it falls under the administrative control of the community's elementary school district. It accommodates children of a broad age range, from 2 to 12 years, and it includes programs for infant, preschool, and after school care. Besides an entire program for toddlers, it also has an afterschool program for children of elementary school age. Our focus was on the 45 to 60 elementary schoolchildren who are bussed there after school and remain until their parents pick them up.

On a typical day, the children arrive in their busses about 3:20 P.M. and line up for attendance. This is more than an empty ritual: the Children's Center has legal responsibility for the children until their parents arrive, and if an expected child is absent, the staff must immediately initiate a search for the child. In this way, the center has a rigid structure for child participation (attendance lists and a follow-up on absences), but it has a very informal structure of activities.

The atmosphere is pleasant and the activities available for the children revolve mainly around play and much less on education. After a small snack, the children are free to choose various activities including a prepared arts and crafts projects, board games, outdoor games of many kinds, and free play. There is a strong positive value in promoting the development of the children and a strong negative attitude toward being "schoollike," "not fun," or "stressing."

The Community Youth Club

The Community Youth Club is a nonprofit, privately funded youth center. It is located in a spacious building that houses the staff of the regional club organization, game rooms, an arts and crafts area, a large gymnasium, a swimming pool, and an outdoor courtyard where various games can be played. The club is part of a national organization and this branch is one of three branches that the parent club organization has founded in this and neighboring communities.

Its costs are born largely by individual contributions and special events, supplemented by corporate contributions, membership dues, and program fees, which are kept very low so that all children can participate, regardless of family economic circumstances.

It is intended as a place where children from elementary to middle-school age can go during afterschool hours. The Club complements the Children's Center in many respects. While the Center has a rigid structure about child participants and a very informal structure of activities, the Club has a very rich structure of activities and a very loose set of rules about who comes when. It is located within easy walking distance of an elementary school and a middle school, and a large number of children have ready access to it and can come without requiring parental assistance or bussing arrangements; but children who live some distance away normally depend on their parents to pick them up. The club provides a wide range of social and recreational activities ranging from indoor and outdoor games and sports to cooking classes, arts and crafts, and so on. These activities are the responsibility of specific staff, who are there to supervise the children.

The basic philosophy of the club is very similar to that of the center: a strong positive value on helping the development of the children and a strong negative attitude toward being "schoollike." In keeping with this philosophy the director of the Community Youth Clubs for the local region stated that part of their policy is to provide the children with a place that "does not taste or feel like school, a place that the children feel is practical and fun" and a place where "the educational objectives must be disguised." Furthermore, the club is self-consciously committed to maximizing the children's freedom of choice, and to allowing them maximum flexibility in participating in different activities with a minimum of supervision. Aside from providing the children with an extensive range of alternatives, there is a general feeling that children ought to be able to begin and end particular activities as they please. Consistent with this "drop-in" philosophy, the children are as free to leave as they are to come. The result, when combined with the wide range of recreational facilities, is a somewhat noisy, boisterous atmosphere, with balls bouncing, children chasing around after each other, a loudspeaker punctuating the activity from time to time to call someone to the phone or announce the start of an activity, and so on.

The library

The library, located in a shopping mall perhaps half a mile from the Community Youth Club, is administratively a part of the metropolitan city County library system. It relies primarily on public funds, supplemented by voluntary contributions of time and money from a community Friends of the Library organization; it charges no fees. Like other local libraries around the country, it attempts to provide a range of informational and educational resources for community members. Thus, in addition to traditional loan services and reference books, it contains a section in Spanish and books on tape. From time to time it puts on special events such as dramatic readings for small children, financial counseling for widows, and in the spring, tax consultations supported by The United Way. Based on this broad range of activities, they were interested in offering special computer activities for children.

Our observations indicated that the number of children present in the library after school fluctuated considerably. On one visit it was estimated that 15 to 20 children between the ages of 6 and 16 were present along with three adults and three staff members. On later visits considerably more adults were present, and quite often one encountered mothers bringing their children in to check out books.

The system of activity – the 5thDimension

Although we entered the project with few preconceived ideas of what forms the activities would take in the different institutions, we assumed they would differ according to local interests. For example, we imagined creating a special "treasure hunt" activity for children at the library. To promote the widest possible range of activity choices, we held a number of workshops for staffs from the different institutions during the first year of the project. As I will explain in more detail later, staff in the different institutions, for various reasons, gravitated toward the 5thDimension as an organizing metaphor for their activities, so I will concentrate here on a description of a generic form of this model system.

Figure 8.1 provides a schematic overview of the 5thDimension as it existed at the three major sites. The central coordinating artifact at the heart of the 5thDimension is shown in the form of a maze divided into 20 or so "rooms," each of which gives access to two activities. The actual maze is constructed of cardboard and is about 1 square meter in size. About three-fourths of the activities are instantiated as computer programs that include computer games and educational software, some of which also have gamelike qualities; the remainder are noncomputer activities that include board games, arts and crafts, and physical exercise. The room which houses the 5thDimension maze also contains a variety of other standard artifacts in addition to computers: A box containing record keeping folders for each child, a computer linked to a modem to enable children to communicate with distant places, maps, task cards that specify how each game is to be played, consequence cards that specify the "next rooms" children can enter when they complete an activity at a specified level of expertise, etc.

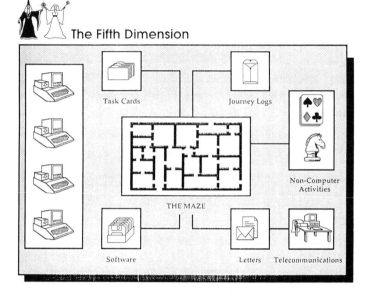

Figure 8.1. A schematic overview of the 5thDimension with the maze used to coordinate access to various games in the center.

According to the rules of the 5thDimension (enshrined in a Constitution, a printed copy of which each child receives upon entering the system), children can make progress through the maze by completing the task cards and selecting their consequences. "Graduation" from the 5thDimension is achieved when children have achieved the good or excellent levels prescribed for the activities in all the rooms of the maze.

In addition to the local goal of completing a task, the rules of the 5th Dimension provide for a variety of other goals, designed to appeal to a variety of children. For example, every child is given a very plain looking token figurine upon entering the 5thDimension. By traversing a path that takes them in one door and out another they may "transform their cruddy creature" and obtain a more desirable figurine. Or they may choose to complete all of the rooms in the maze, thereby earning a special T-shirt, attaining expert status, and gaining access to new activities. In Leont'ev's (1981) terms, the 5thDimension provides a variety of possible effective motives, in addition to motives that are "merely understandable" to the children (such as the need to master new information technologies).

Two other features of the life world of the 5thDimension require mention. First, it is maintained that once upon a time a wizard appeared when the adults working with children could not cope with all of the problems of running and maintaining computers, software, and the computer network that unites children in different after-school programs around the world where telecommunication is available. The wizard is said to be the author of the constitution, provider of the software, designer of the task cards, and arbiter of disputes. The wizard is known to enjoy corresponding with children and to have a terrible sense of humor. Because the wizard is very forgetful, necessary tasks (such as keeping up with needed repairs of computers) are neglected and things go wrong. In such circumstances, the participants in 5thDimension activities (with full justification!) criticize the wizard and send her/him (the wizard changes sexes to fit its mood) sharply worded letters of complaint. And, of course, rules of the 5thDimension can be amended through consensus of its citizens by negotiating with the wizard.

The wizard is also an important artifact for reordering power relations between adults and children in the 5thDimension. This rearrangement comes about in part because when conflicts arise in the 5thDimension, it is the wizard, not the human participants present, who has the power to adjudicate disputes. In such cases, adults as well as children write to the wizard to decide how matters should proceed. It is also important that by pretending to believe in the wizard the adults can collude with the children in the pretension of the wizard's existence and thereby enter into playful relations with them. Finally, because computer technology is not especially reliable and programs or computers often fail to work, adults can off-load responsibility for breakdowns onto the wizard at strategic moments, a possibility that has endeared the wizard to all adults who have worked in the 5thDimension.

Second, it is an important feature of the 5thDimension that it is staffed primarily by undergraduate students who participate in the activity as part of a course in such departments as psychology, education, and communication. Their assignment is to work with the children in the activities in the role of "wizard's assistants." After every session of the 5thDimension they write detailed field notes about their interactions with the children, the wizard, the software, and the life of the 5thDimension. These field notes are primary data about the workings of this cultural system.

At the University of California at San Diego, which divides its academic year into three 10-week quarters, the 5th Dimension goes through three 8-week sessions that children attend from 1 to 4 days a week, depending upon local circumstances. Undergraduates are allowed to take the course three times and children are allowed to attend year after year. Consequently, at any given time, participants include a mix of child and undergraduate "old-timers" and "newcomers" with varying amounts of experience and knowledge about the activities. Among the interesting features of this arrangement is that cultural knowledge and age are not tightly linked. Very often the children have more knowledge about the computers, games, and norms of the 5thDimension than the undergraduates; a situation that helps to reorder everyday power relations with important consequences for the dynamics of the interactions that take place.

Some sample findings

With this sketch of the basic structure of the 5thDimension model system and its initial institutional settings as background, I will now present a sample of empirical findings. My goal is to illustrate a variety of ways in which questions about culture-cognition relations can be illuminated by a research strategy that instantiates model systems of activity in different institutional settings.

The process of enculturation

Perhaps my first task is to establish that the 5thDimension *is* a cultural system. This condition seems necessary if I want to conclude that it can serve as a model for the study of culture-cognition relationships.

This is clearly not the place for me to launch into a discussion of the meaning of the concept of culture within a cultural-historical perspective (see Cole 1992; Cole & Nicolopolou, 1991 for a sample of views on this subject). It is sufficient for my present purposes to draw upon the ideas of Gary Alan Fine (1987) whose work on small group cultures informs my thinking on this topic. Fine (1987, p. 124) remarks that "[c]ulture includes the meaningful traditions and artifacts of a group; ideas, behaviors, verbalization, and material objects." From this very general definition he goes on to characterize the cultural formation that emerges in a small group as an *idioculture*, which he defines as a system of knowledge, beliefs, behaviors, and customs shared by members of an interacting group to which members can refer and that serve as the basis of further interaction. Members recognize that they share experiences, and these experiences can be referred to with the expectation they will be understood by other members, thus being used to construct a reality for the participants. (Fine 1987, p.125)

As pointed out several decades ago by Rose and Felton (1955) when any group of people come together around a common task, they quickly begin to invent, borrow, and repeat new ways of doing things, that is, to create culture. This process at work in the 5thDimension is apparent to anyone who walks into the room while the activity is in progress. At first it seems sort of chaotic and formless: there are children and adults engaged in a wide variety of tasks; they move around in hard to understand patterns, they say odd things ("Wildcat is down!"; "Right 45 degrees"; "Katmandu"; "I hate the Wizard"), and so on.

This casual observer's sense of crossing a cultural border is routinely captured by the difference between the way that (enculturated) old-timers and (unenculturated) newcomers experience the 5thDimension. Routinely the initial field notes written by the undergraduates express their conviction that they are entering a system of shared understandings that is mysterious to them, a condition that generally evokes anxiety and an expressed desire to figure out what it takes to become a member:

As I looked into that room through the windows I had many questions running through my head. How does this program work? What am I supposed to do here? How can I possibly be a leader here when I don't know the first thing about computer games? (Field notes, JG, 01/20/92)

I was anxious about today because it would be the first day with the children. I understood the orientation but had the feeling that the only way to fully understand it was to actually play the games and spend time with the children. I expected to make a lot of mistakes, mostly in not directing the children well since I really had no direction! (Field notes, AO, 10/04/91)

It was really odd having a young adolescent guiding us through the game. I sort of felt helpless in a way, considering that knowledge is power in this society. Here we were, elders who would soon take on the challenge of helping children develop their minds and to help them get through the fifth dimension and we couldn't even finish the first round! Boy was I humiliated in a fun way! ([Field notes, CM, 10/04/91)

Similar evidence is found in retrospective reports about their experience in the 5thDimension that the undergraduates write at the end of each quarter. Many such accounts begin as does the following:

On that first day in the Fifth Dimension site I was totally lost. Everything was foreign to me, and everyone in the room was strangers. In the first week of the class Professor Cole did not clearly explain what we were supposed to do at site, and even if he did, I do not understand the things he was saying.

And with equal frequency, undergraduates report

I got to know everyone at the site very well. We were almost like a little family, because we helped each other and shared ideas about the children. I never would have expected this type of bonding.

My notes started to include statements like, "I asked what I should make. . . . When I explained that . . . I suggested. . . . I told her that . . . I think these statements show that I had begun to define my role in the Fifth Dimension, even though I know this was not a conscious decision.

A second, slightly more subtle indicator of the process of enculturation can be found in a predictable shift in the way in which the artifacts of the 5thDimension mediate the activities of undergraduates once they become familiar with the system. Participants typically reference fundamental artifacts like the wizard, maze, constitution, and task cards in their field notes of daily interaction as they learn to become functioning citizens. Analysis of the field notes reveals the presence of the two modes of interacting with these artifacts. The first mode might be called *orientational*, in which the person treats the artifacts as "things in themselves." The second mode might be called *instrumental* because the artifact is incorporated in some kind of goal directed action as a mediator.

What makes this distinction particularly interesting in the present circumstances is that there is a shift in the relative use of orientational and instrument/mediational patterns as participants become familiar with the cultural system. At first, field note references to 5thDimension artifacts are primarily oriented toward interpreting and understanding their role in the 5thDimension.

Scott proceeded to tell us more about the program: what our role with the children would be, how to use the maze as a guide, the taskcards. . . . We then split into small groups in order to use the computers and different games. (Field notes, LA, 10/1/91)

Here, we learned about the task cards, the hint box, the journey log, the all knowing Wizard and his Wizard's assistants, the Fifth Dimension map, the constitution. Even the Task Cards didn't give you that much advice. (JG, 1/14/91)

Later, as the participants begin to appropriate the culture, they use the task card in an instrumental fashion.

Since he didn't read the instructions, I read him the task card and then asked him to tell me the objective of the game and what he needed to do in order to finish the game successfully. (Field notes, LA, 10/31/91)

Task Card Frequency: Fall Quarter

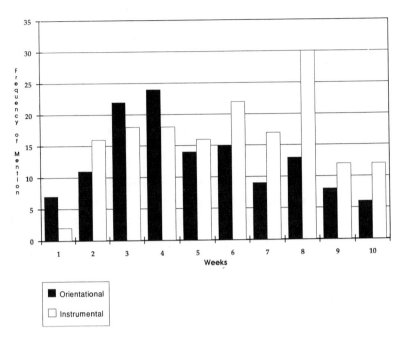

Figure 8.2. The changing frequency of orientational and instrumental uses of the term *task card* in the written discourse of the undergraduate participants in the 5thDimension.

The Task Card mentions that you should start off with all levels at five and gradually increase one of the variables to see which level they belong to, to eventually reach the requested growth of 100cm (Botanical Gardens). (Field notes, CM, 12/5/91)

In the beginning of the game, we were having a really hard time because we didn't know what to do. We both like the sounds that were emitted by the computer, but were frustrated with it. I read the task card again, hoping that it would have more instructs about how to achieve the objective of the game. (Field notes, CM, 04/23/92)

Analysis of the frequency and usage of the two kinds of references to various key artifacts provides a quantitative picture of the shifting understandings that accompany acculturation. Use of the words, "task card" illustrate the trend. As shown in Figure 8.2, in the first weeks of their participation in the 5thDimension, students' use of the task cards is primarily of an orientational nature, but toward the end of the 8-week session, instrumental uses of the task card come to outnumber orientational uses.

Current analyses suggest an additional result. When students continue in the program for two or more "seasons," a third kind of incorporation of such artifacts into their conceptual systems emerges – a reflective/ critical function in which they comment on the way that novices understand (or fail to understand) their uses and ways in which the artifacts could be improved through modification:

The day began with a visit from Romy, she wanted me to tell her whether the task card for Golden Mountain was a good one or a bad one. [Later she wrote, I think that if I had read him the task card straight through I would have lost him. The task card was not challenging for the children. (CM, 11/5/91)

The relationship between culture and its ecological setting

It is a truism of anthropological research that cultures represent qualitatively distinct, historically specific adaptive systems that form over generations of transaction between social groups and their environments. It is equally true, but less generally recognized, that context means more (or other than) "that which surrounds;" rather, "text" and "context" are mutually constitutive of each other. When used in this way, context is a relational concept (Bateson 1972). Our experience with the 5thDimension has made this relational aspect of context too salient to overlook.

In a recent paper, Ageliki Nicolopolou and I compared the cultural systems characterizing two 5thDimensions, one in the Youth Club, the other in the library (Nicolopolou & Cole 1993). These two systems each used the same set of 5thDimension artifacts, ran at the same hour of the day, involved undergraduates participating in the same course, and served children from the same social and economic backgrounds in the same town. Given this commonality of mediational means, institutional purposes, and populations it might be thought that similar, if not identical, cultures would emerge in the two settings. Yet the two systems were remarkably different from each other. Whenever people who had participated in one of the systems for a while journeyed to the other, they remarked on the difference. The 5thDimension at the youth club seemed loud and chaotic as children came and went for reasons that were difficult to fathom. The children worked with undergraduates and played games, but they often did not seem to know each other well, and there seemed to be a relatively contentious atmosphere and a good deal of horseplay. By comparison, the library group seemed intimate and concentrated; children came on time and stayed until the end of the session, often having to be dragged away by their parents or pushed out the door by the librarians. Intense friendships grew between the undergraduates and children and concentration on the games was often intense.

A key to understanding the difference between the two cultural systems is to step outside of them (beyond the walls of the 5thDimension) to examine their local ecologies. When one walks outside the 5thDimension at the Community Youth Club it is a boisterous place with rock music blaring and pool games in progress. Elsewhere children are playing basketball, playing tag, swimming, eating snacks, or gossiping with their friends. The library, expectedly, is a quiet place where decorous behavior is expected at all times; education, not play, is the leading activity of the library. When children left the 5thDimension in the Youth Club, as they were free to do at any time, there were many different activities they could engage in; play being the leading activity. The children could even go home if they liked. But when the children left the 5thDimension in the library, they were expected to read quietly and wait for their parents, who expected them to spend the full 1½ hour session there; literacy was the leading activity.

When we combine the information on the differences between the two 5thDimensions with the information on the different relations of each 5thDimension to its institutional setting, we immediately grasp the way in which the culture of each activity (text) is coconstituted with its context (Figure 8.3). Using the crude variable of noiselevel as a proxy for the qualitatively complex differences between the two locations, we see that while the 5thDimension in the Community Youth Club is noisier than the 5thDimension in the library, the 5thDimension in the library is *noisier* than its institutional context while the 5th Dimension in the Community Youth Club is *quieter* than its institutional context.

The qualitative features of each 5th Dimension are created in the relationship of text to context. Each 5thDimension mixes two leading kinds of activity – education and play. When placed in the institutional context of the Youth Club where play dominates, the educational features of the 5thDimension render it relatively more serious and educationlike (quiet). At the same time, when placed in the institutional context of the library, the play features of the 5thDimension make it noisier and more playlike than its sober-minded educational setting.

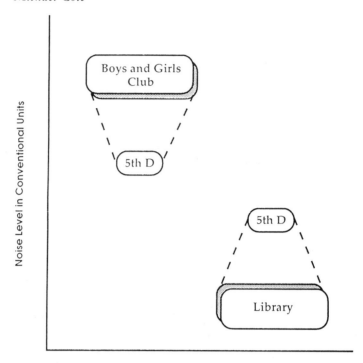

Figure 8.3. A schematic representation of the boisterousness of activity in the library and Community Youth Club 5th Dimensions. Note that while the club is noiser than the library and the 5th Dimension in the club setting is noisier than its counterpart in the library, the library 5thDimension is noisy relative to its context while the club 5thDimension is quiet relative to its context.

The relation between cultural level and cognitive achievement

A long standing issue in the study of culture's impact on the development of thought is the relationship between the level of knowledge characteristic of a culture and the cognitive achievements of its members. As a way of testing the cognitive correlates of these apparent cultural differences, Nicolopolou compared the degree to which each of the two cultural systems fostered the development of shared knowledge using the evidence provided by field notes gathered when children were playing a particular computer game. Figure 8.4 shows the changes in performance on one of the games in the 5thDimension over the course of the year in the two settings. Note that in the Youth Club there is no overall growth in the level at which the game is played; performance at the beginning of the year is low yet better, on average, than at the end of the year. By contrast, performance improves with the growth of the culture of shared knowledge in the library. These and a number of measures of the density and growth of the cultures of the two 5thDimensions confirmed that there was little cultural growth during the year at the Youth Club, but marked and sustained growth at the library.[3]

We are currently investigating a number of other issues relating culture and individual development in the 5thDimension. These include ontogenetic differences in the motivational properties and learning potential of particular computer-based activities, the ways in which new artifacts are invented and diffused, the interpersonal origins of intraperson strategies, the role of inter-site communication as a source of cognitive goals, the conceptual development of the undergraduates who participate in the system, and many more. While these topics are deserving of discussion, I want to spend the remainder of this chapter discussing how the way in which we can study historical change in the 5thDimension activity system affords insights into more traditional questions of historical analysis.

Investigating historical changes in the activity settings

As I noted earlier, when we embarked upon this project a major focus was to determine if it would be possible to create sustainable innovations in activity. By its very nature, research on sustainability requires that one continue research long enough to determine if the new activity system that has been created will continue to develop when it is no longer being force fed by outside research monies.

At the very start of the project, we made it clear that at the end of a 3-year period the external funding for the project would come to an end. We promised that at that time, we would be prepared to continue populating the 5thDimension with eager undergraduates who would be directed by a professor as part of a regularly scheduled course at the university. The university would also continue to provide telecommunications facilities so that the children could communicate with the Wizard as well as children in other parts of the country and the world. But we would no longer provide the computers, software, or the labor of a site coordinator: these would be the responsibility of the local institution.

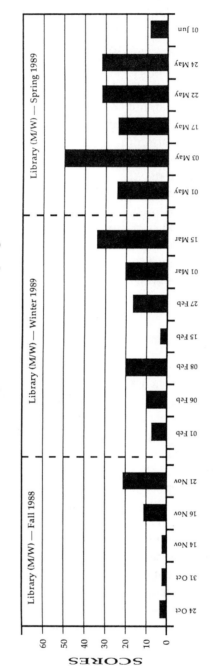

Figure 8.4.   Changes in performance when children play a game in the library and the Youth Club over the course of one year. Note that the improvement is greater in the library, bespeaking of denser culture of shared learning (continued next page).

186

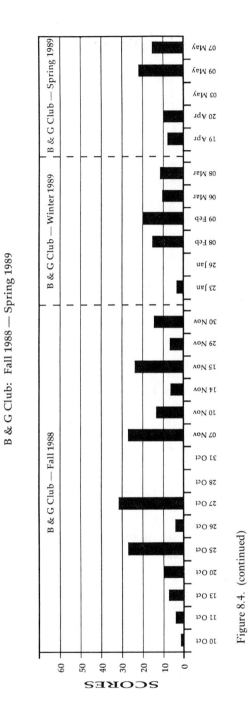

B & G Club: Fall 1988 — Spring 1989

Figure 8.4. (continued)

187

From the field note citations and the general presuppositions of my exposition thus far, it is clear that the 5thDimension has survived for a considerable period of time. As this chapter is being written, the 5th-Dimension is entering its seventh generation of existence. The 5thDimension has not only survived, it has "gone forth and multiplied." In place of the three systems and three community institutions in a single suburban town with which we began in the fall of 1987, there are now 10 5thDimensions spread across 6 communities in 4 states and 2 countries, and more appear to be "in the oven."

This simple quantitative summary is misleading, however. The history of the 5thDimension has not been one of uniform development and continuous growth. Rather, each local 5thDimension has undergone its own distinctive process of development. And for some, development has ceased; these systems have died.

How are we to explain these different developmental outcomes? It is in attempting to answer this question that we return to the difficulty of historical explanation posed by E. H. Carr cited at the beginning of this paper, the fact that our understandings of history can be achieved "only through the eyes of the present."

Many years ago Sigmund Freud pointed to the limitations inherent in such retrospective analysis in the case of human ontogeny:

So long as we trace the development [of a psychological process] from its final stage backwards, the connection appears continuous, and we feel that we have gained insight which is completely satisfactory or even exhaustive. But if we proceed the reverse way, if we start from the premises inferred from the analysis and try to follow these up to the final result, then we no longer get the impression of an inevitable sequence of events which could not be otherwise determined. We notice at once that there might have been another result. (Freud 1920/1924, p. 226)

Precisely this duality of vision, I believe, can be retrieved by the study of "activity genesis" in the model systems I have been discussing. To get a feel for how this process works, I will first describe how matters appeared "looking forward" from the point in 1987 when I interviewed the personnel at each site about their plans and prepared to launch the three activity systems for the first time. My evidence will be the audiotapes of the planning meetings. Then I will give an account "looking backward" at the end of 4 years when, it was hoped, all three systems would have achieved a sustainable state.

Imagining the future: The end of the year interviews

In the beginning, when the future lay before us, we were naturally planning for the long-term success of each of the systems we set up. We had spoken with supervisory personnel in each institution and all had expressed their interest in collaborating with us as a condition of obtaining the grant and undertaking the work. We knew from the very outset that the local institutional goals and arrangements for achieving those goals at each site produced very different patterns of possibilities and constraints for incorporating new activities of the kind we were proposing. But we had no reason to predict success in one case or failure in another.

The first, "goal formation" phase of the research – which extended from July, 1986 to approximately September, 1987 was conducted under the direction of my colleague, Peg Griffin. It was designed to help the participating community institutions to come up with a plan for the content and structure of the future activities that would suit their local institutional goals and to get an overview of the after-school facilities for the children in these institutions as baseline data against which to evaluate later changes. It was evidence from this initial phase that generated the descriptions of the institutions presented earlier in this chapter.

During the year, project staff made regular visits to the sites; they also held seminar/workshops involving representatives of all of the initial community sites. The workshops introduced potential site personnel to a wide variety of activities involving computers and communication. The project director (me) did not participate directly in these activities. I entered the project directly only at the end of this "embryonic" period, when it was time for local institutions to "give birth" to the activity systems they had settled on during Phase 1. In the late summer of 1987 I conducted interviews with staff members at each of the institutional sites. These interviews served a dual purpose. First, they provided me a chance to have the institutional personnel explain their versions of the events of the previous year and to discuss their plans for the start of the activities (which were planned to coincide with the start of the academic year at the university). Second, they gave me my first real glimpse of the challenges I would face in creating a system of activities at the university that would provide the needed support for the community systems to grow and prosper.

In each case, as the interviews clearly demonstrate, the concretization of their plans required concretization of my plans: I had an incoming class of students appearing in a few weeks time, and it was imperative that I learn what I had to do to satisfy whatever plan I agreed to in these interviews. When I told my colleague Roy D'Andrade about this work at the time, I evoked the following, wry, expression of the position I had placed myself in. "Doing social science," he said, "is like being a geologist who studies rocks in a landslide." That captured the phenomenological situation all too well.

The institutions

I will report on interviews with only three of the initial four institutions because the school system dropped out of the project well before implementation of any plans was undertaken. They offered to provide support for the Children's Center as their contribution to the project.

The Children's Center

When I met with the directress of the Children's Center to debrief her on the previous year's experience and to elicit her formulation of goals for the coming year, the directress's first comment was that the teacher she had planned to have specialize in computer activities was leaving. Her goals, she said, remained the same as they had been a year earlier: to find a way to "have the kids, when they are here, be interested and stimulated by the activities." She was especially interested in activities for third and fourth graders, the upper age range of children attending the center after school. Beyond this initial general goal, she found it difficult to be more specific and as a consequence, the conversation proceeded with me asking leading questions, from which she chose alternatives (e.g., "How many kids would you like to have involved?" "How many days a week?" "From the workshops, what kinds of activities would you like to have the kids engaged in?"). The result of this exercise was a decision to have 6 to 10 children play interesting educational games "like Oregon Trails" twice a week with two university undergraduates present each session using the 5thDimension as an organizing metaphor.

Next the discussion turned to computers and telecommunication facilities. The directress was somewhat concerned about the costs of telecommunications and was reassured when she learned that only a local phone call was involved. She was also confident that getting computers for her children to use was not a problem, because she had been assured of support by the computer coordinator of the school system.

One topic that the directress initiated was the process by which we would select the students who would be coming to the center.

One of my concerns . . . I'm not particularly concerned about it but I want you to be aware of it, is that I am not in the classroom and parents, because of day-care problems, if they see a young man on campus, they are going to want to know everything about that young man. So, there isn't someone in that group that . . . you have assistants but that person is not on site. [She was assured that an assistant would always be present] . . . OK, that's the one I could coordinate with.

In further discussion, I explained the entire dynamics of supervision of the students and it seemed that the matter was resolved. However, near the end of this part of the conversation, the directress mentioned the issue again, commenting that she would have to check with the organization that licenses the Children's Center about the proper procedures for dealing with the students.

In this case, it did not take long for our predictions about the future to go awry.

One week following this interview and 1 week before courses began at the university, we held a second meeting at the Children's Center that was attended by the research assistant who would have responsibility for running the activities and the computer supervisor from the school district. It was clear that a good deal had changed in a week's time. The directress opened the discussion with the comment, "You know how I am feeling. I really don't have time for a lot of theoretical kinds of things." I emphasized that this was a meeting to determine as precisely as possible what she wanted the research team to be doing 3 weeks hence when, according to the previous week's discussion, the activity should get under way. The directress replied:

Let me tell you how this was presented to me initially. "E" [a local school official] came to me and presented me with this bountiful platter. I've tied up this wonderful thing at the public university. They will send a student in and they will train your kids on the computer. That's what my goal is, I am very simplistic. Now I am ending up where I am going to in-services, I had to release my secretary to go to an in-service, I had a teacher at in-service two days, all of which costs me money. . . . Now that teacher has left and I do not even have a teacher who can coordinate this thing. . . . So what I was looking for was someone from the university to come in and work with the children. And when I was talking to [the research assistant] the other day she was saying that I had to get a teacher involved.

Here we have a clear example of the failure of the goal formation process during the first year and an expression of additional obstacles to long-term success. But we were undeterred. I assured the directress that all we were asking presently was where physically she wanted us to work and with whom on what basis. She next brought up the fact that "all of these people have to be cleared." We had already taken steps to comply with the clearance procedures and were planning to take responsibility for it, which seemed to relieve her, but her list of concerns was long and pressing.

Next she stated that she needed a limit on the number of people who came because "whether you have someone in charge or not, I still end up being the one who has to supervise. . . . So I don't want several students from the University coming in or various students." Because we had agreed the previous week to have two students come on a Tuesday and two on a Thursday, the somewhat strained way in which this list of concerns was posed was a little disconcerting, but we simply reiterated our understandings, which already relieved the Children's Center staff of all but the most minimal responsibilities and the directress seemed to be reassured. These "internal" issues settled, she now brought up some new concerns with the statement, "Since you were here last week, some things have changed." (Which was certainly clear enough from the change in the atmosphere of the discussion!) The crux of the change was the opening of a new after school center in the same school district but in a neighboring town to which the bulk of the older children attending the center were to be assigned. Since the directress had initially wanted us to work with the older children and had seen software appropriate to older children, this shift in local organization appeared to her as a difficulty, and indeed it turned out to be one.

In the discussion that followed, it was agreed that we would, despite the change in student composition, go ahead with the project, beginning with some new observations of the conditions that obtained at the present moment, and continuing with a plausible form of after school activity that involved children with computers a few weeks hence, once four appropriate undergraduates had been chosen and trained. We emphasized that we were not in a hurry, that whatever we began with would deliberately be incomplete, so that we could cooperate with whatever staff were present to build something that worked for the Children's Center.

Returning to the concrete plans for the start of activities, we suggested that 5 computers be made available for approximately 10 child-participants. At this point, the computer supervisor for the school district, who was present at the meeting as in his role of facilitating the participation of the Children's Center, asserted that although they were a relatively affluent district, they could not provide any help with computers (contrary to prior promises). His justification was an interesting "Catch-22": they had discussed placing computers at the Children's Center, but the rapid staff turnover precluded training a person to work with them. Our response was simply to formulate this difficulty in theoretical terms and to take it in stride as something to be dealt with as part of the project. As I put it in the discussion:

One of the things I see happening over time – this is also a problem at the Community Youth Club but not so much at the Library, each of these institutions being different – is to address the question of how to create a continuous program in the face of discontinuous staffing and computer support. I think this is a problem that the University can really worry about. How can we over the long run provide a kind of continuity that will provide a kind of on-the-job training while helping the teachers to do their thing? I think that's a serious responsibility of ours. (Fieldnotes, September 16, 1987).

To this day we are not certain of all the dynamics at work in this situation. We know that one of the unspoken pressures on the directress was to move our activities from her center to the new facility a few miles away, which she and we were resisting. It is possible that support from the school district was eroded because we would not move our operation from that center to a new one.

The Community Youth Club

At the very outset of our end-of-year interview with the educational director, we were confronted with the problem of unstable staffing; in two weeks she would be leaving the Community Youth Club and no one had yet been hired to replace her. To compensate for this circumstance, the interview was carried out as if she were not leaving so that we could assess how far the process of goal formation had proceeded, even if subsequent development was endangered by the discontinuity of staff changes.

The educational director started her account by pointing to two computers without monitors, which she had checked out with the LCHC staff member who had been making observations at the Community Youth Club in recent months. She had a pretty explicit idea of what she wanted to do.

I am hoping that two TVs will come in [through donations] that I can put these [computers] up to for a permanent thing, like they can be right here so that whenever the kids want they can access the computer. Otherwise I have to set up certain times of day, or one day a week, and that doesn't work for all the kids that come to this club. It's easier to get more kids involved if I leave it set up. I will hopefully start up the Fifth Dimension. I just want to make the box and that type of thing and function just like we were [during the workshops] using the games that we have for these computers in the Fifth Dimension. That's as far as I've gotten so far on the planning. (Interview, Aug. 24, 1987)

Discussion moved on to a consideration of telecommunications plans. At the time of the interview, the Community Youth Club was at a low point in fundraising and the cost of putting in a phone line to secure telecommunications was still a low priority. However, existing phones in a room not too far from the computers were put at our disposal on a "use if available" basis.

As we worked through scheduling, the educational director reiterated that she hoped to see the Fifth Dimension operating on as constant a basis as possible. In practical terms she imagined that this would mean that it would be available from 2:30 P.M. to 5:00 P.M., 4 or 5 days a week. We suggested that perhaps it would be possible to schedule children to come on Tuesday and Thursday or Monday and Wednesday [implicitly thinking in terms of university schedules and a means of providing a structured way of interacting with the children, and using the way that children were scheduled to use the swimming pool].

Cole: "The way the thing works, would it be like a club or would the kids drift in and out?"

Educational Director: "Drift, because they have more of a record with me of doing that. They drift in, they get real excited about it; then they get excited about something in a different area of the club and if I have it here for them to come back to, that is the way it will work."

(Here the linearity of my exposition clashes with the non-linearity of the perspective I now share with the reader. In light of later developments in the Community Youth Club, as the reader knows from reading earlier sections of this chapter, this exchange is especially important, because of the relative degree of structure within the 5thDimension was [and remains] a constant issue in its development, as the comparison with the library indicated.)

A goodly part of the interview was devoted to discussing the possibility that the Community Youth Club's older children, who participated in a service club, might play a special role in the development of the computer activities.[4] This idea appealed to the educational director, who was experiencing difficulty in creating a cohesive teenage service group and thought that the teenagers might find "service" in the 5th Dimension attractive. We liked this idea a lot because it was an obvious source of additional person power for the activities.

The library

Four people representing the library participated in the end-of-year interview, the local librarian and a staff member, as well as two county-wide library employees, one of whom specialized in "technical resources," the other of whom was the supervisor for libraries in the region. In light of staffing problems encountered at the Children's Center and the Community Youth Club, it is worth noting that one staff member who had participated in the workshops had already left the library for another job and that the local staff person present would soon depart.

The interview opened with a review of the library's goals for involving children with computers during afterschool hours. The librarian stated that the basic goal should be to introduce the children to the library through a computer-based educational program that would show them the resources that the library possesses and how to use them. This idea had a history considerably longer than the project, dating back to 1983 when it was raised at a meeting of the local Friends of the Library by my wife, who was a founder of the library support group and who knew about earlier after school work by LCHC. In addition, the librarian reported that a computer had been donated to the library, and they were in the process of figuring out how it might be used by adult patrons.

I asked about the workshops and ideas for activities that arose there. The librarian said that she had been impressed by the afterschool activities that had been reported on during the workshops and that she had especially enjoyed the 5thDimension games where she had learned a lot.

Hence, here too the 5thDimension was chosen as the medium for creating a new form of activity.

When asked about telecommunications, the librarian reported that a telephone line was "in the works" and that the Friends of the Library had provided a budget of $2000.00 for computer activities, a sum that we all agreed was very large. In discussing how this money was to be spent, we explored ways in which LCHC could fill in with certain kinds of equipment in order to allow the library to stretch their budget as far as it could go.

This line of discussion brought the technical resources person into the conversation. She recounted the sad experiences of local libraries which had installed computers for use by patrons, explaining that as a result of prior experiences branch library staff didn't want to have "anything to do with this type of thing." (She offered the interesting rationale that "when a computer breaks down, you have an irate customer.") This concern led to a discussion of ways in which the program for the children would avoid these problems, since we were not proposing to use coin operated computers. This topic brought out the next level of difficulties, that the branch libraries did not have staff who were trained in the use of computers. Our program also seemed to offer a solution to this problem because we had spent a good deal of time working with branch personnel and we were planning to have a knowledgeable staff person present when the computers were in use.

As examples of this variety in the ways that computer could be used, we talked about two different kinds of computer-mediated activity that the librarian had already indicated interest in: an adventure game that would teach children about the library, and the 5thDimension, which had impressed her during the workshops.

We then went over scheduling. The library folk had no clear idea of how often or for how long they wanted the activity to go on. I raised possible problems – if there were too many children or the activity went on a lot of the time, in particular, the possibility that the children would become noisy or disruptive of other activities. Prompted to consider if they wanted the activity every day or less frequently, they decided that twice a week would be about the right level to begin at. The issue of how many children would be involved was not taken up, but it would surface again later, along with other issues signaled in this discussion, to play an important role in the evolution of these activities.

Looking backward

I hope that my brief description of the planning meetings held in 1987 is sufficient to give the reader a sense of how difficult it would be to predict the fate of the systems we were launching. About the only thing I could or did predict about the future of the activity settings we created in 1987 was that they were going to require a lot of work. That each site provided its own set of problems was, of course, obvious. But our ability to deal with those problems in a developmentally productive way was not.

Looking backward is a whole different matter. Here is a synoptic account of how things turned out.

As mentioned earlier, the school's involvement with our project survived barely beyond the time when the grant moneys that launched the projects were made available. The school, of course, had the greatest computer resources for such a program, but it was not willing to run the risk of damage to any of its equipment. Although the school proposed that it remain involved by helping the Children's Center to run its program, this collaboration didn't develop. We later learned that there was hidden antipathy toward our project on the part of the district computer supervisor, who perceived our efforts as criticism of his own program of instruction in the schools.

Next to drop out was the Children's Center, where our activities continued only two-thirds of the 1987–1988 academic year. The "death" of the Children's Center 5thDimension was not the result of the failure of the activities to please the children. In fact, not long after starting the program, at the request of the center staff, we modified our procedures to allow access by more children so that all of the kids could get a chance to participate.

From the interviews between the first and second years of the project two threats to the viability of the 5thDimension at the Children's Center were visible. First, there was the reluctance of the directress to assign staff to work with us. Second was the concern over strange adults coming into the facilities and the concomitant additional work involved.

Staffing the 5thDimension was a problem, but it was not decisive in bringing about its demise. LCHC staff were stretched thin to meet the demands of running the program in three locales more or less simultaneously. This situation was not helped when the school system backed out on its promise of support in terms of computers, as a result of which we found ourselves hauling computers from one part of town to another with fatiguing regularity. But we were managing.

The straw that broke this camel's back was generated by the concern over child abuse. As a result of publicity surrounding the McMartin case in Los Angeles and a high level of concern about child abuse more generally, the agency that licensed the Children's Center insisted that all adults working in a day-care facility register their fingerprints with the Department of Justice and obtain a TB test. Students could obtain the TB test quickly and without cost, but the fingerprinting was time-consuming and cost $16.50 per person, which the project had to pay for. Money was not the problem here. However, when it is remembered that the university works on a system of 10-week quarters, and that the research project had to have checks issued by the university for the costs involved, it is clear that this procedure put a heavy administrative burden on the project, quite apart from any direct costs involved. This effort might have seemed sustainable if we had the impression that the center directress was satisfied with the way the program was going; but she was not. She was pleased with the quality of the activity and the enthusiastic participation of the children, but the administrative overhead of running the program was wearing her out. When a new group of students appeared at the start of the second quarter, her stress was obvious. She was very grateful when we suggested, prior to the start of the third quarter, that we suspend the project.

The library, which was the most successful of our systems from the perspective of its impact on the children, thrived so long as it was run entirely by LCHC research staff. But when it came time for the crucial transition to "steady state," the directress of the Library declined to continue the activities. As in the case of the Children's Center, there is no "villain" in the death of the Library system. Rather, there was a failure to form a working synergism.

During the project we worked with the staffs of the local institutions to build expertise in the running of the 5thDimension and we helped them raise money locally to begin the process of replacing hardware and software. We created special activities in the 5thDimension that required the children to acquire library skills and we met with them periodically to review progress in the program, which they seemed to support. However, when the time came for a shift to shared responsibility, the library staff decided that they did not want to continue the program.

There were many reasons for this decision: the library was short of space, there were administrative difficulties in handling the money needed to pay a site coordinator, they did not have time to train people to work with the children, etc. Each of these problems could have been solved, but the fact of the matter was that even if the money was available, and even if volunteers stepped in to help, the librarians had come to the conclusion that the 5thDimension did not fit closely enough with their main goals as librarians. And that was the end of that.

Looking back at our interviews in the summer of 1987 it seems clear that the reasons for the ultimate failure of the system at the library were articulated during the discussion, although we could not hear them at the time. First, as things developed, we lost sight of the fact that the 5thDimension was planned to be only one element in the activities. The computer-based game that would teach children about how to use libraries did not get written and various plans to have the children use telecommunications for library purposes also failed to develop. This was not a simple oversight, but arose in connection with the fact that our staff was so busy putting together three systems at one time (remember, the most we had ever run before was one), that insufficient resources were put into this aspect of the library activities. While we sought to compensate for this failing by linking various 5thDimension activities to the library in the spirit of the initial plans, the resulting linkages were too few to be readily visible.

By contrast, the 5thDimension at the Community Youth Club not only grew but gave rise to two new 5thDimensions in clubs in two neighboring clubs. The club gave the program an award and embraced it as an important new addition to their program. They did not shy away from picking up responsibility for paying a site coordinator and providing the needed support for computers and telephone lines when the time came. The university also upheld its part of the bargain, making its mainframe computer available for use by undergraduates and children, supporting the teaching of a special course three quarters a year, providing the help of a teaching assistant, and even provided some technical support for computer use by the undergraduates.

The death of the library system and the continued growth of the Community Youth Club system will be recognized as paradoxical from the perspective of a developmental psychologist. There is no doubt in my mind that the library club was a better "garden" for cultivating cognitive and social development, but it was not sustainable and no traces of it are to be found there any more. On the other hand, the very properties that weakened the developmental impact of the 5thDimension in the Youth Club, especially the freedom that children felt to come and go as they pleased, made it an easy-to-assimilate activity from the institution's point of view.

In this context, the relationship of activity to setting depicted in Figure 9.3 takes on added significance. The fact that the library club was noisier than its setting, while being quieter and more studious than the Youth Club, turned out to be a major factor in its eventual demise, while at the same time it was a major factor in shaping its desirable characteristics from a psychological perspective. By the same token, the fact that the Youth Club 5thDimension was quiet compared to its surroundings confirmed its (relatively) educational nature (relative to the other activities at the Youth Club), made it a feather in their cap.

Viewed retrospectively in this manner, the success of the Youth Club 5thDimension and the demise of the other two systems is perfectly understandable and seems almost inevitable. In fact, when I went back to listen to the tape recordings of the planning interviews, I was shocked at how clear it seemed now that the factors which would lead to the demise of the 5thDimesions in the Children's Center and library were clearly present in the conversation in the beginning. The Children's Center directress made no secret of the problems associated with bringing strange adults into her facility, nor did she minimize rapid staff turnover or the difficulty of having any of her staff take responsibility for the activities.

Similarly, the library personnel were pretty clear that they wanted an activity that would help them fulfill their institutional goals. They knew they wanted to have children using computers, but they could not imagine how this would be accomplished, even after a year in which they were exposed to possible models. As in all the sites, goal formation was so feeble, that the most understandable activity, the 5thDimension, served as a stand-in for a specifically tailored activity. Ironically, the better the 5thDimension worked on its terms, the more encapsulated it became within the library. Its "local" success was part and parcel of its "global" failure.

This lesson is clear in a different way at the Youth Club. The porous borders of the 5thDimension at this site were a constant concern for us all during the project. We all felt that the library's 5thDimension represented an almost ideal instantiation of our goals in creating a model afterschool activity involving a large educational component. What we considered to be the sloppiness and chaos of the Youth Club 5thDimension turned out to be its saving features, when viewed in terms of its integration into its institutional context. The shortcomings we perceived in the 5thDimension at the Youth Club were, in important respects, our problem, and not a problem for the children or the staff.

Some concluding comments

Despite the complexity of the topic I have addressed and the brevity of this presentation, I hope that I have made a plausible case that the meso-genetic methodology I have been describing has potential for addressing issues that Sylvia Scribner raised in her work on history and psychology. As noted early in this chapter, Sylvia sought ways to illustrate the idea that historical changes a different systemic levels (genetic domains in Wertsch's [1987] terminology) interact in the construction of development. Moreover, she emphasized that both individuals and sociocultural systems are active agents. Our results are replete with examples of these principles. To take perhaps the most obvious example, we saw that the cultural circumstances created in the 5thDimension at the library afforded a dense culture of collaboration associated with a high level of cognitive development; but the excitement generated by these same circumstances, which were vital to the emergence of the development-enhancing cultural circumstances, were also productive of a high level of excitement. This excitement was manifested not only in higher cognitive attainments, but higher noise levels, which in turn contributed to the rejection of the 5thDimension by its institutional context when extra-systemic resources (in the form of grant support) were withdrawn.

This work also illustrates how one's evaluation of a developing activity system depends upon the level of the system at which it is evaluated. Viewed at the level of individual development within the 5thDimension, the library system was superior to the Youth Club 5thDimension. But viewed at the level of activity system genesis, the Youth Club was superior. The obvious challenge posed by these results is to seek ways of modifying the Youth Club 5thDimension in the direction of greater impact on individual development while retaining its positive synergistic relationship to its institutional setting.

Many potentials of this approach have not been discussed here owing to limitations on space. We have copious data on changes at the microgenetic level which focus in on the processes that result in evaluations of greater or lesser cognitive impact of various 5thDimension cultures. We have also, owing to the continued development and diffusion of such activity systems, had the opportunity to explore a far wider range of institutional ecologies and resulting idiocultural configurations. And, of course, there are our plans for the future, that untravelled world, whose margins continue to recede as we move toward them.

I consider myself fortunate to have been able to count Sylvia Scribner as one of the sojourners on this voyage of discovery and rediscovery. It is one of the gifts of culture that even in her absence, the conversation we began can be continued by those who remain behind . . . or is it up ahead?

Notes

1. Sylvia stated her goal in this paper to be an exploration of the question, "What is history?" in the psychological theory of L. S. Vygotsky. She gave me a copy of the E. H. Carr treatise on this topic from which the second epigraph to this chapter was taken not long after we met.
2. James Wertsch has also written extensively about the importance of including different "genetic domain" within a cultural-historical framework.

References

Bateson, G. (1972). *Steps to an ecology of mind.* New York: Ballentine.

Carr, E. H. (1961). *What is history?* New York: Macmillan.

Cole, M. (1995). Socio-cultural-historical psychology: Some general remarks and a proposal about a meso-genetic methodology. In J. V. Wertsch, P. del Rio, & A. Alvarez (Eds.), pp. 187–214. *Sociocultural studies of mind.* Cambridge: Cambridge University Press.

Cole, M., Griffin, P., & LCHC. (1987). *Contextual factors in education: Improving science and mathematics education for minorities and women.* Madison, WI: Wisconsin Center for Education Research.

Cole, M., & Nicolopolou, A. (1991). Creating sustainable new forms of educational activity in afterschool settings. Final report to the Spencer Foundation, University of California, San Diego.

Cole, M., & Scribner, S. (1977). Cross-cultural studies of memory and cognition. In R. V. Kail, Jr., & J. W.Hagen (Eds.), *Perspectives on the development of memory and cognition*. Hillsdale, NJ: Erlbaum.

Cole, M., & Subbotski, E. (1993). The fate of stages past: Reflections on the heterogeneity of thinking from the perspective of cultural historical psychology. *Schweizerische Zeitschrift für Psychologie, 52* (2), 103–113.

Fine, G. A. (1987). *With the boys*. Chicago: Chicago University Press.

Freud, S. (1920/1924). The psychogenesis of a case of homosexuality in a woman. B. Low and R. Gabler (Trans.). In *Collected Papers*, (Vol. 2). London: Hogarth Press.

Greenfield, P. M. (1993). Historical change and cognitive change: A two-decade followup study in Zinacantan, a Mayan community of southern Mexico. Paper presented at the 60th meeting of the Society for Research in Child Development, New Orleans, LA.

Griffin, P., & Cole, M. (1987). New technologies and the underside of education: What is to be done? In J. Langer (Ed.), *Language, literacy, and culture*. Norwood, NJ: Ablex.

Griffin, P., King, C., Diaz, E., & Cole, M. (1989). *A socio-cultural approach to learning*. Moscow: Progress Publishers (in Russian).

King, K. (1988). The social facilitation of reading comprehension. Ph.D. dissertation, University of California, San Diego.

Laboratory of Comparative Human Cognition. (1983). Culture and cognitive development. In P. H. Mussen (Ed.), W. Kessen (Vol. Ed.), *Handbook of child psychology (Vol. 1)*, pp. 295–356.

Lave, J. (1988). *Cognition in practice: Mind, mathematics, and culture in everyday life*. Cambridge, UK: Cambridge University Press.

Leont'ev, A. N. (1981). *Problems in the development of mind*. Moscow: Progress Publishers.

Mandler, J. M., Scribner, S., Cole, M., & DeForest, M. (1980). Cross-cultural invariance in story recall. *Child Development, 51*, 19–26.

Nicolopolou, A., & Cole, M. (1993). The Fifth Dimension, its play world, and its instructional contexts: The generation and transmission of shared knowledge in the culture of collaborative learning. In N. Minnick & E. Forman (Eds.), *The institutional and social context of mind: New directions in Vygotskian theory and research*. New York: Oxford University Press.

Rose, E., & Felton, W. (1955). Experimental histories of culture. *American Sociological Review, 20*, 383–392.

Saxe, G. B. (1982). Developing forms of arithmatic operations among the Oksapmin of Papua New Guinea. *Developmental Psychology, 18*(4), 583–594.

Scribner, S. (1985). Vygotsky's uses of history. In J. V. Wertsch (Ed.), *Culture, communication, and cognition: Vygotskian perspectives*. New York: Cambridge University Press.

Scribner, S., & Cole, M. (1972). Effects of constrained recall training on children's performance in a verbal memory task. *Child Development, 43*, 845–857.

Scribner, S., & Cole, M. (1981). *The psychology of literacy*. Cambridge, MA: Harvard University Press.

Vygotsky, L. S. (1978). *Mind in society*. Cambridge, MA: Harvard University Press.

Wertsch, J. (1985). *Vygotsky and the social formation of mind*. Cambridge, MA: Harvard University Press.

9 The abstract and the concrete

Rachel Joffe Falmagne

Despite fundamental differences in foundations between activity theory and dialectical logic on the one hand, and mentalistic cognitive science on the other, some particular substantive concerns within these perspectives have points of contact with one another. One such question, the focus of this chapter, has to do with the distinction and the relations between the abstract and the concrete.

Although the analytical categories of abstract and concrete span a range of content areas, this chapter will center on thinking and inference. I will examine some current discussions of the role of abstract/formal processes and contentful/situated processes in language and inference, grounded in the mentalist cognitive framework, and juxtapose these discussions with analyses of abstract and concrete forms of thinking provided within dialectical logic and activity theory. Within their respective aims, both these frameworks have needed to posit and to define distinct modes of thinking and to investigate theoretically the relationship between the two.

The question of the relations between the abstract and the concrete is configured by the conceptual framework of each theory and driven each time by theory-internal problematics. Concepts are never defined in isolation, but rather derive their meaning from their relations to other concepts within a coherent theoretical system (e.g., Wiser, in press). Of necessity, this imposes constraints on the comparability of concepts across theories. Despite those constraints, it is the aim of this chapter to probe the points of contact, of mutual resonance, and of opposition between the two kinds of theoretical descriptions of abstract and concrete phenomena, and to examine how these oppositions are imposed by differences in foundation between the two frameworks. This goal is

I thank Katherine Nelson and Ethel Tobach for thoughtful comments and suggestions. This chapter is dedicated to Sylvia, in memory of our friendship and our conversations on these matters, and with appreciation for bringing Ilyenkov to my attention.

grounded in the belief that juxtaposing alternative theoretical analyses leads to insights that cannot be gained in any other way.

Sylvia Scribner's work embodies a synthesis of both the activity theory and the cognitive science traditions. Developed on an activity theory foundation, Scribner's theory of thinking in action sees cognitive processes as instrumentalities for action in the context of goal-directed, socially purposive activities, yet selectively utilizes analytic tools derived from cognitive theory to this end. The conceptual and functional contrast between abstract and concrete forms of knowledge was of intense and continuing interest to Sylvia Scribner. In particular, this theoretical concern occupies a central place in her analysis of thinking at work (e.g., in Scribner 1985, 1988). After discussing how the concepts of the abstract and the concrete have been treated in dialectical philosophy and in cognitivist approaches to thinking respectively, we will turn to Scribner's discussion of abstract and concrete forms of knowledge in work activities within her rich integrative framework.

Dialectical logic

The categories of the abstract and the concrete have an entirely different meaning in dialectical philosophy than they do in cognitive science and in formal logic, and their epistemological status is entirely different as well. Ilyenkov (1977, 1982), in a brilliant analytical exposition of these constructs reveals their richness and the richness of their relationship within a dialectical materialist framework. Ilyenkov traces the historical roots of dialectical philosophical thinking to Spinoza and, of course, to Hegel, but he himself criticizes the idealist stance of these thinkers and proceeds from a materialist foundation. Although Ilyenkov's analysis draws from Marx's original discussion of the abstract and the concrete in *Capital*, he is, as a philosopher and logician, less concerned with political economy and social theory than with epistemology and thought, and his analysis extends Marx's "objective" notions of abstract and concrete to considerations of thinking, truth, and logic.

With some variations, traditional views on knowledge and concepts view abstract knowledge, or abstract concepts, as revealing the common elements (or properties) in a class of things or phenomena. In contrast, "concrete" concepts are concepts whose extension is a set of real-world entities. The distinction is epistemological, as it contrasts different forms of knowledge, and is typically confounded with the modality of apprehension underlying the concept. It is generally assumed that concrete concepts are perceptually based, perhaps as a legacy of empiricism, and this is indeed one way in which concreteness is defined. Abstract properties, on the other hand, are taken to be objects of thought, abstracted from the object either through a mental or through an epistemological process.

Typically, with the exception of empiricist approaches and, to some degree, of recent "situated" approaches discussed in the next section, abstraction is given the greater epistemological weight; abstract knowledge is superior. Concepts condense information, eliminate unnecessary details, reduce mental processing, get closer to the essence of things, or capture general properties. Abstract concepts do so even more efficiently. For instance, formal logic is generally seen as formalizing the essence of valid deduction, and physical sciences strive to formulate abstract general laws.

Abstractions of this kind are regarded by Ilyenkov (1982) as "lopsided" and impoverished descriptions of reality, "meager" knowledge. True knowledge is concrete, in the dialectical sense that it integrates the diverse aspects of a phenomenon or object and reveals the interconnectedness of these aspects. Thus, Ilyenkov states, "In dialectics, unity is interpreted first and foremost as connection, as interconnection and interaction of different phenomena within a certain system or agglomeration, and not as abstract likeness of these phenomena. . . . The *concrete* [is a] synonym of the real links between phenomena, of concatenation and interaction of all the aspects and moments of the object given to [humans] in contemplation and in a notion. The concrete is thereby interpreted as an internally divided totality of various forms of an object, a unique combination of which is characteristic of the given object only" (1982, pp. 32–33).

Thus, interestingly, both epistemologies are engaged in a search for unity, but the grounds for unity, and the nature of unity, radically differ. Whereas, within the standard view, conceptual unity among objects relies on the commonality of elements, it is the interrelatedness of diverse elements and the integration of opposites that creates unity within dialectics.

The category of interaction is central to this analysis as an ontological category. The essence of interconnection is not sameness but complementarity. Accurate descriptions of reality require that one capture the manner in which individual phenomena complement one another organically.

One important observation is that the mode of apprehension of phenomena is irrelevant to whether or not they are viewed as concrete. It is the structural or dialectical properties of the knowledge, not its perceptual origin, that confers it "concrete" status. Marx's own concerns were ontological, not epistemological. He took concreteness (in the preceding, dialectical sense of unity of diverse aspects) to be an objective characteristic of the object, independent from the manner in which it is known. However, within a dialectical materialist framework, thought is viewed as a reflection of reality. Thus, Ilyenkov, in his analysis of the role of the abstract and the concrete in thought, likewise defines concreteness by the structure of the knowledge, not by the cognitive modality of apprehension, be it perceptual, rational, or linguistic.

Relation between the abstract and the concrete

Far from being separate forms of cognition, the abstract and the concrete are dialectically related in thought. "The concrete in thinking . . . . appears . . . in the form of combination (synthesis) of numerous definitions. . . . Each of the definitions forming part of the system naturally reflects only a part, a fragment, an element, an aspect of the concrete reality, and that is why it is abstract if taken by itself, separately from other definitions. In other words, the concrete is realized in thinking through the abstract, through its own opposite, and is impossible without it" (Ilyenkov 1982, p. 37).

The dialectic of the abstract and the concrete in thought and in theoretical processing is Ilyenkov's primary concern. As is clear from the preceding paragraph, the abstract and the concrete subserve one another in thought through a dialectical interplay. Ilyenkov furthermore problematizes the standard contrast between "real" objects and (abstract) properties taken to be contingent on the existence of an object, by pointing out that neither could exist without the other. As we will see in the next section, I have described a somewhat analogous interdependence between formal and nonformal mental processes in deduction (Falmagne 1989) within an entirely different, cognitivist theoretical framework.

The universal and the particular

Ilyenkov's emphasis on concreteness is not to be mistaken for an exclusive commitment to particularistic descriptions. His ultimate quest is for universal principles. However, universality is to be achieved not through abstract definitions but through genuine synthesis of concrete facts and descriptions (where "concrete" is understood dialectically, as discussed above). "Concrete universal concepts" are those meeting this criterion. One useful illustration of this view, within dialectical and historical materialism, is the statement that "[the human being] is a being producing implements of labour" as a concrete universal definition of ["human being"].[1] The definition is concrete in that it is grounded in the "objective interconnections" between the person and the various aspects of her/his social reality rather than relying on abstracted elements common to all persons. It is universal in that production of labor implements is a universal form of human activity, despite its variations.

As another illustration of this important notion of concrete universal, one might define a mother as a woman having a primary relation to a child, a relation embedded in the social and historical context in which they live. No common, abstract element can be used as definition. Not all mothers are biological mothers, some women mother children born of another woman. The primary relation is not always one of caretaking or of commitment: some mothers do not share their children's lives, yet their relation with them remains primary. The relation need not be unique: African-American culture defines other mothers as women committed to a child, and seen as such, in an extended social network. The notion cannot be captured by a common element, or by other idealizations such as a prototype. Rather, the concept of mothering embraces the range of concrete situations and relations in their full specificity and their particular social and historical context.[2]

Importantly, in the previous examples, this universal concept is not an abstraction away from the particular variations in forms of labor (or of mothering), but rather remains concrete in that it sustains a dialectical relationship with those particulars. Ilyenkov (1982) writes: "But, being an objectively universal basis of [humans'] entire most complex social reality, production of labour implements was a thousand years ago, is now, and will be in the future quite a particular form of [human] activity, actually realized in individual acts performed by individual [humans]. . . . In this conception, *the universal* is not metaphysically opposed to *the particular* and *the individual* as a mental abstraction to a sensually given fullness of phenomena, but is rather opposed, as a real *unity* of the universal, the particular, and the individual, as an objective fact, to other just as objective facts within the same concrete historically developed system, in this case, to [human] social and historical reality" (p. 75).

Thus, the individual object through which the universal is realized is of equal ontological and epistemological importance as the universal itself, a distinctive feature of the dialectical approach. Equally important, the criterion of adequacy for abstract universals is that they subsume each particular fact entirely. An abstract universal law that captures the central tendency of a factual domain is inadequate on this view, because individual facts are of central importance epistemologically: true knowledge must be grounded in individual facts, fully specified and contextualized. Ilyenkov is clearly skeptical about the viability of abstract universals, and argues that real concepts always express concrete universals in the sense just discussed.

The nature of logic

The preceding issues are particularly relevant to considerations of the nature of logic. In particular, as Ilyenkov (1977, 1982) points out, (Aristotelian) syllogisms do not apply validly to concrete universals, as these syllogisms rely on traditional definitions of categories. More generally, since formal logic has been developed precisely to specify the implications of statements based on their form alone, to the exclusion of their content, it is clear that the logical principles and concepts deriving from formal logic are incommensurate with concrete concepts as defined dialectically.

The question of what constitutes a necessary truth is widely debated in philosophy of logic. One focus of the debate has been to define the exact grounds on which logically necessary truths are to be distinguished from contingent (e.g., scientific) truths, and (in some cases) to determine whether there is indeed a fundamental distinction between the two (e.g., Haack 1978, pp. 170–235; Quine 1953). This issue is addressed by Ilyenkov (1982) with limpid eloquence as he contrasts the dialectical materialist view on the matter with that of formal logic: "Is the act of production of labour implements that kind of social reality from which all other human traits may be *deduced in their necessity* or is it not? The answer to this question determines the logical characterization of the concept as a universal or nonuniversal one. Concrete analysis of the *content* of the concept yields in this case an affirmative answer. Analysis of the same concept from the standpoint of the abstract logic of the intellect yields a negative answer. The overwhelming majority of beings that are undoubtedly individual representatives of the human race do not directly conform to this definition. From the standpoint of old nondialectical logic, this concept is too concrete to be justified as a universal one. In [dialectical logic], however, this concept is genuinely universal precisely because it reflects the factual objective basis of all other traits of [humans] which have developed out of this basis factually, historically, the concrete universal basis of anything that is human" (p. 76).

Thus, for Ilyenkov, logic is seen as closely linked with worldview (1982, p. 68), indeed as a network of concrete universal laws and concepts. It does not have the special status of a "detached, abstract universal." In this particular sense, logic is akin to scientific theory, a theory furthermore required to be contextual and fully specific in its descriptions, and a theory resting on interconnections among phenomena rather than on formal structure.[3]

If transposed to our concerns about individual cognition and the nature of deductive inference, this view gives primacy to fully contentful, richly contextualized forms of deductive thought over formal deductive processes. It will be interesting to observe in the next section that some recent "situated" approaches within the cognitive science tradition are likewise stressing the importance of content, context, and general knowledge in deduction. Yet, as we shall see, these analyses, while sharing with Ilyenkov's view a precedence of contextualized knowledge over formal knowledge, critically diverge from it in scope and in presuppositions.

Cognitive approaches to inference

Current discussions of thinking and inference in the cognitive tradition also reflect a theoretical concern with distinct modes of thought, roughly characterized for now as abstract versus contentful. However, within that tradition, the question is framed in mentalistic terms, and not primarily as an epistemological question. The primary aim is not to distinguish different forms of knowledge in terms of their relation to reality, or to define what constitutes "true" knowledge; rather, the aim is to characterize alternative modes of mental representation involved in language and inference and to specify the functional properties of each kind of representation within a cognitive system.

The mentalistic ontology that characterizes much of cognitive science clearly differs from the theoretical base of dialectical logic and, to some degree, of activity theory. Further, the predominant style of theorizing in mainstream work in cognition is decontextualized and builds on formal symbolic descriptions of cognitive phenomena. Though some current approaches are "situated" and do ground cognitive processes in embodied, contextualized agents, they do so in limited ways, as will be elaborated later.

Despite those differences, cognitive approaches to inference have been preoccupied with notions of abstract and concrete as well, within their own problematics. I will focus on the manner in which abstract and concrete processes have been defined and contrasted within some existing theories, and the various functions that those processes have been assumed to have in deduction.

Several intersecting issues, partly distinct and partly overlapping, shape the theoretical landscape. One has to do with the basis of deductive processes, specifically whether human deduction relies on form or on meaning. Another has to do with the extent to which context, biases, and knowledge of the world entirely shape deduction (as opposed to abstract, formal principles).

Both issues have captured the bulk of theoretical debate in recent years, and each has been constructed into an oppositional rhetoric. I will argue, however, that radical debate between extreme proposals is an unproductive path to understanding a phenomenon in any depth, and I will outline how an integrative framework might conceptualize the functional interplay of abstract and concrete processes in deduction. Theoretical style is, therefore, a third feature of the theoretical landscape.

Finally, an issue that centrally affects the concerns of this article, is whether deduction ought to be characterized as a disembodied process or contextualized as a situated activity. Though analyses of the latter kind are few, they do exist in the cognitive literature, and will be discussed in the later part of this section, especially in relation to Ilyenkov's ideas (see Falmagne & Gonsalves 1995, for review).

Form and content

On one view, human deduction is governed by form and relies on a set of deductive principles, represented mentally, that specify what statements of a particular logical form can be derived from what other statements, also described by their logical form alone (e.g., Gentzen 1969; Osherson 1975; Braine 1978). While those "natural logic" models do not posit that human deduction corresponds to standard logic, and instead aim at psychological realism, they share with standard logic the view that deduction is based on the form of the given statements, not on their contents.[4] With few exceptions, on this view, other aspects of reasoning generally have been considered peripheral (However, see Braine and O'Brien [1991] for a recent broadening of this view). One exception is the model described in the next section which, while assuming formal principles as part of long-term knowledge representation, describes these in complex interplay with other, nonformal ingredients of reasoning (Falmagne 1989, 1990a).

Conversely, others have argued that deduction is driven by prior world knowledge, prior content-specific experiences, and beliefs, on the basis of empirical results documenting the effect of those factors in deduction (e.g., Cox & Griggs 1982; Evans 1982, 1989; Pollard 1982). Within the present analysis, the point to notice is that the deductive process suggested by these discussions is primarily "concrete," incorporating as it does diverse specific elements from the reasoner's experience, and mapping onto real-world entities as experienced by the person.[5]

Characteristically enough, discussions of each kind make claims of supremacy. In those analyses stressing content-based processes, the suggestion has been that formal characterizations of logical knowledge ought to be abandoned, and that abstract deductive principles are irrelevant to reasoning. Conversely, most discussions of abstract deductive principles implicitly assume that those principles are used whenever they are applicable, at the exclusion of other processes.

Those are curious conclusions, guided by an oppositional, binary reasoning. There is no question but that content and context affect deduction, yet these observations are neutral with regard to the "formal schemas" assumption if one recognizes that permanent knowledge representation must be distinguished from the ongoing representation of a particular problem, and that in order to utilize a formal deductive principle one must formalize the problem in terms of its logical form rather than construing it in another format. Conversely, contentful processes based on specific knowledge cannot predict how someone, upon being told that "If Sara fibbles, then she thabbles" and that "Sara fibbles," would deduce that "Sara thabbles." Yet, it is intuitively obvious that an adult, untutored in formal logic, would draw that inference, and empirical results indicate that children do as well (Falmagne 1990b).

Harman (1986) provides one coherent theoretical proposal congenial with observations of content effects but balanced. Starting from the view that the proper object of investigations of human reasoning is to identify the determinants of belief revision, Harman argues that, for reasoning so construed, the causal power of current interrelated beliefs and of knowledge of the world far outweighs that of formal processes, although formal schemata may be part of people's knowledge base. Interestingly, this proposal gives epistemological precedence to "concrete" modes of knowledge that integrate various elements of a person's knowledge base over abstract, formal knowledge. From that standpoint, Harman concurs with Ilyenkov's (1982) contention that integration of various aspects of the concrete reality, rather than abstraction, is a sound base for knowledge. An important difference however is that Harman's beliefs remain disembodied and decontextualized. They are mental states whose relation to the world and to the person as a whole remains inexplicit.

Mental model theory, as proposed by Johnson-Laird (1983) and Johnson-Laird & Byrne (1991) is another proposal contrasting with formal schema theory. Models are streamlined mental representations of the state of affairs described in the statements, representations that rely in part on linguistic meaning and in part on knowledge of the world. In that sense, they constitute semantic representations. The contrast between mental model theory and deductive schema theory often has been put as one between a semantically based view on inference and a syntactically based view. The rhetoric, again, has been one of supremacy and Johnson-Laird maintains that mental models are sufficient to account for deduction, and that formal schemata have no place in a theory of reasoning.

Thus, again, formal and contentful processes (in this case, syntactic and semantic processes) are conceptualized as being mutually exclusive as a foundation for reasoning. In the remainder of this section, I will argue that they are not, and describe how they are functionally related within an integrative system. For now, suffice it to point out on conceptual grounds that, as semantic representations, the construction of mental models must exploit the syntactic and logical properties of the sentence; those are, after all, the backbones of meaning.

Toward integration

The road to a mature understanding of cognition lies, I am convinced, in integration of complementary processes, not in competitive opposition between radical views. Reality is complex and so, undoubtedly, is the system of mental representations and processes that underly complex cognitive activities. It is likely that any theory with explanatory power will have an integrative character. Thus, the agenda is to develop a theoretical account that not only affords description of both formal and nonformal aspects of deductive thought, but also that articulates the interplay between the two.

On this view, two requirements seem desirable for a theory of meaning and for a logic, and the conjunction of these requirements generates a dialectical tension. On the one hand, we want to assume that meaning is grounded in people's knowledge of the world, and that thought is contentful. On the other hand, it seems clear that the theory must afford abstract relations. Natural logic consists of such relations between statements, that apply across situations and contents, and in that sense are formal, whatever the notation may be in which we choose to describe them in our theories.

Within this perspective, one key question has to do with the functional interplay between formal and nonformal, or "concrete" modes of representation in the cognitive process. In previous work, I have outlined one theoretical proposal motivated by these integrative aims (Falmagne 1989). The theory distinguishes two levels of mental representation involved in deductive phenomena: the permanent knowledge representation, that includes abstract logical knowledge as a set of deductive schemata based on logical form, amidst other knowledge representation domains such as syntax, event knowledge, concepts, and semantic relations; and a functional, on-line representation of the problem in working memory, where the actual deductive work is done at a specific time for a specific inference token.

Construction of this functional representation is a complex process. To recognize the logical form of the problem, a formalization process is needed that exploits features of the syntactic structure of the sentences, surface cues in the sentences, and semantic and contextual cues. A representation highlighting the logical form of the statement among the other aspects of meaning is then constructed and the pertinent deductive schema operates on it by utilizing logical form explicitly.

However, the formalization process may be overridden by other factors if the surface cues pointing to logical structure lack salience or if other aspects of meaning are more compelling in the problem. The resulting functional representation may then be of various kinds, relatively more "concrete." It may consist of ordinary world knowledge, thus exploiting specific content; it may be driven by domain-specific pragmatic schemas (Cheng & Holyoak 1985); it may be imagistic when the problem is sufficiently imageable (Clement & Falmagne 1986); or it may rely on prototypical exemplars of the relations referred to in the problem (Johnson-Laird 1983, Johnson-Laird & Byrne 1991).

It is plain that this theory is not simply a compromise position between the two extreme views, but rather articulates a distinction, both conceptual and functional between a deep level of (logical) knowledge representation and a functional representation constructed and used during the ongoing deductive action, and that may or may not be formal. This analysis eliminates the previous false controversies by providing a theoretical structure that enables one to consider the functional relations between form, content, and world knowledge in deduction. Indeed, I submit that any theory must include a distinction of this nature, whatever its specific assumptions, in order to avoid the unfortunate conflation of issues just discussed.

The theory further posits that the deployment of nonformal processes based on content or world knowledge crucially depends on logical knowledge to yield valid deductions. Aside from its representational function, discussed previously, logical knowledge has an "executive" function: it controls the construction of the functional representation, even when that representation is nonformal, and it organizes the program of deductive steps whereby consequences from that representation are deduced. Thus, the execution of the entire process is monitored by the logical executive. Although extralogical processes such as world knowledge, mental models, or mental imagery may be sufficient to yield conclusions that fortuitously converge with logic, they are not sufficient to yield valid inferences unless they are directed by a deeper logical understanding.

This assumption is mandated by both conceptual and empirical considerations. For instance it is clear on conceptual grounds that, as semantic representations, the construction of mental models must exploit the syntactic and logical properties of the sentence. The meaning of a sentence includes its logical form. Thus, an understanding of the logic of the sentence is needed to construct the appropriate mental model embodying that logic. Likewise, while mental imagery may be functional in deduction for certain inferences, it only acts as support for logical processes; in the absence of a deeper logical understanding that can provide executive control to imagistic processes, mental imagery does not help. This point has further received empirical support, as have analogous conclusions emerging from studies of representational and executive factors in recognition of indeterminacy in children. (Falmagne 1989).

Thus, formal and nonformal processes are conceptualized not as disjoint or mutually exclusive but as two interdependent poles of the same cognitive process. Despite the differences in foundation and problematic between the cognitive science perspective from which the present analysis derives and the dialectical perspective that grounds Ilyenkov's (1977, 1982) analysis, it is interesting to note the convergence between the present view that formal and nonformal processes are functionally interdependent, and Ilyenkov's observation that the abstract and the concrete are dialectically related in thought and subserve one another, rather than being separate forms of cognition.

Toward contextualization

A different issue, distinct from the preceding concerns (though intersecting with them) has to do more broadly with the theoretical language used to characterize deduction and thought. It is noteworthy that all cognitive approaches described so far offer decontextualized descriptions of inference, based on a mentalistic cognitive process that only referentially connects with the world. This is true in particular of the theory described in the preceding section. Similarly, despite the fact that the mental models described by Johnson-Laird (1983) and Johnson-Laird and Byrne (1991) are semantic representations of the problem, they act as disembodied computations. Though knowledge of the world does enter into the construction of mental models for certain special domains such as spatial relations, it does not affect others, and when knowledge of the world does contribute it does so at the service of building abstract, schematized representations of the referent states of affairs. Thus, again, inference is decontextualized. It is important to recognize this commonality between the mental model view and the deductive schema view, an essential commonality that risks being obscured by the ostensible syntactic/semantic opposition.

In contrast, Cheng and Holyoak (1985; see also Cheng, Holyoak, Nisbett, & Oliver 1986; and Cheng & Nisbett 1993) propose that human inference often relies on "generalized, context-sensitive sets of rules which . . . are defined in terms of classes of goals (such as taking desirable actions or making predictions about possible future events" (p. 395). Specifically those rules are pragmatic schemas having to do with permission, obligation, causation, and the like. Pragmatic reasoning schemas are, in a sense, intermediate in abstractness between formal schemas and domain-specific contentful procedures. The aspect crucial for our present focus, however, is that pragmatic schemas are embedded in goal structures and used by embodied agents. In that sense, Cheng and Holyoak's proposal interestingly constitutes a move in the direction of an activity theory – based analysis of reasoning. However, the proposal is limited in scope, as only a few specific schemas have been examined (permission, obligation, and causation), and, more importantly, its theoretical base has not been elaborated nor its broader commitments made explicit.

The situated approach to inference developed by Barwise (1989) provides an interesting conceptual tool for addressing these issues more broadly. Developed on philosophical grounds as an extension of Barwise and Perry's (1983) situation semantics, the approach sees speech, thought, and inference as situated activities carried by embodied, limited agents and occurring within restricted portions of the environment. Though the theory was motivated by philosophical concerns, it has ramifications that importantly converge with cognitive and developmental analyses. Some of these will be discussed shortly.

Situation semantics describes linguistic meaning and inference within a more general theory of information. Thus, it aims at providing an account of meaning that applies to linguistic as well as to nonlinguistic meaning. In that regard, it provides a useful conceptual bridge for those theories of inference that aim to encompass both the linguistic and nonlinguistic routes to deduction and deductive development, such as the account of logical development that I have proposed in earlier work

(Falmagne 1990a, b). It originated in part as a development of Barwise's prior work on the semantics of perceptual reports (Barwise 1981). The basic building blocks of the theory are situations and cognitive agents, in the same manner as Barwise (1981) took scenes to be the primitives of perception. Objects, relations, and facts arise from uniformities across situations. From a cognitive standpoint, one might say that objects, relations, and facts are abstracted. The theory also defines situation types, abstract situations, and abstract relations between those.

Meaning is defined by systematic relations of a certain kind between different types of situations, to which the agent is attuned. For instance, smoke means fire, under normal circumstances, or the fact that the hands on my watch are in a certain position means that it is four o'clock, under normal circumstances. This makes it clear that meaning is embedded in the circumstances: If I distort my watch, this configuration of hands no longer means that it is four o'clock. Linguistic meaning is treated in a parallel manner.

To simplify, it is not disembodied sentences that have meaning, but rather statements, that is, utterances in context, embedded in their circumstances. The meaning of a statement and the semantic content of a representation depend on its embedding circumstances, a tenet of situation semantics coined as the Situatedness of Content Principle. The theory thus yields a contextual account of meaning.

Meaning and logic are intimately related for any semantic theory, since the meaning of a statement includes the logical relations that it expresses. It is interesting to note that in adopting statements rather than sentences or propositions as the linguistic objects capable of having meaning, the theory makes an important choice as to the primitive objects of logic, that is, those entities capable of being true or false, an issue that has received considerable philosophical attention (e.g., Strawson 1952; Quine 1970; Haack 1978). Here, the primitive objects of logic are statements.

Barwise's (1989) treatment of logic and his formulation of situated inference mechanisms are in the early stages of elaboration, but the requirements for such mechanisms are to exploit environmental constants, to draw circumstantial rules of inference, to make explicit parameters implicit in a situation, and the like (pp. 151–154, 157–160). Situated inference mechanisms are not assumed to capture all deductive thought, but rather are seen as "simple information processing mechanisms that violate the formality condition"[6] and are hoped to lead to "a version of the language of thought hypothesis which recognizes the importance of embedding circumstances on thought and on inference" (Barwise 1989, p. 154).

Within our present focus on contextual perspectives of deduction, one important distinctive feature of situation semantics and situated inference is the manner in which context is conceptualized. Context is now fully incorporated in the primitive of the theory (the situation), rather than being treated as an extraneous factor affecting or modulating semantic interpretation, as it is in a number of analyses of linguistic meaning or in some of the discussions on context effects in deduction in the cognitive literature. Context here is integral to the analysis.

This is a radical reformulation of the notion of context, and it signals an emphasis on contextualized knowledge over formal knowledge, an emphasis consonant with Ilyenkov's (1982) argument, albeit motivated by a different ontology. However, despite this ostensible convergence, it is interesting to note a critical limitation in the scope of contextualization. The theoretically relevant context is the immediate, circumscribed situation rather than the broad social and material context. Situations are small portions of the world, immediately accessible to the agent, and meaning and inference are defined in relation to those.

Returning to the issue concerning the relations between abstract and "concrete" processes, it is important to note that, although Barwise describes situated inference mechanisms only, such mechanisms need not exclude formal processes. These can be postulated within an integrative theory. They are, furthermore, needed. As argued previously, the description of inference in terms of contentful, situated processes needs to be supplemented by abstract knowledge at the knowledge representation level and formal inference processes that apply across situations. Indeed, Barwise himself states rightly that situated inference mechanisms will not solve all the problems involved in inference.

Though developmental concerns are not the primary focus of this chapter, the preceding discussion leads us naturally to ask what is the developmental relation between abstract logical knowledge and either "concrete" or situated knowledge. A developmental proposal addressing this question with reference to semantic and conceptual development is Nelson's (e.g., 1985, 1986), who argues that meaning is grounded in event structures, at least in the early phases of acquisition, and that conceptual structures are derived or constructed from event representations. Along related lines, I have submitted that, in the course of logical development, some logical relations are abstracted from earlier, context-specific, embedded representations of particular relations in particular contexts, akin to those described by Barwise (Falmagne 1990a, b). Thus, abstract deductive principles would be obtained by disembedding situated meaning and situated relations from the range of particular situations in which they are instantiated.

Two features of Barwise's theory are pertinent to examine in relation to Ilyenkov's (1977, 1982) views. First, it is interesting to note that Barwise's position has shifted from an objectivist theory, introduced in *Situations and Attitudes* (1983) as roughly an ecological, realist perspective, to a more cognitive perspective in his 1989 book, *The Situation in Logic*. Unlike Ilyenkov's premise that concepts reflect the structure of concrete reality, Barwise now rejects (1989, p. 232) the notion that situations are "out there in a Platonic sense waiting around to happen and be carved up and characterized," and states that "while some structure is independent of the existence of cognitive agents, a considerable degree of structure is dependent upon the interactions of the world with cognitive agents. What situation an agent can characterize depends upon the cognitive architecture of the agent." This is, of course, a view that has become standard among cognitive and developmental investigators, and it is interesting to observe that philosophical considerations intrinsic to the semantic theory have led Barwise to a similar shift.

Second, despite its situated foundation, the theory implicitly retains its emphasis on abstraction as the privileged form of knowledge. For instance, Barwise (1989) aims at defining situated inference mechanisms that presumably will work in a uniform way across a range of situations, thus implicitly striving towards an abstract characterization of situated processes. Thus, again, it appears that contextualization is limited because of the foundation on which the theory is built. Extensions of a theoretical framework always retain their lineage of origin. Ilyenkov's (1982) concrete universals, by contrast, which he presents as true knowledge, retain the particularities of the phenomenon in their universal formulations: universality is achieved, not through abstraction, but by embracing the range of concrete particulars.

Scribner on thinking at work

Sylvia Scribner's theory of thinking in action offers a rich and elegant description of cognitive processes as instrumentalities for action in the context of purposive, socially meaningful activities (e.g., Scribner 1985, 1988). The approach contrasts in fundamental ways with the perspective dominant in cognitive science, in which mind is seen as a self-contained system of mental processes and representations whose relation to the person's goals and to the social setting in which the person is embedded is not explicitly incorporated in the constructs of the theory, and sometimes explicitly discarded. Scribner (1988), noting the prevailing metaphor of mind-as-computer in cognitive science, wittily remarks that this is "a computer which sits in a room having no transaction with the external environment, a computer that is, so to speak, lost in thought" (p. 1).

In contrast, and consonant with the activity theory framework in which her analysis is grounded, Scribner takes the unit of analysis to be purposive interactions of the person and her/his social and material world. The basic tenets of activity theory need no exposition in this volume, of course. The important point to note, however, is that Scribner (e.g., 1987, 1988) seeks to "concretize and elaborate activity theory constructs." She notes that the fit between activity theory and data is not a close one, and states: "Activity theory is not in itself a theory of cognition. It seems appropriate to consider it, rather, as a metatheory, offering certain basic categories and principles for theory construction in the various fields of psychology" (1988, pp. 10–11).

Scribner's analytic style is jointly guided by preserving the integrity of the phenomenon and providing precision in articulation. Far from rejecting the conceptual apparatus of cognitive science, Sylvia Scribner, after noting the limitations and ontological misconceptions of that framework, selectively utilizes some of its analytic tools, adapted at the service of her broader descriptive and theoretical aims. Thus, the analysis of thought processes is fine-grained, as is typical of a cognitive theory, but it rejects the solipsistic pitfalls of the cognitive approach and describes thought processes as components of complex action systems.

The preceding considerations, while not directly focused on the "abstract" and "concrete" constructs of concern to us here, are important to our discussion, as Scribner's theoretical approach represents an integration of two ostensibly conflicting conceptual frameworks. Whereas Ilyenkov's views (1977, 1982) and the cognitive theories discussed in the preceding section are two separate developments, historically and conceptually disjoint, Scribner's ideas embody a synthesis of both traditions. Thus, her examination of abstract and concrete forms of knowledge, to which I turn shortly, takes on a particular interest.

Though Scribner's perspective on mind in society is broad ranging, in the context of the present discussion I will focus specifically on her analysis of thinking at work, which interestingly pertains to a number of the issues discussed so far.

Sylvia Scribner's research program focused on practical thinking as a "natural kind" of thinking involving operations organized as a purposive system, and its empirical base involves naturally occurring work tasks, embedded in social and material structures and culturally defined practices. She problematized, however, the dichotomous distinction between practical and theoretical modes of thought and examined the complex issues involved in this distinction and in the relation between the two modes of thought in a number of writings (e.g., Scribner 1984a, 1985). A full consideration of these issues is beyond the scope of this discussion, but one aspect of Scribner's distinction is of central relevance to us. While the distinction she draws between practical and theoretical thinking is functional rather than mentalistic and is grounded in the purpose of thinking, it does carry some representational implications, if only implicitly. By its very requirement of compartmentalizing knowledge and yielding streamlined self-contained formulations, theoretical (or formal) thinking, in contrast to practical thinking, severs access to concrete forms of knowledge. It is precisely on those grounds that Harman (1986), from an entirely different framework, argued against the relevance of logic to a theory of reasoning. It is also on those grounds that Ilyenkov (1982) was doubtful about theoretical understanding based on abstract universal laws.

Three interrelated aspects of Scribner's rich analysis have a particular bearing on the present discussion, as they point in various ways to the fundamental importance of the concrete in thought. First, thinking is linked theoretically to action in the world, and, importantly, is seen as "an aspect of concrete activities" (Scribner 1988, p. 3). Thus, thinking and doing are integrated and analytically continuous; thinking is no longer a mental event ontologically separate from action, but rather is grounded in concrete activities. This conceptualization of thinking has important correlates. Scribner rejects the division between internal and external processes, seeing it as a false dichotomy within a functional system analysis of action. On that analysis, the system is conceptualized as the action unit as a whole, including both internal and external operations (Scribner 1987, p. 3). The system also includes the objects of those operations, a point to which I return shortly.

Scribner makes the stronger and more specific claim that mental and manual operations are functionally equivalent. On the basis of her well-known analysis of product assembly work and other tasks, she concludes that, for that particular action system, execution has its mental as well as manual components, and that mental and manual processes can substitute for each other (1988, p. 9). Relatedly, concrete objects can become symbols in their own right, subserving mental rather than manual operations within the same system.

Thus, she notes, "With changing circumstances, different means are brought to bear in the service of an invariant goal. Variation in constituent operations involves, among other things, displacement of some external motor operations (moving milk cartons) by visual search and inner computational or estimation procedures. These inner processes are not interiorized, abbreviated forms of the outer operations they replace. Assemblers do not imagine they pick cartons out of a case. Inner operations involve use of a socially constructed symbol system in arithmetic" (1987, p. 7).

A second, crucial aspect of the theory is that the environment is fully incorporated into the problem solving system. Rather than being a context extraneous to the task and modulating some of its component processes, the environment is constitutive of practical intellectual activities. Furthermore, this occurs through an active "exploitation of the environment" by the problem solver. Properties of the environment assume a functional role only through the initiative of the problem solver and are actively recruited (Scribner 1984b), a constructionist assumption that, while peripheral to our present focus, is critical within the theory.

Central to our concerns, Scribner stresses that the concept of the environment germane to practical problem solving is not merely a physicalist notion, and that "environment" includes not only the physical environment but also "all social, symbolic and material resources outside the head of the individual problem-solver" (Scribner 1985). This broad view interestingly resonates with Ilyenkov's view (1982) on the epistemological primacy of concrete concepts, where concreteness is defined not by the modality of apprehension or by the physical nature of the referent, but by the dialectic property of integrating the diverse aspects of a phenomenon. It may be recalled that, in discussing Barwise's ideas on situated inferences, I pointed out that the context, though incorporated into the primitive of the theory (the situation), was local and circumscribed. I tentatively attributed this feature to the fact that Barwise's theory, despite its situated foundation, derives from the cognitive tradition and that extensions of a theoretical framework always retain their lineage of origin. Scribner's analysis, by contrast, is grounded in the metatheoretical basis of activity theory, supplemented selectively by some cognitive constructs. The context in which problem solving activity is embedded is broad, complex, and constitutive of the activity.

Third, and most significantly, expertise in practical thinking is described as mastery of the concrete. That is, the development of practical expertise entails adapting general problem solving skills and general knowledge through "assimilation of specific knowledge about the objects and symbols the setting affords, and the actions (including cognitive actions) that work tasks require" (Scribner 1984b) and flexible adaptation to the concrete (Scribner 1984a). Thus, the concrete is defined again as that which represents the phenomenon (the task) in its full specificity, including not only physical aspects but symbols as well. It is the nature of the knowledge, not the modality of apprehension, that defines concreteness. In fact, Scribner (1988) notes that in the course of expertise, "the head replaces the hand." This conception is clearly congruous with Ilyenkov's analysis, with which Sylvia Scribner had strong intellectual affinities. Importantly, mastery of the concrete does not dislodge abstraction. Rather, abstraction is a reciprocal process that also develops in the course of expertise, in the form of symbolization and abstract mental representations (Scribner 1984b, p. 40). Thus, the relation between the abstract and the concrete is dialectical, not one of opposition.

Sylvia Scribner's theoretical strategy extended these ideas. Her aim was to describe work tasks and processes in their full particularity while also formulating general features of thinking at work (1984, 1988). She writes: "We are interested, not in whether particulars about practical tasks generalize, but whether we can find general characteristics across a wide range of particular tasks" (Scribner 1988, p. 11). This strategy can be contrasted with the style of description and theorizing dominant in cognitive science, which aims at abstracting away from particularities in the service of abstract structures and general processes. On Scribner's view, by contrast, theoretical generality is to be obtained while retaining the full contextual specificity of the description and preserving the integrity of the concrete phenomenon.

Notes

1. Marx's own terminology, also quoted by Ilyenkov, uses "man" rather than "human being". The latter term is used here to avoid limiting this theoretical analysis to only half of humanity.
2. There may be a misleading surface similarity between this description and Wittgenstein's notion of family resemblance. The two notions, however, differ fundamentally, in that family resemblance provides a noncontextual ground for a concept, based on overlapping sets of (abstract) features. In contrast, crucially, a concrete universal concept is contextually specific in that each particular instance remains fully embedded in its context.
3. Ilyenkov's epistemology is, furthermore, realist: concepts, including logical relations, reflect reality rather than being, for instance, derived from cognitive or linguistic constructions (1982, p. 77), consistent with a dialectical materialist framework in which thought itself is viewed as a reflection of reality.
4. A stronger version of the "formal" assumption is represented by positions which do defend the cognitive relevance of standard logic on conceptual and metatheoretical grounds and which, roughly speaking, conceptualize behavioral deviations from this standard as performance errors (e.g., Cohen 1981, Macnamara 1986).
5. I will use "concrete" in quotations marks throughout to reflect the fact that mental representations cannot, literally, be concrete, nor can their referents in most cases, as even our pragmatic knowledge of certain situations involves abstracting and generalizing over specific experiences.
6. By this, Barwise refers to Fodor's (e.g., 1975, 1985) claim that all thought is formal.

References

Barwise, J. (1981). Scenes and other situations. *Journal of Philosophy, 78*, 369–397.

Barwise, J. (1989). *The situation in logic.* Stanford, CA: CSLI.

Barwise, J., & Perry, J. (1983). *Situations and attitudes.* Cambridge, MA: MIT Press.

Braine, M. D. S. (1978). On the relation between the natural logic of reasoning and standard logic. *Psychological Review, 85*, 1–21.

Braine, M. D. S., & O'Brien, D. (1991). A theory of *if*: A lexical entry, reasoning program, and pragmatic principles. *Psychological Review, 98*, 182–203.

Cheng, P. W., & Holyoak, K. J. (1985). Pragmatic reasoning schemas. *Cognitive Psychology, 17*, 391–416.

Cheng, P. W., Holyoak, K. J., Nisbett, R. E., & Oliver, L. M. (1986). Pragmatic versus syntactic approaches to training deductive reasoning. *Cognitive Psychology, 18*, 293–328.

Cheng, P. W., & Nisbett, R. E. (1993). Pragmatic constraints on causal deduction. In R. E. Nisbett (Ed.), pp. 201–227. *Rules for reasoning*, Hillsdale, NJ: Erlbaum.

Clement, C. A., & Falmagne, R. J. (1986). Logical reasoning, world knowledge, and mental imagery: Interconnections in cognitive processes. *Memory & Cognition, 14*, 299–307.

Cohen, J. L. (1981). Can human irrationality be experimentally demonstrated? *Behavioral and Brain Sciences, 4*(3), 317–370.

Cox, J. R., & Griggs, R. A. (1982). The effect of experience on performance in Wason's selection task. *Memory and Cognition, 10*, 496–502.

Evans, J. StB. T. (1982). *The psychology of deductive reasoning*. London: Routledge.

Evans, J. StB. T. (1989). *Bias in human reasoning: Causes and consequences*. Hillsdale, NJ: Erlbaum

Falmagne, R. Joffe. (1989). *Formal and nonformal aspects of deduction*. Paper presented at the Annual Meeting of the Society for Philosophy and Psychology, Tucson, AZ.

Falmagne, R. Joffe. (1990a). *Situations, statements and logical relations*. Paper presented at the Twentieth Anniversary Symposium of the Jean Piaget Society (Society for the Study of Knowledge and Development), Philadelphia, PA.

Falmagne, R. Joffe. (1990b). Language and the acquisition of logical knowledge. In W. Overton (Ed.), *Reasoning, necessity and logic: Developmental perspectives*. Hillsdale, NJ: Erlbaum.

Falmagne, R. Joffe, & Gonsalves, J. (1995). Deductive inference. *Annual Review of Psychology, 46*, 525–559.

Fodor, J. A. (1975). *The language of thought*. Cambridge, MA: MIT Press.

Fodor, J. A. (1985). Situations and representations. *Linguistics and Philosophy, 8*, 13–22.

Gentzen, G. (1969). Investigations into logical deduction. In M. E. Szabo (Ed. & trans.), *The collected papers of Gerhard Gentzen*. Amsterdam: North-Holland. (Original published by 1935).

Haack, S. (1978). *Philosophy of logics*. Cambridge, UK: Cambridge University Press.

Harman. G. (1986). *Change in view: Principles of reasoning*. Cambridge, MA: Bradford Books.

Ilyenkov, E.V. (1977). *Dialectical logic*. Moscow: Progress Publishers. (Original Russian edition, 1974).

Ilyenkov, E. V. (1982). *The dialectics of the abstract and the concrete in Marx's Capital*. Moscow: Progress Publishers. (Original Russian edition, 1960).

Johnson-Laird, P. N. (1983). *Mental models*. Cambridge, MA: Harvard University Press.

Johnson-Laird, P. N., & Byrne, R. M. J. (1991). *Deduction*. Hillsdale, NJ: Erlbaum.

Macnamara, J. (1986). *A border dispute: The place of logic in psychology*. Cambridge, MA: Bradford Books.

Nelson, K. (1985). *Making sense: The acquisition of shared meaning*. New York: Academic Press.

Nelson, K. (Ed.). (1986). *Event knowledge: Structure and function in development*. Hillsdale, NJ: Erlbaum.

Osherson, D. N. (1975). Logic and models of logical thinking. In R. J. Falmagne (Ed.), *Reasoning: Representation and process in children and adults*. Hillsdale, NJ: Erlbaum.

Pollard, P. (1982). Human reasoning: Some possible effects of availability. *Cognition, 12*, 65–96.

Quine, W. V. O. (1953). Two dogmas of empiricism. In *From a logical point of view*. New York: Harper Torchbooks.

Quine, W. V. O. (1970). *Philosophy of logic*. Englewood Cliffs, NJ: Prentice-Hall.

Scribner, S. (1984a). Studying working intelligence. In J. Lave and B. Rogoff (Eds.), *Everyday cognition: Its development in social context*, pp. 9–40. Cambridge, MA: Harvard University Press.

Scribner, S. (1984b). Toward a model of practical thinking at work. *Quarterly Newsletter of the Laboratory of Comparative Human Cognition*, special issue on Cognitive Studies of Work (S. Scribner, Guest Editor), 6(1–2), pp. 37–42.

Scribner, S. (1985). Thinking in action: Some characteristics of practical thought. In R. J. Sternberg and R. K. Wagner (Eds.), *Practical intelligence: Origins and competence in the everyday world*. New York: Cambridge University Press.

Scribner, S. (1987). Mental and manual work: An activity theory orientation. *Proceedings of the First International Congress on Activity Theory*, Berlin, Germany.

Scribner, S. (1988). *Head and hand: An action approach to thinking*. Occasional Paper no. 3, National Center on Education and Employment, New York, NY. First prepared for oral presentation at the Eastern Psychological Association Annual meeting, Arlington, VA, 1987.

Strawson, P. F. (1952). *Introduction to logical theory*. New York: Methuen.

Strawson, P. F. (1971). *Logico-linguistic papers*. New York: Methuen.

Wiser, M. (In press). Use of history of science to understand and remedy student misconceptions about heat and temperature. In D. N. Perkins, J. L. Schwartz, M. M. West, & M. S. Wiske (Eds.), *Teaching for understanding in the age of technology*. Cary, NC: Oxford University Press.

10 From spontaneous to scientific concepts: Continuities and discontinuities from childhood to adulthood

Katherine Nelson

Conceptual change, a topic of considerable current interest in both developmental and general cognitive psychology, is important to issues in education, knowledge organization, and cognitive development. In this chapter Vygotsky's (1934/1986) ideas about the shift from "spontaneous" to "scientific" concepts are considered in the context of a long-standing issue of conceptual change – the establishment of hierarchical inclusive taxonomic structures in early to mid-childhood – and are related to other specific proposals and problems that have been raised in the recent literature with respect to both developmental change in childhood and conceptual change throughout the lifespan.

Spontaneous and scientific concepts

The problem of conceptual change in childhood from spontaneous to scientific concepts was a central topic of Vygotsky's *Thought and Language*. He hypothesized "two different paths in the development of two different forms of reasoning." In scientific thinking "the primary role is played by *initial verbal definition*, which being applied systematically, gradually comes down to concrete phenomena." In contrast, "the development of spontaneous concepts knows no systematicity and goes from the phenomena upward toward generalization" (Vygotsky 1986, p. 148). In this description his concern was less with scientific thinking than with the acquisition of scientific concepts, very broadly conceived, in contrast to spontaneous concepts formulated by the individual child. Note especially here that Vygotsky assumed that spontaneous concepts were not systematically organized. His idea of systematicity (to be explicated in later sections) rested primarily on the establishment of hierarchical taxonomies.

229

As implied in the statement just quoted, the difference between spontaneous and scientific concepts for Vygotsky was an important aspect of the language-thought relation. He summed up the issue as follows:

The two processes – the development of spontaneous and of nonspontaneous concepts – are related and constantly influence each other. They are parts of a single process: the development of concept formation, which is affected by varying external and internal conditions but is essentially a unitary process, not a conflict of antagonistic, mutually exclusive forms of thinking. (1986, p.157)

For Vygotsky concepts are developed as word meanings, in response to words.[1] Concepts are dynamic; they evolve as an understanding of words and their meanings increases. The move from spontaneous concepts to scientific concepts rests essentially on language, concepts of either kind being the equivalent of word meanings for the individual. The relation of spontaneous concepts and scientific concepts constitutes a whole dynamic interrelated system. The relation is the same throughout life whenever two such systems are constituted, regardless of the cognitive status of the individual: Vygotsky recognized both endogenous stages of cognitive development and generality of process across stages. In his view the most important characteristics of mature thought were (1) generality and (2) systematicity, and he held that these characteristics were absent from the concepts of preschool children. This is the point of greatest contrast with contemporary understanding of young children's thought.

Note that the move from spontaneous to scientific concepts is not the same move as that from "natural" to "sociohistorical" forms of thought. Vygotsky delineated the development of thought and speech in both phylogenesis and ontogenesis. His conclusions from the consideration of the then-available chimpanzee studies are well known: "Thought and speech have different genetic roots" (1986, p. 79). And his strongest claim: "[Human t]hought development is determined by language, i.e., by the linguistic tools of thought and by the sociocultural experience of the child" (1986, p. 94).

It may thus be seen that there are two evolutions of intelligence in Vygotsky's theory: from natural to sociohistorical and from spontaneous to scientific.[2] The latter progression takes place wholly within the sociohistorical phase. The "natural" line of development did not, for Vygotsky, extend to the child's acquisition of word meanings and concepts. Rather, the child's spontaneous concepts, as all development within the sociocultural line, arose in response to external verbalizations.[3] The problem raised by Vygotsky's theory of conceptual development based on the contrast between spontaneous and scientific concepts is essentially the problem of integrating spontaneously developed conceptual knowledge with "scientific" or "theoretical" cultural systems mediated through language. The problem is simply this: How to reconcile individually and informally – often implicitly – constructed knowledge systems with culturally derived, formally organized, explicit systems of knowledge, when the two incorporate different concepts and conceptual relations but refer to the same domain of knowledge. The thesis of this chapter is that the problem in its essential form is pervasive from the beginning of the child's acquisition of language; that the language that the child learns initially implicitly incorporates cultural knowledge systems that are only partially and imperfectly represented – and in important cases not represented at all – in the child's prelinguistic experientially based knowledge system.

Hierarchical categories

The hallmark of scientific categories for Vygotsky was their organization in terms of formal hierarchically organized systems, such as taxonomic categories. That young children treat hierarchical taxonomic categories of objects differently than do older children and adults has been the topic of much research and theorizing over the years. Inhelder and Piaget (1958) set forth the proposition that in order to understand such structures as "all the flowers" and "some of the flowers" correctly, children must come to understand the logical class inclusion relation implied in $A + A' = B$. They must understand that B is necessarily greater than or equal to both A and A'. Inhelder and Piaget argued that younger children did not command the necessary logic of classes and therefore failed to understand inclusion relations.

A great deal of research has proceeded from this and related perspectives. Other research has suggested that children do understand logical quantitative and inclusion relations at a younger age than Inhelder and Piaget found (Smith 1979), while still others indicate that younger children understand hierarchical relations not as inclusion structures but as part-wholes (see Markman [1989] for a discussion of this and related research).

Rosch and her colleagues (Rosch, Mervis, Gray, Johnson, & Boyes-Braem 1976) claimed that young children well understood categorical relations for what they called "basic level categories" (e.g, dog or hat), but had difficulty with superordinate level categories (e.g., animal or clothes). They proposed that the logic of categorization was not missing from young children's thought, but that the structure of higher-order categories was more difficult because instances within them displayed less overall similarity, particularly in shape and function. Subsequent research, however, has demonstrated that under some circumstances even very young children (less than 2 years) will recognize similarity relations among members of superordinate categories (Bauer & Mandler 1989). Mandler (1992) has claimed that children of 1 year or less possess "global" categories that are in some way equivalent to superordinate categories. For example, children this young will tend to group (in action, by touching) "animal" items and distinguish them thereby from other categories such as "vehicles."

The research, however, leaves open the basic issues raised by both Piaget and Vygotsky. Are global categories (recognizing similarities among diverse members) equivalent to superordinate categories (grouping into subclasses and subclasses into higher classes)? Is grouping in action a demonstration of understanding abstract hierarchical inclusion relations? Hierarchical categorization of the type realized as superordinate and subordinate categories – or in semantic terms, in the hyponymic relation – is an abstract relation of asymmetrical inclusion (the "isa" relation – e.g., "a dog is a animal") that can only be realized in a symbolic system such as natural language. Grouping in action can indicate the recognition of similarity but not inclusion. This characterization implies that the research findings with young children, especially prelinguistic infants, have a different meaning.

It is clear that young children see similarity relations of different kinds in the real world, and that they will demonstrate their perceptions through actions on objects. Indeed it goes without saying that young children must be capable of categorizing items in the world. The experimental evidence has verified this for us, but the proposition follows necessarily from what is commonly known about development in infancy and early childhood. Children must be able to categorize in order to learn the language, as Brown pointed out decades ago (Brown 1958). But do these categorization abilities indicate that infants and young children generally organize knowledge in terms of category hierarchies? If so, what is the basis for their formation of higher-order hierarchically organized categories? And how are they related to the categories that adults form in the same domains?

The answer advanced here is that young children naturally form concepts and categories on the basis of their experience with items in real-world activities. Thus items will be conceptualized because of their salient functions within the child's activities. This conceptualization process forms a sufficient basis for the child to acquire words to name all of the items conceptualized within his or her world (Nelson 1974, 1985). As Vygotsky asserted, because the reference of object names overlaps with the reference attributed to those names by adults, young children and adults can use the same words to talk about the same things in their shared world even though their understanding of those things – their concepts of them – may differ. It should be noted that even at this early point the child's conceptualizations, albeit they are individually constructed, are of the cultural world – its artifacts, its social relations, as well as the natural kinds that inhabit it.

The problem of categorization then arises not with concrete items that the child interacts with and the words referring to them, but with words that denote superordinate categories. Because superordinate categories do not exist as such in the real world, but only in the language used to talk about them, the child cannot have a prelinguistic concept that is the equivalent of the adult superordinate concept. The child's problem then is to find a way to form word meanings for superordinate classes that map the adult meaning system appropriately.

Although it is claimed that the young child does not have appropriate meanings for superordinate categories, there is ample evidence that children can use some of these category names in appropriate ways in some situations. What is the basis for this use? What system of categorization is the child using that enables some overlap with the adult use?

Slot-filler categories

The proposal that has emerged from our research is based on the organization of the child's initial conceptualization system, which is held to be primarily in terms of event representations (ERs). The argument here is that the younger child's concepts are not "unsystematic" as Vygotsky claimed, but that the "natural" prelinguistic representational system is one based on understanding events in which social actors and asocial objects take part (Nelson & Gruendel 1981; Nelson 1986). Familiar routine events are schematized in the child's knowledge representational system as scripts, with boundaries, sequences of actions, designated actors, and objects ("props" in script language; see Schank & Abelson 1977).

ERs may include sets of possible alternative actors, actions, and objects that may play the same role or fill the same function on different occasions. For example, in the child's lunch ER, there may be two possible providers, mother or father, and many possible alternative foods (although some children may define only one or a few possible foods). The possible alternative foods might include, for example, peanut butter or cheese sandwich, scrambled egg or cottage cheese, apple or banana, milk or juice. On any given occasion one or more of these might appear to fill the "lunch food slot." These alternative possibilities are designated lunch food *slot-fillers.*

Slot-fillers of this kind form a higher-order category, a category that subsumes basic level object sets; for example, the set of all cheese sandwiches, of all apples, and so on. We can speak then of *slot-filler categories* that are specific to a particular event. Although slot-filler categories are formed on the basis of individual experience, they are constituted in part by the cultural categories of a particular group. Lunch foods vary across families, cultural groups within a society, and societies as a whole. Even the notion of lunch or a meal is variable to this degree. But whatever the experience of foods in specific settings might be for different children, the proposal is that that experience forms the basis for these higher-order slot-filler categories.

There may of course be more than one experiential basis for categorization; for example, Markman (1981) has identified part-whole "collections" such as "family" and "forest" as the primary way in which children understand superordinate terms. Collections are based on the child's perception that all these things together make a coherent group, just as the parts of the body make a coherent whole. Such part-whole structures might explain the child's use of terms like "tool" and "furniture" for example, on the basis of their spatial configuration as a group.

Evidence that children form slot-filler categories comes from a number of studies of preschool children that have verified that slot-filler categories have psychological reality for children in ways that more general abstract taxonomic categories of familiar superordinate terms such as food, clothes, and animals do not. These studies include list recall (Lucariello & Nelson 1985, Rosner & Smick 1989), word association, category production, and forced picture choice (Lucariello, Kyratzis & Nelson 1992, Sell 1992). Moreover, these findings have replicated across children from different cultures (inner-city children in the United States, Korean children in South Korea) for both category production and list recall (Nelson & Nelson 1990, Yu & Nelson 1993). Young children produce items from single events, remember items presented in lists from single events, and choose items from single events in preference to those occurring in different events, all indications of event-based slot-filler categories. Moreover, young schoolchildren (7-year-olds) and adults also cluster items in terms of events when asked to produce category members (Lucariello et al. 1992), although they include and merge more than one script-based category in their productions.

These studies have indicated that when children learn a word like "food" or "clothes" they attach an event-restricted meaning to it. In other words, they interpret the word, not in terms of its conventional cultural system sense, but in terms of their own presemantic system sense. The problem then is to coordinate and integrate the individual conceptual system with the culturally determined semantic one. Research has also shown that parents often provide the linking mechanisms that enable young children to make the connections between their own organizations of objects and events in the world and those that are culturally incorporated into the semantic system of a particular language. Lucariello and Nelson (1986) showed how mothers often provided higher-level terms in situations where children knew the possible alternatives and could respond with a slot-filler. For example, at lunch time mothers asked questions like, "what *kind of juice* do you want?" or "do you want cottage *cheese* or regular *cheese*?" In getting dressed they might say, "Let's *put on* your *clothes* now," and follow with "we have to *put on* your shirt." "Put on" in these constructions provides the link between the superordinate "clothes" and the subordinate members of the clothes category.

A striking example of the kind of parental formatting of cultural categories that enables the child to map her own representations onto those of the adult's comes from transcripts of prebed talk between father and daughter Emily (Nelson 1989). From when Emily was about 2 to 2½ years her father was in the habit of talking with her about what she would have for breakfast after waking up the following morning, as the following excerpts illustrate. The first is from when she was not quite 2 years:

E: What we have on breakfast day? What we have?

F: What will we have for breakfast? You know, tomorrow morning, you're going to have yogurt, and bananas and wheat germ, like mommy gave you this morning, remember that? Instead of an egg tomorrow we're going to have yogurt and bananas and wheat germ . . .

Later, Emily entered into the dialog more actively, specifying what she wanted, as in the following dialog from almost 27 months:

F: We'll get up . . . and we'll go down and have breakfast, you can choose what type of egg you want.

E: I want . . . a boiled egg.

F: Okay. And you can choose what type of cereal you want, you can have either shredded wheat or cheerios.

E: Shredded *wheat!*

A month and a half later, she entered her own suggestions:

E: And, so now tell me about today!

F: Well, today you had a Tanta day also.

E: I want . . . yogurt.

F: And you want yogurt. I know and I think I'll have some raspberries for you tomorrow.

E: And I . . . cereal!

F: Today you had strawberries, tomorrow I think you'll have raspberries.

E: Cereal! Cereal!

F: You'll have cereal? Okay. Cereal and yogurt? You want bananas in yogurt, or raspberries in your cereal?

E: Yeah.

F: Okay. That'll be good.

E: And strawberries in my cereal.

In these discussions, Emily's breakfast food category was highly constrained to the particular situation and did not stray from the alternatives specified by this particular family (e.g. yogurt, cereal, fruit, eggs). It did not wander into domains of pizza, hamburgers, or other items appropriate for dinner. That is, her category of alternatives for breakfast was specific to that event – it constituted a slot-filler category of breakfast foods.

These excerpts provide evidence that at 2 years the language that simultaneously expresses and shapes the child's representations is not the abstract language of categories but the concrete language of experience. To be sure, her language includes category terms, but these are particularized to specific experience. The coordination of the child's language of categories with that of the adult takes place in these everyday activities and the discourse surrounding them. The child's ERs reflect the systematization of her experience in the world, but this system is not the system that organizes the relevant cultural categories. The conventional cultural system is displayed to the child, not systematically as in a school text, but in bits and pieces through adult–child talk, as in the previous examples. The process may be schematized as illustrated in Figure 10.1, revealing some of the problems that may arise.

This figure indicates that the child is acquiring a partial system mediated by both the adult's partial system and by the child's conceptual system. The important points to be noted are (1) that the adult's representation is an incomplete structure in comparison with the cultural system, (2) that its display in speech is a partial and disconnected representation of the adult system as a whole, and (3) that what the child gets from this display is an incomplete, error-prone construction based on both prior (nonhierarchical) concepts and language use. The adult's talk about a category displays certain relations (e.g., that cereal and yogurt are foods for breakfast). The adult language implies a hierarchical relation, and provides a few of the submembers in the hierarchy. The child may recognize these as related members within her event scheme, and form a bond between them, as shown. But event talk about the category is inevitably fragmentary and unsystematic, as the example from Emily and her father showed, sampling bits and pieces from the cultural construction of the category such that the child's mapping may be distorted and full of holes, as indicated in the bottom part of the figure.

Integrating slot-filler and semantic categories

Achievement of an abstract category language depends upon the further development of a differentiated – or abstracted – level of seman-

Cultural System (Langue)

Adult Representational System

Adult Presentation (Parole)

Child Semantic Representation

Child Conceptual System

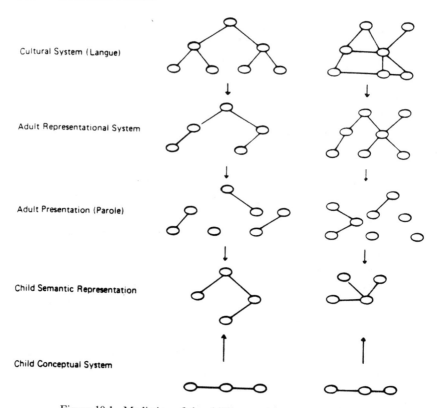

Figure 10.1. Mediation of the child's semantic system by the adult's partial representation and presentation system and the child's conceptual system. Reprinted from Nelson (1985) with permission of the publisher.

tic representation in which linguistic terms and their related concepts are not embedded in the experientially derived event representation system but constitute a semantic system of abstract relations. The development of that level makes possible the representation of a true semantic hierarchy – a taxonomy that is based on hierarchical inclusion relations and not simply on combinations of event-contexted slots. This level, however, is as yet beyond the grasp of even a precocious 2 ½-year-old. Its construction, in collaboration with adult informants, is a major development of the preschool and early school years.

In particular, the child must come to generalize its higher-order categories beyond the single events from which they are constructed, combining for example, the food category across both breakfast and lunch, and other possible occasions of eating all possible foods. Generalization of familiar everyday categories is accomplished during the preschool to early school years. It seems highly probable that it is the linguistic link provided by the superordinate category term (e.g., "food" or "clothes") in conjunction often with direct adult instruction that enables the child to make this generalization.

Beyond this generalization the abstract inclusion relations must be recognized and incorporated into a semantic system. The inclusion relation appears to be much more difficult and to be achieved through direct instruction in school (Watson 1985). Kyratzis (1989) demonstrated that 5-year-olds could generalize a novel category on the basis of common function in an event, but that not until first grade (6 to 7 years) were children able to use inclusion information about a category to construct it in accord with conventional terminology.

We can think of the inclusion relation as a scientific concept (in Vygotsky's terms) that has infiltrated the common language to a greater or lesser extent. Children can learn the superordinate language that incorporates the inclusion relation without yet understanding its implications (e.g., the transitivity and asymmetry of its relations). The question that has not yet been adequately addressed is how children may come to understand these relations, and how the instructional efforts in school advance this understanding. The issue here is the interrelation between conceptual reorganization and restructuring in the face of structures that are simply displayed in cultural talk (as in Figure 10.1) and the explicit instruction that lays out in systematic form how scientific systems (e.g., taxonomic categories) are structured. This kind of restructuring on the basis of both implicit and explicit demands from the culture is likely to be characteristic of a great deal of knowledge acquisition and conceptual change from early childhood and throughout life.

In a study that attempted to examine the results of the integration of event-based categories with scientific instruction in school Panofsky, John-Steiner, and Blackwell (1990) used categorization tasks with fifth-grade children who had completed a course of study in the scientific classification of plants and animals. They found that even after school instruction children of this age relied on a mixture of event-based and formal taxonomic knowledge for forming groups of items. This suggests that in a familiar domain such as animals, scientific instruction may result in intermediate systems, combining aspects of both systems, or in dual representation systems, similar to what we found with adult categories of food and clothes (Lucariello et al. 1992).

The conclusion that emerges from these studies is that the process and problems that are involved in coordinating spontaneous conceptual systems based on experience in the real cultural world with the categories that the culture displays through language in discourse are the same whenever the individual encounters a new mode of knowledge organization. It is characteristic of the process that dual representations of the domain emerge and coexist, each applicable to a specific context. For example, educated adults organize their food categories in terms of meals, as do young children, but adults also can give abstract explications of the concept food, can produce categorizations based on more abstract principles, such as types of nutrients, and can produce other pragmatically based subcategories reflecting, for example, the organization of supermarkets. So long as they remain useful in certain contexts the original organization will not disappear; rather it will be supplemented by the new.

This is not to say that there are no differences between conceptual change in early childhood and change in systems already constituted through linguistic means. Two fundamental shifts seem to be different in kind from later less radical change: the first, from prelinguistic to linguistically organized concepts, and the second from informal to formal (theoretical or scientific) systems. Although Vygotsky's discussion conveys the impression that it is only scientific concepts that represent the "cultural," whereas spontaneous concepts are products of the individual unfettered by cultural knowledge, this impression is misleading. The child's initial conceptual knowledge system derives from experience in culturally arranged activities and scenes; thus there is no sudden discontinuity in human development from the natural to the sociohistorical. Rather, there are a series of accommodations of the individual's organization of experientially derived knowledge to conventional knowledge systems as learning in and through language progresses. The accommodation process may be expected to follow similar paths throughout development, although the nature of both the prior and later systems may change dramatically from the first years of life to the stage of advanced education and theorizing. And as Vygotsky emphasized, the difference between the child's spontaneous concepts and systematic scientific concepts may be quite radical.

Conceptual change in adults and children

The previous section has explicated an important shift in conceptual systems from the first based on individual constructions derived from experience in the cultural world, accommodated to the categories of language used in that world, and subsequently reorganized to comply with the abstract categories and relations that language makes possible, including especially the inclusive hierarchical systems used both in folk systems and in scientific systems of thought. The domains identified in these studies are the basic everyday domains of food, clothes, and animals. To what extent is this process representative of conceptual change in more complex domains and at other points in development? In this section some research relevant to this question, and theories of change, are briefly considered.

An important example of conceptual change is found in Scribner's work on practical thinking in the workplace (Scribner 1986), contrasted with what she termed theoretical thinking. Her studies eventually led her and her students to the problem of the introduction of new technologies that incorporated new languages and new systems of organizing knowledge (Scribner 1990, and Scribner et al. 1992). In this research Scribner and her colleagues studied workers who had organized their production knowledge and working procedures in terms of concrete practices and found themselves having to master formal systems of conceptualizations that not only reorganized the workplace and the process of production, but required thinking and talking about it in different – formal – terms. Some of the studies that have emerged from the analysis of these problems have focused on the distribution of knowledge across the workplace and on the coexistence within individuals of different conceptual systems referring to the same domain of production, as indicated by the use of different "languages" in describing their work practices. This may be analogous to the move from informal language-based systems of concepts to more formal scientific systems.

Scribner's identification of efficient solutions that experienced workers achieved in everyday problem situations also raised the problem of coordinating these solutions with abstract characterizations of the same domains. This problem is analogous, I suggest, to that of the young child who has achieved control over everyday activities sufficient to act intelligently within them, including an understanding of sequencing, duration, and alternative possibilities, but who is faced with the more abstract characterization of these conceptualizations that are encapusulated in the language that adults use to talk about those activities; for example, use of the taxonomic category systems implicit in everyday language. To the extent that this is correct, many of the same processes are applicable to some of the problems in conceptual change in adults that are characteristic of the very young child just coming to master abstract language systems, regardless of the difference in developmental status.

A number of studies of domains such as biology, physics, and psychology and the changes within and between them have been published (e.g., Chi 1978, 1983; Keil 1979, 1989). Carey's (1985) influential work on scientific theory change as a model of conceptual change in childhood provides a challenge to the ideas outlined in the previous section, when they are advanced as reflective of conceptual change in general. Cognitive development in this view is conceived as a series of theory changes, requiring the reorganization of knowledge within a theory domain and the consequent redefinition of concepts in terms of new relations within the domain. Carey's models come from the history of science, such as the shift from an undifferentiated concept of heat and temperature to a differentiated one within a system of physical relations and laws.

The theory change conception appears related to the conceptual change problem that Vygotsky (1986) outlined in terms of spontaneous and scientific concepts, in that the existence of relevant concepts, using the same terms but different conceptual bases, is emphasized in both. However, Carey's model ignores the critical distinction that Vygotsky drew between spontaneous and scientific (and the analogous distinctions drawn here), and does not explicitly recognize the sociocultural/linguistic origin of either system. Indeed, no cognitive mechanism of change from one to the other is proposed beyond the vague notions of cognitive development and growth of (individual) knowledge within the domain.

All the current conceptions of conceptual change, including Carey's, rest on the assumption that the individual encountering a new more advanced, higher-order scientific body of knowledge has in place a pre-scientific conceptual system that applies to some of the same phenomena that the more advanced system does. But except for claims that children arrive in the world with naive theories (Carey 1985, Spelke 1991), there has been little concern for the origin of those prescientific systems. Obviously if we wish to understand the problem of conceptual change from spontaneous to scientific concepts it is necessary to understand both ends – the nature of spontaneous conceptual systems as well as scientific systems. It is too easy to label all of the young child's knowledge as "theoretical" and then discuss any change as the move from one theory to another.

Indeed, the attribution of theoretical knowledge to the young child is deeply misleading, I believe, in obscuring the differences between types of human knowledge systems and thus the problems faced in conceptual change. A scientific theory is a formal system; thus the analogy to theory change in science implies that both the earlier and the later systems have the characterisitics of a formal system, the most important of which for the present discussion are the following:

> A formal system is an internally consistent, closed system
> of relations between elements or concepts.
> It is culturally formulated and maintained and socially
> transmitted; it cannot be "discovered" from experience
> in the world.
> The system is represented in terms of rearrangeable,
> arbitrary signs that are culturally/socially created and maintained.[4]

Given these criteria, it is obvious that the preschool child is not in the possession of any formal system of knowledge, and thus the attribution of "theories" to the preschooler seems fundamentally wrong. Yet the attribution of systematic organization of knowledge of some type is surely right, even at this level of individual construction.

Chi (1992) has discussed the difference between theoretical change that requires reassignment of concepts to different ontological categories (e.g., from substance to process) which require abandonment of the old, and those that retain the same ontological categories, but require differentiating or redefinition within the category. An everyday example of the former type involves concepts of time (Nelson 1991). The prelinguistic child is cognizant of some aspects of time, including the sequence of actions and events and the duration of intervals between events. Thus time enters the cognitive system at this level as relations within ERs. However, to achieve understanding of conventional time concepts incorporated in languages such as English, the child must come to understand time as objectlike units – minutes, hours, days, weeks, months, and years. This is apparently a very difficult shift in thinking; many children do not achieve a well-founded notion of such everyday terms as "yesterday," "tomorrow," and "morning" until the age of 4 or 5 years.

But this is only the beginning. As Piaget's famous experiments have shown, children of 7 or 8 years must go beyond the idea of time as units and again see time as a relation or function between velocity and distance (Piaget 1971). In this connection, Carbery (1992) has demonstrated that children of 5 or 6 years are able to use a simple clock to measure time in units in order to construct accurately the relations of two vehicles moving at different speeds across the same distance. Piaget in contrast held that the latter "logical" knowledge was prerequisite to the former. Indeed, adults in our contemporary society hold several different conceptual systems relating to time, some of which conflict and compete but are applicable to different contexts (McGrath & Kelly 1986).

Conclusion: Three levels of conceptual development

At this point we can summarize the main points brought out in this discussion. First, as Vygotsky outlined, there are major differences in concepts at different developmental levels. However, the differences are not in terms of the onset of generality and systematicity as he thought, but in kinds of generality and of systems. Moreover, the spontaneous and scientific distinction doesn't quite capture the major changes involved. Rather, I would propose that there are two fundamental changes in conceptual systems: the first a shift in the child's thought from the spontaneous presemantic to the conventional "folk" semantic, which must precede a second shift from the "folk" system to the formal or scientific. What Vygotsky termed "spontaneous" actually seems to be characteristic of the second level, achieved through the first transition, the one outlined in the first section of this chapter in terms of hierarchical categories, involving the child's achievement of a system that coordinates the event-based primitive system with the system revealed through adult language use (see Figure 10.1).

The proposal is that within all basic domains of knowledge (those open to encounter by the independent individual) there are two progressions possible, from the individual to the folk/semantic and from the semantic to the scientific. There are thus three basic levels of knowledge organization characteristic of human thought. The first can be constructed by the individual on the basis of direct experience in the world without the mediation of language. But note that even at this level knowledge incorporates cultural systems in so far as these are directly encountered.[5] Even after the internalization of the semantics of one's language, this kind of direct event-based knowledge may be constructed and may be coordinated with informal discourse systems regarding specific contexts, as Scribner's practical knowledge studies demonstrated.

The semantic level of knowledge organization is a product of the language-using community. It abstracts from activities to provide a generalized organization of related knowledge. The "folk taxonomies" observed across the world in different cultures (Berlin 1978) are examples of this kind of knowledge structure, as are the general nonscientific practical taxonomies of our own English language, such as those of food, clothes, furniture, animals, and plants. As noted previously, time concepts are another domain where semantic systems present abstractions from activities. These are each systematically organized domains serving cultural purposes. An individual who has acquired knowledge at the level of the semantic organization of a domain has acquired the tools for viewing activities within a larger context of relationships. Food is not just what you eat at lunch, but anything edible by any organism. A day is not just a sequence of activities, but a unit in an organized temporal system that can be counted, divided, multiplied, and located within an abstract temporal space. But culturally organized knowledge of this kind tends to exist in an informal system that is conveyed to individuals partially through simple exposure to the concepts embedded in language use and partially through informal instruction, in school, workplace, or other contexts. It may result therefore in partial knowledge idiosyncratically organized, as Figure 10.1 implies.

The third level is that of the formally organized cultural system referred to as theoretical knowledge, as characterized previously. This level of knowledge is not accessible informally to the individual through simple exposure to discourse in the domain, but must be mastered as an abstract system. There are no doubt distinctions to be made within this level of knowledge systems, and significant, often radical, conceptual change takes place as one formal system displaces another in the domain, as Carey and Chi have both discussed.

There are commonalities and continuities of process in any conceptual change that reaches across a system organizing a domain of knowledge. But there are also substantial differences in the problems involved depending on the type of systematic knowledge involved in both the old and the new systems. One important difference is that noted by Vygotsky between moving from the abstract to the concrete or from the phenomena to generalizations of them; the one based on formal instruction, the other on informal learning processes. While similar structures and processes are observable throughout life, it is also true that different structures and processes may be involved in the construction of different knowledge organizations. One model cannot fit all cases of conceptual change, but we can hope to identify a set of processes that such changes involve, and try to facilitate movement from one level to another, while recognizing the utility and importance of different levels of organization in different contexts of activities.

Notes

1. This idea is most developed in Vygotsky's well-known studies of stages in the development of preconcepts in early childhood prior to the stage of true concepts, which is achieved only in early adolescence. The strong – and from a contemporary perspective, wrong – implication of Vygotsky's stance on the relation of concepts and words is that concepts do not exist prior to or independently of words.
2. These evolutions do not seem to be well integrated with his more familiar claims about private speech and the emergence of inner speech as verbal thinking. No doubt, given more time, he would have made these connections clearer.
3. The view that there is a strong break in human cognition involving the onset of verbal thought, and that verbal thought is not "natural," is at present quite unfashionable in either philosophy or psychology. Certainly Vygotsky's knowledge of primate thinking and communication was exceedingly limited by today's standards. But the attempt to connect evolutionary phylogenetic development with problems in ontogenetic development is currently being revived with more success and decidedly better data. It seems quite probable that at least some part of Vygotsky's position may receive support from these studies. (See Donald [1991] for some interesting evolutionary proposals that conform well with his position.)
4. Many people have written on the construction of formal systems, a topic that was central to the considerations of Scribner and her colleagues in their work on conceptual system change from practical to theoretical. The characteristics cited here were outlined in an unpublished 1989 paper by one of Scribner's students, Lia DiBello.
5. For an interesting account of the possibilities of this kind of individual construction by adults independent of language see "A Man without Words" (Schaller 1991),

describing the mental life of a deaf man never exposed to conventional language of any kind.

References

Bauer, P. J., & Mandler, J. M. (1989). Taxonomies and triads: Conceptual organization in one- to two-year-olds. *Cognitive Psychology, 21*, 156–184.

Berlin, G. (1978). Ethnobiological classification. In E. Rosch & B. B. Lloyd (Eds.), *Cognition and categorization*, pp. 9–26. Hillsdale, NJ: Erlbaum.

Brown, R. (1958). *Words and things*. New York: The Free Press of Glencoe.

Carbery, M. (1992). *The development of objective time: The integration of logical and cultural conceptual systems*. Unpublished Ph.D. dissertation, City University of New York Graduate Center.

Carey, S. (1985). *Conceptual change in childhood*. Cambridge, MA: MIT Press.

Chi, M. T. H. (1978). Knowledge structures and memory development. In R. S. Siegler (Ed.), *Children's thinking: What develops?* Hillsdale, NJ: Erlbaum.

Chi, M. T. H. (1992). Conceptual change within and across ontological categories: Examples from learning and discovery in science. In R. Giere (Ed.), *Cognitive models of science: Minnesota Studies in the Philosophy of Science*. Minneapolis: University of Minnesota Press.

Chi, M. T. H., & Koeske, R. D. (1983). Network representation of a child's dinosaur knowledge. *Developmental Psychology, 19*, 29–39.

Donald, M. (1991). *Origins of the modern mind*. Cambridge, MA: Harvard University Press.

Inhelder, B., & Piaget, J. (1958). *The growth of logical thinking from childhood to adolescence*. New York: Basic Books.

Keil, F. C. (1979). *Semantic and conceptual development: An ontological perspective*. Cambridge, MA: Harvard University Press.

Keil, F. C. (1989). *Concepts, word meanings, and cognitive development*. Cambridge, MA: MIT Press.

Kyratzis, A. (1989). *The role of language in superordinate category formation*. Unpublished Ph.D. dissertation, City University of New York Graduate Center.

Lucariello, J., Kyratzis, A., & Nelson, K. (1992). Taxonomic knowledge: What kind and when. *Child Development, 63*, 978–998.

Lucariello, J., & Nelson, K. (1985). Slot-filler categories as memory organizers for young children. *Developmental Psychology, 21*, 272–282.

Lucariello, J., & Nelson, K. (1986). Context effects on lexical specificity in maternal and child discourse. *Journal of Child Language, 13*, 507–522.

Mandler, J. M. (1992). How to build a baby II. *Psychological Review, 99*, 587–604.

Markman, E. M. (1981). Two different principles of conceptual organization. In M. Lamb & A. Brown (Eds.), *Advances in developmental psychology* (Vol. I). Hillsdale, NJ: Erlbaum.

McGrath, J. E., & Kelly, J. R. (1986). *Time and human interaction: Toward a social psychology of time*. New York: Guilford Press.

Nelson, K. (1974). Concept, word, and sentence: Interrelations in acquisition and development. *Psychological Review, 81,* 267–285.

Nelson, K. (1985). *Making sense: The acquisition of shared meaning.* New York: Academic Press.

Nelson, K. (1986). *Event knowledge: Structure and function in development.* Hillsdale, NJ: Erlbaum.

Nelson, K. (Ed.). (1989). *Narratives from the crib.* Cambridge, MA: Harvard University Press.

Nelson, K. (1991). The matter of time: Interdependencies between language and thought in development. In S. A. Gelman & J. P. Byrnes (Eds.), *Perspectives on language and cognition: Interrelations in development.* (New York: Cambridge University Press.

Nelson, K., & Gruendel, J. (1981). Generalized event representations: basic building blocks of cognitive development. In M. Lamb & A. Brown (Eds.), *Advances in Developmental Psychology* (Vol. 1). Hillsdale, N.J.: Erlbaum.

Nelson, K., & Nelson, A. J. (1990). Category production in response to script and category cues by kindergarten and second grade children. *Journal of Applied developmental psychology, 11,* 431–446.

Panofsky, C. P., John-Steiner, V., & Blackwell, P. J. (1990). The development of scientific concepts and discourse. In L. C. Moll (Ed.), *Vygotsky and education: Instructional applications of sociohistorical psychology.* Cambridge, UK: Cambridge University Press.

Piaget, J. (1971). *The child's conception of time.* New York: Ballantine.

Rosch, E., Mervis, C., Gray, W., Johnson, D., & Boyes-Braem, P. (1976). Basic objects in natural categories. *Cognitive Psychology, 8,* 382–439.

Rosner, S. R., & Smick, C. (1989). Cueing maintenance of slot-filler and taxonomic categories. Poster presented at Society for Research in Child Development meetings. Kansas City, MO.

Schaller, S. (1991). *A man without words.* New York: Summit Books.

Schank, R. C., & Abelson, R. P. (1977). *Scripts, plans, goals, and understanding.* Hillsdale, NJ: Erlbaum.

Scribner, S. (1986). Thinking in action: Some characteristics of practical thought. In R. J. Sternberg (Ed.), *Practical Intelligence,* pp. 13–30. New York: Wiley.

Scribner, S. (1990). The character of knowledge systems in the workplace from the perspective of activity theory. Paper presented at the Second International Congress for Research on Activity Theory. Lahti, Finland.

Scribner, S., DiBello, L., Kindred, J., & Zazanis, E. (1992). *Coordinating two knowledge systems: A case study.* City University of New York Graduate School, Laboratory for Cognitive Studies of Work.

Sell, M. A. (1992). The development of children's knowledge structures: Events, slots, and taxonomies. *Journal of Child Language, 19,* 659–676.

Smith, C. L. (1979). Children's understanding of natural language hierarchies. *Journal of Experimental Child Psychology, 27,* 437–458.

Spelke, E. S. (1991). Physical knowledge in infancy: Reflections on Piaget's theory. In S. Carey & R. Gelman (Eds.), *The epigenesis of mind: Essays on biology and cognition*, pp. 133–170. Hillsdale, NJ: Erlbaum.

Vygotsky, L. (1986). *Thought and language*. Cambridge, MA: MIT Press.

Watson, R. (1985). Toward a theory of definition. *Journal of Child Language*, *12*, 181–197.

Yu, Y., & Nelson, K. (1993). Slot-filler and conventional category organisation in young Korean children. *International Journal of Developmental Psychology*, *16*, 1–14.

11 The psychology of Japanese literacy: Expanding "the practice account"

Giyoo Hatano

In this chapter I will try to expand and enrich "a practice account of literacy" proposed by Scribner and Cole (1981), by applying it to the question of literacy in standard Japanese orthography. Scribner and Cole's account or framework conceptualizes literacy not as "simply knowing how to read and write a particular script" but as "applying this knowledge for specific purposes in specific contexts of use" (p. 236). It assumes that both how literacy is acquired and what cognitive consequences it has depend on a set of socially organized literacy practices in which people engage. I will examine issues related to Japanese literacy relying on this assumption. Although it is not possible to compare literates and nonliterates or the schooled and unschooled in Japan, I will discuss the role of a school in the acquisition of literacy, and also whether literacy has generalized effects on linguistic communication.

Scribner and Cole (1981) made a significant contribution to the field of culture and cognition, as most investigators in the field agree. Theoretically, their work stands as a monument in the history of our understanding of cognitive outcomes produced by everyday activity, alongside Cole, Gay, Glick, and Sharp (1971) and Rogoff and Lave (1984). Empirically, their book reports two rather surprising results: (1) the dissociability of literacy from schooling, and (2) the localized cognitive consequences of literacy. Unlike earlier investigators including Scribner (1968), Scribner and Cole stress that schooling and the acquisition of literacy not only should be distinguished conceptually but also may be separable in practice. Whereas earlier works assumed that literacy produced qualitative and generalized changes in individual thinking, their book

I would like to thank Drs. Laura Martin, Kayoko Inagaki, Keiko Kuhara-Kojima, and Michael Cole for their comments on earlier drafts of this chapter.

250

shows that literacies developed and used in different contexts tend to produce correspondingly differentiated patterns of cognitive competence. In other words, it indicates that repeated use of literacy skills produces more or less general, transferable cognitive skills that promote the practice, but that the effects of literacy on "general" thinking and problem solving are often negligible.

What we can learn from a single study, however, is necessarily limited. Literacy may be acquired without schooling, as Scribner and Cole demonstrate, but this is not always the case. As predicted from the practice account, whether the acquisition of literacy requires schooling or not depends primarily on how appealing and how easy it is to participate in major literacy practices. Participation depends heavily on technology and the knowledge involved in the practices: among other things, the nature of orthography (the type of scripts and how they represent spoken words). Thus another example of an extreme case – the case of Japanese literacy – will be informative. Different from the case of the Vai literacy, for which about 200 syllabaries (characters representing syllables) have to be learned, the literacy for the standard Japanese orthography requires learning several thousands of morphograms (characters representing morphemes) in addition to 71 syllabaries. It does not seem warranted to generalize from the Vai case to the Japanese case. After a brief description of Japanese orthographies and literacies, I will discuss how children are motivated to become literate in the standard orthography that imposes a heavy burden on beginners, and what roles a school seems to play therein.

As for literacy's cognitive effects, I am afraid that Scribner and Cole (1981) are concerned too much with, if not "misled" by, the Anglo-American intellectual tradition of viewing literacy as a potential mechanism for the development of logical thinking (Serpell & Hatano, in press). Although I would expect that their findings of the localized effects on thinking will be replicated for any literacy separated from schooling and used in a specialized context, this does not mean that it has no general cognitive consequences. I assume that cognitive skills developed through practicing literacy are generalizable in linguistic communication, but probably not to logical thinking for the following two reasons: (1) the practice of literacy is primarily not for thinking but for communication, and (2) even if modes of communication are internalized into modes of thinking, cognitive processes involved in literacy-based communication (e.g., understanding a text) are directed more to the satisfaction of multiple constraints rather than to rigorous inference of a logical nature.

Based on the practice account of literacy, I predict marked effects of literacy on modes of communication that apparently do not depend on the target script but that involve skills used in major literacy practices. More specifically, engaging in Japanese literacy practices repeatedly enables people to understand and effectively acquire knowledge from text in another orthography or text given aurally. I will present data confirming this line of reasoning in the second half of the chapter.

Japanese orthographies and literacies

There are, in fact, two orthographies in the Japanese language: Standard Japanese Orthography (SJO) and Children's Japanese Orthography (CJO). Whereas SJO sentences in newspapers, books, journals, and letters are written by using both *kanji* (morphograms originated in China and thus called Chinese characters) and hiragana (one of two kinds of *kana* syllabaries; characters representing syllables) in combination, CJO sentences in picture books and magazines for young children are written by using hiragana only. (In addition, katakana, for representing words of foreign origin and onomatopoeic expression, and Arabic numerals are also used, but infrequently.) When the target audience is younger grade-school children, a small number of kanji are added. Those kanji are usually accompanied by hiragana, which show their pronunciation. Figure 11.1 presents an SJO sentence and a CJO sentence, which are exactly the same when pronounced and identical in meaning.

Major literacy practices for CJO are reading children's books and recording simple information (e.g., the name of the owner, the day of a week, etc.). Children are almost always willing to participate in these practices, because they are either fun or significant, and it is not hard for them to do so because of the nature of the orthography. In contrast, typical SJO literacy practices include reading newspapers and magazines, enjoying literary works, reading professional or technical books and articles, and writing an elaborated document in ways educated people do. These practices are often not appealing to school-age children. Therefore, literacy in CJO, like the Vai literacy, may be acquired without schooling, and is almost always acquired in the lower grades of elemen-

(SJO)

スクリブナー博士はアフリカへ行き、ヴァイ族の人達の読み書きについて
さまざまな調査をした。

(CJO)

スクリブナーはかせは　アフリカへ　いき、ヴァイぞくの　ひとたちの
よみかきについて　さまざまな　ちょうさを　した。

(Meaning)
Dr. Scribner went to Africa and conducted many studies on Vai people's
literacies.

Figure 11.1. Japanese sentences written in Standard Japanese Orthography
(SJO) and Children's Japanese Orthography (CJO).

tary school at the latest. Its complete acquisition prior to schooling is not
unusual (e.g., National Language Research Institute of Japan 1972). In
contrast, literacy in SJO is mastered gradually through the elementary,
junior high, and high school years. Its acquisition requires, as will be
argued later, strong cultural pressure and systematic teaching.

Sentences in CJO are usually divided into segments by placing some
space before each "substantive" word, as shown in Figure 11.1. This is to
reduce the trial and error for segmentation that is often seen in the case
of Vai readers. Therefore, by knowing hiragana and a few processing
rules for special syllables and case particles, one can easily read every
sentence in CJO. The SJO sentences, in contrast, are separated by two
kinds of punctuation marks, roughly corresponding to the comma and
period in English, and words are not separated from one another. Thus,
the very first task for a reader after recognizing letters is to segment the
string of letters between the punctuation marks into a sequence of
words. Because there are several rules of thumb governing whether a
word is written in hiragana or kanji (nouns and verb/adjective stems are
usually written in kanji, while inflections, auxiliary verbs, and particles
are written in hiragana), it is fairly easy for an experienced reader to
divide a sentence written in a combination of kanji and hiragana into
words and to parse it syntactically.

Types of scripts	Examples	Numbers of kinds	Script-sound correspondence
hiragana (syllabary)	はかせ	71	nearly one-to-one
kanji (morphogram)	博士, 族	2,000 +	many-to-many

Figure 11.2. Two major types of Japanese scripts.

A few more words about the major scripts (see Figure 11.2). Hiragana are 71 simple-figured characters, each representing one syllable (more precisely, a *mora*, a subsyllabic rhythmic unit). The script-sound correspondence is nearly one-to-one, with minor exceptions for special syllables and case particles. Since the number of kinds of syllables are limited in the Japanese language because no two consonants appear consecutively, 71 hiragana characters, with a few ways of combining them for special syllables, are enough to represent effectively any Japanese word.

Kanji are complex-shaped characters representing morphemes. In Japan, about 2,000 kanji are designated as "kanji for daily use," but educated adults are able to read at least a few times this number. About half of the 2,000 are taught in elementary school. Kanji characters usually have a prototypical meaning and unique but multiple pronunciations, sometimes consisting of multiple syllables.

The script-sound correspondence for kanji is highly complicated. A unique characteristic of kanji in the Japanese language, not shared by Chinese characters in the Chinese or Korean language, is that most of them are given a Japanese reading as well as a Chinese reading (i.e., two pronunciations). Each Japanese reading was historically originated by attaching to a Chinese character a native Japanese word representing the meaning of the character. Therefore, the Japanese reading is sometimes called the semantic reading, while the Chinese reading is regarded as the phonetic reading. A rough approximation in English is found in *etc.* : "et cetera" could be called the Latin (phonetic) reading and "and so on" the English (semantic) reading. The Chinese and Japanese readings are usually quite dissimilar. For example, the Chinese reading for 水 is *sui*, while its Japanese reading is *mizu*. However, irrespective of the reading chosen, the character has the core, prototypal meaning of "water," which may be expanded to such other meanings as "sea," "flood," or "moisture" when combined with other kanji. Some kanji have several different meanings in the Japanese language and thus several Japanese readings. Other kanji have several different Chinese readings because of the historical changes of their pronunciation. (However, when a kanji is combined with other kanji or hiragana to make a compound word or derivative, only one reading is usually given.) Since the Japanese language has many fewer kinds of syllables and less clear intonation or accent differences than the Chinese language, many kanji must share one and the same Chinese reading. For example, more than 70 of the 2,000 kanji used everyday have the Chinese reading of *ko*. Technical terms and other infrequently used words can often be distinguished from their homonyms only by being written in kanji.

How are children motivated to acquire two literacies?

Japanese children can easily acquire literacy for Children's Japanese Orthography (CJO) because its major practices are attractive, and because the orthography consists of only 71 hiragana syllabaries, corresponding one-to-one with sounds. In contrast, the acquisition of literacy for Standard Japanese Orthography (SJO) is hard.

Many authentic SJO practices, like reading newspapers and writing a report in a mature fashion, are not appealing to children. The use of the basic 2,000 kanji in SJO is apt to be inhibitory for beginners, in both reading and writing. However, though it takes many years, most Japanese people eventually learn SJO literacy and this learning starts at the latest in the middle childhood. Why are children motivated to acquire it? Why are they not satisfied with CJO, which is adequate for writing informal letters and keeping personal records? I offer my answers to these questions in the next paragraph and then try to justify them later in this section.

I believe that Japanese children almost unanimously try to learn SJO literacy because of the cultural sanction. One has to be an expert in SJO literacy if he or she wants to be regarded as an educated member of Japanese society. It is almost impossible for a person to occupy a key position in a big company or an important organization if he or she is unable to read and write SJO documents. Having a good command of spoken Japanese and/or being literate in CJO is not enough. Unlike the acquisition of the Vai literacy, the acquisition of SJO literacy is not an optional enterprise. The Japanese culture, both in and out of school and in various forms, urges children to learn SJO literacy and its component skills as extensively as possible. For example, it assigns some privileged status to those who are gaining expertise in SJO literacy, especially those good at writing kanji, which requires much exercise. Schools are considered to be responsible for the acquisition of SJO literacy, though not every aspect of these literacy skills is taught intensively or effectively in language classes or in other lessons.

From CJO literacy to SJO literacy by school instruction. Expertise in SJO literacy includes the learning of many component skills. It is a formidable job to learn to read, write, and know the prototypal meaning of a great number of kanji. In a sense, children learn the "conceptual structure" of the Japanese culture through kanji. The morphograms constitute a complex network of concepts, ideas, and beliefs – in short, a condensed set of conceptual tools of the culture. Choosing the right kanji among many characters sharing the same pronunciation while writing and, to a lesser extent, choosing the right pronunciation while reading are possible only with knowledge of their prototypal meanings. Furthermore, as our experiments to be described later suggest, expertise in SJO literacy includes the acquisition of compounding schemata by which kanji are combined to make new words with more extended or precise meanings. It also includes cognitive skills to use prototypical meanings of component kanji, compounding schemata and other constraints to solve homonymic ambiguity and to infer the meaning of unfamiliar words, sometimes by assigning likely kanji to an aurally given word.

These skills do not seem to be acquired by participating directly in SJO practices. There are some intermediate practices between CJO and SJO literacies that are expected to facilitate a smooth transition, for example, reading story books (for school-age children), keeping a short diary, etc. Participating in these practices is recommended by schools and parents. The acquisition of the skills also requires some exercise, and, in fact, considerable time is devoted to it in Japanese schools. How much time is assigned for such exercise in language classes varies from skill to skill. How necessary and how effective the exercise is also seems to vary among skills.

Although we cannot compare schooled and unschooled children, the contribution of school to the acquisition of the target skill can be estimated by comparing between-grade and within-grade variances of students' performances. The within-grade variance would be minimal if the skill is acquired only in schools, because the curriculum, under the central control of the Ministry of Education, is highly similar across schools. Based on a few small-scale surveys and informal observations of this kind (Hatano 1986, Kaiho & Nomura 1983), let me describe ways in which children gain expertise in SJO literacy.

First, to associate a kanji with one of its readings is fairly easy. If children spend time reading books, they are likely to learn the readings of many kanji outside of school. In other words, acquiring this component of the SJO literacy skills does not depend heavily on formal instruction. Some children are much more advanced than their agemates and the academic standard. One subject in the intensive study by the National Language Research Institute of Japan (1972), a 6-year-old boy, could read 566 kanji in addition to hiragana, katakana, Arabic numerals, and English alphabet letters. It was reported that he could read an adult newspaper without much difficulty. He said that he had learned these kanji by reading books in which hiragana were attached to kanji, because he liked books so much. His parents' educational principle was, as reported, laissez-faire.

Second, even though the prototypical meaning of a kanji is not explicitly taught but left to be discovered by children, some of them can quickly find it through induction or semantic analogy, though their understanding often remains intuitive. For example, a 4.1-year-old boy, who is my colleague's nephew, understood that the prototypal meaning of 停 is "stoppage," when he learned that the meaning of 停電 is "electricity stoppage." He said, with a smile, "(this must be) the same as in 停車 (i.e., the stopping of a car)."

Compounding schemata are not explicitly taught either, but, again, it is not hard for children to acquire them by induction or analogy. It is easy for a child to infer analogically that "x – meat" means "meat of x," using a primitive, concept-specific compounding schema, when the child has learned that "cow-meat" means "beef" and "pig-meat" means "pork." Our preliminary study indicates that even elementary school children can use some compounding schemata, though they have not yet grasped them consciously. It is conceivable that, as a child accumulates learning experiences about kanji compound words, compounding schemata become more and more abstract and generally applicable. Skills for solving homonymic ambiguity and inferring the meaning of unfamiliar words by relying on the compounding schemata as well as prototypal meanings of constituent kanji also develop informally, and later, by learning to assign proper kanji, can be extended to aurally given words.

In contrast, learning to write kanji characters accurately is difficult and much delayed compared with learning to read them. It is also difficult to learn to choose proper kanji in writing from among the characters sharing one pronunciation. Because being able to write kanji correctly and properly is regarded by our culture as a sign of cognitive maturity and general understanding, as prescribed in the Course of Study issued by the Ministry of Education, school teachers tend to spend a large amount of time drilling children in the writing of kanji. Kanji dictation quizzes are given often, sometimes every day. A student is punished for making an error by being asked to write the kanji many times. As revealed by *kusho* behavior (i.e., writing kanji in the air), figural memory of kanji is enhanced by the motor element (Sasaki 1987), so repeated writing seems to be a good exercise. However, the exercise is usually mechanical and boring, and thus is motivated primarily by external reinforcement like an exam in school.

For kanji compound words, there is a big gap between ease of reading and of writing, even when a very lenient criterion is applied to the latter (e.g., accepting a character that is recognizable but which has some incorrect details). This probably implies that in some entries of the mental lexicon the kanji code is not described in its complete form but has to be assembled at the time of writing. Yoshida, Matsuda, and Shimura (1975) showed that most dictation errors involved choosing identically pronounced but semantically different characters. Even when students know the prototypical meaning of kanji satisfying a given phonetic code, this knowledge is not sufficient for the selection of the correct kanji out of the many kanji with the same sounds.

The skill for choosing a semantically appropriate kanji character that satisfies the phonetic constraint also develops through the experience of writing. Although some children are intrinsically interested in writing letters, keeping a dairy, or even submitting an article to a student newspaper, writing a composition or essay in classes seems to be the most common opportunity for such an experience.

The use of kanji as a sign of cultural maturity. Our culture provides children with special rewards for writing kanji; that is, being able to write many words in proper kanji is regarded as the sign of intellectual maturity. A recent experiment I conducted captures this. Two sets of two texts, allegedly a young boy's message to his mother (consisting of 49 characters) and a composition by an elementary school child (about 300 characters), were constructed. In one version of the first, there were no kanji written, while in the other, four kanji were written. Two versions of the second differed also in the number of kinds of kanji involved (9 and 27). The two versions were exactly the same in other features. Junior college students, divided into two groups and shown one of the two versions from each set, were asked to give an age or grade estimate of the writer.

Results clearly revealed that in each set, the use of kanji in writing made a considerable difference in the age or grade estimate. For the first set, the message having four kanji had the mean age estimate of 7.6 (SD=1.3), whereas the message without kanji was 6.5 (1.3). For the second set, the composition with 27 kanji had the mean grade estimate of 5.2 (1.4), whereas that with 9 kanji was 4.4 (1.1). The difference was statistically significant for both sets of materials. The subjects were told the fictitious age or grade of the writer later and were asked to guess what the child was like. Writing more kanji produced a higher estimate of intellectual ability, when the age or grade was constant. I would expect similar results for subjects of middle and later childhood.

The role of school in the acquisition of SJO literacy. As mentioned earlier, cultural pressure seems to be critical for the acquisition of SJO literacy because it is not easy to acquire and because for most communicative and documenting purposes CJO could be used effectively. The pressure works both in and out of school. Whether an intensive lesson is provided by schools for SJO literacy or the quality of the lesson may not be critical except, possibly, for skills for writing kanji. Some can learn SJO literacy without good lessons, others may fail to do so in spite of good lessons.

However, the very fact that it is taught in schools, as symbolizing the cultural pressure, is important.

In this sense, I believe that without schooling SJO literacy could not be acquired by a great majority of Japanese, and the very high SJO literacy rate in Japan has been a product of widespread general education. Thus, if Japan's rapid modernization was due to the high literacy rate in SJO, which allowed people to participate in practices like reading professional and technical books and articles, it was certainly based on the widespread system for general education, which was established just after the Meiji restoration.

Literacy enhances the acquisition of knowledge

Considering that every Japanese word can readily be represented by hiragana characters only, one might ask: Isn't the use of kanji unnecessary? Why does the Japanese culture bring pressure on children to acquire SJO literacy, spending so much time and effort? It is often claimed, by scholars as well as laypeople, that we should stop using kanji in order to increase practical efficiency (e.g., Unger 1987), and we could do so without much sacrifice.

I believe, to the contrary, that kanji characters play important roles as part of the technology of SJO literacy practices. More specifically, they serve to enhance understanding of unfamiliar or uncommon words and thus of the written sentences containing them. Moreover, I predict that based on the practice account, repeated processing of kanji in SJO literacy practices produces skills generalizable to other, related activities, especially understanding and acquiring knowledge in aural communication. Let me present some experimental data supporting this prediction.

It was Suzuki (1975, 1977) who suggested these functions of kanji convincingly for the first time. He specifically claims that kanji help readers resolve homonymic ambiguity and infer meanings of unfamiliar words. However, properly interpreting an ambiguous word or making an educated guess about the meaning of a new word significantly contributes to the process of linguistic communication, more specifically, understanding and acquiring knowledge from presented sentences.

Suzuki's (1975) argument for the kanji's function in resolving homonymic ambiguity is straightforward. Because the Japanese language has a small number of kinds of syllables, as no two consonants appear consecutively, there are many homonyms, especially for short words, and

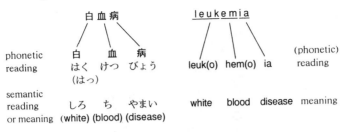

Figure 11.3. An example of the construction of kanji compound words in Japanese and Greek-derived compound words in English.

they can usually be distinguished only by describing them in kanji. Even in aural communication, we often refer to the kanji used to represent a target word when it is ambiguous.

Suzuki's (1975) argument for kanji's function in inferring the meaning of unfamiliar words is as follows. Many unfamiliar words are compound words (e.g., technical terms). Those words transcribed in kanji are superior to the corresponding hiragana transcriptions because prototypical meanings of component words are clearly and unambiguously indicated by kanji. The kanji transcribed words are also better than Greek- or Latin-derived compound words in English in terms of inferability of meaning, because the component kanji are semantically understood far more easily than the component Greek or Latin words: they are already imbued with Japanese or semantic readings, and, unlike Greek or Latin components, the component kanji are not deformed by the influence of modified pronunciation. Figure 11.3 gives an example, which, I hope, makes this claim convincing.

It should be noted that, although Suzuki refers exclusively to the effect of available specific kanji, we can expect, based on the practice account of literacy, that Japanese readers tend to develop more and more sophisticated skills for using kanji for the resolution of homonymic ambiguity and inference of meanings of unfamiliar words through their repeated engagement in SJO literacy practices. In other words, the acquisition and use of SJO literacy may have "general" cognitive consequences within the practices and, as will be seen later, the consequences may well be extended to other modes of linguistic communication.

Kanji's function: A cross-national study. Now let me describe a series of five experiments in which my associates and I have examined kanji's

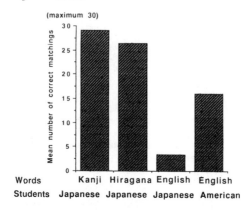

Figure 11.4. Mean number of correct matchings of definitions with words (Experiment 1).

function in inferring the meaning of unfamiliar words. In Experiment 1, which was a cross-national investigation, undergraduates were asked to match 30 unfamiliar, technical terms with their definitions or descriptions (Hatano, Kuhara, & Akiyama 1981). We selected 30 Latin- or Greek-derived English technical terms and their Japanese translations, which were kanji compound words with two to five component characters, from a list compiled by Suzuki (1978). The terms were mostly from botany, zoology, medical science, psychology, or linguistics. Two examples of the technical terms and their definitions are *limnology* – the scientific study of physical, chemical, and biological conditions in lakes and ponds – and *piscivorous* – eating fish as a regular diet.

Three groups of Japanese college students were asked to match the words with their definitions in Japanese. The word lists were presented in kanji, hiragana, and English, respectively. A group of American college students were tested using the English definitions and word list.

The results are shown in Figure 11.4. The order of performance of the four conditions was kanji, hiragana, English/American students, and English/Japanese students. The inferability in the kanji condition was almost perfect. Why was it so easy to infer meanings from the kanji expressions? The kanji expression for *limnology* is constructed of three characters, which have semantic readings roughly corresponding to "lake(s)," "pond(s)," and "study (studies)," respectively, and these semantic readings can easily be understood even by children. Similarly, the component kanji of the Japanese word corresponding to *piscivorous* are literally "fish-eat-nature." It is not hard to infer rough meanings of these difficult unfamiliar words if they are expressed in kanji.

That the kanji condition was superior to the English for Americans is consistent with our prediction, that is, that the words in kanji have higher inferability of meanings than the words in English. Another interpretation is possible, however: Japanese students were already more familiar than Americans with the technical terms. To check this, we asked other groups of Japanese and American students to write the words corresponding to the 30 definitions. When the students did not know the word, they were encouraged to invent one. The mean number of correct responses, which included inventions, was 7.2 for the Japanese students and 5.0 for the American students. The difference in the mean number of correct responses between the two groups was small, and could not explain the large difference in matching performance.

The reader may wonder if meanings of component kanji are really sufficient cues for inferring the meaning of most compound words. It is true that the meaning of a compound word, even an artificially constructed word like a technical term, cannot be determined solely by the meaning of its component kanji. For example, a compound word consisting of fish, eat, and nature may mean "the nature of fish's eating," "natural bait for fish," etc. However, there are other constraints on the range of possible meanings for the word. First, experienced readers have acquired several compounding schemata by which kanji words are constructed. For example, when two nouns are compounded, the new word belongs to a family of the last noun. Thus, "milk-cow" means a cow for milking and "cow-milk" means milk of a cow, as shown in Figure 11.5. Second, our world knowledge can be used to exclude some possible meanings and also to choose other, more likely ones. This is similar to English speakers' differentiated interpretation of structurally similar phrases like "horse-shoe" and "alligator shoe." Finally, the context of the sentence, passage, or work as a whole can give additional clues to the meaning of the word

乳牛 = milk-cow = a cow for milking

牛乳 = cow-milk = milk of a cow

Figure 11.5. A compounding schema for words consisting of two kanji representing a noun.

in question. In addition, college students are expected to have developed skills for inferring the meaning of an unfamiliar word by using these constraints. Therefore, meanings of component kanji only partly increase the inferability, but this increment is often very helpful.

The latent cognitive function of kanji

As seen in Figure 11.4, the undergraduates in Experiment 1 matched hiragana-transcribed, unfamiliar technical terms with definitions fairly well. The performance in this condition was only a little lower than that in the kanji condition. I assume, following Suzuki (1975), that this is because, in addition to their general skills for inferring the meaning, students in the hiragana condition, by using the definitions as contextual information, often succeeded in retrieving the appropriate kanji that satisfied the phonetic constraint of the hiragana and then utilized the kanji to infer the meaning. Using the present terminology, this skill for inferring the meaning of an unfamiliar word transcribed in hiragana (or given aurally) by tentatively assigning a series of kanji is a general cognitive consequence of SJO literacy practices, because 1) it is almost certainly derived from the skill for inferring the meaning of an unfamiliar word transcribed in kanji, and 2) it generally enhances the understanding of and the acquisition of knowledge from a sentence containing the unfamiliar word.

Of course, there are many possible kanji codes that satisfy the phonetic constraint, and a subject may have to try a number of combinations of component kanji. Take *gyoshokusei*, for example. According to the *Iwanami* dictionary of Japanese, there are three characters read *gyo*, ten read *shoku*, and 33 read *sei*. Therefore, even when the phonetic code is correctly segmented, there are 990 possible combinations of kanji to examine. However, in the case of *gyo*, one of the three characters is salient because its Japanese reading (i.e., *sakana* – fish) appears in one of the 30 definitions. (For the other two characters *gyo*, no Japanese readings appear in the definitions.) Thus, the number of likely candidates is nowhere near 990.

If the above assumption is right, namely that the subjects' inferring meaning was mediated by the kanji code, then the correctness or incorrectness of the inferred meaning would depend upon their finding the correct kanji. To test this, we examined the kanji representation of the technical terms chosen by the students in the hiragana condition. After matching the definitions with the words, the students in the hiragana condition were given a kanji encoding test. In the test, they were given the correct combinations of 30 definitions and corresponding hiragana words and were asked to change the hiragana into kanji. We examined the proportion of correct matchings of the definitions with the words as a function of correctness in this kanji encoding test. When kanji encodings were correct, that is, the hiragana words were encoded into the correct combination of kanji, the mean proportion of the correct matching to definitions was 0.89; but when kanji encoding responses were incorrect or missing, the mean proportion was 0.69.

This difference is statistically significant, but the latter proportion is still fairly high. This is almost certainly due to the fact that one must get only the critical character(s) correct in order to make the correct matching. For example, the Japanese word corresponding to *laryingal* consists of three kanji, but only the last one, meaning "sound," is critical to matching the word with the definition, "a sound articulated between vocal cords when breathing out," because there were no other definitions regarding sounds.

In order to examine in more detail the correspondence of inferred meanings and the kanji representations of technical terms, we conducted Experiment 2 (Hatano, Kuhara, & Akiyama 1981), in which subjects were required to indicate the inferred meanings of unfamiliar words instead of matching them with definitions. Ten technical terms sampled from Experiment 1 were presented in a weak sentential context. As shown in the following examples, each of the sentences included one target word written in hiragana and underlined: (1) He is a specialist in *koshogaku* (limnology) and has studied everywhere in Japan; (2) This animal lives by the river bank and is *gyoshokusei* (piscivorous).

A group of Japanese undergraduates were asked to write the meanings of the hiragana target words and, after this test sheet was collected, to change the target words into kanji. Both inferred meanings and kanji encodings were classified into three categories: correct response, incorrect response, and no-answer, including incomplete response. The correspondence between inferred meanings and kanji encodings was very close, as can be seen in Table 11.1. When the students made correct kanji encodings, they inferred correct meanings in most cases. When they retrieved incorrect kanji, inferred meanings were also incorrect. Where the students failed to give kanji, they could not indicate meanings.

Table 11.1. *Relationships between inferred meanings and kanji encodings*
(Experiment 2)

| | Kanji encodings | | |
Meanings	Correct	Incorrect	No answer
Correct	51.2%	4.2%	0.8%
Incorrect	2.7%	16.9%	1.5%
No answer	6.5%	6.2%	10.0%

Close correspondence was also observed within erroneous responses. Three different incorrect responses were given for *koshogaku* (limnology), all having the target pronunciation, in the kanji encoding test. The component kanji had the meanings of "old-document-study," "old-artist-study," and "old-naming-study," respectively. As expected, the meanings of the word inferred by the students were highly similar to the integration of the meanings of the three component kanji. For example, students who gave "old-artist-study" in the kanji encoding test inferred that *koshogaku* was a study of great artists in old days.

Kanji code in the process of inferring meaning

Experiment 2 clearly showed the close correspondence between inferred meanings and kanji encodings. However, we cannot conclude that the kanji code is used as a mediator in inferring the meaning. A rival interpretation is that several possible meanings are activated from the context (either simultaneously or in sequence) and then a kanji code is selected that is semantically appropriate and satisfies the pronunciation constraint (kanji as a selection cue interpretation).

To exclude this rival interpretation, Keiko Kuhara-Kojima and I conducted three more experiments (Experiments 3–5). In Experiment 3 college students were individually asked (1) to guess, then (2) to choose from among alternatives the meaning of an unfamiliar word, and (3) to verbalize as much as possible the process of inferring. Ten Japanese kanji compound words were embedded in contextual sentences similar to those used in Experiment 2. At the end of the experiment, the subjects were asked about their general strategy for figuring out the meaning, such as what cues had been used. The experimenter carefully avoided suggesting the subject use or refer to kanji.

Of the 23 college students experimentally given kanji compound words, 22 replied when asked about their general strategy that they had used kanji in inferring the meaning. All 23 spontaneously referred at least once to kanji with verbalizations like ". . . if I change it into kanji . . . ," ". . . to assign kanji. . . ." For guessing the meaning of the 10 items, spontaneous reference to kanji occurred 45% of the time.

The subjects often stated that they could not figure out the meaning because they could not think of appropriate kanji. The following are a few examples:

Tape-recorder: *Koshogaku*. He is a specialist in *koshogaku* and has studied everywhere in Japan.

Subject's verbalization: *Koshogaku* – a name of a science – because *gaku* is attached last – this must be the *gaku* of *gakumon* – I thought this by trying to imagine the kanji – but I don't know what *kosho* is.

Tape-recorder: *Tosokurui*. There are many foreigners who reject *tosokurui*, although they can eat shellfish.

Subject's verbalization: *Soku* may be *ashi* (the Japanese reading that means foot or feet) – I cannot figure out what *to* means – I guess the word means a living thing with feet.

When subjects selected incorrect kanji that shared the same pronunciation, they usually guessed the corresponding incorrect meaning, as Experiment 2 had suggested. Moreover, in the second phase of Experiment 3, where subjects were asked to choose the correct meaning out of four alternatives given aurally, they tended to choose a different meaning from the one they had guessed in the first phase, when they thought of another kanji while examining the alternatives.

Those results again strongly suggest that the kanji code is used in inferring the meaning of unfamiliar words, but do not give conclusive evidence for it. The alternative interpretation still cannot be excluded. The process of inferring the meaning proceeds so rapidly that it is almost impossible to decide from a subject's verbal protocols whether the kanji code is a mediator or a selection cue for inferring meaning.

Experiment 4 relied on the selective interference paradigm. Assuming that the kanji code takes a figurative form (i.e., mental imagery of kanji characters), we predicted that preloaded visual-spatial memory would be more interfering than aural-verbal memory when subjects try to use the kanji code for inferring the meaning, whereas the reverse would be true when they use the phonetic code. We decided to present aurally an unfamiliar English word as typical of those inducing the phonetic code.

Inference of the meanings of unfamiliar words

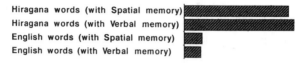

Hiragana words (with Spatial memory)
Hiragana words (with Verbal memory)
English words (with Spatial memory)
English words (with Verbal memory)

Recall of preloaded items

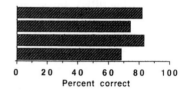

Spatial (with hiragana)
Verbal (with hiragana)
Spatial (with English)
Verbal (with English)

    0   2 0   4 0   6 0   8 0   1 0 0
              Percent correct

Figure 11.6. Mean number of correctly inferred meanings and retained pieces of preloaded information (Experiment 4).

Forty-eight college students were randomly assigned to one of four conditions, in each of which subjects were given 10 unfamiliar words embedded in the same weak context sentences and were asked to guess their meanings. In two of the conditions, the unfamiliar words were in English, in the other two, in hiragana. Only the latter would be coded in terms of mental imagery of kanji. In one of the two conditions for English and hiragana words, visual-spatial memory was preloaded, while in the other, aural-verbal memory was preloaded. These memory tasks were similar to those constructed by Brooks (1967): a spatial item consisted of a sequence of seven moves – either to the left, to the right, up, or down – from the fixed starting point in a four-by-four square matrix (e.g., to the right, up, to the right, down, down, down, to the left), and a verbal item, a list of four randomly chosen adjectives – quick, slow, good, and bad (e.g., good, quick, good, bad). Subjects were first presented a memory item, then were required to infer the meaning of a word in context, and finally were asked to reproduce the memory item.

The results are shown in Figure 11.6. Compared with subjects tested with the English words, the subjects tested with the hiragana words that could be encoded into kanji not only made many more correct responses as shown, but also generated a much more limited range of erroneous responses. In other words, the subjects' guessing the meaning of unfamiliar words was strongly constrained by the need for finding a series of kanji that satisfed the phonetic code.

However, no interaction effect was significant, either in inferring the meaning or retaining the preloaded information. Thus we cannot exclude the rival interpretation (kanji as a selection cue interpretation). The kanji code may not be used in inferring the meaning, or, if used, it may not be figuratively detailed and therefore its use may not be incompatible with visual-spatial memory.

This latter possibility was also suggested when we extended Experiment 3 to five blind college students who had not learned to read or write kanji. (Japanese braille is limited to syllabaries.) Unexpectedly, four of them almost always referred to kanji spontaneously. Even though they did not know the configuration of the kanji whose Chinese reading was *sui*, they did know it had another reading, *mizu*, and had the prototypal meaning of water. Since SJO constitutes an integral part of the Japanese culture, even the blind in order to be successful in the academic world have to learn multiple readings of kanji and use that knowledge in inferring the meaning of unfamiliar words, although their kanji codes must be nonfigurative.

In the final experiment (Experiment 5), we tried to enhance retrievability of component kanji and examine whether this would facilitate the inference of the meaning of unfamiliar words. If component kanji are a mediator, not a selection cue, of inferring the meaning of an unfamiliar word, we will observe a better performance in the inference of the meaning when the component kanji are more readily retrieved.

Prior to the task of inferring meaning, college students were shown and asked to remember six or seven lists of five kanji characters, each satisfying a given pronunciation (or fewer if there aren't five such characters), so that they could write them down later. (Based on the results of a pilot experiment, we made the number of kanji presented relatively small so that subjects could readily recall the target component kanji and possibly use it as a mediator in inferring the meaning of an unfamiliar word.) About half of the subjects were thus exposed to 28 kanji that included 6 critical component characters of three unfamiliar words to be presented later. The other half were exposed to another set of 28 kanji including 6 other kanji, which constituted four unfamiliar words. They were not told, either before or after this exposure and the recall of kanji immed-

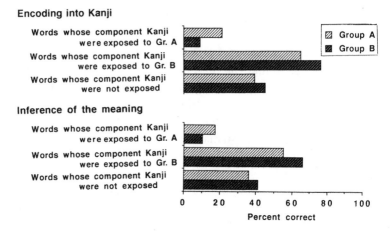

Figure 11.7. Mean number of correctly inferred meanings for words consisting of presented and unpresented kanji (Experiment 5).

iately following, that it was related to the task of inferring meaning, and in fact almost none of them recognized the relevance. A kanji encoding test of the unfamiliar words was administered after the critical task of inferring the meaning.

As shown in Figure 11.7, enhancing the retrievability of component kanji facilitated not only the encoding of the words into correct kanji but also inferring the meaning of unfamiliar words, and this facilitation effect was observed irrespective of the baseline retrievability of the constituent kanji. Moreover, the prior exposure to the constituent kanji reduced failures to infer the meaning rather than incorrect guessings. We can now exclude the alternative interpretation because this pattern of facilitation effects on the inference of the meaning could not be predicted from kanji as a selection cue interpretation.

In summary, these experiments demonstrate a kanji's latent cognitive function. Experienced readers of Japanese try to find a combination of kanji satisfying a given phonetic code of hiragana transcription that seems to be appropriate in the context, then they infer the meaning. This is the opposite of what has been demonstrated by several psycholinguistic studies (e.g., Rubenstein, Lewis, & Rubenstein 1971), where a word written in English is transformed into a phonetic code before its meaning is retrieved. (Such phonetic transformation may occur in the Japanese language provided the word is written in hiragana.)

That kanji have such a latent cognitive function has an important implication. Readers of Japanese can understand unfamiliar words, spoken or in hiragana, with the help of kanji codes stored in long-term memory. We can reasonably conclude that SJO literacy has some general effects on linguistic communication, more specifically on understanding in and the acquisition of knowledge through communication, either in a written or aural form.

Multiple mental lexicons. From the above findings and those from other experiments on cognitive functions of kanji (e.g., Kuhara & Hatano 1981), we now think that experienced readers of Japanese have, in addition to the usual mental lexicon of words, a mental lexicon of kanji or the corresponding morphemes as building blocks for compound words. The latter lexicon has a complex structure so that the component kanji can be retrieved either phonetically or semantically. Suppose Japanese readers fail to find the word in their word lexicon that matches a given wordlike utterance or string of characters. They will recognize that they do not know the word as a word, but will still try to figure out its meaning by using the kanji lexicon. Compounding schemata, world knowledge, and contextual information may also be relied on.

Readers can continue reading or aural conversation without break if the inferred meaning of the unknown compound word seems correct. Even when the inferred meaning has proven to be incorrect, they can easily learn the word by using the kanji lexicon. After the inference or learning, they may add the word to their word lexicon or store the word temporarily. For the purpose of the efficient processing of linguistic information, the word lexicon should not be very large, and must be comprised of frequently used words. The kanji lexicon can potentially generate a great number of compound words, though it may not give precisely specified meanings. Inferring word meanings using the kanji lexicon tends to take a longer time. Thus two lexicons can be used most effectively in combination, producing a flexible, large vocabulary.

Because of this multiple mental lexical system and the skills for using the system effectively, experienced Japanese readers are able to increase and reorganize their vocabulary quite easily. Kanji, when appropriated, not only serve as the basis for expanding one's vocabulary, but also enhance the acquisition of knowledge through aural as well as written communication. Most of ordinary Japanese people can make educated guesses about technical terms with the help of kanji. This is important because we are exposed to a large number of new technical words almost every day, but it was even more so in the period of rapid modernization. According to a newspaper interview with S. Ohno (*Mainichi-shinbun*, June 17, 1980), about 15,000 words were invented in the first 20 years of the Meiji period to represent Western ideas, customs, and things, and many of them were incorporated into the vocabulary of ordinary Japanese people. Most of the invented words were, as expected, compound kanji words. Thus we may credit kanji with playing an important role in the rapid modernization of Japanese society.

It will be interesting to speculate what will happen in the future if modern technology and science are brought into the Vai community and thus Vai people have to talk about the conceptual entities involved in these new enterprises. Are they willing to use those new words borrowed from English or another Western language or will they try to translate them? How will these words be written? These questions challenge the practice account of literacy.

Concluding remarks

Although pictures of literacy drawn in this chapter are considerably different from those offered by Scribner and Cole (1981), probably because of the differences between the Vai and standard Japanese orthographies, I believe that my theoretical stance is not far from theirs and that the preceding case study of Japanese literacy reinforces the practice account of literacy. Because an orthography, that is, the type of script and how it represents words, is a critical constituent of literacy practices, how readily people participate in them and what skills they develop through the participation may vary according to orthographies. Although this point is not emphasized in Scribner and Cole's book, it is almost a corollary of the practice account of literacy.

Speaking generally, because many skills for everyday activities can easily be learned and are apparently useful for the activities they want to engage in, motivating children to acquire them poses no problem. Skills needed for production, ritual, and other complicated practices are more elaborated and require some training, but their acquisition through apprenticeship is still straightforward. Skills involved in Vai literacy practices (e.g., writing letters) and Japanese literacy practices in CJO (reading books) are of this kind. Scribner and Cole (1981) found that the

Vai literacy skills can be acquired in an exceedingly short period, and always outside of school. Likewise, CJO literacy skills can be learned rapidly, easily, and usually without systematic teaching.

Unlike these skills, many literacy skills, including those for SJO, require a large amount of exercise for acquisition. Partially acquiring them does not allow learners to participate in a set of appealing practices and thus is not very useful. Therefore, even when people desire to participate in the target literacy practices, not all of them successfully acquire needed literacy skills unless they are systematically taught in school and/or strongly urged by the surrounding culture to learn them. I believe that a majority of children would never acquire SJO literacy skills unless the task of learning them is culturally imposed (and enforced institutionally). Although what specific purposes the orthographic knowledge is used for and in what specific contexts it is applied are critical for its acquisition, we cannot ignore the effects of the type of scripts and their correspondence with sounds on its acquisition. It seems reasonable to assume that when the target literacy skills deal with thousands of morphograms, their acquisition cannot be separated from schooling.

As for literacy's cognitive consequences, I would suggest, following the practice account, that we direct our attention to a specific literacy's effect on a specific cognitive ability. Moreover, I would suggest, we might investigate the effect on aspects of linguistic communication first, because it is highly unlikely for us to find any effect on thinking and problem solving if the effect on communication is negligible, and second, because enhanced communication ability may have a large long-term effect on a body of acquired knowledge and thus on problem solving based on it. Scribner and Cole (1981) found that the Vai literacy practices improve an aspect of aural communication, that is, integrating syllables pronounced separately. Kanji or other morphograms, once acquired, will produce a much greater facilitation effect on aural communication than Vai, hiragana, or other syllabaries, because morphograms serve to form an enriched representation of spoken words. For example, the experiments reviewed in this chapter have demonstrated that kanji help experienced readers infer the meaning of unfamiliar words.

This and related functions of kanji are probably reasons why Japanese still use them in spite of the time and the effort needed for learning them and technological inconvenience their use produces. We sometimes encounter people who speak daily Japanese reasonably well but write hiragana (and a small number of kanji) only. They are, almost without exception, foreigners other than East Asians, second- or later-generation Japanese, or Japanese who have spent many years in a foreign country. They seem to suffer when they are involved in professional or technical conversation in Japanese, or when they have to get a quick overview of an issue they are not familiar with. In this sense, engaging in SJO literacy practices repeatedly induces more or less general cognitive consequences, for example, facilitated abilities to understand and acquire knowledge from aurally presented sentences and passages.

I believe this idea of SJO literacy's generalized effects on linguistic communication is quite compatible with the practice account of literacy, because Scribner & Cole (1981, p. 258) indicate that "particular practices promote particular skills" and that we may find "more generalized skills, or different skills in other societies." I would like to emphasize, once again, that the orthography is an indispensable aspect of literacy practices, and also part of the culture as a set of artifacts. The present practices are not entirely free from the past or historically accumulated artifacts. Literacy practices, which induce cognitive consequences, are constrained by the nature of the orthography involved in them.

References

Brooks, L.R. (1967). The suppression of visualization by reading. *Quarterly Journal of Experimental Psychology, 19*, 289–299.

Cole, M., Gay, J., Glick, J., & Sharp, D.W. (1971). *The cultural context of learning and thinking*. New York: Basic Books.

Hatano, G. (1986). How do Japanese children learn to read?: Orthographic and eco-cultural variables. In B.R. Foorman and A.W. Siegel (Eds.), *Acquisition of reading skills: Cultural constraints and cognitive universals*. Hillsdale, NJ: Erlbaum.

Hatano, G., Kuhara, K., & Akiyama, M.M. (1981). Kanji help readers of Japanese infer the meaning of unfamiliar words. *The Quarterly Newsletter of the Laboratory of Comparative Human Cognition, 3*, 30–33.

Kaiho, H., & Nomura, Y. (1983). Psychology of kanji processing. Tokyo: Kyoiku-shuppan [in Japanese].

Kuhara, K., & Hatano, G. (1981). *Comprehension and memory of a short oral discourse involving homonymic ambiguity: Effects of headings.* Paper presented at the Meeting of the American Educational Research Association.

National Language Research Institute of Japan. (1972). *Reading and writing ability in pre-school children*. Tokyo: Tokyo Shoseki [in Japanese].

Ohno, S. An evening edition interview with Dr. S. Ohno. (1980, June 17). *The Mainichi-shinbun*, p. 3.

Rogoff, B., & Lave, J. (Eds.). (1984). *Everyday cognition*. Cambridge, MA: Harvard University Press.

Rubenstein, H., Lewis, S. S., & Rubenstein, M. A. (1971). Evidence for phonemic recoding in visual word recognition. *Journal of Verbal Learning and Verbal Behavior*, *10*, 647–657.

Sasaki, M. (1987). Why do Japanese write characters in space? *International Journal of Behavioral Development*, *10*, 135–149.

Scribner, S. (1968). The cognitive consequences of literacy. Unpublished paper, Albert Einstein College of Medicine, printed in *The Quarterly Newsletter of the Laboratory of Comparative Human Cognition, 1992, 14*, 84–102.

Scribner, S., & Cole, M. (1981). *The psychology of literacy*. Cambridge, MA: Harvard University Press.

Serpell, R., & Hatano, G. (In press). Education, schooling and literacy in a cross-cultural perspective. In J. W. Berry, P. R. Dasen, & T. S. Saraswathi (Eds.), *Handbook of cross-cultural psychology, Vol. 2: Basic processes and developmental psychology*. Boston, MA: Allyn and Bacon.

Suzuki, T. (1975). On the twofold phonetic realization of basic concepts: In defense of Chinese characters in Japanese. In F. C. C. Peng (Ed.), *Language in Japanese society*. Tokyo: University of Tokyo Press.

Suzuki, T. (1977). Writing is not language, or is it? *Journal of Pragmatics*, *1*, 407–420.

Suzuki, T. (1978). Are Kanji compound words loan words from Chinese? *Gekkan Gengo (Language Monthly)*, *7*(2), 2–8 [in Japanese].

Unger, J. M. (1987). *The fifth generation fallacy*. Oxford, UK: Oxford University Press.

Yoshida, A., Matsuda, Y., & Shimura, M. (1975). A study on instruction of Chinese characters: An approach from an analysis of children's errata. *School of Education Research Bulletin, University of Tokyo*, No. 14, 221–251 [in Japanese].

12   Voices of thinking and speaking

James V. Wertsch, Fran Hagstrom, and Eve Kikas

Over the course of her career Sylvia Scribner made numerous contributions to our understanding of how human activity is related to psychological functioning. Her focus on activity is most explicit in the ingenious analyses she conducted near the end of her career on cognitive processes in the workplace, analyses that were specifically grounded in the theory of activity outlined by Leont'ev (1981) and others. In our view, however, Scribner made major contributions to what may be termed an activity oriented approach to psychology even before she began explicitly grounding her claims in the writings of activity theorists. For example, her decades of work on the relationship between literacy and psychological processes are perhaps best understood in terms of what she and her colleagues came to call a "practice account of literacy" (Scribner & Cole 1981, p. 235). This and other earlier research concerned with literacy, language, and thought focused consistently on how "socially organized activities may come to have consequences for human thought" (p. 235). In one way or another, then, much of Scribner's research can be viewed as being grounded in the assumption that the study of human mental functioning is best approached from the perspective of socioculturally situated activity.

In an attempt to explicate the forms of activity Scribner considered in her studies of literacy we shall harness the notion of "mediated action" (Wertsch 1991; Zinchenko 1985). Our use of this notion reflects the intellectual heritage we share with Scribner, a heritage grounded in the works of authors such as Vygotsky (1977, 1978, 1981, 1987), Leont'ev (1981), Tulviste (1991), and Zinchenko (1985). The primary claim at

The writing of this chapter was assisted by a grant from the Spencer Foundation to the first author, who also wishes to express his appreciation to the University of Seville for its support during 1992–93. The second author was assisted by a grant from the National Medical Enterprises Foundation, and the third author was supported by a special grant from the Frances L. Hiatt School of Psychology at Clark University. The statements made and the views expressed are solely the responsibility of the authors.

276

issue here is that the use of "mediational means," or "tools" such as language shapes human action in essential ways. According to Vygotsky, "by being included in the process of behavior, the psychological tool [i.e., one form of mediational means] alters the entire flow and structure of mental functions. It does this by determining the structure of a new instrumental act, just as a technical tool alters the process of a natural adaptation by determining the form of labor operations" (1981, p. 137). When considering literacy practice as mediated action, the mediational means employed are the forms of language used in this activity setting, and the issue is how these mediational means are actively employed by humans such that they are appropriated, or incorporated into concrete action, thereby shaping the form this action takes.

One of the major contributions Scribner and her colleagues made to our understanding of literacy is that language is incorporated into action in a variety of ways, reflecting a variety of sociocultural settings and resulting in a variety of literacy practices (e.g., Scribner 1977; Scribner & Cole 1981). The roots of this claim can be found in the writings of Vygotsky (1977, 1978, 1981, 1987) about the role of "technical" and "psychological" tools in organizing human mental processes, but it goes beyond Vygotsky's formulation in its analysis of the range of cultural, historical, and institutional contexts that shape mediational means and hence human action.

In general, Vygotsky did not carry out detailed analyses of sociocultural context. He was only beginning to devote attention to this issue near the end of his life. This becomes apparent if one considers differences between chapters 5 and 6 of *Thinking and Speech* (1987). Chapter 5, "An experimental study of concept development," was probably written sometime in the early 1930s. In it Vygotsky reported on research he had conducted with Sakharov (1930) in the late 1920s. Chapter 6, "The development of scientific concepts in childhood," was written specifically for the volume *Thinking and Speech*, which was published in 1934.

Although both chapters are concerned with concept development, there is a major difference between them in how this development was viewed as taking place. Chapter 5 deals with concept development in terms of individual mental functioning as measured in a clinical experimental setting. Results from the Vygotsky–Sakharov block-sorting task were used to document the nature of various kinds of complexes and the transition to pseudoconceptual and conceptual levels of functioning.

In chapter 6, the concern with concept development continues to occupy center stage, but there is an important shift to considering concept development in terms of how it is tied to forms of discourse in a specific institutional context, namely, formal schooling. This shift is reflected in the terminology Vygotsky employed. In contrast to chapter 5, where he wrote of "complexes," "pseudoconcepts," "genuine concepts," and other constructs that apply to individual mental functioning, chapter 6 deals with "scientific concepts," a term Vygotsky had not employed in the previous chapter. The Russian word involved here *nauchnyi* can also be translated as "academic" or "scholarly" instead of "scientific;" the term "scholarly" actually being used in the English translation of one of Luria's works (Luria 1976).

This shift in Vygotsky's terminology reflects a more general shift in focus and a growing concern with how specific forms of mediated action are tied to the institutional context of the classroom. His focus had expanded beyond individual ("intramental") as well as dyadic or small group ("intermental") functioning construed in a narrow way. In place of searching for the social origins of individual mental functioning solely in intermental processes, he was concerned with how individual and social processes are situated in a broader sociocultural context. Scribner extended this line of inquiry in her studies of literacy and workplace activities. In both realms her research led her to identify important differences in socioculturally situated, material practice. For example, her studies of literacy led her to conclude that rather than being a monolithic essence or process, literacy activity and the psychological processes associated with it take on various forms and that these forms reflect aspects of the institutional settings in which they appear.

Modes of thinking and ways of speaking

One of Scribner's most interesting analyses of how forms of speaking and thinking are tied to activity settings can be found in her chapter "Modes of thinking and ways of speaking: Culture and logic reconsidered," which appeared in the 1977 edited volume *Thinking: Readings in Cognitive Science*. Based on her review of numerous studies of differences between schooled and nonschooled subjects in solving verbal logic problems (typically syllogisms), Scribner concluded

the overall level of performance of nonschooled traditional people and the within-culture differences in performance between schooled and nonschooled groups suggest that logical problems pose special difficulties for traditional nonliterate people. Uniformities in patterns *across* cultures indicate that the source of these difficulties is not likely to reside in aspects of culture that are unique to any one of the given cultures. (1977, p. 487)

In trying to account for the sources of the consistent differences she found between schooled and nonschooled peoples, Scribner turned to the notions of genre and performance as outlined by Hymes (1974).

[G]enre refers to stylistic structures or organized verbal forms with a beginning and a end, 'and a pattern to what comes between. '. . . Greetings, farewells, riddles, proverbs, prayers, are among well-known elementary genres, and tales and myths representative of complex genres, *Performances* refers to the use of genres in particular contexts. Both genres and performances may vary from one speech community to another, and the relationship between them may vary as well: certain genres in certain communities may be context-bound while in others they range over diverse events and situations. (Scribner, 1977, pp. 497–498)

The specific issue that concerned Scribner in her analysis of literacy activities and their psychological correlates was the nature of what she termed the "logical genre."

Let us entertain the proposition that verbal logic problems . . . constitute a specialized language genre that stands apart from other genres in ways that may be difficult to define but are readily recognizable (just as poetry may be distinguished from prose by readers who may never exactly agree on what 'poetry' is). (Scribner 1977, p. 498)

In developing her account of the logical genre Scribner was dealing with a specific form of what we are calling mediated action and with the more general issues of a theory of activity. The mediational means involved are the genres or "organized verbal forms" used by participants in her studies, and the concrete instantiation of these mediational means occurred in the form of performance, the "use of genres in particular contexts." Furthermore, Scribner made a series of claims about how the form that mediated action takes is related to the activity setting in which is appears. All this points to the idea that even though Scribner was not explicitly formulating her claims in the 1970s in terms of a theory of activity, she had important insights into what would constitute an activity-oriented approach and this approach played a major role in determining what she saw as research issues and how she approached them.

Voices, genres, and modes of speaking and thinking

In recent years, a figure who has come to be recognized as a major contributor to our understanding of the motion of genre is Mikhail Mikhailovich Bakhtin (1981, 1984, 1986; see also Clark &

Holquist 1984; Todorov 1984). Although Bakhtin was not in search of a Marxist approach to psychology, and although there is no indication that he was in direct contact with Vygotsky, his ideas provide extremely valuable complements and extensions of Vygotsky's notion of mediation (Wertsch 1991). Of particular interest for our purposes is Bakhtin's notion of "speech genre."

When writing of speech genres, Bakhtin was specifically focusing on *speech*, which occurs in the form of *utterances*, in contrast to linguistic forms (e.g., sentences) abstracted away from the form of action he called "speech communication." This focus on speech as action rather than on linguistic structures abstracted out of action also characterized Vygotsky's writings, a point that is sometimes overlooked because of the mistranslation of the title of his best known volume as *Thought and Language* instead of *Thinking and Speech*.

Bakhtin insisted that an adequate account of speech communication could be derived only by focusing on "the *real unit* of speech communication: the utterance" (1986, p. 17) since "speech can exist in reality only in the form of concrete utterances of individual speaking people, speech subjects" (1986, p. 71). In his view an essential key to understanding the nature of utterances is recognizing a level of organization between abstracted linguistic form or structure, on the one hand, and unique, contextualized utterances, on the other. This is a level that has been largely missing in linguistic analysis since Saussure. As Holquist (1986, p. xvi) has noted

Saussure conceived the individual language user to be an absolutely free agent with the ability to choose any words to implement a particular intention. Saussure concluded, not surprisingly, that language as used by heterogeneous millions of such willful subjects was unstudiable, a chaotic jungle beyond the capacity of science to domesticate.

Bakhtin, on the other hand, begins by assuming that individual speakers do not have the kind of freedom *parole* assumes they have: the basic unit for the study of actual speech practice is the "utterance," which "with all its individuality and creativity, can in no way be regarded as a *completely free combination* of forms of language, as is supposed, for example, by Saussure . . . who juxtaposed the utterance (*la parole*) as a purely individual act, to the system of language as a phenomenon that is purely social and mandatory for the individual."

The intermediate level of organization that Bakhtin proposed in order to deal with this issue is to be found in categories of utterance categories, or types such as speech genres. Speech genres are "relatively stable and normative forms of the utterance" (1986, p. 81). It is this level of organization that makes it the case that the utterance, with all its properties of individuality and uniqueness, is nonetheless not a *"completely free combination* of forms of language" (Bakhtin 1986, p. 81). According to Bakhtin (1986, p. 87)

A speech genre is not a form of language, but a typical form of utterance; as such the genre also includes a certain typical kind of expression that inheres in it. In the genre the word acquires a particular typical expression. Genres correspond to typical situations of speech communication, typical themes, and, consequently, also to particular contacts between the *meanings* of words and actual concrete reality under certain typical circumstances.

There are many similarities between Bakhtin's treatment of speech genre and utterance and the account of genre and performance, which Scribner invoked to develop her notion of a logical genre. As is the case in Hymes's account, Bakhtin's approach emphasizes that genres are associated with particular kinds of situations. This, of course, was an essential point for Scribner in her attempt to deal with the fact that the logical genre is so closely tied to experience in a particular institutional setting – formal schooling. It is the mediating role of genres that creates the link between individuals' performances or utterances on the one hand and institutional settings on the other. Furthermore, both Bakhtin and Hymes focus on the tension between a genre, which is "impersonal" (Bakhtin 1986, p. 88), and the utterances produced by appropriating a genre. Every utterance occurs in a unique way in a concrete setting and hence has personalized and contextualized properties specific to it and it alone.

The essential contribution Bakhtin's ideas make to this general line of inquiry derives from his account of "dialogism." As authors such as Holquist (1990) and Todorov (1984) have noted, dialogism, or dialogicality, is the most fundamental theoretical construct in Bakhtin's approach. It is a notion that is analytically prior even to that of the utterance or voice since the production of utterances always involves a speaker's appropriating, invoking, or ventriloquating through the voices of others, thereby entering into a dialogic encounter with them. The fundamental Bakhtinian question is, Who is doing the speaking?, and the fundamental Bakhtinian answer is, At least two voices. This claim about "multivoicedness" comes through very clearly in Bakhtin's (1986, p. 78) comments on speech genres.

We speak only in definite speech genres, that is, all our utterances have definite and relatively stable typical *forms of construction of the whole*. Our repertoire of oral (and written) speech genres is rich. We use them confidently and skillfully *in practice*, and it is quite possible for us not even to suspect their existence *in theory*. Like Moliere's Monsieur Jourdain who, when speaking in prose, had no idea that was what he was doing, we speak in diverse speech genres without suspecting that they exist. Even in the most free, the most unconstrained conversation, we cast our speech in definite generic forms, sometimes rigid and trite ones, sometimes more flexible, plastic, and creative ones.

In this view it is no more possible to produce an utterance without invoking a speech genre than it is possible to produce an utterance without invoking a "national language" such as English, French, or Thai.

The resulting picture is one in which speaking is inherently a process of appropriating the words of others, be they concrete, identifiable other individuals or groups of others, as in the case of "social languages" (Wertsch 1991). Speech is therefore a form of mediated action in which speech genres (along with other aspects of language) serve as mediational means. As is the case with all forms of mediated action (Wertsch 1991) this implies that there is an inherent and irreducible tension between the mediational means, that is, an "impersonal" tool, on the one hand, and the unique and personal use or instantiation of this tool in a concrete performance, on the other. In Bakhtinian terms

Our speech, that is, all our utterances (including creative works), is filled with others' words, varying degrees of otherness or varying degrees of "our-own-ness," varying degrees of awareness and detachment. These words of others carry with them their own expression, their own evaluative tone, which we assimilate, rework, and re-accentuate. (Bakhtin 1986, p. 89)

Speech genres and the logical genre

A complete account of the implications of Bakhtin's claims for Scribner's account of literacy would need to address two basic issues. First, it would need to produce a more complete explication of speech genres in general and of the genres associated with literacy in particular. What are the specific properties of speech genres used in literacy practice? How do they differ from other speech genres? Second, the problem of how these speech genres can be appropriated in unique performances needs to be addressed. What processes are involved in invoking or ventriloquating through a speech genre in order to produce concrete utterances? How do these processes vary depending on contextual factors?

These two research agendas may be distinguished analytically and hence investigated, at least to some degree, independently. This is so even though they must eventually be related in order not to lose sight of the irreducible connection between mediational means and their use, a point Bakhtin was alluding to in his critique of traditional linguistic analyses when he noted that "speech can exist in reality only in the form of concrete utterances" (1986, p. 71). In what follows, we shall focus primarily on issues of mapping out the properties of speech genres used in literacy practice and spend less time on the dynamics of their use (for the latter, see Wertsch & O'Connor, 1994). In particular, we shall be concerned with ways in which Scribner's "logical genre" might shape speaking and thinking processes.

On the basis of her review of several studies of verbal logical problems, Scribner (1977) argued that the major difference between schooled and nonschooled participants was that the former tended to use only that information explicitly provided by the experimenter, whereas the nonschooled participants' answers often reflected a tendency to take other information into consideration.

The critical factor [in the performance of the nonschooled subjects] is that the 'evidence use by the subject', in many cases . . . bore little resemblance to the evidence supplied in the experimental problem. Cole et al. (1971, p. 188) concluded: 'The subjects were (or seem to have been) responding to conventional situations in which their past experience dictated the answer. . . . In short, it appears that the particular verbal context and content dictate the response rather than the arbitrarily imposed relations among the elements in the problem.' (Scribner 1977, p. 488)

Further analyses by Scribner suggest that the pattern of nonschooled subjects' performance was *not* attributable to faulty logical procedures or logical procedures that were even qualitatively distinct from those employed by the schooled subjects. Instead, the differences between schooled and nonschooled participants derived from different patterns in what they took to be the content on which operations were to be performed.

In her analysis of studies that specifically asked participants to justify or explain their answers, Scribner employed a distinction between "theoretical" and "empirical" explanations. Theoretical explanations were defined as being based strictly on information supplied by the experimenter, whereas empirical explanations were defined as being based on information that the subjects themselves introduced. As an example of this distinction Scribner gives the following problem and types of explanation:

> All people who own houses pay a house tax.
> Boima does not pay a house tax.
> Does Boima own a house?

A theoretical justification: 'If you say Boima does not pay a house tax, he cannot own a house.' An empirical explanation: 'Boima does not have money to pay a house tax.' (1977, p. 489)

Scribner found that by incorporating the distinction between empirical and theoretical explanations into the analysis of data from several studies the differences between schooled and nonschooled participants became even more pronounced:

> Nonschooled villagers overwhelmingly support their answers by appeals to fact, belief or opinion [i.e., facts known to them but not explicitly stated by the experiment]. . . . This appeal to real world knowledge and experience, which for the time being we will call 'empirical bias', is the single most prominent characteristic of villagers' performance. (1977, pp. 489–490)

As Scribner notes, an empirical bias does not disappear completely from the reasoning of even very highly educated individuals. Furthermore, she was certainly not implying that it *should* disappear from the thinking processes of individuals as they go about their everyday business in a variety of activity settings, only one of which may be formal schooling. Instead, the implicit claim is that the logical genre is one tool in a "cultural tool kit" (Wertsch 1991) that emerges in response to participating in certain activity settings. Instead of replacing other cultural tools, or mediational means, the emergence of the logical genre is more likely to add to the "heterogeneity" (Tulviste 1991) of this took kit, a heterogeneity that reflects the "activity relativism" (Tulviste 1991) of sociocultural settings in which humans live.

In the particular case of Scribner's logical genre, a defining property of the mediational means is a distinction between what we shall term "activated" and "nonactivated" information. When schooled participants invoked the logical genre to solve syllogisms, activated information was defined as that information which has been explicitly stated by the experimenter. Nonactivated information was any other information known to either the experimenter or subject or both, but information that had not been made known through the explicit statements of the experimenter. In this particular context, because it was not made known through such explicit assertions, it was deemed irrelevant to the task.

At first glance it might appear that the distinction between activated and nonactivated information is grounded in an objective assessment of what information is available (through explicit statements or otherwise) to the interlocutors in a context. Such a view would parallel assumptions that underlie accounts of given versus new information (Halliday 1967; Chafe 1974, 1976; Clark and Haviland 1977), psychological subject versus psychological predicate (Vygotsky 1987), and so forth. In these accounts the focus is on how information is established in consciousness or in the context of speaking and how this "given information" is then used as the foundation for interaction.

It is certainly true that knowledge of given information plays a role in producing and understanding utterances and is a necessary factor in determining what counts as activated information. Specifically, if something is not given information – the psychological subject, the theme, and so forth – it cannot be activated information. However, *not all given information is activated* in the sense of "activated" that we are using. The distinction between activated and nonactivated information differs from the others in an essential way. This is because the distinction between activated and nonactivated information is grounded not only in what information is available for one reason or another in a discourse setting, but in the speech genre as well. That is, *specific speech genres entail specific assumptions about what is activated and nonactivated information*, and this fact often operates independently of whether or not the interlocutors in a speech context share knowledge of certain information.

The difference we are talking about here concerns relationships between utterances and their contexts. On the one hand, utterances must occur in some already existing context and as a result have certain presuppositions. Notions such as given information, psychological subject, and theme are grounded in this observation. On the other hand, making an utterance defines or transforms this context in some way. This is the "performative" or "creative" dimension of speaking analyzed by theorists such as Austin (1962) and Silverstein (1976, 1985). The specific claim we wish to make derives from the observation that producing an utterance involves a speech genre and any speech genre shapes the creative dimension of utterances in certain ways. Of particular interest at this point is that the invocation of a particular speech genre carries with it a specific assignment of activated and nonactivated information, and this assignment may be independent of the given-new distinction.

As an illustration of this claim, consider the examples reviewed by Scribner in her account of what she called the logical genre. The major difference between schooled and nonschooled participants in the studies she reviewed was that the former were more likely to operate solely on the basis of activated information (in this case defined as information explicitly provided by the experimenter), whereas the nonschooled participants tended to take other information into account. The fact that activated information is defined in the context of this speech genre as that information explicitly provided by the experimenter cannot be reduced to facts about what the experimenter and subject knew in general and how their knowledge overlaps. For example, in the case of the syllogism about Boima, both the experimenter and subject may have in fact known that "Boima does not have money to pay a house tax" (Scribner 1977, p. 489). However, by invoking the logical genre, this shared background knowledge is not defined as activated information and hence is deemed irrelevant when drawing a conclusion.

Scribner's "theoretical" explanations are associated with invoking her logical genre and hence using activated information as defined by this genre, whereas "empirical" explanations are associated with using nonactivated information (in some cases alongside activated information). Similarly, the definition of the "empirical bias" derives from the distinction between activated and nonactivated information, and again this distinction is grounded in the invocation of the logical genre and not from some distinction between types of information, which has an independent, objective existence. The mastery of this genre therefore involves mastery of a particular distinction between activated and nonactivated information.

The essential point here is that the difference between activated and nonactivated information is not grounded in some objective property of the information itself. Instead, it is grounded in the properties of the speech genre used to carry out the mediated action at issue. By invoking the logical speech genre, one creates a very circumscribed discourse space in which certain information is defined as irrelevant independently of what the interlocutors might actually know or share as background information. As a result, what counts as an empirical explanation cannot be determined by analyses of information that do not take into account the particular distinction between activated and nonactivated information entailed by the particular speech genre at issue. In cases involving Scribner's logical genre, this means that information invoked to produce an empirical explanation could have produced a theoretical explanation *if* it had been explicitly stated by the experimenter rather than deriving from some other source.

The logical genre and literacy activity

As we argued earlier, Scribner was utilizing a kind of activity-oriented approach to issues in literacy several years before she explicitly invoked ideas and terms from others' activity theories. In our view much of her career was devoted to developing an activity theory approach to a range of phenomena. In general, this approach was grounded in the claim that mental processes of individuals can be understood only by understanding how they fit into culturally, historically, and institutionally situated activity. Scribner pursued this claim by examining concrete forms of practice, or action, with one eye toward their psychological correlates and the other toward the sociocultural settings in which they occurred. As noted earlier, this line of reasoning is consistent with the perspective Vygotsky was developing near the end of his career when he expanded his notion of scientific concepts to say that such concepts must be understood in terms of their role in discourse peculiar to formal instructional settings rather than in terms of more narrowly defined social processes.

Given this context of concerns and issues, Scribner's account of the logical genre can be seen to have major implications for how we can understand literacy activity. Specifically, it raises the question of what it is in literacy practice that might lead to differences between schooled and nonschooled people's approaches to syllogistic reasoning. Neither Scribner nor others have argued that it is extensive practice with tasks that are explicitly organized in syllogistic form that has this effect. With a few possible exceptions (e.g., story problems in mathematics), there seem to be few direct parallels between the requirements of syllogistic reasoning tasks and those of ongoing literacy practices in the classroom.

Instead, we would argue that the patterns of using the logical genre Scribner found derive from extensive experiences with various forms of the distinction between activated and nonactivated information. In contrast to the relatively simple and clear distinction entailed when invoking the logical genre to solve syllogisms (a distinction grounded in what has been explicitly stated in the immediate context), this distinction is often less simple and less clear in classroom discourse. However, it is no less strongly imposed. This latter fact is an indication that it has one of the major properties of a cultural tool, or mediational means, in an account of mediated action. It is socioculturally situated in the sense that it is preferred, or "privileged" (Wertsch 1991), over others in a particular cultural, institutional, and historical setting.

In contrast to the experimental settings reviewed by Scribner (1977), the distinction between activated and nonactivated information in classroom discourse does not rest on whether something has been explicitly stated in the immediate context. Instead of this relatively simple and clear criterion for making the distinction, the speech genres found in classroom discourse tend to be grounded in a more general distinction between activated and nonactivated information. It is certainly true that something may be activated information by virtue of its just having been stated, but many other criteria seem to be used as well. For example, information that has been covered in previous classroom discourse, information that comes from shared background reading, and information from other sources that are presumed to be shared all may qualify as activated information.

However, as in the case of Scribner's logical genre, the distinction between activated and nonactivated information cannot be reduced to what is shared background and what is not. It always involves the element of contextual creativity or performativity, and what is created is conventionally associated with the speech genre. Thus, to master a speech genre is to master a particular distinction between activated and nonactivated information.

The specifics of this line of reasoning are obviously still in the process of being worked out. However, the general framework of the argument has begun to emerge quite clearly, thanks to the insights of scholars such as Scribner. Indeed, Scribner's career can be understood as a continuing attempt to address the complex issues of a theory of activity that would allow us to understand relationships between human mental processes and sociocultural setting. For her, a starting point was the claim that human mental processes are best understood in terms of human action. Given that such action always occurs in cultural, institutional, and historical contexts, she was constantly led to address the issue of how mental functioning is inherently socioculturally situated.

Scribner's elaboration of these claims generated insights that will be the focus of research and action programs for years to come. The fact that her ideas continue to appeal to people from such an array of professional and cultural backgrounds speaks volumes about the ingenious insights she brought to her work. Perhaps even more importantly, this appeal reflects the deep commitment she had to respecting the perspectives of the weak as well as the powerful. Her convincing demonstrations that there is more than one intelligent way to understand the world around us provides an important starting point for pursuing one of her deepest desires – to make the world a better place for all of us.

References

Austin, J. L. (1962). *How to do things with words.* London: Oxford University Press.

Bakhtin, M. M. (1981). *The dialogic imagination: Four essays by M. M. Bakhtin.* M. Holquist (Ed.). C. Emerson & M. Holquist (Trans.). Austin: University of Texas Press.

Bakhtin, M. M. (1984). *Problems of Dostoevsky's Poetics*, Caryl Emerson (Ed. and Trans.). Minneapolis: University of Minnesota Press.

Bakhtin, M. M. (1986). *Speech genres and other late essays.* Caryl Emerson & Michael Holquist (Eds.). V.W. McGee (Trans.). Austin: University of Texas Press.

Chafe, W. L. (1974). Language and consciousness. *Language, 50*, 111–133.

Chafe, W. L. (1976). Givenness, contrastiveness, definiteness, subjects, topics, and point of view. In C. N. Li (Ed.), *Subject and topic.* New York: Academic Press.

Clark, H., & Haviland, S. E. (1977). Comprehension and the given-new contract. In R. Freedle (Ed.), *Discourse production and comprehension*, pp. 1–40. Hillsdale, NJ: Erlbaum.

Clark, K., & Holquist, M. (1984). *Mikhail Bakhtin.* Cambridge, MA: Harvard University Press.

Cole, M., et al. (1971). *The cultural context of learning and thinking.* New York: Basic Books.

Halliday, M. A. K. (1967). Notes on transitivity and theme in English, II. *Journal of Linguistics, 3*, pp. 199–244.

Holquist, M. (1986). Introduction. In M. M. Bahktin (1986). *Speech genres and other late essays.* Austin: University of Texas Press.

Holquist, M. (1990). *Dialogism: Bakhtin and his world.* London: Routledge.

Hymes, D. (1974). *Foundations in sociolinguistics.* Philadelphia: University of Pennsylvania Press.

Leont'ev, A. N. (1981). The problem of activity in psychology. In J. V. Wertsch (Ed.), *The concept of activity in Soviet psychology.* Armonk, NY: M. E. Sharpe.

Luria, A. R. (1976). *Cognitive development: Its cultural and social foundations*. Cambridge, MA: Harvard University Press.

Sakharov, L. S. (1930). O metodakh issledovaniya ponyatii [Methods for the investigation of concepts]. *Psikhologiya, 3*(1).

Scribner, S. (1977). Modes of thinking and ways of speaking. In P. N. Johnson-Laird & P. C. Wason (Eds.), *Thinking: Readings in cognitive science*. New York: Cambridge University Press.

Scribner, S., & Cole, M. (1981). *The psychological consequences of literacy*. Cambridge, MA: Harvard University Press.

Silverstein, M. (1976). Shifters, linguistic categories, and cultural description. In K. Basso & H. Selby (Eds.), *Meaning in anthropology*. Albuquerque: University of New Mexico Press.

Silverstein, M. (1985). The functional stratification of language and ontogenesis. In J. V. Wertsch (Ed.), *Culture, communication, and cognition: Vygotskian perspectives*, pp. 205–235. New York: Cambridge University Press.

Todorov, T. (1984). *Mikhail Bakhtin: The dialogic principle*. W. Godzich (Trans.). Minneapolis: University of Minnesota Press.

Tulviste, P. (1991). *Cultural-historical development of verbal thinking: A psychological study*. Commack, NY: Nova Science Publishers.

Vygotsky, L. S. (1977). Iz tet'ryadei L. S. Vygotskogo [From the notebooks of L. S. Vygotsky]. *Vestnik Moskovskogo Universiteta: Seriya psikhologii* [Moscow University record: Psychology series], *15*, 89–95.

Vygotsky, L. S. (1978). *Mind in society*. Cambridge, MA: Harvard University Press.

Vygotsky, L. S. (1981). The instrumental method in psychology. In J. V. Wertsch (Ed.), *The concept of activity in Soviet psychology*. Armonk, NY: M. E. Sharpe.

Vygotsky, L. S. (1987). *The collected works of L. S. Vygotsky. Volume 1: Problems of general psychology*. N. Minick (Ed. and Trans.). New York: Plenum.

Wertsch, J. V. (1991). *Voices of the mind: A sociocultural approach to mediated action*. Cambridge, MA: Harvard University Press.

Wertsch, J. V., & O'Connor, K. (1994). Multivoicedness in historical representation: American college students' accounts of the origins of the United States. *Journal of Narrative and Life History, 4*(4), 295–309.

Zinchenko, V. P. (1985). Vygotsky's ideas about units of analysis of mind. In J. V. Wertsch (Ed.), *Culture, communication, and cognition: Vygotskian perspectives*, pp. 94–118. New York: Cambridge University Press.

Part IV

Activity in work and school

13 The qualitative analysis of the development of a child's theoretical knowledge and thinking

Mariane Hedegaard

The aim of this chapter is to contribute to the analysis of a basic problem that is central in both Vygotsky's and Scribner's work, namely, that of how educational practice becomes reflected in children's general psychological functioning. This problem is related to the more epistemological problem of how societal practice effects qualitative change in the higher intellectual functioning of humans. The study presented here is a qualitative study of the effect of *Developmental Teaching* on a child's skill acquisition and general psychic development.

Developmental Teaching is an approach based on the epistemology of the cultural-historical or sociohistorical school in psychology inspired by Markova, Davydov, and Lompscher (Markova 1978–79; Davydov 1982, 1988; Lompscher 1984). It is also inspired by Jerome Bruner's curriculum, *Man a Course of Study*. Developmental Teaching, however, transcends both these approaches on several essential points: by introducing a "double move" in instruction, by working directly with goal formation as a phase of instruction, and by using children's cooperation to facilitate their acquisition of knowledge and skill in the subject matter.

Developmental Teaching was carried out as part of a three-year intervention project in biology, geography, and history in a Danish elementary school.

A microstudy of one child's skill acquisition and general psychic development is presented in order to trace the learning process in detail. The teaching process has been the focus of earlier reports of the project (Hedegaard 1988, 1990a, 1990b, Hedegaard and Sigersted 1992). Specifically, the focus of the analysis will be a child's development of motivation, social interaction, theoretical knowledge, and thinking skills. The societal practice of history teaching in Denmark will be outlined as well,

293

to give a context for the change in teaching practice represented by Developmental Teaching.

For both Vygotsky and Scribner, the central problem in psychology has been conceptualizing and analyzing the relations between social practice, skill acquisition with tools (manual as well as intellectual), and qualitative change in people's general functioning (Scribner & Cole 1981; Vygotsky & Scribner 1978, 1985–1987, 1984a, 1989b). This relation can be characterized as the germ cell of the cultural- or sociohistorical approach. Through her interpretation of Vygotsky and of the sociocultural–historical approach to psychology and through her cultural studies of literacy with Cole, Scribner has contributed to the logic and possibilities of a methodological approach based on this scientific epistemology. Since the research project described here used the methodological approach of the sociohistorical school, a first step will be to relate the project to the methodology as it is based on Scribner's categorical outline of its basic concepts.

The general categories of the sociocultural-historical approach

Scribner presents two ways of systematizing the sociohistorical approach that can be very helpful as an epistemological orientation for identifying the level and type of problems dealt with in the current study. The first is an analysis of different levels of historical change of human psychic activity (Scribner 1985). The second is an analysis of the relation between function, structure, and mode of development as an integrated whole (Scribner 1990).

Historical levels of analysis

Scribner, inspired by Vygotsky's work, characterized four levels of historical analysis which focus on the transformation and development of humankind, society, persons, and skills, respectively (Scribner 1985, p. 110).

The first level is the transformation of biological evolution into historical development. The conceptualization of tool production in the form of both material and intellectual tools is the prime focus in explaining this transformation. In the project described here, this level is reflected on the general methodological plane through the choice of an intervention study of teaching and learning activity. It is also conceptualized on a more specific plane by the selection of the teaching themes of the experimental teaching, which were the evolution of animals, the origin of humans, and the historical change of society.

The second level in Scribner's system is the analogy of the relation between societies and levels of humankind's ontogenetic development. The interaction between practice in societal institutions and the child's psychic development is the relation to be explained on this level. This is also the question of how the biological and cultural lines interact in the ontogenetic development of humans. When practice in an institution changes, or when a child goes from one social institution to the next – kindergarten, school, professional education, and work – the child develops new psychic capacities or gets to a new stage in development. In the project here, the analysis of the interaction of the practices of history teaching in the Danish school system and ideals of character formation occur at this level.

The third level focuses on the life history of the individual. The relationship between a child's psychic development and her interaction with others in an institutional context is the topic to be explained at this level. It is this kind of analysis that is of prime importance in the project described here.

The fourth level of historical analysis is of the development of specific psychological systems. This level is conceived in the research project in the analysis of development of motivation, social interaction, and cognition in relation to acquiring and using historical concepts and methods.

Structure, function, mode of development, and content

Scribner points to structure, function, and mode of development as the basic dimensions of human activity and points out that the theoretical characteristics of these three dimensions determine the logic, possibility, and limitations of the research methodology.

In Scribner's interpretation of the sociohistorical school (1990, p. 110), structure is mediated by tools and signs; function is characterized by goal-directed activities; and the mode of development is historical and social. The characterization of these three dimensions will be used to further explicate the aim of this project and its roots in the cultural and sociohistorical tradition.

A fourth dimension will also be taken into consideration: subject matter, or the content of the activity, a dimension that has to become integrated into the analysis of activity to make it truly cultural-historical. Practice has to be practice in relation to something, and activity has to be activity in relation to an object (Leont'ev 1978), where objects are understood in a broad sense conceptually as well as materially.

The structure of human activity and cognition is the cultural mediation between organism and environment. According to Vygotsky, this mediation is basically characterized by tool mediation. Scribner adds an important extension to this: mediators include culturally developed technologies, knowledge, and skills, which she characterized as cultural practice (Scribner & Cole 1981, p. 259; Scribner 1984a, p. 2–3).

Scribner and Cole conceptualize the relation between culture and psychology as two different perspectives on practice. Practice is defined as "a recurrent, goal-directed sequence of activities using a particular technology and particular systems of knowledge," and the psychological aspects of the cultural practice are skills defined as "the coordinated sets of actions involved in applying this knowledge in particular settings." Practice is characterized by three components: technology, knowledge, and skills, which can be applied "to the spheres of activity that are predominantly conceptual (for example, the practice of law) as well as to those that are predominantly sensory-motor (for example the practice of weaving)" (Scribner & Cole 1981, p. 236). This change of focus from tool to practice is a step forward, because it enriches our understanding of the specific characteristics of human beings' relation to the environment.

The concept of mediation is basic to Developmental Teaching in the more broad sense that Scribner explicates because both the models and procedures for exploration and structure of the classroom activity make up classroom practice that transcends a narrow sense of acquisition of intellectual tools and knowledge. The notion of interdependence between technology, skill, and knowledge creating a specific cultural unity is the heart of the cultural- and sociohistorical approach. In this research it means that school practice, in the form of 1) knowledge of subject areas, 2) procedures for how this knowledge has been acquired, and 3) technologies in the form of written records, pictures, historical films, and systematized collections (i.e., museums) have to be taken into consideration as the content of the teaching.

This approach further characterizes activities so that they are always motivated or goal directed, both when they are looked at as traditions and practice in the culture as well as when they are conceptualized as the subjects' personal ways of tackling their environment. The relation between cognition and motivation has been described in Davydov's (1982) formulation of the structure of the teaching activity. He points to three phases in this structure: goal formation, learning acts, and evaluation. The importance of working with the pupils' motivation has become central in educational psychology (Pintrich 1991), but the transcendence between the cultural or social goals and the personal goals in instruction are not generally problematized. How the society, the community, the school, and the teacher's goals for learning become reflected in pupils' goals and how they influence the students' understanding and formation of their own goals for the activities in the classroom has only been researched on a formal level. In Developmental Teaching, goal formation has been taken seriously as a special phase of problem formulation in the instructional period. An analysis of this phase of our project will be presented in the "Results" section.

The developmental importance of the social interaction between teacher and student inside the zone of proximal development has been a central issue in instruction based ón the cultural-historical tradition (Vygotsky 1978; Griffin & Cole 1985; Tharp & Gallimore 1988). In Developmental Teaching, the importance of students' cooperation is conceptualized as essential for a child's development inside the zone of proximal development. Cooperative learning is not seen as a natural process, but as one that also has to be developed in the instructional setting (Cowie & Rudduck, 1990). In Developmental Teaching, children's cooperation and group work become topics of special concern. This is especially important to point out because the presentation following focuses on an individual child in fourth-grade history class. To be able to follow her acquisition of skill and knowledge about history and how this influences her psychic development, we have to take her interactions into consideration, especially those with her classmates.

The fourth dimension to be considered is the subject matter to be related to, or the content of the activities. In this project the central activity is learning historical concepts and methods and the subject is historical aspects of reality. The different ways of relating to this subject in

Danish school practice will presently be introduced from the perspective of teaching.

Problem formulation

At the institutional level, the school's objective is to develop an effective practice of teaching and mediating knowledge and skills among the children. The aim of this project was to combine this objective with the development of tasks that would motivate the pupils to engage in a research activity that established a connection between the pupils' own questions and questions in the subject area. This aim is based on the presupposition that the motive for learning develops from the child's participation in teaching activity, and that the interest the children bring to this teaching has to be a starting point for this development of motivation (Hedegaard 1988a; Schiefele 1991). In teaching it is important to cultivate a motive for learning. It is also important that the learning motive becomes connected to the school subject because it is the basis for the child's development of a reflected and theoretical orientation to the world.

The objective of this chapter is to evaluate the process of how a single child's acquisition of knowledge in history becomes a tool for her thinking and knowledge acquisition and influences her motivation and social interaction. Evaluation of the teaching itself is not conducted directly, but is so indirectly through the child's learning activity. Since social interaction is one of the basic categories of this approach, cooperative group work has been a key. So though the focus is on a single child, the importance of this child's interaction with her fellow students is essential to an evaluation of her gain in interest for and acquisition of theoretical knowledge and thinking related to historical concepts.

It is important for understanding the analysis of skill acquisition and general development of this child to point to the specific theory of knowledge that Development Teaching builds upon. This theory of knowledge will be outlined later and related to the specific paradigm of Developmental Teaching that is the core of the "social practice" described in this project.

A theory of knowledge

A child is born into a society where knowledge already exists. Knowledge exists as practice and procedures for tool use, tool production, and interaction between persons – in both manual and intellectual forms. The standard procedures that exist in a society to tackle and solve societal problems can be seen as culturally developed skills which each generation has to acquire and transcend. Knowledge as it exists in different media (language, text, diagrams, pictures, movies, computer programs, etc.) is the result of societally developed procedures for solving social problems. The development of medicine and of computer science are typical examples of this development. Societal practice comes before societal knowledge (Wartofsky 1979, Juul-Jensen 1986) and therefore knowledge can never be knowledge of essence independent of the societal practice, but is in constant change and development.

When societal knowledge can be characterized as reflected knowledge, which means that it can become communicated, two forms of knowledge can be distinguished, which can be connected to different trends in scientific development. The importance of distinguishing between theoretical and empirical knowledge in the educational context has been pointed to by Davydov (1977, 1982, 1988). His characterization of the difference between these two types of knowledge can be formulated thus: theoretical knowledge deals with a connected system of phenomena and not separate, individual phenomena. It has arisen through a historical process of knowledge development connected to an institutional approach to the pressing problems of society. In contrast, empirical knowledge deals with the differences and similarities of a single phenomenon abstracted from its context. Both forms of knowledge can be found in both practical and scientific domains (Hedegaard 1990b), and theoretical knowledge should not be equated with abstract knowledge. The aim of Developmental Teaching is the mediating of theoretical knowledge.

Developmental teaching
Theoretical knowledge and the germ cell as tools for learning and teaching

Theoretical knowledge is best characterized in relation to the basic structure (the germ cell) of a problem area where thinking is the procedure and process for acquiring, using, and evaluating knowledge of that problem area. By this definition, it is fruitful to look at empirical knowledge as subordinated rather than opposed to theoretical knowledge, as Davydov does (1977).

Models can become important tools for acquiring theoretical knowledge and a theoretical orientation to the problem area under investigation. The model of a germ cell as formulated by Ilyenkov (1977), Davydov (1977) and Engeström and Hedegaard (1986) is seen as such a tool.

The two main characteristics of a germ cell as an intellectual tool are that 1) it depicts the basic relations in the subject area or problem area studied so that if one aspect changes the influence of this change can be traced in the other aspects depicted in the germ cell, and 2) the basic relations can be recognized in the concrete surrounding phenomena.

A germ cell as an intellectual tool for teaching/learning activity has two main functions: (1) as the teacher's planning tool for organizing and motivating the teaching, and (2) as the pupils' tool for organizing their active research of the problem area in question.

An example of a germ cell that we have used in part in our teaching experiment is found in Figure 13.1.

This germ cell depicts the relations between nature, tools, and people's living conditions. By examining these relations it is possible to analyze the following kind of changes: if nature changes, then people's use of tools will also have to change if existing living conditions are to be preserved, or if tool use changes, people's living conditions change if nature remains unchanged.

Teaching history in the Danish public school

In Denmark, the Ministry of Education's requirements for history teaching have changed very drastically in recent years (1960, 1975, 1981, 1984). This has not been true for other subjects and shows the weight the ruling parties place on history teaching.

The different emphases in teaching that can be found in these requirements relate to (1) objectivity in presentation, (2) critique of sources, (3) pluralism in presentation, and (4) unity and continuity in presentation. These, in turn, can be related to two dimensions of values: the formation of personality through history teaching, and the relation between the science of history and the school subject of history.

The formation of personality through history teaching. A special part of the content of history as it is taught in schools has been determined by different ideals of character formation. In Scandinavia and in Denmark

The Developmental Steps of the Germ-Cell Model

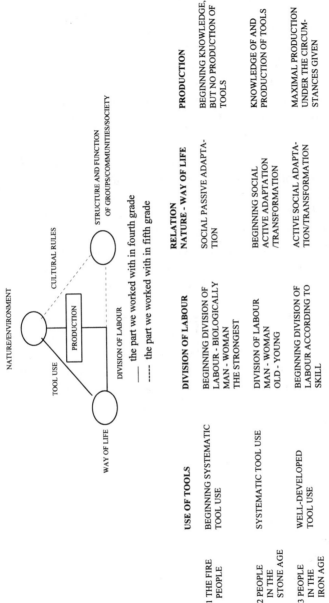

the part we worked with in fourth grade
----- the part we worked with in fifth grade

	USE OF TOOLS	DIVISION OF LABOUR	RELATION NATURE - WAY OF LIFE	PRODUCTION
1 THE FIRE PEOPLE	BEGINNING SYSTEMATIC TOOL USE	BEGINNING DIVISION OF LABOUR - BIOLOGICALLY MAN - WOMAN THE STRONGEST	SOCIAL PASSIVE ADAPTATION	BEGINNING KNOWLEDGE, BUT NO PRODUCTION OF TOOLS
2 PEOPLE IN THE STONE AGE	SYSTEMATIC TOOL USE	DIVISION OF LABOUR MAN - WOMAN OLD - YOUNG	BEGINNING SOCIAL ACTIVE ADAPTATION /TRANSFORMATION	KNOWLEDGE OF AND PRODUCTION OF TOOLS
3 PEOPLE IN THE IRON AGE	WELL-DEVELOPED TOOL USE	BEGINNING DIVISION OF LABOUR ACCORDING TO SKILL	ACTIVE SOCIAL ADAPTATION/TRANSFORMATION	MAXIMAL PRODUCTION UNDER THE CIRCUMSTANCES GIVEN

METHOD: VARIATION OF THE MODEL ON THE BASIS OF TOOL USE AND DIVISION OF LABOUR

Figure 13.1. The Developmental Steps of the Germ Cell Model.

these ideals have changed from the first days of history teaching in school until today (Sødring Jensen 1978, Mainfest 1983, Engelund 1988). Before World War II, history in Denmark together with classes in religion had the task to shape the moral and national identity of the child. This objective changed in the 1950s when the aim became to mediate the rational objective truth of the past. History became a descriptive subject. Today, discussion of the formation of personality has reappeared though in a more modern version, related to the formation of personal identity (Historididaktik i Norden 1988, 1990).

The relation between the science of history and the school subject of history.
Another topic of discussion is how close history teaching can be connected to the scientific study of history (Dickenson, Gard, & Lee 1978; Lee 1983). In Denmark, the question has been whether the task of school is to present scientific history based on chronology or to motivate children by making teaching project oriented. That is, should the children learn to ask questions the same way as professional historians or should history teaching be related to the children's experience?

If the concepts we base our teaching on are viewed as psychic tools, practices, and procedures in the sense described by Vygotsky and Scribner, teaching cannot be based only on the child's experience but has to be related to societal knowledge. Therefore, in this project we asked which aspect of scientific history can become relevant knowledge for children's life of today and for the development of their future competence. We also asked about how we integrate these aspects with the motivation children bring into the teaching situation in the form of interests, experience, and previously acquired knowledge.

The aims of the project's teaching approach (see Hedegaard in press) were

1. To develop conceptual models as tools for analyzing historical material. The models and procedures should be characterized by central concepts of history accepted broadly in different scientific approaches to history.
2. To use a time line and historical periodization.
3. To promote skills and procedures analogous to methods of doing research in human science.
4. To foster use of the acquired models and procedures for analyzing society of today.

The double move in teaching

The instructional plan in the teaching experiment can be characterized as a double move from the abstract to the concrete and from the concrete to the abstract. The teacher guides instruction from general aspects of the problem area, as formulated in the germ-cell model. At the same time, the children's activities and ways of formulating questions give substance to the teaching activity in the classroom. This means that the teacher formulates tasks and activities, based on the abstract principles of the problem area as well as on his or her knowledge of the children's conceptual frames and experiences. At the beginning of a teaching unit the task is to provide children with experience. Practical activities such as museum visits or viewing films and pictures become important events. The mediation of general relations through practical material implies the use of examples where the general laws of the area can become visible to the children.

In the experimental teaching situation, two core examples were used to establish the basic germ-cell relation of tool use and tool production as a mediating link between nature and living conditions. In these activities abstract concepts of the model were used to structure the children's activities, but the interrelation of its elements was brought forward during class activity through the examples the teacher brought up. The teacher provoked the children to formulate the relation through contrasting examples and by asking the children to reflect upon and analyze the contrasts that could be experienced with different material. The first example was taken from a film about the !Kung people's way of living. Their living conditions were compared to those of Stone Age people, as viewed in pictures and on a museum visit. A contrasting example was Iron Age people's production and use of tools to create living conditions in a cold environment. The experience of the importance of tool use and production was created through a workshop at an outdoor museum.

Structuring the classroom activity

The model of the social science research process was used for teaching history in this experiment. The teaching process, however, is not the same as the scientific research process. Rather, the model of social science research was used analogically in modeling teaching activity.

A general research model inspired by Lewin (1946) was adapted as a procedure for the children's research and was used for structuring the daily activities. The component questions of this cyclical model are

1. What is the research area?
2. What do we know and what do we not know about this area?
3. How can we relate the known to the unknown in a model?
4. What means do we have for exploring this model?
5. How are the results of the exploration related to the research problem?

The procedure guided the daily activities in the class: planning the day, engaging in dialogue about the previous session and relating this summary to the model and to the task of the day, and the evaluation of the activities. These steps can also be recognized in the phases that guide the children's activities over the whole year (see Figure 13.2, pages 292–293). These were problem formulation, model formulation, model use/extension, model variation, construction and evaluation of tasks, and evaluation of one's own performance.

Research method

The three-year teaching experiment consisted of one year of teaching the subject of evolutionary history (third grade) and two years of teaching human history and the historical periods in society (fourth and fifth grades).

Participant observation was conducted during all sessions of the experimental teaching, resulting in extensive research protocols from each. In addition to general observations of the class, three children were followed closely throughout the study. Cecilie is the child we followed most closely, and an analysis of her activities in fourth grade are presented here.

The second year of the teaching experiment is then the focus of our analysis, when the teaching of human history and historical periods in society started. The experimental teaching year consisted of 26 teaching sessions, each session comprising three lessons.

The lessons took place in a Danish elementary school with 600 students located in a commune that can be characterized both as a village and a suburb to a moderately sized town (250,000 inhabitants).

Evaluation of the learning activity

The frame for the interpretation of the protocols was developed in earlier work, on the basis of theoretical and empirical analyses (Hedegaard 1986, 1990a). The basic categories of the frame are teaching activity and learning activity, each of which have subthemes. The topics of the teaching activity are differentiated into concepts, process, activities, and problems. Learning activity is differentiated into motivation, social interaction, knowledge acquisition, and development of problems and strategies for solving them.

This frame of interpretation is based on the assumption that interaction between subjects is the prime factor in a child's learning activity (Vygotsky 1971–1974, 1978, 1985–1987). The frame is further characterized by the integration of content matter into the questions. Since the focus of our analysis will be Cecilie's learning activity only the frame for evaluation of learning activity is shown in Figure 13.3.

Results and analysis

Before discussing the development of Cecilie's theoretical thinking and knowledge of historical time, an overview of all the students' competence in evolutionary history as reflected in their explanations and use of models will be presented. Table 13.1 shows that the first year of teaching resulted in almost all the children acquiring a mental model for evolutionary history. Cecilie's development can be compared to that of her classmates. She is obviously not the only person to have acquired theoretical concepts. Furthermore, the results can be compared to those of a control class (see Table 13.2), which did not perform as well as the experimental class. Hence it can be concluded that the first year of teaching influenced the children's concept acquisition.

Cecilie's learning activity in fourth grade is structured around the six learning phases: problem formulation, model formulation, model use/extension, model variation, construction and evaluation of tasks, and evaluation of her own performance. The interpretation of the first phase will be presented in detail. A condensed description of two protocols is presented in the Appendix, covering the first two of the three sessions of the problem formulation phase, to illustrate the difference between the protocols.

Activities in Fourth Grade

1 PROBLEM FORMULATION

PICTURE ANALYSES OF DIFFERENT HISTORICAL PERIODS AND DIFFERENT SOCIETIES OF TODAY (FOCUS: TYPES OF WORK AND DIFFERENCE IN TOOLS, IN LIVING CONDITIONS, AND IN DIVISION OF LABOUR)

ROLE-PLAY OF RESEARCHER AT WORK

2 MODELLING

THE !KUNG PEOPLE'S WAY OF LIVING ANALYSED THROUGH A SERIES OF TASKS IN RELATION TO A FILM PRESENTATION

ANALYSES OF STONE-AGE PEOPLE'S WAY OF LIVING FROM READING TEXT

MAKING ANALOGY BETWEEN THE !KUNG PEOPLE'S WAY OF LIVING AND THE STONE-AGE PEOPLE'S WAY OF LIVING

TWO DAYS EXCURSION TO AN OPEN-AIR MUSEUM WITH ACTIVITIES IN TOOL USE IN THE IRON AGE. VISITING FARMS AT THE MUSEUM FROM 1700, DESCRIBING MALE AND FEMALE TOOLS

MODEL MAKING OF HISTORICAL PERIODS:

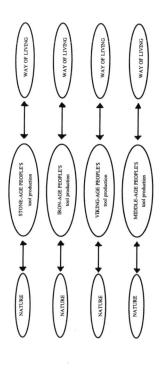

PLAY MAKING AND PERFORMANCE SHOWING DIFFERENT WAYS OF LIVING WITH FOCUS ON DIFFERENCE IN TOOLS IN THE STONE AGE, THE IRON AGE, THE VIKING AGE. BOOKS ARE USED FOR INFORMATION SEEKING.

SOLVING WRITTEN TASKS WITH FOCUS ON WAYS OF LIVING, TOOLS, DIVISION OF LABOUR, BELIEFS AND SOCIETY IN THE IRON AGE.

Figure 13.2. Activities in fourth grade (continued next page).

307

MODEL EXTENSION
MODEL MAKING OF THE FOUR THEMES THE CHILDREN HAVE WORKED WITH IN THIRD GRADE AND THE THEMES THEY ARE GOING TO WORK WITH IN FOURTH GRADE: THE EVOLUTION OF ANIMALS, LIVING CONDITIONS FOR HUMANS, DEVELOPMENT OF HUMANS, DEVELOPMENT OF SOCIETIES.

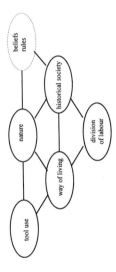

MODEL VARIATION
MODEL MAKING OF THEIR CONCEPTUAL KNOWLEDGE OF

THE STONE AGE - THE IRON AGE
THE VIKING AGE - THE MIDDLE AGE

THE CLASS LIBRARY IS USED AS INFORMATION SOURCE

CONSTRUCTION OF TASKS AND EVALUATION OF OWN SKILLS
FORMULATION OF TASKS IN SMALL GROUPS FOR THE FOUR PERIODS.
ONE GROUP FORMULATES FOR THE STONE AGE, THE OTHER GROUPS SHOULD SOLVE THESE TASKS, AND SO ON.
CLASS DIALOGUE ABOUT CREATION OF GOOD AND BAD TASKS FOR THE DIFFERENT PERIODS.
VISITING AN EXHIBITION OF THE VIKING AGE. THE TASKS ARE TO CREATE GOOD QUESTIONS ABOUT THEIR WAY OF LIVING, DIVISION OF WORK, BELIEFS, SOCIETY AND TO CREATE PLAYS WITH FOCUS ON THESE TOPICS.

Figure 13.2. (continued)

Frame for interpretation of a child's learning activity

1   **MOTIVATION**
WHAT ARE THE CHILD'S INTERESTS AND WISHES?
WHAT NEW INTERESTS ARE PRODUCED THROUGH THE PROCESS OF TEACHING?

2   **SOCIAL INTERACTION**
   I   HOW IS THE INTERACTION BETWEEN CHILD AND TEACHER?
      DOES THE CHILD FOLLOW THE TEACHER'S ADVICE?
      DOES THE CHILD ASK THE TEACHER FOR HELP?
   II HOW IS THE INTERACTION WITH OTHER CHILDREN?
      IS IT RELATED TO THE CONTENT OF THE TEACHING?
      DOES THE CHILD HELP OR SEEK HELP FROM THE OTHER CHILDREN?

3   **DEVELOPMENT OF THEORETICAL KNOWLEDGE AND THINKING**
   I   CONCEPTUAL RELATIONS:
      WHAT CHARACTERIZES THE CHILD'S TIME CONCEPTION?
      WHAT CHARACTERIZES THE CHILD'S MODEL USE?
      WHICH PROCEDURES DOES THE CHILD ACQUIRE FOR RESEARCHING HISTORICAL
      PROBLEMS?
   II CHARACTERISTICS OF THINKING
      DOES THE CHILD PARTICIPATE IN THE PROBLEM FORMULATION?
      DOES THE CHILD ANTICIPATE PART OF THE TEACHING PROCESS?
      IS THE THEME KEPT IN FOCUS?
      ARE WHY-QUESTIONS FORMULATED?
      DOES THE CHILD SEEK FOR RELATIONAL INSTEAD OF CATEGORIAL SOLUTIONS?
      DOES THE CHILD RELATE THE CONCEPTUAL KNOWLEDGE INTO A MODEL?
      DOES THE CHILD QUESTION THE MODEL'S BORDERS?
      DOES THE CHILD'S MODEL CHANGE AND DEVELOP?
      DOES THE CHILD'S IMAGINATIVE PRODUCTION EVOLVE?
      DOES THE CHILD CRITICISE THE CONTENT OF THE TEACHING?
      DOES THE CHILD CREATE NEW TASKS FOR HIM/HERSELF?
      DOES THE CHILD HAVE A CRITICAL ATTITUDE TO HER OWN PRODUCTION AND
      CAPACITY?

4   **PROBLEMS IN THE LEARNING ACTIVITY**
HOW DO PROBLEMS ARISE, HOW DO THEY PROCEED, AND HOW ARE THEY SOLVED?

Figure 13.3. Frame for Interpretation of Child's Learning Activity.

The analysis of the problem formulation phase and the five following phases is the basis of my conclusions about Cecilie's learning process in fourth grade.

The problem formulation phase

Motivation. In the first teaching session, where the topics are problem formulation and the relation to an earlier model of evolution, Cecilie is obviously engaged in the content as well as in the other children and

Table 13.1. *Experimental Class: Evolution Concepts*

	Evolution explanation[1]	Evolution/ time dimension[2]	Variation climate/nature[3]	Model[4]
Cecelie	G	ET	Climate	G
Morten	G	ET	Climate	G
Lilian	G	ET	Climate	G
Didrik	G	ET	Climate	G
Sanni	G	ET	Nature	Seal
Lisbeth	S	ET	Nature	Seal
Lise	S	E	—	Seal
Allan	S	E	—	G
Jarl	S	E	Climate	G+polar bear
Loke	S	E	—	G
Mikkel	S	E	Climate	G
Bente	S	E	Climate	G
Louis	S	E	Climate	G
Susanne	I	E	Climate	G
Jette	I	ET	Nature	G
Juliane	I	ET	—	G
Jens	I	E	Climate	G
Jørgen	I	E	—	G
Niels	I	E	—	Drawing
Lea	O	E	Climate	G

[1] Evolution explanation key:
   G = General explanation of evolution through offspring
   S = Specific example used for explanation of evolution through offspring
   I = The species changes through individuals
   O = The individual will adapt or die
[2] Evolution/time dimension key:
   ET= Evolution dimension includes the time dimension
   E = Evolution dimension without time
   O = No conception of evolution/time
[3] Variations in Climate/nature key:
   The evolution/adaptation of the animals is linked up with variation in change of
   climate or nature.
[4] Model key:
   G = General model
   Specific models: seal, polar bear

Table 13.2. *Control Class: Evolution Concepts*

	Evolution explanation[1]	Evolution/ time dimension[2]	Variation climate/nature[3]	Model[4]
Dan	G	ET	—	Drawing
Mads	S	E	—	—
Thomas	S	E	—	Drawing
Jesper	S	E	—	—
Hans	O	E	Nature	—
Kim	O	E	—	—
Morten	O	ET	—	—
Jan	O	ET	—	Drawing
Martin	O	ET	—	—
Rikke	O	ET	—	—
Linda	O	E	—	—
Tina	O	E	Climate	—
Tommy	O	O	—	—
Anja	O	O	—	—
Mikael	O	O	—	—
Trine	O	O	—	—
Karen	O	O	—	—
Casper	O	O	—	—
Helle	O	O	—	—
Torben	O	O	—	—
Jacob	O	O	—	—

[1] Evolution explanation key:
  G = General explanation of evolution through offspring
  S = Specific example used for explanation of evolution through offspring
  I = The species changes through individuals
  O = The individual will adapt or die

[2] Evolution/time dimension key:
  ET = Evolution dimension includes the time dimension
  E = Evolution dimension without time
  O = No conception of evolution/time

[3] Variations in Climate/nature key:
  The evolution/adaptation of the animals is linked up with variation in change of climate or nature.

[4] Model key:
  G = General model
  Specific models: seal, polar bear

their contributions. This impression is confirmed in the following: Cecilie expresses interest in the general goals of the historical topics which can be seen in several examples from the sessions. In the first session, she anticipated the teacher's explanation and characterized a poster of the historical time periods as a calendar of time. In the second teaching session, she brought a model for historical research into class, which she had prepared at home. She also showed her interest in the form of the teaching: in the first session she pleaded for group work, and in the second she criticized the teacher for writing too many items on the agenda, so that they would not have much time for each. The latter criticism was connected to the preparation of a play, for which she wanted more time to prepare. She was the organizer, and contributed the main theme of the play in the second session as well as in the third session. She also functioned as the storyteller so the audience could understand the performance of her group.

Social interaction. Cecilie was active in commenting on the teacher's proposal and in organizing the other children during group work. In the second session she explained her model to the other children. During the performance of the play she took care that everybody understood what happened by acting as the commentator. She criticized one of the other groups for not being serious because they exaggerated their performance. The other pupils listened to her and the teacher took her comments seriously. The teacher used Cecilie's model about the research procedure for the different historical time periods in several of the following teaching sessions.

Theoretical thinking and knowledge. In the first session Cecilie demonstrated that she had an understanding and a model of the evolution of animals. She was able to describe the connection between changes in the hare species and the change in nature when the hare was imported to the Faeroe Islands, and that the change developed over several generations of hares. Jarl and Allan drew a model of the evolution of animals and a parallel model for humans on the blackboard. Cecilie could point to the similarity, but not to the difference between the two models.

Cecilie already had a rough conception of historical time, as indicated by her comments on the poster of historical time periods and in her formulation of a procedural model.

In the third session Cecilie demonstrated that she had some ideas about how researchers explore the past.

Difficulties in the teaching activity. In the second session Cecilie exemplified her procedural model for historical time with the evolution of the sparrow through different historical time periods. By choosing a sparrow to illustrate differences in historical time periods, however, she mixed up evolutionary history with human history. This perhaps reflects the difficulties she showed in the second and third session in seeing the model of human development as different from the model of the evolution of species.

Cecilie's ideas about researching the historical past lead her to propose digging in a kitchen garden in the play performance. This shows that she confused the Danish kitchen midden as a research object with digging in the kitchen garden. Although she had misconceptions, she also had a conception about finding things from the past that can explain something about the people who lived at that particular time.

Conclusions about the phase of problem formulation

Cecilie tried to formulate an overview of what the class was going to work on, as seen in her characterization of the historical chronology poster as a calender of time and in her model, also showing a historical chronology. In addition, from the beginning, she formulated the idea of researching historical times by writing what the class members knew and what they did not know about the different historical periods.

She was motivated to cooperate around the content of the teaching, and tried to be active, anticipating and contributing both to the tasks set by the teacher and in relation to the other pupils in the class.

She demonstrated that she understood historical time perspective, but she still had difficulties in distinguishing between human history and the history of species. She demonstrated how historical findings provide a foundation for knowledge about the past, but her knowledge about methods was still bound up with her knowledge of researching fossils, which were part of the previous year's curriculum.

Thus we conclude that Cecilie started to conceptualize the goals of the research area but her conception was still rudimentary and not very detailed at the end of these three teaching sessions where problem formulation was the primary focus of teaching. Problem formulation for both Cecilie and the class became an ongoing process in later learning phases, but became subordinated to the dominating activities here: model formulation and model use.

Cecilie's learning activity in fourth grade

The evaluation of Cecilie in this section builds on all 26 experimental teaching sessions in the fourth grade. It is a condensed interpretation of all six learning phases, resulting in a characterization of the development of Cecilie's motivation, social interaction, theoretical thinking, and knowledge and strategies for solving problems.

Development of motivation

Cecilie engaged in problem formulation, and from the start she oriented towards a historical problem formulation where the dimension of time is central. In the model formulation phase, Cecilie was still engaged when the children researched and collected information from a film about the !Kung people, and during an excursion to an outdoor museum with reconstructions of buildings from the Stone Age, the Iron Age, and the Viking Age as well as original buildings from the Middle Ages. At this museum the children worked with reconstructions and tools from the Iron Age. They worked inside a reconstruction of a farm house from the Iron Age where they prepared food, made textiles, and worked in the field using a plough. They also made pots in a potter's shed and iron tools in a forge.

At that point, Cecilie was not that engaged in model formulation because she could not see a new aspect to these first phases of the modeling: to her it was merely a repetition of the well-known model for the evolution of animals. However, in the tenth teaching session, which was part of the model extension phase, her motivation rose when the model was used for formulation of four poster boards depicting the research goals: evolution of animals, development of humans, development of different ways of living, and the historical change of society. Then her understanding of the goals of the class activity became more explicit and her interest level rose. This could be seen in the activity where the model was used to concretize four different historical time periods (the Stone Age, the Iron Age, the Viking Age, and the Middle Ages). Working with the posters, Cecilie did not want to stop for breaks and was very eager to make a contribution. Thus, we see her development: in the first phases Cecilie's motivation was mostly concerned with the process of teaching and the well-being of everybody – her fellow pupils and the teacher. She had a vague understanding of the goals of the classroom activity connected to an idea of historical chronology, but because she knew very little about the concepts of the model this did not capture her interest. In later phases, where the model is used and varied, as in the four different historical time periods, the content of the subject became her prime concern. She was still helpful and still concerned with the well-being of everybody. She also urged the others to contribute to the class's common production of a goal/results boards. In the last phase, her interest in the content became so dominating that she did not hold back on her evaluation of the other participants in the group, and offered mild criticism. She was happy that they could decide on the content of the play they were going to produce about the Viking Age, and she was very active in researching information for the play.

Development of social interaction

At the start, Cecilie was oriented toward the concerns and well-being of her fellow pupils. She organized the activities in her group and was supported by her classmates. She protected weaker students and tried to make sure that everybody in her group accepted and participated in the activities. But gradually the content of the subject matter became important to her, and she started to criticize her classmates' contributions, sometimes pressing them to engage more in the instructional activities. In fact, she became so engaged that in the last session (the 26th), when the class visited the Viking museum, she was able to accept the fact that the other children did not want to use their free time to collect information for the play but preferred to use the play area. Cecilie continued to work alone for half an hour after the others had stopped, seeking help from the observer.

The development of theoretical thinking and knowledge

During the problem formulation phase, Cecilie formulated the dimension of historical time by using the model research process. She thereby contributed to one of the goals of instruction: to help children create a research procedure. Variations of her model were used over the following months and became the foundation for developing a procedural model for other children's research of time periods.

In the next phase, model formulation, Cecilie continued to have difficulties in seeing that a model of human history needed to differ in quality from a model of the evolution of animals. She was active, though, in contributing to making poster boards about what they knew and did not know about the four areas of investigation – the evolution of animals, the development of humans, the development of different ways of living, and the historical change of societies. In fact, she pointed to the difficulty in distinguishing between different ways of living and the development of humans. Her observation resulted in these categories being combined, reducing the number of research areas to three.

In the model extension phase, Cecilie started to symbolize the different ways people live in different cultures and in different historical time periods. She helped to make models of these relationships cooperatively with her group. In the model use phase, she was able to adapt the model for different societies. Later, she was able to use the model to formulate and evaluate good and poor questions for exploring different historical time periods.

Problems in the learning activity and the process of change in problems

Cecilie's biggest problem was how to change her model of the evolution of species to include historical concepts. For several months into fourth grade she continued to explain and conceive historical conditions with concepts and methods that she acquired from her work with the history of evolution. With the help of her groupmates' comments she ended up understanding the differences between the evolution of animals and historical change in human ways of living. Her first step towards the acquisition of a conceptual model for historical development of societies was understanding about the meaning of tools and their changes in different historical time periods. This understanding arose as she worked with posters of the four different research areas and later with the posters of the four different historical periods. It was through comparing her work with the other children's and their pointing out to her what they did that gave her some conceptual insight on the tool as mediating between nature and living conditions.

The second type of problem Cecilie faced most often was how to categorize different pieces of historical knowledge into relevant time periods. But she approached this problem with an attitude, which continued to develop, that she could use books, pictures, the children's models, and the goal/results posters to check the correctness of her categorizations. In particular, she became oriented toward using the children's models as a check after they created four models of the different time periods.

Discussion

Stigler and Stevenson (1991) describe how teaching practice differ between two highly industrialized countries (Japan and the United States) and how this creates differences in the types of knowledge and skills the children acquire. Ames and Ames (1984) theorize that different types of motivation for engaging in school activity are derived from the particular goal construction that determines classroom activity. They distinguish between competitive, cooperative, and individualistic goal structures, which reflect the social reality constructed in the school. These two articles, though about social reality on different levels, emphasize the importance of taking teaching practice into account for understanding differences in the types of knowledge, skill, and motivation that children acquire.

The study reported here, conducted in a Danish elementary school, gives perspective to how teaching practice effects psychic development. The effect of Developmental Teaching on the processes of knowledge development, motivation, and social interaction for a single child was evaluated. The result of the study can be seen as a conceptualization of the theoretical hypothesis that valid teaching should take into account both the basic concepts of a subject area and children's interests.

How educational practice can become reflected in children's general psychological functioning is exemplified through the categories developed and used in the analysis of a single child. This analysis can then become the basis for a reformulation of the question into more specific subquestions: How do we promote theoretical knowledge and thinking through teaching? How do we develop motivation and support cooperative learning? The analysis of Cecilie's development through fourth grade is illustrative of how these questions are applied and suggest questions to think about in the future.

Theoretical knowledge and thinking

The analysis of Cecilie's learning process demonstrates that it is a process of knowledge construction. Through class dialogue, problem solving connected to films and texts, play performance, and modeling she demonstrated the constructive aspect of how she learned central and basic information in the area of history. The relation between humans and nature mediated by tools was a basic theoretical conception she acquired through exploratory and cooperative activity with her classmates in the first month of fourth grade. This relation became a germ cell of knowledge that she was able to use and differentiate in further learning activity.

The results also demonstrate how much Cecilie drew upon the teaching of the previous year and theoretical conceptions derived from the evolution of animals to develop new understanding of historical relations. One of her major problems was how to overcome and transcend this previously acquired knowledge in her first conceptual model of the historical development of humans. In fact, she transcended it through her cooperation with her fellow students. This demonstrates an embedding of situational learning in a social context.

At the end of fourth grade Cecilie had a model to characterize different ways of living in different historical time periods that she could use to formulate tasks and guide her own collection of information. But her model was not so well developed that she was able to explain changes in societies through historical time, and she was still operating only at the level of formulating independent tasks. She did not yet have a critical relation to the content of the model or her own contribution. When we followed her into fifth grade we saw the development of these aspects of her learning activity.

What becomes important to analyze further is the dialectic between knowledge construction and theoretical thinking on the one hand and the development of motivation and cooperativeness in learning on the other.

Motivation and cooperative learning

Cecilie's motivation grew as her knowledge of the research area grew and as the challenge for independent activity and evaluation grew.

As she created models, she was absorbed in the work of symbolizing her conceptual understanding.

In his study of high school students' engagement, Stevenson (1990) demonstrated that the challenge for the students are tasks that involve "higher order thinking" in the form of inferences and value judgements. This is confirmed by the analysis of Cecilie: her engagement really grew when she had to conceptualize and work with models of the investigative areas and the four different historical periods.

We also saw that she liked to work with her peers and that they influenced her acquisition of conceptual understanding. They especially helped her overcome the problem of being bound up with the evolutionary model and acquire a model of a historical change of human ways of living. The possibility of interdependence of peer interaction in classroom learning and its importance for knowledge construction is supported by Pontecorvo (1985), Brown and Palinscar (1989), and Cowie and Rudduck (1990). However, Cowie and Rudduck point to the fact, that this is not a natural process that unfolds easily. They describe that "teachers who introduce cooperative work into their classes often meet with initial difficulties as pupils encounter educational demands, which they have rarely met before" (Cowie & Rudduck 1990, p. 250). The experimental teaching in our project overcame these initial difficulties, and Cecilie lived up to the criteria put forward by Cowie and Ruddick for cooperative group work (1990, p. 253): participation, supportiveness and turn taking, being tolerant as a group member, and having emphatic awareness of other people's feelings.

Appendix: Condensed description of the two first teaching sessions in fourth grade
1st session, 10 August 1987

Focus: Cecilie. This is the first period after the summer holiday. The teacher plans to connect to last year's teaching and introduce the general problems for this year.

He writes the plan for the period on the blackboard:

1. What is the researcher doing in our classroom?
2. What do we know? (Written test about last years concepts and models – the model for the evolution of animals)

3. What are we going to research?
4. A task with pictures.

Item 1: The researcher tells the children what she will be doing. She also starts the tasks under item 2: she wants the children to tell her what they learned last year. The first response comes from Sanni who gives the general formulation: about the evolution of animals, the origin of man, and the development of the earth.

Lise's answer is more specific.

Lise: We also learned about the snow hare and the desert hare.

Loke: We explored what would happen if we moved the snow hare to the desert.

Cecilie then says: We also worked in groups.

This is surely an important aspect for Cecilie because later, when they get the test about last year's content and model, she asks if they can do it in groups and is disappointed when the teacher says no.

Cecilie has a good understanding of last year's teaching. When the researcher asks how they used the model, Cecilie answers that they compared the models for the snow hare and the desert hare and found out that they ate different food.

The researcher then asks if they found anything important about the evolution.

Louis explains that if the climate changes then the animals change.

Allan tells about the earliest periods in the history of animals, and that the climate changed, and if it changed too suddenly the animals would not have time to change.

Cecilie responds to this and says that the change does not happen so quickly. The animals do not change so quickly.

Loke goes on and says that the offspring change, not the animals.

The children then answer written questions and draw models about last year's research area – the evolution of animals.

When they have finished this task, Jarl is asked to draw the model of the evolution of animals on the blackboard. They have never worked with the model of the origin of man, so the teacher asks if one of them would try to create it.

Allan volunteers and is asked to draw it on the blackboard.

The teacher asks: What are the connections between the model of the evolution of animals and the model of the origin of man? Are they the same or are there differences?

Cecilie: Family and living together means the same.

She hereby suggests that the models are the same. She also answers affirmatively when the teacher asks if the conditions for survival of man and animal are the same.

Cecilie: Because they all need food, to live together with others, and parental care.

The teacher then proceeds to the next topic and asks: What are we going to research this year?

Some children formulate their ideas about history.

The teacher then shows a poster of humans characterizing the development of inventions and clothing throughout history.

Cecilie characterizes the poster as a time line and says further that it can be used instead of a calendar.

Morten elaborates Cecilie's answer by saying that on this poster one can actually see the way things were abroad and at home in Denmark, and that our time counting starts at zero.

The teacher then introduces the first general research theme by asking: Throughout time people have lived differently, if we take nowadays, are all people alike?

The children get the picture task which contains pictures of four different cultures in the twentieth century. They are asked to discuss and sort the pictures into four different piles relating to the four different societies. The children have difficulties in solving the task; later, in a class discussion, it mostly becomes a talk about and discussion of what looks different in the pictures showing different societies. The same is happening to pictures showing four different historical periods in Denmark.

2nd session, 17 August

Focus: Cecilie. The topic of the teaching is still to formulate the research goals and to combine them with that which they explored last year. This time the teacher has seven items on the agenda, and first Louis and then Cecilie complain that there are too many items. Today's items are

1. The genealogical tree of the animals.
2. Formulating the research question for this year.
3. Finishing the task from last session.
4. Cecilie's model.
5. How did the first humans live?
6. Make a poster with an overview of last year's research and what we are researching now.
7. Start creating a play about scientists at work.
8. Evaluation.

The children get a sheet of paper with the genealogical tree of the animals, and they describe and discuss it in the class dialogue. Niels says that in some ways we are animals ourselves. The children are very interested in the pictures of the different animals on the genealogical tree and spontaneously tell about some of the prehistoric animals. Then the children are asked to add a picture of man into the drawing of the genealogical tree.

Cecilie tells about leeches, and the teacher asks her to locate them in the genealogical tree. Then they start item 2. Cecilie reads the item aloud from her paper: "The development of humans." The teacher shows the children pictures of how humans lived in different places in different time periods, and then he says: We also have to make a journey in thought. Imagine what this town was like 100 years ago, 1000 years ago, 10,000 years ago.

Niels: Then there were mammoths.

Cecilie's model. All the children in the class have a piece of paper so that they can draw Cecilie's model.

Cecilie goes to the blackboard and starts drawing. She draws the following:

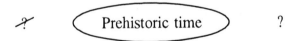

Then she says: This shows what we know about the sparrow and what we know about it in prehistoric time. Then she explains the part with all the different times. She draws and writes:

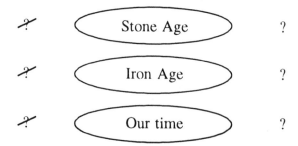

The teacher then asks: If you were to work with this model, what would you then look for?

Cecilie: How the earth has changed for the sparrows.

She would write what she knew and what she did not know about the sparrow in the different times.

Under the next item, how the first humans lived, the teacher draws Allan's model from the last session about the first humans, and the children draw it next to Cecilie's model on their paper.

Then the teacher says: We can compare the models, but he does not go further into this. The teacher asks: What do we know about how the first humans lived?

The children make suggestions about what they eat: berries, meat, fish.

Cecilie asks: Why do we never write what they drink?

Sanni says milk, and the teacher asks: Where would they get it from? She answers: From the animals.

Then the children continue to mention characteristics of the way the first humans lived: First, that they lived together in tribes.

The teacher asks: Do we all agree on this? How can we be sure we know?

Allan says: By looking into books. He then tries to find something and shows a book with a picture, where one can see a settlement.

Second and third, the children mention that the earliest humans mated and took care of their children.

It is obvious that the children use the concepts from the model of evolution of animals. A child mentions a fourth characteristic of the early humans: They defended themselves against enemies.

Allan continues and says that they fought a lot. The teacher replies that he has heard a theory about the first humans: That they were actually more peaceful than we think. Only later did humans start to fight.

Cecilie supports the teacher by saying that she has seen a picture about the earliest people and they looked really sweet.

As planned, the teacher and the pupils finish the goal result board.

They only got a very short time to start planning their play performance about how researchers of history work.

The last item is evaluation, and the children try to evaluate by telling what was the most important for each of the items on today's agenda.

References

Ames, C. & Ames, R. (1984). Systems of students and teacher motivation: Toward a qualitative definition. *Journal of Educational Psychology*, *76*, 535–556.

Brown, A. L. & Palinscar, A. S. (1969). Guided, cooperative learning and individual knowledge acquisition. In L.B Resnick (Ed.), *Knowing, learning and instruction: Essays in honor of Robert Glaser*. Hillsdale, NJ: Erlbaum.

Cowie, H., & Rudduck, J. (1990). Learning from one another: The challenge. In H. C. Foot, M. H. Morgan, & R. H. Shute (Eds.), *Children helping children*. London: Wiley & Sons.

Davydov, V. V. (1977). *Arten der Verallgemeinerung im Unterricht.* (Types of Generalization in Teaching). Berlin: Volk und Wissen.

Davydov, V. V. (1982). Ausbildung der Lerntätigkeit (Development of Learning Activity). In V. V. Davydov, J. Lompscher, & A. K. Markova, (Eds.), *Ausbildung der Lerntätigkeit bei Schülern*. Berlin: Volk und Wissen.

Davydov, V. V. (1988). Problems of developmental teaching. *Soviet Education*, *30*, (8–10), 1–97, 1–83, 1–41.

Dickenson, A. K., Gard, A., & Lee, P. J. (1978). Evidence in history and the classroom. In A. K. Dickenson & P. J. Lee (Eds.), *History teaching and historical understanding*. London: Heinemann.

Englund, T. (1988). Historieemnets selektive tradition set ur ett legitimitetsperspektiv (The selective tradition of the subject of history seen through a perspective of legitimacy). *Historiedidaktik i Norden 3*. Malmö, Sweden: Lärerhögskolan i Malmö.

Engeström, Y., & Hedegaard, M. (1986). Teaching theoretical thinking in elementary schools. In E. Bol, J. P. P. Haenen, & M. A. Wolters (Eds.), *Education of cognitive development*. Proceeding of the Third International Symposium on Activity Theory. Den Hague, SVO/SOO.

Griffin, P. & Cole, M. (1984). Current activity for the future: The zo-ped. In B. Rogoff & J. W. Wertsch (Eds.). *Children's learning in the "zone of proximal development"*. San Francisco: Jossey Bass.

Hedegaard, M. (1986). Methodology in evaluative research on teaching and learning. In F. J. Zuuren, F. J. Wertz, & B. Mook (Eds.), *Advances in qualitative psychology*. North America: INC/Berwyn.

Hedegaard, M. (1988). *Skoleborns personlighedsudvikling set gennem orienteringsfagene* (School children's personal development seen through subject teaching). Aarhus, Denmark: Aarhus Universitetsforlag.

Hedegaard, M. (1989). Motivational development in school children. *Multidisciplinary newsletter for Activity Theory*, 30–38.

Hedegaard, M. (1990a). *Beskrivelse af småbørn* (Describing small children). Aarhus, Denmark: Aarhus Universitetsforlag.

Hedegaard, M. (1990b). The zone of proximal development as basis for instruction. In L. Moll (Ed.), *Vygotsky and education: Instructional implication and applications of sociohistorical psychology*. Cambridge, UK: Cambridge University Press.

Hedegaard, M. & Sigersted, G. (1992). *Undervisning i samfundshistorie. [Teaching Historical change of societies]*. Aarhus, Denmark: Aarhus Universitetsforlag.

Hedegaard, M. (In press). History education and didactics. In Y. Engeström & R. Miettinen (Eds.), *Perspectives on activity theory*. Cambridge, UK: Cambridge University Press.

Historiedidaktik i Norden 3 [History Didactics in the North 3]. (1988). Malmö, Sweden: Lärerhögskolan Malmö

Historiedidaktik i Norden 4 [History Didactics in the North 4]. (1990). Kalmar, Sweden: Högskolan Kalmer.

Juul-Jensen, U. (1986). *Practice and progress: A theory for the modern healthcare system*. Oxford: Blackwell Scientific Publications.

Leont'ev, A. (1978). *Activity, consciousness, and personality*. Englewood Cliffs, NJ: Prentice Hall.

Lee, P. J. (1983). History teaching and philosophy of history. History and theory. *Studies in the philosophy of history*, *12*, 19–80.

Lewin, K. (1946). Behavior and development as a function of the total situation. In M. Carmichael (Ed.), *Manual of child psychology*. New York: Wiley.

Lompscher, J. (1984). Problems and results of experimental research. In M. Hedegaard, P. Hakkarainen, & Y. Engeström (Eds.), *The formation of theoretical thinking through instruction*. Aarhus, Denmark: University of Aarhus, Institute of Psychology.

Manifest 83. Historie i folkeskolen [History in Comprehensive School]. (1983). Copenhagen, Denmark: Centrum.

Markova, A. K. (1978–1979). The teaching and mastery of language. *Soviet Education*, *21*, (2–4), 1–281.

Ministry of Education (1960–1977–1981–1984). *Undervisningsvejledning for folkeskolen: Historie. [Teaching guidelines for comprehensive school: History]*. Copenhagen, Denmark: Ministry of Education.

Pintrich, P. R. (1991). Editor's comment. *Educational Psychologist*, *26*, 199–205.

Pontecorvo, C. (1985). *Peer interaction in learning contexts: Suggestions for some general mechanisms and subject-content effects*. Paper presented at Peer Based Learning in Primary Schools Workshop, Nijmegen, The Netherlands.

Schiefele, U. (1991). Interest, learning, and motivation. *Educational Psychologist*, 26, (3–4), 299–323.

Scribner, S., & Cole, M. (1981). *The psychology of literacy*. Cambridge, MA: Harvard University Press.

Scribner, S. (1984a). Cognitive studies of work. *The Quarterly Newsletter of Comparative Human Cognition of the Laboratory of Comparative Human Cognition*, 6, 1–4.

Scribner, S. (1984b). Studying working intelligence. In B. Rogoff & J. Lave (Eds.), *Everyday cognition*. Cambridge, MA: Harvard University Press.

Scribner, S. (1985). Vygotsky's use of history. In J. V. Wertsch (Ed.), *Culture, communication and cognition: A Vygotskian perspective*. Cambridge, UK: Cambridge University Press.

Scribner, S. (1990). A sociocultural approach to the study of mind. In G. Greenberg & E. Tobach (Eds.), *Theories of the evolution of knowing*. Hillsdale, NJ: Erlbaum.

Stevenson, R. B. (1990). Engagement and cognitive challenge in thoughtful social studies classes: A study of student perspectives. *Journal of Curriculum Studies*, 22, 329–341.

Stigler, J. W., & Stevenson, H. W. (1991). How Asian teachers polish each lesson to perfection. *American Educator*, 12, 14–20, 43–47.

Søring Jensen, S. (1978). *Historieundervisningsteori [The theory of history teaching]*. Copenhagen: Christian Ejlers's Forlag.

Tharp, R. G., & Gallimore, R. (1988). *Rousing minds to life*. Cambridge, UK: Cambridge University Press

Undervisningsvejledning for folkeskolen. Historie (1977–1981–1984). [Teaching Guidelines for Comprehensive School]. Copenhagen, Denmark: Ministry of Education.

Vygotsky, L. S. (1985–1987). *Ausgewälte Schriften [Selected texts]*. Cologne: Pahl Rugenstein.

Vygotsky, L. S. (1978). *Mind in society*. Cambridge, MA: Harvard University Press.

Vygotsky, L. S. (1971–1974). *Sprog og tænkning [Language and thought]*. Copenhagen: Reitzel.

Wartofsky, M. (1979). *Models – Representations and the scientific understanding*. Dordrecht and Boston: D. Reidel.

14 Innovative organizational learning in medical and legal settings

Yrjö Engeström

Organizational learning: Adaptation or creation

The notion of organizational learning has become a household term in literature on management and organizations (for reviews see e.g., Shrivastava 1983, Fiol & Lyles 1985). The notion holds two promises. First, it implies a departure from the individualism that dominates laboratory- and school-based theories of learning. Second, the notion of organizational learning is closely connected to notions of innovation and change, implying a departure from the obsession with reception, adaptation, and acquisition dominant in laboratory- and school-based theories of learning.[1]

One source of the organizational learning literature comes from the idea of learning curves. During the life cycle of a certain production technology or product, firms are able to reduce their unit costs of production because of the experience gained by the workers in repeated cycles of production (Ghemawat 1985). This notion of organizational and technological learning assumes that learning occurs as a "natural" result of cumulated experience, as if automatically. The concrete mechanisms that lead to the observed reduction of unit costs have been largely neglected (Abernathy & Wayne 1974, Kibria & Tisdell 1985, Lilja 1989). Bell and Scott-Kemmis (1990) argue that the experiential learning curve approach is fundamentally flawed in that it ignores the continuous technological improvements and product innovations brought about by workers, managements, and clients. March, Sproull, and Tamuz (1991) point out another crucial problem: accumulation of experience cannot

The research reported in this paper has been partially funded by the Academy of Finland for the project Learning and Expertise in Teams and Networks. I thank the editors of this volume for their insightful comments and suggestions.

explain how organizations learn from unique events, or "samples of one or fewer."

In their pioneering book, Argyris and Schön (1978) characterized organizational learning as error detection and error correction. Using Gregory Bateson's (1972) ideas as their springboard, they distinguished between single-loop learning and double-loop learning in organizations. Single-loop learning aims at keeping the organization stable in a changing context. This is done by modifying organizational strategies so as to keep organizational performance within the range set by organizational norms. The norms themselves remain unchanged. Double-loop learning leads to a creative questioning and modification of the norms themselves.

This basic distinction between adaptation and creation, or between experience and experimentation, is echoed in the literature time and again. Dodgson (1991, p. 111) differentiates between short-term tactical learning "which has an immediate problem-solving nature" and strategic learning which "extends beyond immediate issues" and provides the basis "for future, perhaps unforeseen, projects." Garratt (1990, pp. 80–81) speaks of first-order change and second-order change, the latter being a process where "one rises above the day-to-day routines of managing the operational deviations from plans." Senge (1990, p. 14) writes that "survival learning" or "adaptive learning" is necessary. "But for a learning organization, 'adaptive learning' must be joined by 'generative learning,' learning that enhances our capacity to create."

While it is easy to agree in principle with the emphasis on creative or innovative learning, the state of concrete research and detailed theorizing in such learning processes is less than satisfactory.

It is difficult to find concrete analyses of innovative learning in literature. One of the few relevant studies is Rittenberg's (1985) analysis of the care of Mary, a patient hospitalized in a pediatrics ward for cystic fibrosis (for further inspiring studies, see Bowers & Middleton 1991, Middleton 1991).

Based on an intricate division of labor, the care of ward patients requires on-going collaboration between ward staff. In this setting, a routine process of care for Mary became threatened by alarming medical and social problems, centering on the actions of the attending physician. In response to these threats, the other caretakers formulated an interpretation of what had happened and what should happen in Mary's care.

And precisely because this interpretation arose through a team effort to deal with shared work problems, the meaning expressed in the interpretation was publicly emphasized, propagated, and agreed upon among the caretakers. (Rittenberg 1985, p. 148)

Rittenberg calls an innovation process such as this 'the objectification of situated meanings.' He points out that disturbances are an important condition for such a process: "an interdependent work group is faced with unexpected and serious threats to its work" (Rittenberg 1985, p. 149).

However, Rittenberg defines the process exclusively as an *inter*-mental, not *instru*-mental event: "by the mechanism of attracting vivid collective attention, the meaning of a transitory action may get established as part of public knowledge: as something which individuals know that everyone knows" (Rittenberg 1985, p. 150). Rittenberg himself (1985, p. 151) notes that in Mary's case the newly objectified meaning (or innovation) "began to pass out of social existence when the hospitalization ended." The only alternative for him is that a meaning is swept into a larger social arena, for example by becoming embroiled in the courts and by being propagated over the media to a larger audience.

This view privileges language and discourse as the only mediators of innovation. It neglects the power of *material artifacts* as means of consolidating innovations and turning them into practical and theoretical tools of activity. A narrowly interactionist and inter-mentalist notion can be contrasted with the recent interest in artifacts as mediators of socially distributed cognition (e.g., Goodwin & Goodwin in press, Heath & Luff in press, Hutchins & Klausen in press). Predecessors of the latter approach may be found both in Deweyan pragmatism (e.g., Hickman 1990) and in the cultural-historical theory of activity (Leont'ev 1978, 1981).

Another problem in Rittenberg's account is its exclusive emphasis on the situational and improvisational nature of innovative learning processes. There is no provision for deliberately planned and systematically conducted *collaborative design* of innovations.

If innovative and creative learning is indeed an integral aspect of organizational life and especially of teamwork, then we should be able to observe and analyze it in detail. Furthermore, such learning should be analyzed both as a socially distributed and as an artifact-mediated process, allowing for both situational improvisation and deliberate design.

In this paper, I will make an attempt at such concrete analysis. I will use data from two sets of ongoing studies. The first one is focused on teams in Finnish health centers, responsible for the primary care of the population in their respective municipalities. The second set of studies deals with court settings in the United States and Finland.

Before presenting and discussing actual examples, the notion of innovative organizational learning has to be elaborated. In my studies in various work settings, three kinds of innovative learning may be identified. I will characterize schematically those three kinds of innovative learning. After that, I will present a series of examples from medical and legal settings and discuss their theoretical implications.

Three kinds of innovative learning

To describe the innovative learning processes, I use the conceptual framework of activity theory. Activity is seen here as a collective, systemic formation that has a complex mediational structure. Activities are not short-lived events or actions that have a temporally clear-cut beginning and end. They are systems that *produce* events and actions and evolve over lengthy periods of sociohistorical time. I use the schematic diagram of Figure 14.1 to represent the mediational structure of an activity system.

To differentiate between the psychological mechanisms of adaptive and innovative learning, an observation made by Karmiloff-Smith and Inhelder (1975) is useful. The authors presented young children with a relatively difficult block-balancing task. The first approach taken by the subjects was that of seeking an immediate solution and concentrating on the *outcome* of one's effort – the "action response." The children were

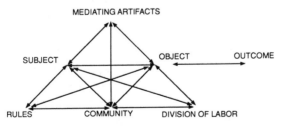

Figure 14.1. The mediational structure of an activity system (Engeström 1987).

happy when when they got the blocks balanced, unhappy when they failed. However, another approach emerged almost as an interruption in the midst of the first one.

Frequently, even when children were successful in balancing an item on one dimension . . . they went on exploring the other dimensions of each block. It was as if their attention were momentarily diverted from their goal of balancing to what had started as a subgoal, i.e., the search for means. One could see the children oscillating between seeking the goal and seeking to 'question' the block. (Karmiloff-Smith & Inhelder 1975, p. 201)

This latter approach was named "theory response." Within that approach, the subject does not measure his or her success with the immediate outcome (balanced or not balanced), but rather with the verification or falsification of a hypothetical model created and used as a tool, as a "mediating artifact" in the effort to understand and predict how the system works.

At this point we witness experimentation for the experimentation's sake; for attending to the means implies seeking knowledge of the approximate range of possible actions on an object. (Karmiloff-Smith & Inhelder 1975, pp. 207–208)

The difference between focusing on the outcome (success-orientation) and focusing on the means, or rather on the relationship between means and outcomes (theory-orientation), is extremely important. In Figure 14.1, the former may be depicted as a straight line from the subject to the object (task) to the outcome. The mediating artifact (model or algorithm for the solution of the task) is constructed tacitly, on the basis of blind trial and error, without questioning why and under what conditions the model will work. This is a prototype of adaptive learning, or empirical generalization as Davydov (1990) would call it.

In Figure 14.1, the theory-orientation should be depicted as pausing before the subject moves from the object-task to the outcome. The subject stops and looks at the task, trying to create an explanatory model, an artifact that enables him or her to predict the outcome of any action upon the object. This experimental triangulation between the subject, the object, and the tool (or rule, or pattern of division of labor) is the origination of innovative learning, or theoretical generalization.

The situational innovative learning described previously produces a novel solution to a problem, typically a new mediating artifact, or a new rule, or a new form of the division of labor in the organization. I will call such innovations limited to one component in the activity system *solution innovations*. The learning that leads to solution innovations has typically a two-step structure. First, there is a disturbance, tension, or conflict in the routine flow of activity. Secondly, along with or instead of straightforward "action responses," there is a moment of reflection and experimentation – or remediation – that leads to an attempted or completed nonroutine solution.

The trajectory of an object from raw material to a finished product or outcome is crucially important in the determination of the rhythm of organizational practice.[2] In the data, I have found innovation efforts aimed at altering the nature of this entire trajectory. I will call these *trajectory innovations*. The time span and scope of impact of such innovative learning processes are significantly wider than those observed in solution innovations. Solution innovations require that the subject's focus is widened from the outcome alone to include the potential mediating artifact, or rule, or form of division of labor. The decisive characteristic of trajectory innovation is that here the subject refocuses on the object and redefines and models it as a multistep procedural achievement rather than a once-and-for-all entity. Because it changed the care of only one particular patient, not the trajectory in general, the case of Mary described by Rittenberg was a solution innovation, not a trajectory innovation. It led to the situational adoption of a new artifact – the altered regime of care for Mary.

Finally we have witnessed a third kind of innovative learning. This involves processes where a group of subjects design a new model for their activity system over an extended period of time. In other words, the focus is again shifted from the object to the mediating components of the activity system – but this time those mediating components are analyzed and reconceptualized as an interconnected system. I will call these processes *systems innovations*.

Learning that leads to systems innovations is a long-term process of internalization and externalization, appropriation of available cultural resources and design of a novel form of practice. I have called processes of this kind *learning by expanding,* or expansive learning (Engeström 1987). The notion of expansion refers to the phenomenon of going beyond the initially given context of specific problems and refocusing on the wider context that generates those specific problems.[3]

The three kinds of innovative learning characterized earlier are schematically depicted in Figure 14.2. The light bulb symbolizes the typical location of the innovative breakthrough in the activity system. The light

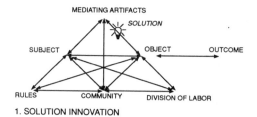

1. SOLUTION INNOVATION

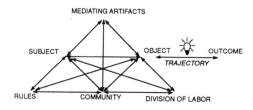

2. TRAJECTORY INNOVATION

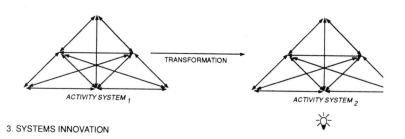

3. SYSTEMS INNOVATION

Figure 14.2. Three kinds of innovative learning.

bulb that symbolizes solution innovation could equally well be located between the object and the rules or between the object and the division of labor, indicating that a solution innovation may lead to a novel tool, a novel rule, or a novel collaboration pattern.[4]

The three kinds of innovative learning differ in the nature of errors detected. In solution innovations, the errors detected and corrected are immediate and limited in scope. In trajectory innovations and especially in systems innovations, the errors are latent "resident pathogens" in the activity system, to use Reason's (1990) terminology.[5] In all innovative

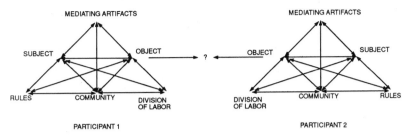

Figure 14.3. Collaboration as encounter of activity systems (see Engeström 1990, p. 128).

learning, there is an oppositional flavor of questioning the prevailing norms and conventions.[6]

Now the diagrams in Figure 14.2 are still inadequate in that they depict innovative learning as basically a process realized by a single subject, albeit a subject embedded in a community. In an attempt to depict interaction in team meetings and other potentially collaborative encounters with the help of the general structure of activity, I have used the following extension of the basic diagram (Figure 14.3).

For the sake of simplicity, the encounter is depicted in Figure 14.3 as consisting of two participants only. In principle, any number of activity systems could form such an encounter. The crucial feature of such an encounter is that a shared object cannot be taken for granted. Each participant, representing a specific position in the organizational context, enters the encounter with a more or less clear preconstructed notion of the object of the meetings, as well as with preconstructed mediating artifacts, rules, etc. Although an encounter, such as a meeting, may have relatively clear-cut rules, even they are not automatically interpreted in the same way by the different participants. The key issue is whether or not a shared object will be constructed in the meeting.

Emergence of a solution innovation in a health center team

The following example is taken from a videotaped joint meeting of two primary health care teams held in the fall of 1991 (Engeström 1992, pp. 86–91). The teams operated at a health station where we conducted a developmental work research project (Project LEVIKE) from

1986 to 1990 (see Engeström 1991). The multiprofessional teams of this station were launched in the fall of 1989. They were the key organizational and functional units in the health center district that served a population of approximately 40,000 inhabitants. The identity of the teams involved in the example was strong, based on direct responsibility to the population of the area and on the fact that the activity system was redesigned by the practitioners themselves. The teams were quite autonomous in decisions concerning their daily work. The teams did not have designated leaders. The task of coordinating the team meetings rotated between team members. Both teams met regularly and roughly once a month the two teams had a joint meeting.

Both teams consisted of four doctors, a nurse, two assistant nurses, and representatives of the home health care for the elderly. Each team had a geographical area and the corresponding population as its responsibility. Several functions of the health center remained outside the teams however: laboratory, x-ray services, the preventive work of public health nurses in schools and maternity clinics, etc. These functions were organized in the traditional sectorial fashion so that each function had its own vertical line of management in which the decisions were made by a head nurse or a head doctor located in the city's central board of health, miles away from the station.

This meeting focused on the problematic relations between the teams and the laboratory of the station. The laboratory employed two laboratory nurses supervised by the head laboratory nurse. There was a history of tensions between the laboratory and the teams, manifested in disagreements concerning the opening hours and services offered by the laboratory. The two laboratory nurses were invited to attend this meeting.

One of the lab nurses presented their problems and grievances to the meeting which was attended by some 15 team members. She complained at length about the way laboratory work was constantly disturbed by patients coming at a wrong time, and not being well enough informed and instructed by the staff in the teams. This was a disturbance in a dual sense. The laboratory staff felt that their work was being disturbed by the teams, which sent patients to the lab without considering the lab's rules and its need for peace and quiet in work. The team members felt that their work was being disturbed by the lab, which would not serve the patients who needed services. This dual disturbance was not a life-

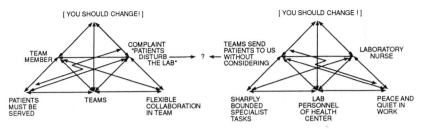

Figure 14.4. Structure of the tension in the team meeting.

threatening danger like in the case described by Rittenberg. But it was a serious source of tension and disruption.

This tension is exemplified by the way a team assistant nurse interrupts the complaints presented by the lab nurse.

Excerpt #1

01 Lab nurse: . . . So that patients should not be sent in vain to our door. But maybe they come even on their own . . .

02 Team assistant nurse: I do think lots of them come on their own. After all, they have been waiting for 2-½ months.

In turn 01, the lab nurse crystallizes her complaint by stating that the patients should not be sent by team members to the laboratory without first securing an appointment. She modifies her implicit criticism by continuing that maybe patients come to the lab even on their own, without anybody sending them. In turn 02, the team assistant nurse interrupts and says that patients indeed come on their own because they have been waiting for 2-½ months while the lab has been closed during the summer due to budget cuts. The implicit structure behind this tension is depicted below in Figure 14.4.

As shown in Figure 14.4, the object for the lab nurses is the problem of patients coming without appointments, supposedly sent by the team members. This is in contradiction with their rule of securing peace and quiet in analyzing lab samples – thus, the two-headed, lightning-shaped arrow in between the object and the rules in their triangle. The lab nurses don't seem to have other instruments for dealing with this problem except complaining, with the obvious message "you should change!"

The structure of the activity of the team assistant nurse is almost a mirror image of the lab personnel's triangle. For team members, the object is the lab personnel's complaint "patients disturb our peace in the lab." This is in contradiction with the rule of serving the population with maximum flexibility, worked out by the team members themselves during the recent redesign of their activity. Here, too, the only tool seems to be the implicit demand: "you should change!"

The rather straightforward character of the latent confrontation in the meeting was altered at one point. The change was initiated by a team general practitioner (GP) who had kept careful notes during the meeting. After the lab nurse had presented her grievances, the GP asked whether it was so that patients who do not have appointments can go to the laboratory of the next, bigger station (named L) at any time without appointment. The lab nurse answered affirmatively. After this exchange, the discussion proceeded as follows:

Excerpt #2

01	Team GP:	Would it help if you put a big sign on the door of the laboratory, which would say "Only with appointment and acute samples . . . ?"
02	Lab nurse:	. . . We can put there such a sign.
03	Team GP:	And "If you don't have an appointment, you can go to the L station lab without appointment." Not too much text, but so that patients will realize that there is such an arrangement in place. . .
04	Lab nurse:	Yes . . .
05	Lab nurse 2:	As little text as possible.

During this exchange, there is a visible change in the atmosphere. The team physician and the laboratory nurse both lean forward to look each other in the eyes. The laboratory nurse and the physician are suddenly talking about the same concrete object, out there in the "real-time" activity. The object nicely brings together the interests of the population responsibility and the interests of the laboratory specialists: informing the patients will enhance their self-reliance and it will also help the lab get some peace and quiet.

This is a small but important example of a solution innovation. It did not resolve the tension between the team (population responsibility) and the laboratory (sectorial specialism) in any permanent manner. But it demonstrated that the tension is not unsurmountable. It is also important that the innovation proposed by the team physician did actually materialize. The sign was placed out there, a material artifact on the laboratory door. It functioned as a remediating instrument for at least a year.

Instead of merely suggesting the solution, the physician used two important linguistic tools. First, she initiated the innovation by asking a question (turn 01: "Would it help if . . . ?") and listening to an answer. Secondly, she concretized her proposal by using reported speech, that is, quotations from the possible text to be put on the laboratory door (turns 01 and 03; for the uses of reported speech as a tool in innovation, see Engeström, Brown, Christopher, & Gregory 1991).

It is impossible to confirm with certainty the role of the GP's notes as a cognitive artifact mediating the innovation. But throughout the entire meeting the GP can be seen as the only one in the room making detailed notes, and she read her notebook just before initiating the exchange that led to the innovation.

However, the innovation was not achieved by the GP alone. It was a socially distributed achievement in that without the active appropriation by the lab personnel it would never have been realized. The lab nurses turned the innovation into a mediating tool at the same time as they temporarily reconstructed their object as informing the patients. The structure of this solution innovation is depicted in Figure 14.5.

As a form of learning, solution innovations like this are still very vulnerable. This case was more robust than Rittenberg's purely inter-mental innovation in that it was fixed in a mediating material artifact that is to some extent relatively independent of the particular persons interacting in the setting. But being a very specific solution, it may easily become compartmentalized and thus have little impact on the overall contradictions and tensions of the activity systems.

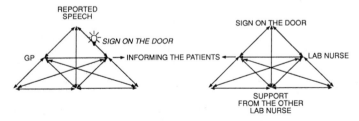

Figure 14.5. Structure of the solution innovation in the health center team meeting.

Interdependence of solution innovation and systems innovation at a health center

My second health center example is from another city in Finland where the staff of a health center district constructed a new team-based model for their work through a 3-year process of systems innovation (Engeström 1993). In the fall of 1992, after the new model was designed but shortly before its implementation in practice, a disturbance occurred in the health station. The handling of this disturbance and the accounts given by the different participants illustrate the interdependence of solution innovations and systems innovations in the learning that was going on in the setting. In the following, the events are reconstructed on the basis of accounts given by key participants some time after the incident.

Before the new division into teams, we had a physician on duty for each day and all patients needing urgent care were directed to see this doctor. Appointment times for the physician on duty could be given only in the morning because the health center assistants "opened" daily at about 7:45 A.M. the appointment times to be given for the day.

At about 8:00 I heard that one of the physicians had become ill and he should have had appointments at the maternal guidance clinic of the district. On most days I habitually looked over the appointment situation of the day and that's what I had done that day, too. I noticed that one physician had not been given any appointments (due to a change in the night shift duty). I pointed out to the head physician of the district that Kimmo could perhaps go and do the appointments at the maternal guidance clinic since he had not been given any appointments.

However, the day had started so that Sinikka, Kimmo's assistant, "opened" Kimmo's appointments as urgent care slots because she did not know about Kimmo's possible transfer to the maternal guidance clinic. The urgent care slots were filled immediately.

The physicians agreed in their morning meeting that Kimmo will go to the maternal guidance clinic and do the appointments there. Information on that change came too late to the assistants and all of Kimmo's urgent care slots were already given out to patients.

The physicians came from their meeting and told Ritva, who worked as assistant for Auli and Jouni, that Kimmo will go to the maternal guidance clinic. Ritva said that all Kimmo's appointment slots were already given out. Auli and Jouni (who was the physician on duty that day) said that those appointments must be canceled. Ritva was angered by that and told the doctors that they cannot be canceled because some of the patients are already on the premises and some are on their way to the health station.

The situation was thought over together. Jouni said that he'll see as many patients as he can and the urgent patients assigned to Kimmo can be transferred to him. Olavi (another physician) was to see patients in the home care that day; he rearranged his work schedule so that he came from the home care at about 10 o'clock A.M. to see how the morning had gone and he said that he, too, can take some of Kimmo's patients.

By being flexible and by reorganizing together that morning's situation was handled appropriately and patients did not have to be returned home. A physician enlarged his job and went to the maternal guidance clinic to take care of the appointments. Thus, clients did not have to make a visit in vain and the public health nurse did not have to reschedule appointments and arrange new ones within her already tight schedule. (District nurse's account)

The accounts given by Ritva, a health center assistant, and by Kimmo, a physician, illuminate the events further.

Naturally I was angered by the possibility of unnecessary work in the middle of all the rush. It is easy to say that appointments must be canceled when one doesn't have to do it oneself. It is unpleasant to explain that a moment ago we had appointment slots but now we don't anymore.

After some further thinking I came to the conclusion that we don't know enough of what another group of employees is doing. Or hopefully it is not so that we don't care about what some individual employee does. The group won't work if all employees are not taken into account. (Health center assistant's account)

In the morning meeting among the physicians the situation was assessed and I was apparently the only one at that point who had experience of working in a maternal guidance clinic; I had five or six years of experience of it. However, my last visit to maternal guidance clinic was about five to six years ago. We knew that all appointment slots in the maternal guidance clinic had been given out with quite a high frequency and including cases which could not be much postponed. So I decided to go and see it through and try to handle it with the knowledge and skill and experience that I had. On the other hand, we knew that a replacement person cannot be found anywhere in that situation, and we would face canceling all the appointments which at the moment seemed like a very heavy decision from the clients' viewpoint. (Physician's account)

The district nurse pointedly summarized her assessment.

Had a similar situation occurred a couple of years earlier, Kimmo's appointment slots would probably have been canceled without opposition. The gap between the different professional groups was so great and the physicians dictated how one acted in such a situation. (District nurse's account)

As a solution innovation, this case occurred between the object (patients) and division of labor in the activity system. The professionally sectorized and compartmentalized division of labor was temporarily overcome. There is no transcript of the actual discussion in which the solution was worked out. Thus, we have no direct evidence indicating what kinds of mediating artifacts were constructed and used by Ritva and the other participants of the discussion. But it is more than likely that the new collectively designed team-based model of work functioned as a shared mediating artifact, or common frame of reference, in the process.

This case indicates the presence of several facets of systems innovation and expansive learning. First, there was willingness on the physicians' part to go beyond traditional job descriptions and fixed duties, to take risks by accepting nonroutine tasks.

Secondly, there was courage and ability on the health center assistant's part to challenge the decision of the physicians and to argue for an alternative course of action. The health center assistant broke the boundaries of the traditional ladder of power and the associated code of silence.

Thirdly, and most importantly, "the situation was thought over together." The multiprofessional collective was capable of reassessing the situation and reaching a relatively complex novel solution under time pressure – a solution that involved contributions from several participants.

This case also demonstrates the limitations of the old model of work. The physicians had their own meeting while the health center assistants were working on their own. This in fact triggered or at least escalated the disturbance. In the new model, teams meet and handle problems like this multiprofessionally. In the new model, the multiprofessional meeting that was able to solve the problem expansively is not anymore an ad hoc solution innovation but a continuous and fundamental feature of the daily practice.

In sum, the particularly expansive nature of this solution innovation was dependent on the ongoing and more pervasive process of systems innovation at the health center. Had the practitioners not been engaged in design and implementation of a new model based on multiprofessional teamwork, the solution innovation would probably not have occurred in this fashion. On the other hand, the process of systems innovation, or expansive learning, was certainly enriched and pushed forward by a disturbance and solution innovation of this kind. The notion of flexible job descriptions and mutual responsibility embedded in the new model were actualized and put to a practical test, which in turn called forth anticipations and concretizations of the future way of working.

I would say that some days of refreshment study of new methods of care and examination that have evolved in the field [of maternity care] during the last five years would be useful before I'll go and do appointments in the maternity guidance clinic again. But in the near future, the situation will be such that if one of the colleagues gets sick and all other physicians' appointment slots have been given out, we need to consider which appointments will be canceled and which ones will be held, and which clients will be seen. Some kind of priorization must be done. In the maternity guidance clinic, too, those patients must be selected whom the public health nurse regards as urgent, and the so-called normal routine check-ups will be deleted. (Physician's account)

Solution innovations in courts

I will now turn to some examples of innovative learning in courts. My first example is from a complex civil case tried in a municipal court in southern California (Engeström, Brown, Christopher, & Gregory 1991). The dispute was about alleged construction defects in a condominium complex for which the plaintiffs demanded monetary restitution. In the United States, the organizational routine for handling problem situations during the trial is a brief sidebar conference held between the judge and the attorneys out of the presence of the jury. In this case, we obtained the official court reporter's records of the conversations in sidebar conferences. The following is a verbatim excerpt from the official record. However, the names have been replaced with initials, Mr. G. referring to the plaintiff's attorney and Mr. S. to the defendant's attorney. Necessary additional explanations have been added in brackets [ ].

Excerpt #3

Direct examination by Mr. G:

01	Q.	What did Mr. M say about why he permitted the two-hour wall not to be completed in this particular case?
02	Mr. S:	Objection. Hearsay, your honor.
03	The court:	Sustained.
04	Mr. G:	Okay. Your honor, may I be heard?
05	The court:	You may.

(The following held in chambers between court and counsel:)

06	Mr. G:	Your honor, I believe I have a legitimate exception to the hearsay rule, that being a prior inconsistent statement. And I would make an offer of proof that, when asked and answering that particular question, Mr. C [the witness] will happen to say that Mr. M's best recollection is that he made a thumbnail guestimate of the square footage area and just let it go by, –
07	The court:	All right.
08	Mr. G:	– which is in contradiction to what he said yesterday on the stand.
09	The court:	Mr. S?

| 10 | Mr. S: | Well, my opinion – or, my position is, your honor, that it is still hearsay, anyway you look at it. He testified under oath and in his deposition consistent with that. And I don't think that this is the proper way that a prior inconsistent statement is to be used. |
| 11 | The court: | All right. I am going to allow it. |

In this example, the judge first reacts to the violation detected by the defense attorney (line 02) by applying the hearsay rule in an adaptive straightforward manner – as an "action response" (line 03). The structure of this step is shown in Figure 14.6.

In the sidebar, the plaintiff's attorney introduces the alternative rule of "prior inconsistent statement" (line 06), which forces the judge to question the validity of the hearsay rule in the face of this particular object. The judge changes his ruling and allows the line of questioning he first denied (line 11). The structure of the innovation is depicted in Figure 14.7.

The innovation here takes place between the object and the rules. The innovation is not a product of an individual practitioner's reasoning. One might argue that the innovation was created by the plaintiff's attorney. But without the judge's decision, the innovation would never have materialized. The judge conducts an interactive thought experiment – a "the-

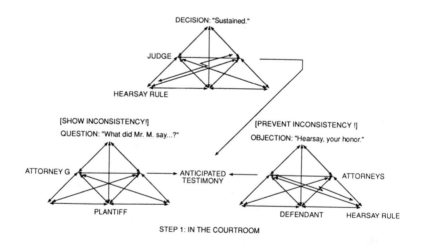

STEP 1: IN THE COURTROOM

Figure 14.6. Structure of the tension in the courtroom.

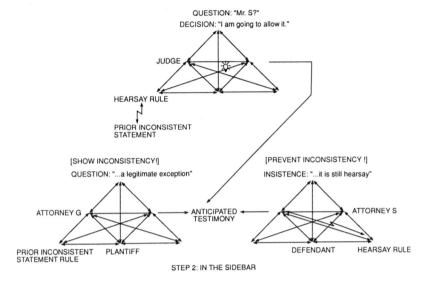

Figure 14.7. Structure of the solution innovation in the sidebar.

ory response" – with the alternative rule of "prior inconsistent state-ment" by asking for the defense attorney's opinion (line 09). The ques-tion seems to function as an important mediating artifact in this solution innovation. The defense attorney's response is negative and contains no new argument (line 10). For the judge, this seems to confirm the hypoth-esis of the validity of the alternative rule. We are dealing here with a socially distributed innovative learning process.

Trajectory innovations in courts

Trajectory innovations are more planful and more visibly delib-erate than solution innovations. In courts, trajectory innovations are typ-ically attempts to reorganize or monitor more effectively the processing of a case. The following example of trajectory innovations is taken from a traffic court in southern California (Engeström 1992, pp. 29–63). On a typical day, a single judge handles a large number of cases ranging from driving without a valid license to driving under the influence of alcohol. There is no jury, but the cases are processed collaboratively by prosecu-tors, public defenders, bailiffs, court interpreters, clerks, and the judge, all working within or next to the same large courtroom.

The following excerpts, transcribed from taperecorded court proceedings, demonstrate how the judge we observed handled typical problematic situations with the clients. Here, the original names have been replaced with fictional ones.

Excerpt #4

01	Bailiff:	Brian Ferguson. Requesting conversion of public service to fine.
02	Judge:	All right . . . ah . . . Mr. Ferguson, you failed to complete seven days of public work service in lieu of a $498 fine. If I convert it back to a fine, when can you pay the $498?
03	Defendant:	Ah, I did complete two days.
04	Judge:	You completed two, let me see . . . I have . . . it shows you completed one day. Public work service reported that you completed one day of the seven leaving the balance due of six. Mr. Ferguson was terminated in error, it says. Did you have 20 days to do in the beginning? Yeah, you had 20 days and you did 13, that brought it down to 7. And, ah, then you were reassigned to do seven and they are saying you did one which leaves six. So is it six days?
05	Defendant:	I think it was eight. They messed up, on the first day I went back to work in the office and they gave me credit for that day. Then I worked one day after that.
06	Judge:	Okay, well, let's assume for the moment for the sake of argument that you did. So that what you owe is five days which comes out to fifty . . . how much is five days? Five days is $250, right? So it's $250. Are you prepared to pay the $250 today?
07	Defendant:	Yeah.
08	Judge:	All right, then that will be the order and I will give you credit for the extra that you say you did.

Excerpt #5

01	Bailiff:	Next Johnson.
02	Judge:	This is a further proceedings matter where, ah, your fine of $250 was due on October 22. Are you prepared to pay that today?
03	Defendant:	No, I am not.
04	Judge:	How much are you prepared to pay today?
05	Defendant:	I can't pay any of it.

06	Judge:	All right, then ah . . .
07	Defendant:	I need an extension also on work days due because I can't do anything with my arm.
08	Judge:	Let me see. You were sentenced in May. It's been five months and you haven't paid *anything* [emphasizing the last word].
09	Defendant:	That's right.
10	Judge:	When can you pay something?
11	Defendant:	Well, I'm on disability right now and I'll get off disability on the first of December and I'm living on my own, so. I mean I only get $500 a month on disability. It goes to my rent and all my bills, and I'm not working right now because of my arm.
12	Judge:	All right. I'm going to trail this one to let you talk to a counseling attorney. Ah, you are going to have to give a higher priority to this matter. I appreciate that you have a limited amount of income and that you want to pay your bills. But this is probably your only creditor who can put you in jail and revoke your probation. I am willing to work with you and give you more time, but you haven't done anything and you're still not offering me anything except a vague statement that maybe in December you'll have some money. I, I need concrete facts, "on this date I will pay *x* number of dollars and I need this much more time to pay the balance." Then I'll work with you but not with vagaries.
13	Defendant:	I . . . I can pay it on the first of December.
14	Judge:	You can pay the whole thing on the first . . . ?
15	Defendant:	The whole thing.
16	Judge:	All right, all right then.
17	Defendant:	I just overlap on some checks and hold off, it is no big deal.
18	Judge:	All right, then I will, ah, continue this matter until December one, and if you have the money on December one, great.
19	Defendant:	Can you pay it before?
20	Judge:	Absolutely, you can pay it any time before then.
21	Defendant:	I understand, if I do get any money. What about the work days?
22	Judge:	Okay, on the work days, ah, your disability is a temporary disability. So, ah, just tell them when you'll be phy-

sically able and just make your arrangements with them. It's negative reporting, and as long as you do whatever you tell them you're going to do, you won't have a problem. If you need me to reassign you, I hereby reassign you. But just say, "I have trouble with my arm and I won't be well until January," and they'll just have you do it then. Okay? All right.

In a postsession interview, the judge explained her behavior as follows:

Interviewer: You sometimes get into some sort of discussion with the defendant. It is often concerning whether or not she or he needs time to pay, and also whether or not she or he has a place where the work will be performed.

Judge: Right.

Interviewer: Little things like this seem to be more personal than one would imagine normally happens.

Judge: Not all judges do that. For example, somebody else was here yesterday and the clerks told me that that judge said that "I don't want to talk to anybody about time to pay," and he also ordered the clerks not to have any pauses between cases. . . . But the reason I do that, I have a lot of reasons why I do that. One of them is that a lot of the cases on my calendar are people who were sentenced before by another judge. Since I've only been here 30 days and, well, not even 30 days, and I'm only going to be here 30 days more. I see, I don't know, 10 or 20 people a day who are sentenced by other judges, probably more than that, and haven't done what they said they were going to do. I sincerely believe that if the last judge had worked with them a little bit more when they were being sentenced, they might have been more realistic at the outset and they wouldn't be back seeing me again. What we can't afford to do is keep seeing these people over and over and over again. So, the reason I say "How much time do you need to pay" is that I am very very liberal in the amount of time I'll give them to pay. I am real hard on the people who come back and have had a long time and still haven't paid. I am very tough with them and I threaten to put them in jail and I'm sure that somebody is going to go to jail. But on the front end, I'll capitalize on their sincerity and I want to be realistic. I would rather they took a really long time to pay than that they come back to the court over and over and over again. So I'll give anybody six months to pay a driving under the influence fine, which is about $1,000. The guidelines before I got here from the last judge were four months. I don't think four months is enough time. I would have a hard time paying a fine of

$1,000 in four months, and I think that I'm probably better situated than a lot of these people. . . . The other thing is, I told you once before, that my philosophy is how can I help the system to become law-abiding, how can I make law-abiding accessible. Because if it's not accessible, then they are going to be nonlaw-abiding. They are going to break the law. I want everybody, as soon as possible, to have a driver's license and to have insurance, to have registration.

The judge's explanation is actually her account of a deliberate trajectory innovation she has designed and implemented. She has questioned and changed the norms of "not talking about time to pay" and "four months to pay a driving under the influence fine." Instead, she has adopted alternative rules that might be called "acquiring realistic commitment" and "making law-abiding accessible." But these new rules are not just passing situational solution innovations. They are used to shape and monitor the trajectories of cases: to prevent defendants from coming back and overloading the court system. Such a trajectory innovation is not only based on questioning the previous rules, above all it is based on a reconceptualization of the objects, that is, the defendants, in terms of their realistic possibilities in time.

This trajectory innovation is also a socially distributed achievement. It has to be reconstructed time and again in collaboration with each defendant, as well as with the prosecutor and the public defenders.

Systems innovations in courts

A systems innovation is much more difficult to trace and document than trajectory innovations and solution innovations. Over a period of 3 years, my research group followed and supported a process of analysis and redesign of the activity system in two Finnish municipal courts (see Engeström, Haavisto, & Pihlaja 1992). I will use a part of this process as an example of systems innovations.

In this particular court, the caseload has increased rapidly and the personnel feel they are working at the upper limits of their capacity. During 1990, we collected interview, observational, and historical data on the court and conducted workshops with the personnel where they reflected on their work. The work was led by a project group consisting of practitioners from the court and members of my research group. In February 1991, five multiprofessional planning groups were formed, with the task of designing different aspects of a new overall working model for the court. The first group got the task of redesigning the organization and the internal division of labor of the court; the second group was to redesign the procedures for handling civil cases; the third group was to redesign the procedures for handling criminal cases; the fourth group was to redesign the handling of real estate matters in the court; and the fifth group was to redesign the customer services of the court. The planning groups presented interim reports on their work at a seminar in August 1991. They submitted their final reports in February 1992.

The work of the first planning group became decisive for the evolution of an overall concept of the new organization of the court. In the following, I will look into the work of this planning group as an example of systems innovations. It should be noted that the implementation of the proposals of the planning groups in practice is going on presently and thus cannot be fully evaluated until later.

The first planning group consisted of three judges and three clerks. The presiding judge of the court took part in approximately half of the meetings. One of the judges acted as chairman of the group. The group met 18 times, including one meeting the group organized for the entire personnel of the court to discuss the provisional proposals of the group. The group started out by discussing and designing future job profiles for court secretaries (clerks). This phase took the first seven meetings and 5 months. In July, the group quite suddenly embarked on drafting a framework for the new organization of the court. The initial model for the organization was elaborated in four meetings over a period of 3½ months. In the next three meetings, the group concretized its model and introduced the idea of work teams; the implementation of the teams was started at the beginning of December by dividing the clerks into teams. This phase took place over a period of 6 weeks. After this phase, one meeting was used to discuss the filling of a specific position. Finally, the last three meetings (a period of roughly 4 weeks) were used to finalize the report of the group. The phases of the work are summarized in Table 14.1.

An analysis of the complex interactions and cognitive processes that took place during this 1-year period is not possible within the scope of this paper. The crucial question here is, In what way was this a process of systems innovation?

Three traditional organizational principles dominate in Finnish courts: the principle of the autonomous judge, the principle of seniority,

Table 14.1. *Phases of the work of planning group 1.*

Period	Number of meetings	Topics discussed	Outcomes of the phase
February to July 1991	7	Job descriptions of court secretaries (clerks).	Proposal for new job descriptions.
July to October 1991	4	New organization of the court; revision of the new model to eliminate rigid specialization of judges.	Interim report; draft model for the new organization.
October to December 1991	3	Work teams; their implementation starting with the clerks.	The team idea accepted; implementation launched in December.
January to February 1992	3	Finalization of the group's report; preliminary placement of personnel in teams.	Final report submitted; organization model in a finished form.

and the principle of departmental specialization. These principles have made the courts captives between traditional craft professionalism and bureaucratic division of labor.

The three traditional principles mentioned previously were available to the planning group in the form of concrete organizational solutions. The Swedish model of "personal dockets" (*rooteli* in Finnish) designated to each judge is commonly presented as a modern version of the principle of the autonomous judge. The principle of seniority is connected to departmental specialization. In the municipal courts of certain large cities, typically Helsinki, judges are divided into specialized departments and senior judges occupy positions of department heads.

These traditional principles were present in the interviews of the members of the planning group obtained before the group began its work. However, rudiments of two alternative principles were also identified in the interviews, though only in very vague forms. These two alternative principles are the principle of many-sided, flexible job descriptions and the principle of group collaboration. There were no concrete organizational models available in Finnish courts to exemplify these alternative principles in practice.

The work of the planning group can be seen as a stepwise struggle between these two sets of organizational principles. In the second phase of its work (see Table 14.1 above), the group initially proposed a model in which the judges were divided to departments, some of which were specialized in civil cases, some in criminal cases. This model did not include any rotation between the departments. After receiving criticism from colleagues, the group revised the model on the basis of many-sided, flexible job descriptions plus rotation in the few necessary specialized tasks. This revision seems to have created something of an ideational vacuum: the departments' original function of achieving effectiveness through specialization was eliminated, so they needed another function and way of achieving effectiveness. In the third phase of its work, the group filled this vacuum by formulating the idea of teamwork and group collaboration.

This stepwise process was definitely one of questioning and gradually giving up previously dominant norms of organization design. It can also be seen as a process of collective concept formation.

Notes toward theorizing innovative learning

In the examples presented in this paper, various kinds of mediating artifacts have been indicated. In the solution innovations, I pointed out the role of questions, reported speech, and notebooks. In trajectory innovations, deliberately constructed novel rules or scripts seem to be crucial. And in systems innovations, we are dealing with complex models of alternative past, present, and future versions of the activity system. All these artifacts seem to serve in revisioning the problematic object, in turning the self-evident into an object of inquiry and experimentation.

These different types of mediating artifacts, constructed and used to re-vision the object, seem to appear in complex hierarchies where the different levels interact and inform each other. Inspired by Wartofsky's (1979) discussion of levels of artifacts, I have suggested a typology of four kinds of artifacts (Engeström 1990, pp. 187–195). *What* artifacts are used to identify, describe, and classify objects. *How* artifacts are used to guide and monitor ways of proceeding and acting with objects. *Why* artifacts are used to justify, direct, and explain objects and actions. Finally, *where to* artifacts are used to explain, predict, and direct the evolution and change of systems over time.

I argue that there is an important vertical or hierarchical dimension to learning and human cognition more generally. The typology of artifacts sketched above is one important aspect and indicator of this dimension. Moreover, it is interestingly related (though not identical) to theories of different levels of learning suggested by Bateson (1972) and Engeström (1987). Accounts of learning and innovation that only operate with horizontal or "flat" notions of cognition miss a crucially important resource in failing to explore the particular complementary potentials and limitations of the different levels of mediational means.

Arguments for the importance of this vertical dimension have sometimes been interpreted as falling back to deterministic models of developmental stages leading to a fixed end point. For example, this is how Klaus Holzkamp interprets Bateson's (1972) levels of learning and my use of them (Engeström 1987) as an ingredient in a theory of expansive learning: "development depicted as learning passage through a logically preconstructed matrix of stages of learning" (Holzkamp 1993, p. 238).

Does an argument for a vertical dimension of hierarchical levels automatically imply a fixed course of development? Holzkamp overlooks here the dialectics of universality and context-specificity in development. This very issue was discussed by Sylvia Scribner (1985) in her seminal analysis of Vygotsky's uses of history.

But just as Vygotsky does not offer a 'progression of cultural stages,' he does not offer a stagelike progression of higher forms of behavior. One reason, I believe, is that he does not represent higher systems as general modes of thought or as general structures of intelligence in a Piagetian sense. *Vygotsky addressed the question of general processes of formation of particular functional systems, a project quite at variance from one aimed at delineating a particular sequence of general functional systems. . . .* Vygotsky's comparisons are always made with respect to some particular system of sign-mediated behavior – memory, counting, writing . . . each of these systems has its own course of development; all of them ('higher' or 'cultural' by definition) advance from rudimentary to more advanced forms. But there is no *necessity* in theory for all functional systems characterizing the behavior of an individual, or behaviors in a given social group, to be at the same level. (Scribner 1985, p. 132; first italics added by Y. Engeström)

In the context of my own argument for levels of artifact mediation and learning, the spirit of Scribner's point translates as follows. I maintain that levels of learning and artifact mediation represent "general processes of formation of particular functional systems." As general processes or general mechanisms, they contain no fixed order of progression, nor a fixed end point. They are continuously present as resources for the formation of specific innovations and transformations in particular organizations. It is characteristic to the levels of artifact mediation and learning that they appear in various combinations and that there is continuous interplay between the levels. In this sense, consider the levels as a kit of wrenches of successive sizes. The kit is pretty general – it may be used in a tremendous variety of specific tasks. There is definitely a hierarchy in the kit. Yet there is no inherent necessity that the wrenches must be used in a specific order.

The context specificity of innovative learning requires that attention be paid to the horizontal dimension as well. How to differentiate between and analyze contexts of learning?

Perhaps the most commonly held and pervasive distinction is that between formal and informal settings of learning. Much of the literature on formal learning in educational institutions seems to ignore or dismiss informal learning in the workplace. Correspondingly, much of the literature on organizational learning overlooks the potential of formal, intentionally organized learning and instruction. The underlying assumption in both camps seems to be a belief in the superiority of one's own realm.

Research done by Sylvia Scribner and her co-workers on knowledge acquisition at work questions the validity of such dichotomous views.

Although this research could not disentangle the educational contributions of formal study and practical work experience in a systematic manner, we have suggestive evidence that these two types of activity may be functionally equivalent in certain respects. . . . In terms of our initial formulation: formal and nonformal practical activities may be substitutable for each other with respect to mastery of some aspects of a formal domain.

. . . On the basis of this study, we cannot claim absolute substitutability, but it is clear that the workplace itself is a learning environment. It is clear, also, that *how* the workplace is set up either enhances or constrains learning. (Scribner, Sachs, Di Bello, & Kindred 1991, pp. 49–50)

At the first glance, it would seem that all the examples presented in this paper deal with informal workplace learning only. However, this is not true of the examples illuminating systems innovations in health centers and courts. An expansive learning process that leads to a transformation of an entire activity system typically contains various complementary learning events and sequences. Many of these events are formal training sessions or courses, occurring side by side with informal interactions facilitating externalization and internalization of a new model of work.

The crucial precondition for such complementarity is that events and specific sequences of learning and instruction are subordinated to a long-term process of encompassing systems innovation. Such a motive and vision puts the debate between formal and informal learning in a perspective. Substitutability is no more only a question of allowing various individual paths of learning. It becomes an issue of facilitating the collective innovation by any useful means available. Individual substitutability becomes collective complementarity, or joint exploitation of the potentials of multivoicedness in expertise.

Notes

1. Jean Lave (1988) points out the strong affinities between the basic assumptions about learning and problem-solving in cognitive laboratory experiments and in school instruction.
2. I owe the notion of trajectory to Anselm Strauss. See especially his *The Social Construction of Medical Work* (Strauss et al. 1985).
3. The concept of expansive learning corresponds to Bateson's (1972) concept of Learning III. This level of learning in Bateson's theory has been systematically neglected by Argyris and Schön (1978). Also Schön's (1983) notion of reframing does not correspond to the expansive notion of recontextualization. Schön sees the mechanism of reframing in problem solving as a process of pattern recognition based on analogy and experience, not as a process of constructing a context for the context and thus not requiring any particular new mediating tools.
4. The categories suggested here have some resemblance to the common distinction between product innovations, process innovations and organizational innovations. However, the logic behind my categorization is entirely different from the one behind the common typology. My categories are based on the originally Hegelian epistemological differentiation between primary centering, de-centering, and re-centering (or coordination, cooperation and communication), analyzed by Raeithel (1983), Fichtner (1984), and Engeström (1987, 1992).
5. See also Engeström (1991) for a critical discussion of Reason's framework.
6. This oppositional aspect has mostly been neglected in discussions of the psychology of innovation. For a nice related analysis, see Litowitz (1990).

References

Abernathy, W. J., & Wayne, K. (1974). Limits of the learning curve. *Harvard Business Review*, September–October, 109–119.

Argyris, C., & Schön, D. A. (1978). *Organizational learning: A theory of action perspective*. Reading, MA: Addison-Wesley.

Bateson, G. (1972). *Steps to an ecology of mind.* New York: Ballantine Books.

Bell, M., & Scott-Kemmis, D. (1990). *The mythology of learning-by-doing in World War II airframe and ship production.* Science Policy Research Unit, University of Sussex.

Bowers, J., & Middleton, D. (1991). Distributed organizational cognition: An innovative idea? Paper presented at the Franco-British Seminar 'Information and Innovation: The Management of Intellectual Resources', Paris, April 16, 1991.

Davydov, V. V. (1990). *Types of generalization in instruction.* Reston, VA: National Council of Teachers of Mathematics.

Dodgson, M. (1991). *The management of technological learning: Lessons from a biotechnology company.* Berlin: Walter de Gruyter.

Engeström, Y. (1987). *Learning by expanding: An activity-theoretical approach to developmental research.* Helsinki: Orienta-Konsultit.

Engeström, Y. (1990). *Learning, working and imagining: Twelve studies in activity theory.* Helsinki: Orienta-Konsultit.

Engeström, Y. (1991). Developmental work research: Reconstructing expertise through expansive learning. In M. I. Nurminen & G. R. S. Weir (Eds.), *Human jobs and computer interfaces.* Amsterdam: Elsevier.

Engeström, Y. (1992). *Interactive expertise: Studies in distributed working intelligence.* Research Bulletin #83. University of Helsinki, Department of Education.

Engeström, Y. (1993). The working health center project: Materializing zones of proximal development in a network of organizational innovation. In T. Kauppinen & M. Lahtonen (Eds.), *Action research in Finland.* Helsinki: Ministry of Labour.

Engeström, Y., Brown, K., Christopher, C., & Gregory, J. (1991). Coordination, cooperation and communication in courts: Expansive transitions in legal work. *The Quarterly Newsletter of the Laboratory of Comparative Human Cognition, 13,* 88–97.

Engeström, Y., Haavisto, V., & Pihlaja, J. (1992). *Alioikeudet uuden työtavan kynnyksellä: Kehittävän työntutkimuksen sovellus tuomioistuinlaitoksessa* (Municipal courts facing a new way of working: An application of developmental work research in the court system). Helsinki: Yliopistopaino (in Finnish).

Fichtner, B. (1984). Co-ordination, co-operation and communication in the formation of theoretical concepts in instruction. In M. Hedegaard, P. Hakkarainen & Y. Engeström (Eds.), *Learning and teaching on a scientific basis: Methodological and epistemological aspects of the activity theory of learning and teaching.* Aarhus: Aarhus Universitet, Psykologisk Institut.

Fiol, C. M., & Lyles, M. A. (1985). Organizational learning. *Academy of Management Review, 10*(4), 803–813.

Garratt, B. (1990). *Creating a learning organisation: A guide to leadership, learning and development.* Cambridge, MA: Director Books.

Ghemawat, P. (1985). Building strategy on the experience curve. *Harvard Business Review,* March–April, 143–149.

Goodwin, C. & Goodwin, M. H. (in press). Formulating planes: Seeing as a situated activity. In Y. Engeström & D. Middleton (Eds.), *Cognition and communication at work*. Cambridge: Cambridge University Press.

Heath, C. & Luff, P. (in press). Collaboration and control: The use and development of a multimedia environment on London Underground. In Y. Engeström & D. Middleton (Eds.), *Cognition and communication at work*. Cambridge: Cambridge University Press.

Hickman, L. A. (1990). *John Dewey's pragmatic technology*. Bloomington: Indiana University Press.

Holzkamp, K. (1993). *Lernen: Subjektwissenschaftliche Grundlegung [Learning: Subject-scientific foundations]*. Frankfurt am Main: Campus.

Hutchins, E. & Klausen, T. (In press). Distributed cognition in an airline cockpit. In Y. Engeström & D. Middleton (Eds.), *Cognition and communication at work*. Cambridge: Cambridge University Press.

Karmiloff-Smith, A., & Inhelder, B. (1975). If you want to get ahead, get a theory. *Cognition, 3*, 195–212.

Kibria, M. G., & Tisdell, C. A. (1985). International comparisons of learning curves and productivity. *Management International Review, 25*(4), 66–72.

Lave, J. (1988). *Cognition in practice: Mind, mathematics and culture in everyday life*. Cambridge: Cambridge University Press.

Leont'ev, A. N. (1978). *Activity, consciousness, and personality*. Englewood Cliffs, NJ: Prentice-Hall.

Leont'ev, A. N. (1981). *Problems of the development of the mind*. Moscow: Progress.

Lilja, K. (1989). *Epics and epochs: Organisational learning and the Kaskinen pulp mill*. Working Papers # F-232, Helsinki School of Economics.

Litowitz, B. E. (1990). Just say no: Responsibility and resistance. *The Quarterly Newsletter of the Laboratory of Comparative Human Cognition, 12*, 135–141.

March, J. G., Sproull, L. S., & Tamuz, M. (1991). Learning from samples of one or fewer. *Organization Science, 2*, 1–13.

Middleton, D. (1991). *Team collectivity in discursive action: Improvising innovations*. Paper presented at the Fourth European Conference for Research on Learning and Instruction. Turku, Finland, August 24–28, 1991.

Raeithel, A. (1983). *Tätigkeit, Arbeit und Praxis: Grundbegriffe für eine praktische Psychologie*. Frankfurt am Main: Campus.

Reason, J. (1990). *Human error*. Cambridge, UK: Cambridge University Press.

Rittenberg, W. (1985). Mary; Patient as emergent symbol on a pediatrics ward: The objectification of meaning in social process. In R. A. Hahn & A. D. Gaines (Eds.), *Physicians of western medicine: Anthropological approaches to theory and practice*. Dordrecht: Reidel.

Schön, D. A. (1983). *The reflective practitioner: How professionals think in action*. London: Temple Smith.

Scribner, S. (1985). Vygotsky's uses of history. In J. V. Wertsch (Ed.), *Culture, communication, and cognition: Vygotskian perspectives*. Cambridge, UK: Cambridge University Press.

Scribner, S., Sachs, P., Di Bello, L., & Kindred, J. (1991). *Knowledge acquisition at work.* Technical Paper No. 22. Laboratory for Cognitive Studies of Work, City University of New York.

Senge, P. M. (1990). *The fifth discipline: The art and practice of the learning organization.* New York: Doubleday.

Shrivastava, P. (1983). A typology of organizational learning systems. *Journal of Management Studies, 20*(1), 9–28.

Strauss, A., et al. (1985). *The social organization of medical work.* Chicago: The University of Chicago Press.

Wartofsky, M. (1979). *Models: Representation and scientific understanding.* Dordrecht: Reidel.

15 Intellectual and manual labor: Implications for developmental theory

Joseph Glick

Tensions of developmental theory: Need for a critical perspective

Developmental theories operate with two principles in tension with one another. On the one hand, developmental analysis must meet ordinary tests of analytic adequacy by providing an account of the organization of behavior as it is manifested in a particular setting, related to the demands and structure of that setting. This mode of analysis involves the construction of linkages between behaviors and/or thoughts "here and now" with conditions "here and now" – from which descriptions of the organization of behavior, here and now, are derived.

But developmentalists try to do more. The essential move in developmental analysis is to compare behavioral organization at one time with behavioral organization at some other time. These analytic "moments" (Glick 1992) are then linked into a series. The linked moments are treated as defining a trajectory, which can then be taken to be informative about development and the differences between the less developed and the more developed. However, in order to do this, in many instances, the "here and now" conditions must be changed so as to allow for situations to be used or observed which are appropriate to different age groups. When this has been done, the construction of a developmental description involves a balancing of the evidentiary requirements for understanding behavior here and now with the comparative requirement for making statements about the relationships among behaviors which differ in their here and now conditions.

The tension in trying these enterprises together is that they embody, in fact, different principles of analysis. The here and now analysis is oriented toward an understanding of behaviors as situated in the particulars of setting and of organism at a given point in time at a particular place. For those, in particular, who take a "levels of organization" point of view

357

it is axiomatic that this sort of situated and embedded analysis is critical to making any sense out of measured phenomena (e.g., Werner 1937; Werner and Kaplan 1963; Schneirla 1972; Sroufe 1979; Kaplan 1983; Tobach & Greenberg 1984; Vygotsky 1987; Glick 1992). These theorists work on the principle that "what looks similar" isn't necessarily similar, since a behavioral outcome can be achieved by any number of rather different underlying processes (Werner 1937; Kaplan 1983; Glick 1992).

These analytic considerations suggest that there are some formidable barriers in the way of constructing a developmental trajectory out of an extrapolation of the relationship between points of developmental measurement. If the points which are linked are, in fact, subserved by very different behavioral process organizations then the construction of a linkage may be on external features only. Sroufe (1979), for example, has examined the methodological and theoretical consequences of this point for analysis of social behaviors.

The basic problematic is that *if* the "linking" of behaviors at different time periods within developmental theory violates the analytic necessities of understanding behavior in relation to its local conditions, *then* the principles of linkage, and indeed the notion of development, must come from sources other than the empirical phenomena. *Developmental description then, is basically theoretical although it presents itself as empirically grounded in comparative measurements.*

Theories fill the gap created by the tension between grounded situational analysis and the need to compare. It can be argued that theories impose their own ordering on phenomena and so must be understood not only in terms of their empirical adequacy but also in critical terms that consider the ways in which theories construct their theoretical objects (Glick 1983). Such critical understanding is an understanding that attempts to be reflective about the processes and practices by means of which theoretical understanding is constructed.

Metaphors and theoretical choices

Theories operate on at least two levels. The first level is explicit. Whether framed in the positivistic terminology of "prediction and control" or in more hermeneutic terms. The explicit level of theory makes statements that are easily recognizable as theoretical and contains operations that seem to link the theory to empirical phenomena. Most often this explicit level is what is taken to be the theory.

However, underlying the theory in its explicit form there is an implicit and presuppositional, pretheoretical level where choices are made about what phenomena are to be theorized. This level of theory is seldom focused on, although compelling cases have been made that the implicit and presuppositional level of theory determines the possible forms that the explicit level of theory can take.

Pepper (1942) identified this level in terms of the concept of "root metaphor" (see also Reese & Overton 1970; Overton & Reese 1973). Pepper's basic notion is that the root metaphor gives the phenomena to be "theorized about" an object-like status that invites certain ways of inspecting the object. This then selects certain ways of posing the theoretical questions. The notion of root metaphor suggests that theories are built upon basic "image models" (metaphors) – with associated categories of analysis appropriate to the image model. For example, if the theory "imagines" the human to be a complex machine, it is led to ask questions about how the parts of that machine are connected, or, where it is plugged in (how it is motivated). If the image is instead the image of an organism, questions change: One might wonder what accounts for the direction of the organism's motion (not the source of it) and about the relationship between various organism systems (rather than the connection of part to part).

Glick (1983) has identified similar questions in terms of the related but somewhat different notion of the "conceptual object" of a theory – that which the theory is trying to explain. The idea of the conceptual object of theory links the critical question closely to the operations of theorists. It suggests that theorists, of whatever "metaphoric" school, make critical choices about the topic of their inquiry, and that theories may best be compared and contrasted on the level of what they "topicalize." If topicalization is understood, much of the theoretical apparatus posited as an explanation of development can be predicted. Indeed, it can be argued that many of the differences between major theorists are, in fact, differences between the topics that the theorists address – a fact that tends to become obscured when developmental theories are involved. Since "the child" is a compelling natural kind, seeming to provide the conceptual target for theory in a straightforward way, it is easy to forget that the child in question is a "theorized child" depicted and interrogated within the framework of the conceptual topicalization moves that theories make. We shall later be looking at the way in which these topicalization moves are related to "the child" but in a less direct way than is currently understood.

Most recently, we have come to understand that there is a third level of the function of theories as well – a level that characterizes them not so much in terms of their internal structure, but in terms of their external function and setting which has consequence for their internal structure. This is a level that characterizes theories not so much in terms of what the theory has to say about it conceptual topic, but a level that sees theories as the products of theorists who are themselves involved in the situated practices of the places where theorists work – usually universities and research labs, and engaged in extended discourses with those similarly located.

Pierre Bourdieu (1988) suggests in his deeply unsettling book on Homo Academicus - us – that we are situated as members of academic communities that follow certain institutionalized forms of procedure and discourse. He suggests that what "counts" as the principled study of a topic is composed of both the canons of scientific study and the institutional rules, techniques, and membership practices that format inquiry in a way that is manifestly recognizable as scientific. This institutional apparatus privileges certain methodologies whose semiotic function is to guarantee a sense and feel of objectivity, rigor, logic and well-formedness – which thus makes assertions seem like truths beyond a particular and situated observer.

Often the "ordinary practices" of academic work involve techniques of inscription which themselves provide an order and an inner logic to what is found (Clifford & Marcus 1986; Mehan 1993). For example, Clifford and Marcus (1986) have collected a number of essays that show the influence of the "written" form of ethnographies on the rendering of ethnographic "fact." Indeed, even for the ethnographer, there is a gap between the experienced and the written forms of ethnography. There is a translation process at work that inevitably bends toward the logic and form of the inscription devices used as a part of professional practice (e.g., the "writtenness" of ethnography). The gaps that this produces between the written form of "understanding" by the ethnographer and the understandings (often multiple and unclear) of both the ethnographer and the ethnographized in situ (and not in writing) have been elegantly documented by Bourdieu (1977) with respect to the production of an agricultural calendar – which is orderly when constructed between anthropologists and informants and something quite different when the agricultural seasons indicated by the calendar are understood and experienced by either anthropologists or informants as they are involved in the activities of farming. Thus, the institutional participation of theorists in the life of the academy provides not only a location where theoretical thinking happens, but also a set of location-specific devices and tactics that define legitimate membership in the academic community.

It might also be cogently argued that since developmental theories generally work with either an implicit or explicit notion of the "telos" of development (that toward which development is developing), the institutional location of those studying development may deeply affect the choice of developmental topics studied. Indeed it often seems that the enterprise of "studying cognitive development" constructs development as the acquisition of knowledge structures whose telos is to be inherently university-like: abstract in form, literate in organization, and counted as true cognitive development when it is formulated and rationalized in an acceptable "public" and logical form.

The academic form privileges knowledge of a certain type, and elevates that form of knowledge to universal and moral status as the kind of knowledge that people should have if they are said to have knowledge at all. In Wittgensteinian terms, some language games count more heavily than others as the only game in town.

Such selection practices can serve to fundamentally skew accounts of the phenomena under study and obscure certain essential elements that "do not fit" into theoretical idealizations. For example, studies of activity in scientific laboratories (e.g., Knorr-Cetina 1981; Knorr-Cetina & Mulkay 1983; Lynch 1985; Latour & Woolgar 1986; Latour 1987; Suchman 1987; Suchman & Trigg 1993) attest to the distance that may be found between actual laboratory practices and their cognitive idealizations.

There is a directionality to all of this. Alfred Sohn-Rethel (1978), in a remarkable little book, identified this as a privileging of an "idealized" over an "activity" perspective. This in turn relates to a privileging of the "intellectual forms" over the other forms often associated with "doing." He related these tendencies to the dynamics of the particular form of social/economic organization of capitalism which establishes a value hierarchy between those activities that are "intellectual" (cognitive) and those that are "merely activity" (manual). In developmental theory the "intellectual over manual" formulation is, at the least, a warrant for hierarchical social organization, where those who have more of the "intellectual" gain, in some manner the natural right, to manage, scaffold, teach, or otherwise impact on those who are manually engaged, or "sensorimotor."

Cognitive developmental theories

Most developmental theories treat cognitive development as if the core issue to be addressed is the way in which new behaviors or organizations of behavior enter the repertoire. The general developmental question is posed in somewhat the following form: "Something was not in the child's repertoire, and later it was. How did it get there? What was its getting there based upon? What are the mechanisms of development?" (e.g., Sternberg 1984). As we shall see the emphasis on "the new" involves a particular stance toward "the old" as something that will be supplanted or otherwise transformed.

A second feature of most developmental accounts is that they pose a "trajectory" that specifies at its end point a particular notion of what "most developed" is like. In general the idea is that "the most developed" is "the most abstract." It seems quite natural to a developmental account to pose the issue in these terms. Whether the source is considered as innate or acquired, or somewhere in between there seems to be agreement that the essential problematic of development may not be in its source but in its direction. Abstract knowledge is generally considered as a telos for development, and if not for developing children, certainly for developmental theory (Piaget 1983; Vygotsky 1987, chapters 5, 6).

The "move" from concrete to abstract is most often considered as the essential hallmark of developmental progress – and indeed as often distinguishing "true" development from "mere" learning. Any developmentalist worth his or her salt is ready and eager to engage in a heated discussion of how learning, insofar as it involves exposure to concrete forms of information, cannot be equal to development, because development entails a "structuring" of the concrete into the more abstract. Though learning may account for how the "new" arrives, only development can account for how the "new" is abstract and general.

The characterization of development as the development of "increasingly abstract" abilities is not uncontested. Considerable attention may be paid in some theorist's accounts to the "mediational means" or "representational systems" that concretely underlay performance on tasks that presumably measure abstract functioning (e.g., Klahr 1984; Nunes, Schleimann, & Carraher 1993). Nonetheless, these more concrete factors are generally treated as being the kind of "performance" or "operational" factors entangled in the measurement and display of abstract abilities. The general "telos" of increasing abstraction is not seriously challenged.

Sudies of developmental issues in well-structured knowledge domains have begun to suggest that there must be some relationship between learning of the "knowledge base" and developmental structuring. For example, studies by Chi (1979) and Chi, Glaser, & Rees (1981) have begun to detail the contingency between having a rich knowledge base and those abilities that seem to presuppose abstract structuring. In particular, the strategic consequences that have been attributed to abstract knowledge can be seen instead to be the consequences of having a rich knowledge base that affords many alternative paths through it.

A third feature of most developmental accounts is that they treat the "unit" of development as "the organism and its identifiable history." Testing, when testing is the means by which developmental assertions are done, generally focuses on the performance of individuals.

Piagetian accounts (e.g., Piaget 1983) most notably "individuate" the relevant history, so that development is seen as either a "self-construction" or as the joint construction of selves and other's demands. Similarly, Vygotskian theory (1978, 1987), while it makes room for "sociohistorical" factors (Scribner 1985), nonetheless tends to yield studies whose focus is on the impact of sociohistorical factors on individual and time-bounded lives. While notions of cultural development and/or other aspects of material transindividual developments may "inform" the shape and form of Vygotskian theory, it is still the "child as impacted upon by others" who remains the topic.

The questions traditionally posed by developmental theories seem natural to ask, and the assertions upon which they are based seem quite natural as well. But these questions and assertions are not necessarily the most productive. Indeed, some of the blinders imposed are most clearly to be seen when a point of contrast is provided.

A start in this direction has been opened up in the groundbreaking work of Sylvia Scribner (1984, 1986). Sylvia was deeply interested in the problem of how "topics" emerge for theoretical treatment, and how these topics are themselves open to critical analysis, not as "the" topics but as "selected" topics that have a particular social function and location.

In particular Sylvia was engaged in comparing the classical formulations of development with formulations of development that emerge within an activity theory perspective (Leont'ev 1978, 1981; Engeström 1990; Scribner 1990). The question addressed by these comparisons concerned the relationship between the formulation and description of abilities and their development in the measurement situations typically applied by developmental and cognitive researchers and formulations of development and ability that might be found in activity settings, where intellect is not seen as a thing in itself but is seen rather as an integral part of people's activities and lives. As a part of this effort Sylvia redirected attention to the issues of development as they are encountered in workplaces where adults are expected to function after they have done their developing in schools and families.

I will be exploring some of the further developments of this approach. But given all of the levels on which theory operates, this chapter will not be so much about the relation of results obtained in work on adult development to results obtainable in studies of child development, but rather it will be looking at some of the reconfigurations of ways of understanding, ways of speaking, and shifts in unit of analysis that flow from a full engagement with adult development in the workplace.

School and work – locations and agendas

There is an "invisible" structuring principle in most developmental analyses, which is in part generated by a convergence between the institutional location of the children who are the topics of the developmental study and the institutional structure of the places where studying is done.

Most developmental models focus on periods of life when children are in families and in schools – both institutions have a unique social structure and status. Schools and families are not only "locations where learning and development happens," they are also institutions that have an agenda that is very much related to their status as *transitional institutions from which people eventually are expected to leave.*

Yet, to the extent that the concept of development is a general concept, the institutional narrowing of perspective afforded by these settings is a limiting factor. Studies of "situated cognition" (e.g., Suchman 1987; Lave 1988; Lave & Wenger 1991; Chaiklin & Lave 1993) typically examine developmental and cognitive issues in very different sorts of settings.

If one refocuses, instead of looking at development in traditional settings, one thinks of development as a process that can happen in a number of different sorts of settings. Such examination might allow an appreciation of the relationship between the manner in which the category of development is defined, the manner in which the invisible constraints of developmental theorizing are acquired, and the perhaps "unique" features of setting within which developmental topics are studied.

In the following we shall be examining such issues as how is development recognized as development?, and what counts as an account of it?

For starters let me pose a question. Where do people who do the developing (in our theoretical accounts of development) end up? Where does development go? (Glick 1993). Many, if not most, "developed" people do not end up in universities, nor do they end up in other institutions that privilege logical and abstract knowledge structures. Many people end up in jobs. And although it may be argued that jobs are becoming more "intellectualized" as technology invades the workplace, the work environment does not yet resemble the sort of environment that characterizes either schools or universities.

To begin with, look at some of the differences that may be found when we consider the "location" aspect of development, in particular contrasting the school and the workplace. This can be seen in Table 15.1.

In constructing this contrastive table I have attempted to identify not only the ordinary practices of school and work, but have striven to more clearly identify their "institutional agendas" and the topics and theoretical concerns that would flow from these different settings.

At first this identification of the different institutional agendas of school and work might feel like a strange contrast for the reader. This is understandable since, for most teachers and professors, the school identified in the table is actually a workplace, and for the university embedded academics, in particular, the workplace is really a school.

The identifications represented in the table are based upon "what" constitutes a normal conversation that might be had about the mission of the setting and the understandings of the problem as seen from an institutional perspective. And, indeed, in reading these charts in the vertical dimension, there is an implicit argument structure laid out. This is not so much a script as it is a "normative conversation" or narrative appropriate to and natural to the environment.

Table 15.1. *Child development versus adult practices (work)*

Schools	Work
A place people leave - People "graduate" or "grow up"	*A place people stay* - Long standing position in place
Notion of multiformed future - Understanding that the tasks of school/family are preparatory for some unknown future destination	*Notion of a rationalized future* - Progress will be organizationally defined
Knowledge to be carried with the person - Transportable skills - Generative skills	*Knowledge a part of the environment* - Efficient artifacts - Effective skills - Technology solutions
Organization for "flexibility" - Generalized/abstract skills - Progressively achieved - Transferable knowledge	*Organization for efficiency* - Specialized skills - Maximally adapted - Some transfer from person to machine
Long time for formative contact	*Formation needed "now" but under ideal circumstances contact will be long term*
Architectural notions of progress - Younger to older - Agenda for progress - Progress in person	*Historical notions of progress* - Novice to expert - Agenda for success - Progress isn't necessarily in people
Efficacy seen in individuals - Measures of success based on individual progress - Frustrations derive from behavioral or organizational interference	*Efficacy seen in organizations* - Profit/loss - Organizational worth - Individuals make way within institutional possibilities - Defend "selves" within institutional constraint
Guidance toward progress - Teaching, scaffolding - Piggybacked demands - Development as constraint	*Guidance toward efficiency of function* - Apprenticeship - On-the-job training - Retraining
Focus on knowledge acquisition - Completeness - Integrity	*Focus on knowledge integration* - Adaptedness - Coordination
DEVELOPMENT THE TOPIC!	EFFICIENT FUNCTION THE TOPIC!

A master narrative of schooling

People who problematize development from the imaginal perspective of the school are presented with a situation predicated on the idea of "school leaving." Because the school is to be left, the ultimate "deployment" of knowledge gained in school is inherently unknown. Thus, future knowledge demands are likely to be "multiformed." Therefore, the knowledge-related mission of the school is to impart just that sort of knowledge that will travel well. The most likely form of knowledge that will travel well to multiformed futures is knowledge that is "transferable." And "everybody knows" that abstract and formal knowledge is most likely to be most flexible and transferable.

Fortunately the school has a long time to accomplish this job. Children are in school for at least 12 years. Therefore it is "normal" to talk in terms of a "progressivist" agenda. Issues of "sequencing" and/or "readiness" take on great importance. It is perfectly "normal" school and developmental theory talk to focus on "what goes before what" in the process of building knowledge of the flexible sort required by the condition of graduation to an unknown future. Most often the concept of building such knowledge and/or development is architectural. Talk is in terms of building "foundations" for higher levels of functioning. "Foundations" are necessarily both educationally and developmentally prior, and what is higher than a foundation is necessarily more abstract. The task of the institution, and the theory, is to orchestrate an understanding of, and practice of, progressively building from foundations to higher levels of functioning.

The progressivist architectural model of both educational and developmental theories has as its critical focus the building of individuals who are, as units, prepared to meet the multiformed and not fully knowable tasks that society will pose. While children in schools and in families are part of a collective group, it is well known and an intrinsic part of the "agenda" that their fates will be either as individuals or in collectivities whose composition is currently unpredictable. Thus, the "knowledge that counts" is that knowledge which is possessed by individuals. Thus school, and even developmental theories, acquire a secondary agenda, that of "sorting out" those who are meeting the progressive architectural agenda in a comparatively appropriate manner. Timeliness to achieve agenda performance levels acquires central importance in the conceptual structure of the school culture (McDermott 1993), and the "timetables of development" are so deeply embedded in our thinking that any theory will, in some manner, address the issue of timetable.

Work

People who look at work do not necessarily do so from the kind of developmental perspective outlined above. After all, in a work environment the "topic" is not people and their development, it is the survival of the work environment in a competitive framework. Rather than people being the competing parties (as in school), workplaces are the competing parties in business.

This simple difference makes for a rather huge difference in the way that the workplace "problematizes" development within it. Rather than rendering this difference in narrative form I will instead shift to outlining issues involved in conceptualizing work in a theoretical form. I could afford to be narrative in areas where I can assume the reader has a general grasp of the relevant theories. I will become theoretical for those areas where I feel that many of my readers may only have narratives.

In the development of the theoretical perspective on development as might be ferreted out of the environment of work, the argument will be contrastive – in general, contrasting the "school-based" developmental perspective with a possible "work-based" view.

The unit of analysis

V. P. Zinchenko (1985), in an attempt to characterize the theoretical uniqueness of Vygotsky's theory, focused on the problem of the "unit of analysis" as being a core issue around which theories divide.

It is interesting that in the history of psychology one can observe quite complex relationships between the analytic unit and the theoretical structure as a whole. Contradictions emerge more sharply at the level of units than they do at the level of overall theoretical structures. This frequently testifies to the fact that the founders of schools of psychology have given more content to the units of analysis than their opponents, or even their followers understand. (Zinchenko 1985, p. 95–96)

Zinchenko goes on to say:

Nonetheless, contemporary psychology, which is characterized by an unprecedented accumulation of new facts, has shown insufficient interest (and occasionally an astounding carelessness) in isolating and defining units of mental analysis. This is particularly characteristic of cognitive psychology. (Ibid, p. 96)

Perhaps the sharpest distinction between typical developmental accounts (as outlined in the school narrative) and developmental accounts that are situated in the workplace concerns the unit of analysis, in particular with respect to the issue of what is knowledge? and where does it reside?

In workplaces, there is little presumption that knowledge exists, or even should exist, solely in an individual. To be sure, people in work environments might talk about prerequisite skills or about "levels of training" of workers, but *as they practically function* workplaces actually obey a set of different principles:

Since workplaces are places where people are expected to stay, there is a tendency to adapt the workplace and its structure to functional requirements, which is at least as strong as the tendency to adapt the worker. To the extent that work environments are "enduring" in time, the "knowledge" of the workplace can exist either in the worker or in the environment. In particular, there is a tendency for modern machine design and/or "computerization" to embed within their artifact structure many of mental operations that may have formerly been in workers. This has precipitated many debates about the issue of "de-skilling" of work (e.g., Shaiken 1984).

"Knowledge" may be located either in the worker, or in the work environment. Knowledge can be "distributed." Technical manuals abound that hold within them many of the things that schoolkids might be expected to hold either in memory or in cognitive structure. Most work environments house "artifacts" constructed either by workers or by technical designers, which "embed" needed knowledge within the artifact structure. For example, workers at the "electric bench" in the Transit Authority of New York have to deal with the problem of the proper spacing of switches in 16-switch electronic transmissions. This can be achieved by close measurement operations, but it is in fact achieved by the construction of "templates" that can be laid over an array of switches and which dictate their required spacing. To a great extent it is not a stretch of the imagination to say that the "knowledge of spacing" is in the template and not in the worker.

Knowledge resources are inherently social, distributed over people rather than necessarily residing within a person. Many people do closely related, if not redundant, jobs. In the work environment there are acknowledged "masters" who can be appealed to in order to deal with vexing problems that are not within individual competence.

Use of knowledge is inherently social, often requiring the coordination of disparate skills, which are located in different perspectival relations to the workplace. Since the unit of functioning is the business, which requires the orchestration of many different functions, there is a constant problem of coordinating activities in one part of the workplace with activities in other parts. However, because each job entails its own logic and perspective, the coordination is often a coordination across perspectives.

All of these (and many other) features of life in the workplace suggest a basic unit of analysis that is quite different from the unit of analysis presupposed by the school/development narrative structure. In the work environment it is virtually impossible to conceive of matters of knowledge as if they were matters of individual psychological development. At the very least, conceptions of knowledge must take into account the question of "what is known?" and must also raise the question of "where is it known?" In many cases the answer to the "where" question involves the necessity of seeing the environment structure in cognitive terms that may either be reciprocal to or supportive of individual aspects of knowing (Scribner, DiBello, Kindred, & Zazanis 1991).

Knowledge as activity: Activity as knowledge

The shift in unit analysis from individual to individual-in-structured-environment is a part of the conceptual reconfiguration involved in the perspective of development based on the view from work. There is a second major part as well, the idea of work itself.

Lave (1988); Lave & Wenger (1991); McDermott (1993); Nunes, Schliemann, and Carraher (1993); Cole, Hood, and McDermott (1978); and Newman, Griffin, & Cole (1989) among many others have pointed out the essentially "abstracted" features of conceptualizations of development examined either from the perspective of school or the experimental tradition. Knowledge is expected to be "displayed" for its own sake, as if the "having of" that knowledge was the most centrally relevant issue.

The concept of knowledge in such "abstract" and "disengaged" form varies considerably from conceptualizations of knowledge when it is considered as a constituent element of a larger unit of analysis. Knowledge in work or in the course of activity looks quite different from knowledge when it is considered as, in itself, the "topic." The conceptualization of the relationship of knowledge and activity can take many forms, some of which are less useful than others.

Knowledge can be "knowledge of," "knowledge for," or "knowledge in."
School and developmental theory–based on conceptions of knowledge tend to treat knowledge as "something as acquired" and as "something as displayed" in settings that make the having of knowledge or not (either classrooms or experiments) the core topic. Activity theory-based conceptions of knowledge place conceptual acquisitions more squarely within the context of situated accomplishments (Scribner & Sachs with DiBello & Kindred 1991). The knowledge in question could be conceptualized in terms of "that knowledge which is ingredient in and necessary for" accomplishing some task. This conception of knowledge keeps many of the elements of the "knowledge of" conception intact. The main question raised by the "knowledge for" conceptualization is that of embedding.

There is a more radical conceptualization – that of "knowledge in" action. The essential feature of this conceptualization is that the "knowing" in question may not be something that is describable by the knower. It is rather a regulative principle of the knower's activity, and may not have the status of something that can be talked about. Scribner (1984, 1986) has studied this sort of knowledge in exquisite detail. The basic point of studies of this sort is that they expose knowledge structures, often mirroring the knowledge structures demanded in the more formal "knowledge of" situation, but existing as "operating principles" that do not find explicit formulation. Scribner's dairy workers (Scribner 1984, 1986), for example, use in their activities principles of cognitive economy based upon "calculations," which they do not explicitly formulate. What makes this sort of knowledge so "unformulatable" is that it is knowledge that makes intrinsic use of environmental features and incorporates them as a part of the "calculation." Thus, a dairy worker makes use of the ordinary structure of "the case" (that holds containers) as a sort of computational base for minimizing physical labor. The knowledge in this case is "distributed" between the knower and, in some very direct sense, the case that holds the product. Thus the knowledge in question is best thought of as "what you do with a case" than as "how you do calculations." As with dairy works, so with many others.

Knowledge as replacement, acquisition, or transformative coordination.
Many developmental models problematize the issue of knowledge development as a particular form of "acquisition." The Piagetian model, for example, looks at new knowledge as not coming "de novo" into an organism, but rather as a transformation of earlier knowledge systems into more advanced ones, differing in terms of possessing a more advanced and more abstract structure.

More work-based models, for example, Chi, Glaser, and Rees (1981), see the issue in terms of the development of "expertise," and hence as a matter of developing a rich knowledge base, which provides certain opportunities for strategic operations in such areas as problem solving. While the "novice to expert" shift has been spoken of by many as being a work-based surrogate for more developmentally structural models, it appears to me that it is still, in kind, a developmental model of the school-based sort. This is so because the basic conception of development is essentially "transformative," with experts being separated from novices by the knowledge base divide.

In her last work Sylvia Scribner was exploring an alternative conceptualization of the issue, more informed by an engagement with the dynamics of change in the workplace than by an abstract conception of what it takes to be an expert. The model, which made an early appearance in a posthumous paper (Scribner, DiBello, Kindred, & Zazanis 1991) begins to conceptualize developmental issues in the workplace as the development of higher-order structures that allow the successful coordination of systems which do not replace one another, but which reside "side by side." We might term this model a model of "transformative coordination," as opposed to a model of "growing expertise" or a model of "transformative replacement" which is more characteristic of classical developmental models.

In the remainder of this paper, I would like to explore some the implications of the "transformative coordination" point of view for a reconfiguring of some of the fundamental developmental questions which may be addressed from either the "school" or the "work" perspective.

Transformations in the workplace

Industrial transformations since World War II have seen the increasing encroachment of "abstract" systems into the world of what was formerly dominated by manual work (see for example Sobel 1991;

Moss-Kanter 1991). For example, machining has been revolutionized by the use of computer numerical control systems, which substitute programming for hand, eye, and micrometer control. Manufacturing resource planning (MRP) techniques similarly involve the importation of a new form of planning, aided by computers, requiring a massive reconceptualization of the manufacturing process and the ways in which manufactured objects are thought about.

These systems, of which MRP is an example, have the basic function of "rationalizing" functioning in the workplace. And, as with all systems that attempt such rationalization, they reinstantiate some of the fundamental social and "intellectual" disparities that serve to hierarchize the workplace.

As Sylvia Scribner described the situation in a paper delivered at the activity theory conference in Lahti, Finland:

MRP is a theory of the management of manufacturing and the planning, organizing and control of production – precisely those functions whose separation from the doing of production was the historical basis for the division of so-called intellectual from so-called manual labor. Therefore, in addition to this being a program which indeed takes on very important functions with respect to production, it is an ideology. Although management theories were formalized in some respects before the advent of computer systems, they were integrated into management practice, if at all, using technical means that severely limited the capacity of theory to influence practice. Empirical knowledge systems dominated management practice. MRP and similar systems allow theory to regulate practice more directly. (Scribner 1990)

There are four unspoken principles underlying this description, all of which are critical to our analysis:

First, there is an assumption that the "logic" of management guided production and the "logic" of production systems as they exit in practice, are different.

Second, that management systems had previously been unable to "control" production systems, but that with the increasing availability of computers integrated into manufacturing the "control" aspect of management practice is increasingly possible.

Third, that the "embedded rationalities" of production will have to meet, at some point, with the ideological rationalities of management control.

And fourth, that "progress" in this environment of change will require either the total supplanting of one system by the other, or that a point of "integration" must be found.

Much would depend on the degree of "fit" between the system of production as it existed and the new demands of the "rationalized" production system.

Without going into unnecessary detail about the precise nature of the MRP system, suffice it to say that its logic is quite different from the logic of production on a number of key points. Rather than thinking of manufacturing production as a process that moves *forward in time*, from available materials, upon which labor and machine processes are applied to yield a finished product, MRP thinks of manufacturing as a process that moves *backward in time* from customer orders. Thus, the system plans backwards. In order to do so it needs several key pieces of information. It needs to know the "structure" of items so that it knows the constituent parts. But not only must it know the structure of items, which could be specified in a simple parts list, it also needs to know the "assembly logic" of the part so that it can plot "what comes before what." This is represented in an "indented bill of materials" which outlines the relations between the parts in terms of a family structure – of "parent-child" relations among raw parts and the subassemblies into which they go. Once the system knows the item structure and the parent-child relations, it can then introduce into planning the concept of "lead times" for the acquisition of materials so that the various parts come together in an assembly process just as they become needed.

The "logic" of the MRP system introduces, along with it, a new language for describing things. Thus, a "finished item," which we are likely to call "the thing that is made" or "an x," is redescribed as a "0 level item") composed of "levels" beneath the "0 level" which represent the necessary parent-child relations of assemblies to subassemblies to constituent parts of subassemblies.

Once the system is "armed" with its bills of materials, level labeling processes, and parent-child relations (which, for those of you who like the arcane can be "pegged up and down" to trace family relations and the parts involved), it can then apply a fairly rigid logic to yield a number of "planned order recommendations," which are really recommendations for what to order when. But these recommendations are often "unreal" and fatally unconnected to the reality of factory life. Indeed, the recommendations are "theoretical" in both the best and worst sense of the word.

In order to gain analytic power, certain assumptions are left out of the materials ordering process. For example, the machine has no knowledge of "the outside world," so it doesn't know whether there is bad weather (pardon the pun) between the part supplier and the plant. It doesn't know about whether there might be a strike. It assumes that materials are "where it's at" and can make recommendations that are unrelated to either machine capacity or availability of labor hours. It assumes a work force that can be hired and fired in relation to fluctuating demand. And its cycles for making such decisions are not long term enough so that they can be rationally connected to business flow, but rather fluctuate on a day-by-day or order-by-order basis. In other words, only a fool would automatically follow the recommendations. Skilled human judgment must be inserted into the equation to evaluate the recommendations against everything else that is known about the actual practices of real business with real labor forces in a real world.

In order to evaluate the recommendations of the computer program two things must be known: "reality" and "the logic of the system, and where and how it might be unreal." Typically, people engaged in production "know reality:" they have real relations with real suppliers in a real industry in a real plant. What is generally not known is the constraint on the logic of the computer program, and the many ways in which it can be unreal. Thus, it is not surprising that such systems work to a greater or lesser degree across implementations. In some cases the computer "fouls things up" and becomes progressively less used – or more precisely, ignored – while in other cases it helps a manufacturing plant to become more smoothly efficient in its operations.

In short, the "more abstract" and "more rational" system embedded in MRP is a system that *cannot work* unless it is adapted to the real conditions of the workplace.

There are a number of important points embedded in this too quick description. First, as technological systems of great abstraction impinge on the workplace, working for those who participate in such systems becomes a matter of integrating the manual routine of manufacturing with the intellectual processes of manufacturing control. The workplace becomes neither manual nor intellectual, but a place where manual and intellectual processes become coordinated.

But the precise nature of this "coordination" will be differentially achieved for different members of the work force. The system can either be a "tool" for people to use or a remote source of orders for people's jobs. A key issue becomes the issue of "participation" in the use of the system.

For those who do not participate in using such systems as tools, working becomes more "order driven" than before, except this time the orders emanate from a computer that has an abstract and hegemonic authority – it is management in "technological drag." While one can argue with a boss, it is infinitely more difficult to argue with a computer-generated requirement.

In the research it has been found that the issue of whether a new system is a "tool" or a new source of "top-down control" depends heavily on the degree to which workers (actors) are given freedom to act within the workplace.

In comparative studies of two plants where the MRP system had been implemented it was found that the ability to use the system as a tool relates most directly to the degree to which the organization of jobs in the workplace allows for tool mediated problem solving (DiBello & Glick 1992, 1993; Zazanis & Glick 1993). It has been found, for example, that achievement of knowledge of the relation of the principles of the abstract system to actual production processes does not relate at all to either formal education or specific training in the logic of the system ($r = .06$), but does relate to the "constructive opportunity" afforded by existing jobs ($r = .67$).

A look at development through the perspective of change

There are some aspects of the story told so far that may be quite familiar to developmentalists. Activity counts. Less abstract systems are overlaid by more abstract systems. It seems tempting to obliterate the distinction between the "school narrative" and work-based conceptions of development. But I invite anyone tempted to do so to look a little closer at the issues.

First, the kind of "knowledge" for which "activity counts" is not knowledge that is "knowledge for itself." The knowledge for which "activity accounts" is knowledge of how to integrate systems of different levels of construction into a seamless integrated functioning unit. Some of the knowledge that has been measured (Scribner, DiBello, Kindred, & Zazanis 1991) is perfectly abstract knowledge of the perfectly abstract system. Those who hold such knowledge are not the same people who have achieved the kind of knowledge integration that makes the system work in a real environment. Thus, "activity counts" for knowledge related to activity, and not for knowledge that is disembodied from it.

Second, the knowledge that is at issue is not knowledge which is "outside of" its embodiments. It is not knowledge carried around in heads, but rather it is knowledge "embedded" in artifacts – a computer screen, a read-out of a Lotus spreadsheet. Thus, it is not quite clear as to where the knowledge resides. To be sure, some is in the thinking process, some is in the "eyes" which can see the meaning in the artifact; but it is just as much in the artifact, where it exists to be seen. It is not as if the knowledge is the "text" that might be in a mind or an eye and the artifact is the context for that mind or eye – the distinction between text and context blurs (see also Latour 1987; Suchman 1987; Cole 1990; Salomon 1993).

Third, if knowledge can be said to reside in the environment, then one of the essential developmental problems is not "having knowledge" but "having access" to where knowledge may be found. I have already pointed to data that implicates "opportunities for constructive activity" as a key to knowledge coordination. There are more radical implications of this point as well.

Workplaces can be either full of opportunity or dead ends. Many industrial settings contain both elements, unequally distributed among its inhabitants. Some jobs are routine, others are challenging. Being developed would have very different meanings depending on the structure of opportunity within the work setting. The state of "being developed" in the school/development narrative structure is an unquestioned value – the goal toward which the logic of the system points. However, in actual settings, settings moreover which are of long duration – as a place for the living of lives rather than a place of transition to a life yet to be lived – the issue of the relation of "being developed" to environmental opportunity is a serious problem. Martin and Beach (1992) have clearly documented the "search for" opportunity that characterizes many of the workers they studied (machinists in environments where hand and eye machining was being transformed to CNC or programmed machining), and, as clearly, they have documented the frustration of these aspirations to opportunity which meet many workers.

The advent of new technological systems has major import for the structuring of opportunity within the workplace. It has been observed (field notes: Kindred, Zazanis, DiBello, and Glick) that the "bringing in" of a new technological system such as MRP to an environment where it had not existed before, mobilizes many aspirations and opportunities for gaining greater freedom of action within the organization.

Newness presents opportunity. Some people make use of the new system and become its first "volunteers" and servants. By doing so they enter into a community of "new practice" (apologies and thanks to Lave 1991) which has the potential for new access and new opportunity, perhaps supplanting the constraints of old practice. At the least a "de-heirarchicization" of work relations occurs (Moss-Kanter 1991), since most new technologies are accompanied by a new team who are responsible for its implementation in situ. These implementation teams cut across existing boundaries. It thus becomes an important developmental issue as to how "membership in communities of new practice" is accomplished.

Some earlier research suggests one of the possible means of accomplishing the task of "membership" in such new communities. It was found, for example, that knowledge integration shows up in a distinctive "way of speaking" where discursive devices such as intrapropositional code switching (between production terms and MRP terms) is closely related to attained knowledge states (Zazanis & Glick 1993). Use of language may also be a way of gaining entrance to new communities, even before knowledge has been attained.

Since coexisting systems each have their own "language," they tend to create discursive communities within the factory who speak the language of the system. The most interesting thing about this is that not everybody gets it, and at a functional level, there are few consequences. Jobs are done much the same as before. But "speaking the language" is a powerful social signal of membership. In one of the observations, "the boss" of the operation being studied was captivated by the fact that some of the people on the floor were speaking knowledgeably within the terminology and concepts of the MRP system. This led to some job changes where people were allowed to "run their own business" using the system, in competition with managers.

In conclusion, it seems fair to say that when you look at issues from the situated standpoint, not of an intellectual, but of a worker, the layout of phenomena looks different. When analyses are done from that perspective we tend to subordinate the dialectical view of "supplanting the lower by the higher" to a dialogical view that looks at the issue as one of systems in conversation. And within the dialogic perspective, the issue shifts from "what are the grades of knowing?" to "where is there room for a subject's voice and participation in the activity of knowing?"

In school and other traditional "developmental" settings the institutional format and the master narrative seem sufficiently well known that they are seldom questioned. In work settings the game is a bit more open and the preferred starting point for research becomes ethnographic, which is at least an attempt to come to grips with the perspectives of those who live within the world we wish to study.

In closing I would like to suggest that there is perhaps more to learn from the work setting than from the setting where everything seems clear. Indeed, many educational "subversives" have been pursuing the ethnographic route and applying it to the school (e.g., Newman, Griffin, & Cole 1989; Tharp & Gallimore 1988; Kvale 1993; McDermott 1993; Mehan 1993; Minick 1993; Saljo & Wyndhamm 1993). The new conceptions of knowledge that are emerging from research in the workplace and on ethnographic and deconstructionist approaches to schooling suggest that there are grounds for a rapprochement between theorizing development in school and theorizing development in work (Chaiklin & Lave 1993; Forman, Minick, & Stone 1993). However, not so strangely, it will be the master narrative of schooling that will be what is most changed.

References

Bourdieu, P. (1977). *Outline of a theory of practice*. New York: Cambridge University Press.

Bourdieu, P. (1988). *Homo Academicus*. Peter Collier (Trans.). Stanford, CA: Stanford University Press.

Chaiklin, S., & Lave, J. (Eds.). (1993). *Understanding practice: Perspectives on activity and context*. New York: Cambridge University Press.

Chi, M.T.H. (1979). Knowledge structures and memory development. In R. Siegler (Ed.), *Children's thinking: What develops?*. Hillsdale, NJ: Erlbaum.

Chi, M.T.H., Glaser, R., & Rees, E. (1981). Expertise in problem solving. LRDC preprint 1981/3, published in *Advances in the psychology of human intelligence, Vol. 1*. Hillsdale, NJ: Erlbaum.

Clifford, J., & Marcus, G.E. (Eds.). (1986). *Writing culture: The poetics and politics of ethnography*. Berkeley: University of California Press.

Cole, M. (1990). Cognitive development and formal schooling: The evidence from cross-cultural research. In L.C. Moll (Ed.), *Vygotsky and education: Instructional implications and applications of sociohistorical psychology*. New York: Cambridge University Press.

Cole, M., Hood, L., & McDermott, R.P. (1978). *Ecological niche picking: Ecological invalidity as the basic category of educational psychology*. Working paper no. 14. Laboratory of Comparative Human Cognition, Rockefeller University.

DiBello, L., & Glick, J. (1992). *The relative roles of on the job training and classroom education for workers learning MRP-II effectively*. Presented at APICS Society meetings, special academic session. Montreal, Canada, October 1992.

DiBello, L., & Glick, J. (1993). *Technology and minds in an uncertain world*. National Society for Performance and Instruction, Chicago, IL, April 1993.

Engeström, Y. (1990). *Learning, working and imagining: Twelve studies in activity theory.* Helsinki: Orienta-Konsultit Oy.

Forman, E., Minick, N., & Stone, A. (Eds.). (1993). *Contexts of learning: Sociocultural dynamics in children's development.* New York: Oxford University Press.

Glick, J. (1983). Piaget, Vygotsky and Werner. In S. Wapner & B. Kaplan (Eds.), *Toward a holistic developmental psychology.* Hillsdale, NJ: Erlbaum.

Glick, J. (1992). Heinz Werner's significance for contemporary developmental psychology. *Developmental Psychology, 28*(4).

Glick, J. (1993). *What happens to development?* Presented at the annual meetings of the American Educational Research Association, Atlanta, GA, April 1993.

Kaplan, E. (1983). Process and achievement revisited. In S. Wapner & B. Kaplan (Eds.), *Toward a holistic developmental psychology.* Hillsdale, NJ: Erlbaum.

Klahr, D. (1984). Transition processes in quantitative development. In R. J. Sternberg (Ed.), *Mechanisms of development.* San Francisco: W.H. Freeman.

Knorr-Cetina, K. (1981). *The manufacture of knowledge: An essay on the constructivist and contextual nature of science.* Oxford, UK: Pergamon Press.

Knorr-Cetina, K., & Mulkay, M. (Eds.). (1983). *Science observed: Perspectives on the social study of science.* Oxford, UK: Pergamon Press.

Kvale, S. (1993). Examinations reexamined: Certification of students or certification of knowledge? In S. Chaiklin & J. Lave (Eds.), *Understanding practice: Perspectives on activity and context.* New York: Cambridge University Press.

Latour, B. (1987). *Science in action: How to follow scientists and engineers through society.* Cambridge, MA: Harvard University Press.

Latour, B., & Woolgar, S. (1986). *Laboratory life: The construction of scientific facts.* Princeton, NJ: Princeton University Press (originally published in 1979 by Sage Publications, Inc.).

Lave, J. (1988). *Cognition in practice.* New York: Cambridge University Press.

Lave, J., & Wenger, E. (1991). *Situated learning: Legitimate peripheral participation.* New York: Cambridge University Press.

Leont'ev, A. N. (1978). *Activity, consciousness and personality.* Englewood Cliffs, NJ: Prentice-Hall.

Leont'ev, A.N. (1981). The problem of activity in psychology. In J.V. Wertsch (Ed. and Trans.), *The concept of activity in Soviet psychology.* Armonk, NY: M. E. Sharpe.

Lynch, M. (1985). *Art and artifact in laboratory science: A study of shop work and shop talk in a research laboratory.* London: Routledge & Kegan Paul.

Martin, L.M.W., & Beach, K. (1992). *Technical and symbolic knowledge in CNC machining: A study of technical workers of different backgrounds.* Technical report for the National Center for Research on Vocational Education, University of California at Berkeley.

McDermott, R.P. (1993). The acquisition of a child by a learning disability. In S. Chaiklin & J. Lave (Eds.), *Understanding practice: Perspectives on activity and context.* New York: Cambridge University Press.

Mehan, H. (1993). Beneath the skin and between the ears: A case study in the politics of representation. In S. Chaiklin & J. Lave (Eds.), *Understanding practice: Perspectives on activity and context.* New York: Cambridge University Press.

Minick, N. (1993). Teacher's directives: The social construction of "literal meanings" and "real worlds" in classroom discourse. In S. Chaiklin & J. Lave (Eds.), *Understanding practice: Perspectives on activity and context.* New York: Cambridge University Press.

Moss-Kantor, R. (1991). The future of bureaucracy and hierarchy in organizational theory: A report from the field. In P. Bourdieu & J.S. Coleman (Eds.), *Social theory for a changing society.* Boulder, CO: Westview Press & Russell Sage Foundation.

Newman, D., Griffin, P., & Cole, M. (1989). *The construction zone.* New York: Cambridge University Press.

Nunes, T.M., Schliemann, A.D., & Carraher, D. W. (1993). *Street mathematics and school mathematics.* New York: Cambridge University Press.

Overton, W.F., & Reese, H.W. (1973). Models of development: Methodological implications. In J.R. Nesselroade and H.W. Reese (Eds.), *Life-span developmental psychology: Methodological issues.* New York: Academic Press.

Piaget, J. (1983). Piaget's theory. In P.H. Mussen (Ed.), *Handbook of child psychology. Vol. 1: History, theory and methods.* New York: Wiley.

Pepper, S. (1972) (orig. 1942). *World hypotheses.* Berkeley: University of California Press.

Reese, H.W., & Overton, W.F. (1970). Models of development and theories of development. In L.R. Goulet & P. B. Baltes (Eds.), *Life-span developmental psychology: Research and theory.* New York: Academic Press.

Saljo, R., & Wyndhamm, J. (1993). Solving everyday problems in the formal setting: An empirical study of the school as context for thought. In S. Chaiklin and J. Lave (Eds.), *Understanding practice: Perspectives on activity and context.* New York: Cambridge University Press.

Salomon, G. (Ed.). (1993). *Distributed cognition: Psychological and educational considerations.* New York: Cambridge University Press.

Schneirla, T.C. (1972). Levels in the psychological capacities of animals. In L.A. Aronson, E. Tobach, J.S. Rosenblatt, & D.S. Lehrman (Eds.), *Selected writings of T.C. Schneirla.* San Francisco: Freeman. Reprinted from Sellars, R.W., McGill, V.J., & Faber, M. (Eds.). (1949). *Philosophy for the future: The quest for modern materialism.* New York: McMillan.

Scribner, S. (1984). Studying working intelligence. In B. Rogoff and J. Lave (Eds.), *Everyday cognition: Its development in social context.* Cambridge, MA: Harvard University Press.

Scribner, S. (1985). Vygotsky's uses of history. In J. Wertsch (Ed.), *Culture, communication and cognition.* New York: Cambridge University Press.

Scribner, S. (1986). Thinking in action: Some characteristics of practical thought. In R.J. Sternberg & R.K. Wagner (Eds.), *Practical intelligence*, pp. 13–30. New York: Cambridge University Press.

Scribner, S. (1990). *The character of knowledge systems in the workplace from the perspective of activity theory*. Paper presented to The Second International Congress for Research on Activity Theory, Lahti, Finland.

Scribner, S., DiBello, L., Kindred, J., & Zazanis, E. (1991). Coordinating two knowledge systems: A case study. Unpublished working paper, Laboratory for Cognitive Studies of Activity, City University of New York.

Scribner, S., & Sachs, P., with Dibello, L., & Kindred, J. (1991). *Knowledge acquisition at work*. Technical paper no. 22, Institute on Education and the Economy. New York: Teacher's College.

Shaiken, H. (1984). *Work transformed*. New York: Holt, Rinhart, and Winston.

Sobel, C. (1991). Moebius-strip organizations and open labor markets: Some consequences of the reintegration of conception and execution in a volatile economy. In P. Bourdieu & J.S. Coleman (Eds.), *Social theory for a changing society*. Boulder, CO: Westview Press & Russell Sage Foundation.

Sohn-Rethel, A. (1978). *Intellectual and manual labor: A critique of epistemology*. Atlantic Highlands, NJ: Humanities Press.

Sroufe, L.A. (1979). The coherence of individual development. *American psychologist, 34*, 834–841.

Sternberg, R.J. (Ed.). (1984). *Mechanisms of development*. San Francisco: W.H. Freeman.

Suchman, L.A. (1987). *Plans and situated actions: The problem of human-machine Communication*. New York: Cambridge University Press.

Suchman, L.A., & Trigg, R.H. (1993). Artificial intelligence as craftwork. In S. Chaiklin and J. Lave (Eds.), *Understanding practice: Perspectives on activity and context*. New York: Cambridge University Press.

Tharp, R.G., & Gallimore, R. (1988). *Rousing minds to life: Teaching, learning and schooling in social context*. New York: Cambridge University Press.

Tobach, E., & Greenberg, G. (1984). The significance of T.C. Schneirla's contribution to the concept of levels of organization. In G. Greenberg & E. Tobach (Eds.), *Behavioral evolution and integrative levels*. Hillsdale, NJ: Erlbaum.

Vygotsky, L. S. (1978). *Mind in society*. Cambridge, MA: Harvard University Press.

Vygotsky, L.S. (1987). *Collected Works*, Vol. I. New York: Plenum.

Werner, H. (1937). Process and achievement: A basic problem of education and developmental psychology. *Harvard Educational Review, 7*, 353–368.

Werner, H., & Kaplan, B. (1963). *Symbol formation*. New York: Wiley.

Zazanis, E., & Glick, J. (1993). *Discursive measures of cognitive structure*. Unpublished working paper, Laboratory for Cognitive Studies of Activity, City University of New York.

Zinchenko, V.P. (1985). Vygotsky's ideas about units for the analysis of mind. In J. Wertsch (Ed.), *Culture, communication and cognition*. New York: Cambridge University Press.

16 Visionary realism, lifespan discretionary time, and the evolving role of work

Howard E. Gruber

Factory windows are always broken – Vachel Lindsay

The idea of work is set in an old mythology extolling it. Long before the rise of the Protestant work ethic, there is Jacob toiling for his father-in-law, patiently waiting twice seven years for Rachel. There is Hercules heroically cleaning out the Augean stables and accomplishing the other eleven labors set for him by the gods. Closer to our own times there is John Henry and his hammer, vying with the steam drill. And the Soviets had the miner, Alexei Stakhanov, who performed wonders of socialist labor, thus helping to create a non-Protestant work ethic.

In phrases such as "the nobility of toil" are we not in danger of confusing the toil with the toiler? Does the nobility of the toiler lie not in superhuman accomplishments, but rather in the courage and forbearance with which heavy burdens are born? In his essay "The myth of Sisyphus" did Camus mean to extol the condemned hero's futile and senseless rolling of the rock up the mountain, or did he extol the human ability to go on in the face of adversity? Camus's answer is a little mysterious but he does conclude that ". . . Sisyphus teaches the higher fidelity that negates the gods and raises rocks" (Camus 1942/1955, p. 91).

Women do not figure in this mythology, probably because "woman's work" was not perceived as work. But there was the grass widow Penelope, forever weaving and unweaving the shroud; there was the wartime worker Rosie the riveter, rising to the emergency; and there is the great chef in exile, Babette of *Babette's Feast*.

To some extent this essay represents the counterpoint to Sylvia Scribner's rightful emphasis on the constructive cognitive activity neces-

The author thanks many friends and colleagues for the conversations that led up to this paper including Lee Benson, Tom Bregman, Ray Franklin, Simon Gruber, Neil Mendoza, Ethel Tobach, Jacques Vonèche and Doris B. Wallace.

383

sary for much, perhaps most, work. Illuminating and celebrating the intelligence required of and exhibited by working people even in very modest jobs is a valuable antidote to elitism. Nevertheless, work has its darker side: it can be mind-numbing, soul-destroying, brutalizing. Even in its Biblical origins work is seen as punishment. For violating God's injunction against eating of the Tree of Knowledge, Adam and Eve are driven from the Garden of Eden in which no work was necessary. Henceforth, the Almighty tells them, "In the sweat of thy face shalt thou eat bread" (Genesis 3:19).

As a pioneer in the psychological study of work Sylvia Scribner was noted especially for her demonstration of the intelligence and ingenuity that ordinary workers exhibit in doing very modest jobs. Her research reflected a positive, optimistic attitude toward life and work. But as a seasoned trade unionist and labor activist in her earlier career she was also well aware of the darker side of work, and of the way in which every step forward in improving the conditions of workers has been won through prolonged struggle and often at great human cost.

In what follows I will examine some of the motivations to work and some of the positive and negative characteristics of work. Since the motivations for work depend in good part on its historical circumstances, I have tried my hand at comparing the nineteenth, twentieth, and twenty-first centuries as an important aspect of situating the lifetime of working hours and of discretionary time expected of people living in those periods. Indeed, the challenge of maximizing and then coping with lifespan discretionary time (LDT) was the starting point for this essay. The term *discretionary time* is intended to be more inclusive than *leisure* or *play*. It embraces everything we do that is neither for earning a living (the job) or for sleeping and other maintenance functions. It can include very serious and prolonged projects and enterprises, and games such as chess that do not always feel very playful.

Since such discussions inevitably involve epistemological considerations, there is a brief interlude later in which I discuss several alternative attitudes toward change and sketch my own point of view, which I call here *visionary realism*. If this term suggests a seeming penchant for oxymoronic juxtapositions (as in "creativity in the moral domain" [Gruber 1993a]), it does not reflect insensitivity to paradox but rather the evolving need to sort out new categories for dealing with a world in great flux.

We can divide people into those who love their work and those who do not. Among the former there are many who would like to work as many hours in the week and as many years in the life as possible. Among those who do not like their work there are many who are willing to do their share of the world's work, who are even eager to hold down a job, but who can also dream of a sudden Edenic windfall liberating them from work. They say in effect, "If I won the lottery I would quit my job."

Finally, there are many for whom a future permitting such an option is wholly unthinkable, undreamable. The present essay is primarily about the second group, those who work but do not like their work. They are alienated from it but they know that they must do it. If given the opportunity they can do it, but they can dream too.

The complexity of capturing the experience of work can be seen in reactions to works of art depicting workers' lives. The Marxist, Ernst Fischer writes:

Millet, an artist of peasant origin who supported the revolution of 1848, presents the work of the peasant in the capitalist world as a modern form of slavery and hideous dehumanization. (Fischer 1963, p. 135)

But Gombrich writes of the same people in the same painting:

Just three hard-working people in a flat field where harvesting is in progress. They are neither beautiful nor graceful. There is no suggestion of the country idyll in the picture. These peasant women move slowly and heavily. They are all intent on their work. . . . Thus his three peasant women assumed a dignity more natural and more convincing than that of academic heroes. (Gombrich 1972, p. 402)

Another perspective on the life and work of peasants is expressed in a recent biography of Van Gogh. The author describes Van Gogh's early masterpiece, *The Potato Eaters*:

By distorting the perspective, by creating the crudest features for his subjects by making them stare into the void in so disturbing a way, Vincent had deliberately undermined any possibility of associating this meal with a form of peasant Mass; these figures are not holy, they are deprived, nor are they to be admired nor pitied, their dignity is their own not ours to grant them. (Sweetman 1990, p.189)

Over a century ago, the young Karl Marx wrote about alienated labor and characterized existing society as one in which the artificial and sometimes brutal division of labor made for a conflict between individual desire and the common good. He imagined a world in which

nobody has one exclusive sphere of activity but each can become accomplished in any branch he wishes, society regulates the general production and thus makes it possible for

me to do one thing today and another tomorrow, to hunt in the morning, fish in the after-
noon, rear cattle in the evening, criticize after dinner, just as I have a mind, without ever
becoming hunter, fisherman, shepherd or critic. (Marx 1846/1939, p. 22)

This romancing of labor has often been a component of Utopian
thought. What is new now is not only the changed nature of work but the
prospect of a world in which working for a living is no longer the main
thing that people do.

Motives for work

Although there are many ways of conceptualizing it, I have in
mind the idea that motivation for work is an internalization of a set of
social arrangements arising out of the interaction between person and
society. Even the person completely absorbed in doing a task for its own
sake ("intrinsically motivated") relies on the tacit knowledge that he or
she will be left free to pursue the task. In the evolving systems approach
to creative work (Gruber 1989) we must take some account of motives
other than the almost completely task-oriented idealization inherent in
describing creative activity as "purposeful work." These other motives
include the "planetary motivation" that arises out of increasing concern
for the future of our habitat in the solar system (see Gruber 1993b).

I know what it means to love one's work. Having been a teacher for 46
years, with minor exceptions I have always loved it and still do. The same
for my career as a research scientist. I think my main motive for this
work has always been intrinsic. That is, I do it for the pleasure of doing it.
When I am engrossed in it I don't feel or think much about my other
motives. Being absorbed in good work can be one of the great pleasures
of life. For that, other worlds are well lost – or almost so. But of course
there are other motives operating. Fortunately so, for not all work feels
good. We need other motives to carry us through.

A reasonable list of motives for work might include

1. Intrinsic motivation.
   a. The actual pleasure of the activity.
   b. The desire, once having begun a task, to get on with it, see it
      through, complete it.
   c. To enjoy the finished product for its usefulness, its beauty, its nov-
      elty, its embodiment of tradition, etc.

2. Ego motives.
   a. The self-esteem that stems from appreciation of one's work, the praise of others.
   b. To maintain identity: the need to do this work because "this is how I conceive of myself."
3. Other orientation.
   The desire to help others, an activity that may be a substantial part of a research and teaching career. The empathic response to someone in need. Also included under this heading may be what I call the *squad mentality*, things one does for the good of the group. To these motives might be added the pleasures of working with others, to some extent independent of the nature of the work.
4. Planetary motivation.
   Things we do for the sake of the world. This may really refer to the whole planet, as in the Green movement, or it may refer to more local needs.
5. Livelihood.
   Let us not forget, most people work to earn a living.

Probably one could construct a profile for an individual, representing the relative strengths of these motives, summed over the life span. It would be better, if feasible, to make a dynamic profile showing how different motives come to the fore at different times. Although he dealt with a somewhat different list of motives, Maslow's (1954) need hierarchy was a kind of dynamic profile in which movement was from lower to higher motives, with self-actualization at the top, only striven for when "lower" needs are satisfied.

Evidently, hierarchies with other sequences than Maslow's are conceivable. For example, not everyone would put self-actualization above belongingness and love needs. More important, hierarchical structure is not the only possibility. For example, if several different motives are each *necessary* to account for the activity of working, then hierarchical structure among them is precluded. In a systemic approach one vital function is not more necessitous than another. Necessary is simply necessary.

My introduction to the idea of task orientation, or intrinsic motivation, came in a course on personality given at Brooklyn College by Rosalind Gould. She was then an ardent Lewinian and the romantic youth in her class resonated, even thrilled, to the idea of a life motivated, not by money grubbing or esteem cadging, but by work for its own sake. Note how well the "work ethic" was built into this aproach.

About 5 years and a war later, but still very young, meeting Professor Gould again I alluded to those ideas and how important they had been for me. "Ohh, that silly idea," she said as I remember it, "How can something that absorbs you totally not engage your ego too?" Some of her own research dealt with the Lewinian concept of "level of aspiration" which draws both upon task and ego orientations (Gould 1939; Lewin et al. 1944).

Gould's remark was for me a beginning of wisdom. Although I did not surrender easily, I moved away from the ideal of work purely for its own sake and toward the idea of multiple motives shifting dynamically in response to the totality of one's psychosocial situation.

Some of the complexities of such a motivational structure are revealed in an interview with the biologist Gunther Stent:

Interviewer   And the gratification of publishing is really so that other people will see your work – it's sort of an ego trip?

Stent: I don't want to deny that. The expectation of admiration probably is there too, but I think it's not only that, I think it is just the pleasure. I like conversation very much, and to make conversation you have to have something to say . . . the final excitement, the real source of the gratification, is not so much beating nature as being able to tell it . . . if I was on a desert island, Robinson Crusoe, I think I wouldn't do science. (Interview reported in Wolpert & Richards [1988])

Needless to say, other scientists would describe themselves differently. And a mercurial character like Stent might tell a different story on a different day. Getting a clear and comprehensive picture of someone's motives is not a task for a single interview. Compare Stent with a recent study of 34 inventors. In response to the question "What do you do for fun?" almost all responded, "I work" (Colangelo, Assouline, Kerr, Huesman, & Johnson 1993).

Amabile (1983) has given an excellent account of the role of intrinsic motivation in creative work. Nevertheless, other motives are both inescapable and indispensable.

Livelihood

Eventually, I came to recognize and want now to include in the conception of motivation for work something else that everyone knows:

most people work to earn a living. Moreover, there are some interesting interactions between the quality of work required in a job and the remuneration one receives for it. I will examine a few of the factors affecting the psychological quality of work, leading into a discussion of the struggle, past and future, for a shorter work week.

The quality of work

On a day-to-day basis, most work probably ranges from mildly satisfying to mildly unsatisfying. And unfortunately, some jobs are truly rotten.

Csikszentmihalyi (1990) has studied the experience of *flow*, the psychological state of emotional well being that may come about when the activity in which one is engaged is just challenging enough to stretch performance to the limits of the possible – the possible for that individual at the given point in his or her development of mastery. As Csikszentmihalyi points out, this may require successive escalations in the level of mastery called for and in the individual's level of aspiration. Many games are designed so as to optimize flow experience by manipulating these variables.

At the same time, it must be recognized that such escalation and design may not always be possible. In fact, the social and economic demands of work may often militate against progressive change in individual conduct at rates maintaining flow. As an example of the protection or achievement of flow while performing a boring office job, Csikszentmihalyi describes the "great gift" of a man who could produce marvelous renditions of great music while doing the work. From the description it is apparent that the flow experience lay not in the office work, which remained boring, but in the "peripheral activity."

Sometimes, of course, the experience of work is wonderful. But even the best things in life may pall, even highly rewarding work. *Burnout* is not a term commonly used to describe the problems of a laborer; it is reserved for college professors, executives of large corporations, and the like.

Why is so much of work simply boring?

Boredom is built into the nature of work in modern society (and elsewhere too). To be productive, much work must be repetitive. The worker does over and over what works. One way to break this monotony is to change jobs, but the cost may be too high. Even highly skilled jobs, like computer programming, may become boring. One way of relieving boredom is to make the work automatic and mentally peripheral – to sing or daydream while one works. Even this can pall. The more skilled jobs don't permit such a degree of inattention, a constraint which in the long run may make them even more boring. In this connection it pays to reread Lewin's description of Karsten's research on "psychic satiation" – the disorganization of behavior that can set in under extreme conditions of repetitive activity – an experimental version of burnout? (Lewin 1935, Karsten 1928). As I have written elsewhere (Gruber 1976), in an unfortunate case of the transformation of quantitative into qualitative change, a moderate amount of repetition with spontaneous variation may be fruitful, even essential, for creative work; but long-continued repetitive work has the baleful consequences described by Lewin (1935) and Karsten (1928).

Even with repetitive work there are variations in interest level and in the cost to the worker (in terms of energy expenditure and fatigue). Thus, Ryan (1947, p. 186) wrote: ". . . extrinsic incentives like pay in the absence of the interest factor, increase output at the expense of increased cost of work, and . . . are not even very effective in increasing output."

When all is said and done, the perennial and intense discussion of the unresolved problem of work motivation – such as today's worries about the decline of the "work ethic" – reflects the fact that much work is not inherently attractive, not intrinsically motivating.

Why is so much work dangerous or deleterious to health?

Danger is not an unalloyed evil. Some workers really take pleasure in the element of risk involved in their work; but not everyone. Moreover, it is probably very difficult to find anyone who actually prefers working conditions that impair health. Yet some jobs seem to be inherently deleterious. This is in good part because work involves the transformation of the material world; this entails the use of tools that can injure, the moving of heavy materials, the creation of waste products that must be disposed of, etc. – all characteristics that may lead to injury or disease. The prolonged repetitiveness of some work can itself be harmful, to the mind or to the back, as in the work done by truck drivers, telephone operators, and secretaries.

Although danger is inherent in the physical nature of some work, it should not be forgotten that much danger is a result of the sociopolitical nature of work; in particular, that those making the arrangements under which the work is done ("the bosses") are not themselves directly affected by the risks incurred. Only a little while ago, 12 May 1993, the newspapers carried the story of the toy factory in Thailand in which over 200 workers were burned alive: when fire broke out they could not escape because they were locked in "to prevent pilferage." In its magnitude this tragedy is unusual but not unique.

More damaging, probably, are the unnoticed, undramatic risks taken everywhere by workers exposed to radiation and other pollutants, workers endangered by the removal of safety devices from tools, and so on. These should not be regarded as exceptions: they are inherent in the nature of work under the social arrangements that have prevailed hitherto. It would be a convenient shorthand to say "prevailed under capitalism," but then Chernobyl comes to mind and we are forced to suppose that there are even deeper reasons for the chronically purblind organization of production that leads to such tragedies.

Recently, Kwong (1988) has given an account of "American sweatshops 1980s style: Chinese women garment workers." He shows how the main characteristics of sweatshops – brutally long hours (e.g., 12 hours per day, 6 days per week), low pay, miserable working conditions – are not merely a part of our historical past but continue today. The particular ethnic group that is victimized changes with the waves of immigration (Jewish, Italian, Chinese), but sweatshops survive. They are not an aberration but a phenomenon predictable from a given, long-enduring social organization of production. Kwong also describes the growth of solidarity and militance among Chinese women workers in New York's Chinatown. Who will be the next victims?

Are some jobs inherently brutal and rotten?

There are a few literary classics that describe the soul-destroying nature of some jobs. George Orwell's *Down and Out in Paris and London* (Orwell 1933/1961) depicts the life of a menial worker, and Upton Sinclair's *The Jungle* (Sinclair 1906/1965) depicts the brutality of the lives of slaughterhouse workers. Today there are in some countries regulatory agencies charged with ameliorating these conditions. But almost any day's newspaper carries stories that show the violation of human worth going on today or in the recent past: sweatshops for women from the Caribbean, uranium mines for Navajos, and so on.

It is hard to escape the conclusion that much of the rottenness of work – boredom, brutality, danger, futility – stems not from the inherent attributes of the job, but from the social organization and control of the productive process. In any event, we are still a long way from making a world in which work is as pleasant, or as little unpleasant, as possible. Beyond that, we have hardly begun to ask, How might ordinary work be designed so as to elicit positive experiences such as flow?

The quantity of work

When my father first came to America, 17 years old in 1910, he worked in a high-class hotel, first as a busboy and then as a waiter. He worked a split shift, 14 hours per day, 6½ days per week, for a total of 91 hours per week. By the end of his life he was working less than 40 hours per week, having participated in the struggle for a 60-hour week, a 48-hour week, and a 40-hour week. I should add that in 50 years of work he never had a paid vacation.

Those 91 hours seem so inhuman as to be implausible, so that sometimes I fear there must be some fault of memory at work. But no: if you browse through the *Encylopedia Britannica* for 1911 under such headings as "children" and "labor" you come to realize that such experiences were not so exceptional. In England in 1819, thanks in good part to the efforts of the Utopian socialist, Robert Owen, a law was enacted limiting the working day to 12 hours for children under 18. In 1833 children under 11 could work no longer than 9 hours per day, 48 hours per week; and children 11 to 18 could be worked no more than 12 hours per day, 69 hours per week. That is, if the law was enforced, which is questionable.

In industrialized countries these conditions prevailed with some slow improvements until after World War I. At that point the movement intensified for an 8-hour day, 48-hour week (still no norm of a vacation with pay). The rise of trade unions and the fear of Bolshevisim contributed to a desire to improve working conditions. Moreover, thanks to advances in applied psychology, it had become apparent that long hours of work diminished efficiency and did not pay. So the thrust for a shorter work week was multiply motivated: by the workers' desire to escape from the heavy burden of work, the employers' desire for efficiency and profit, and broader political considerations. Although there are important exceptions, the 8-hour day, 5-day week, and 2-week vacation – sometimes paid, sometimes not – have become the national norm in the United States. In more advanced European countries shorter work weeks and longer vacations (such as 1-month paid) prevail.

To be sure, not everyone wants to "escape" from the burden of work. To further their careers, young corporate lawyers may work incredibly long hours, with the ultimate goal of acquiring personal wealth. People doing creative work often work longer than 60 hours per week. Many academics view vacations as times when they can "really work." And although the mean age of retirement continues to drop (the norm under Social Security is 62 to 65), resistance to retirement is often fierce. On the one hand, then, there is work that invites dreams of winning the lottery and never working again; on the other hand, people who love their work want to go on doing it, want to be consumed by it.

Lifetime working hours and lifespan discretionary time (LDT)

Contemporary discussion of economic problems places great emphasis on the need for endless growth of the economy and on the need to raise the level of skill in the potential work force so that unemployment would be reduced by matching workers to the new high-tech jobs that will become available. I question this line of argument. There is reason to doubt the feasibility of maintaining endless growth, and perhaps still more reason to question its virtues at a time when there is urgent need for conservation as well as growth. There may be even more reason to doubt how much unemployment can be reduced by raising skills. It may be true that, right now, some jobs go begging for lack of adequately trained applicants. But over the long haul, advances in technology have made it possible for fewer and fewer people to do the world's work. In agriculture, in manufacturing, in shipping, in business – earth movers, assembly lines and robots, containers, and computers have meant the phasing out of many jobs. If these technological trends continue, and if armaments and war drain less and less of our resources, we will need to cope with large numbers of people whose labor power is not needed.

Recently, expressing an idea that has become a contemporary theme, the economist Richard Barnett wrote

Across the planet, the shrinking of opportunities to work for decent pay is a crisis yet to be faced. The problem is starkly simple: an astonishingly large and increasing number of human beings are not needed or wanted to make the goods or to provide the services that the paying customers of the world can afford. (Barnett 1993, p. 47)

In the same article Barnett remarked

shortening the work week could encourage job sharing. This, in turn, would create more jobs, accommodate working mothers, and perhaps encourage the healthy notion that a job is not the whole of life. (Barnett 1993, p. 51)[1]

An alternative far more preferable than massive, chronic unemployment on a global scale would be to distribute work in new ways. Assuming we follow this second course, what consequences will follow for the working person, and for the motivation to work?

There are various ways in which we can model changes in the amount of labor performed in a lifetime by any individual: hours per day, days per week, weeks per year, and years per life can all be modified. Periods of nonwork can be treated as misfortunes, unemployment, or they can be treated as retraining, vacation, sabbaticals, or retirement.

In Tables 16.1 and 16.2 I have done some of this modeling for three cases that I have labeled nineteenth, twentieth, and twenty-first century. There is some historical realism about the numbers I have used for the nineteenth and twentieth centuries. For the twenty-first century I have chosen to make assumptions of relatively moderate changes from the present: a 7-hour day and 4-day week; vacations of 1 month per year; sabbaticals of 6 months per decade worked; a retirement age of 60 and a mean life expectancy of 80.

Table 16.1 outlines three hypothetical sets of norms, one for each century. Taking these hypotheses as points of departure, the sketches of LDT for each century follow, as shown in Table 16.2. To be sure, the norms in Table 16.1 do not apply to everyone. Most notably, taking account of the influx of women into the work force would lead to other sets of norms. Moreover, the tables are "ethnocentric" in that they are based primarily on American experience. Other norms would apply in other societies. Nevertheless, I believe these sketches are useful in showing the enormous potential that exists for increases in LDT.

As Table 16.1 shows, there has been, in industrialized countries, a radical change from the nineteenth to the twentieth centuries. The LDT has almost tripled. For a person working full-time, the ratio of discretionary hours per working year to working hours per working year has approxi-

Table 16.1. *Hypothetical working lives*

	Century		
	19	20	21
Working day (hours)	12	8	7
Workdays per week	6	5	4
Weeks worked per year	52	50	48
Working hours per year	3,744	2,000	1,344
Sabbaticals (6 months/decade worked)	—	—	2 years
Start work (age in years)	15	20	25
Retirement age	—	65	60
Life expectancy	50	65	80

mately quadrupled. From the twentieth to the twenty-first century, in this model, LDT will almost redouble, and the ratio of discretionary hours to working hours will increase significantly.

Probably the most radical change in the LDT estimated for the twenty-first century arises out of the combination of two assumptions, neither one of which is very extreme:

1. That the norm for retirement will be about 60 years.
2. That life expectancy will be about 80 years.

Table 16.2. *Lifespan discretionary time*

	Century		
	19	20	21
Lifespan discretionary hours during working years	47,320	139,320	123,816
Lifespan discretionary hours during nonworking years	0	0	112,112
Lifespan discretionary time	47,320	139,320	235,928
Ratio of discretionary hours to work hours during working years	0.4	1.6	2.8

Note: Education accomplished before starting work is treated neither as work nor as discretionary time. Periods of unemployment are also not considered in this sketch.

This means that there will ordinarily be a period of 20 years of good health and vigor during which discretionary time will approach 100%. And this time could come, not after an oppressive working life, but after a far better working lifetime than most people now experience.

To be sure, much in these tables is both approximation and speculation. But I have tried to be more or less realistic. For example, the notion of a 4-day week may seem extreme, especially at a moment in history when many people are desperate for more work. But the Volkswagen corporation has recently announced a shift to the 4-day week and the French Senate debated the question recently. My suggestion in Table 16.2 that lifespan discretionary hours during nonworking years currently approaches zero may provoke some objections, since the norm for retirement under Social Security is 62 to 65 years of age. But the Social Security pension level (about $800 per month) is kept fairly close to the official definition of poverty (about $600 per month), so "retired" people do have a motive to work and they often do work.

It should be emphasized that the choices to be made in the use of LDT are made by the individual and/or the family unit. Larger social units determine or powerfully influence the range of choices available. The manifold interactions among these different societal levels create the uncertainty and tension that characterize the struggle for a normal life.

Prospects for the near term

The best bet for the immediate future, say from now until the year 2000, is that present well-entrenched trends will continue.

Phasing out of labor-intensive jobs

In this century we have seen an astonishing change in the pattern of employment. Around the turn of the century, when my parents were children, most people in the United States lived and worked on farms. Today agriculture absorbs about 2% of the labor force. Fertilization and farm machinery are responsible. Containerization, automation, and computerization have dramatically altered shipping, manufacturing, and white collar employment needs and prospects.

Acceptance of chronic unemployment

The present level is reputed to be about 7%, with much higher percentages for disadvantaged groups, especially black youth. This is coupled with acceptance of a permanent sector of the population called the "working poor." They earn close to the legal minimum wage, often at jobs that have little or no intrinsic reward, and they cannot live on what they earn. As a result, subsidization through unemployment benefits, Social Security, tax credits, and other economic devices are necessary to maintain a veneer of humanity in the treatment of the permanently un- and underemployed. Needless to say, these people are largely youth, minority groups, and recent immigrants. Obviously also the palliative measures are not expected to lift people out of poverty but to keep them in it. Moreover, many labor-intensive jobs will not really disappear but will be done by people in or from other countries.

It should be noted that at present it can hardly be said that everyone in the United States is ready for so much LDT. In fact, as Schor (1992) points out, the number of hours per year worked, both by individuals and by family units, has increased in the last 25 years. To some extent this has come about because some workers have traded leisure for the commodities that extra work can pay for. But it is also true that often it simply takes two people working, possibly with some moonlighting, for a family to earn its living.

In spite of these severe and intractable problems, there will be a large sector of the population who live reasonably well and who have a very large amount of LDT. This sector exists now and will probably increase in number. They will be perpetually looking for something to do, something to soak up their liberated energies. Undoubtedly, the commodification of time-killing and energy-absorbing devices (exemplified at one extreme by computer games and at the other by violence and pornography in the media) will continue to absorb a great deal of this time and energy.

During some interim period, while intense social problems persist, there will also be continuing growth in planetary morality and volunteerism of all sorts. There will also be sharp and prolonged struggles between competing interests.

Toward a vision of the future

Let us suppose that, without a revolution, the powerful middle class (as the term is now used, this includes a goodly fraction of what was once called the *working class*), looking for something to do, discover that they can have a better life if all of the well-known social evils are eliminated. Let us suppose that the country discovers that it can really afford these blessings. Just as we once learned, the hard way, that our nation could not survive half slave and half free, we might now learn that democracy cannot flourish if we are half poor and half rich. Let us suppose, then, that "the better angels of our nature" (Lincoln, First Inaugural, 1860) prevail.

The question will remain and intensify: What do we do with our increased LDT? Suppose that by the year 2050 we have solved some of the most vital problems of un- and underemployment, perhaps by the creation of new jobs, systems of job sharing, increases in LDT, and some sort of guaranteed minimum income plan. We may still have a severe problem of underoccupation, many people with time on their hands and no adequate way of using it to make a happy, satisfying life, doing their share of the world's work and having their share of the world's pleasures.

Putting the problem in this way is a step toward recentering the discussion. For the moment, take adequate production and distribution of the necessities of life for granted: What lies beyond? We try to escape from the narrow choice between a few social systems, such as capitalism and socialism, both focused mainly on the goal of productivity. We recognize that, of the thousands of patterns of social organization conceivable in modern societies, only a very few have been tried (Gruber 1993). Instead of setting ourselves the task of dreaming up one or another entire social system, our Utopian thinking can take another direction – to explore the disposition of LDT.

This stratagem is not merely an interesting and amusing avenue for reflecting on human potentiality. By definition, discretionary time is only loosely coupled to the main social institutions organized for production and distribution of goods. Consequently, the historical evolution of LDT can go forward without settling everything else. Moreover, large enough changes in the amount and use of LDT may open the way to other societal changes affecting the economic base.

The autobiography of Frederick Douglass (1845/1960), escaped slave and great orator, gives a hint of how such openings can come about even under the most adverse conditions. As a slave boy, for no better reason than an insatiable hunger for knowledge, he began to use his very limited, stolen discretionary time to learn to read. In this he was aided for awhile by his owner's wife, who did so for reasons unknown to us, but probably just normal empathy for an engaging 12-year-old boy. When her husband, the owner, found out, he forbade his wife from this practice, for it would give slaves ideas about equality and freedom. Overhearing their conversation, Frederick had a beautiful insight: his owner was right – if he could learn to read that would be a decisive move toward freedom. In telling the story Douglass adds that the slave system did his owners more harm than it did him, for they – both husband and wife – were brutalized as they brutalized him. In spite of difficulties, Douglass did learn to read, then he taught other slaves in a clandestine study group.

How much more freedom we have and how much greater is our discretionary time? What change will there really be in LDT? What can we expect and demand of ourselves in deploying it?

Attitudes toward reality and change

Aspirations for change do not necessarily depend on deep dissatisfaction with the existing state of affairs. This remark applies both to areas of potential change in the objective state of affairs and to our knowledge and understanding of the world. There is more than one path to the future. Let us consider three of the major alternatives.

Establishmentarianism

This does not mean clinging to the present at all costs. It also includes the aim of maintaining a rate of change slow enough so that the existing power structure remains intact. In the search for new knowledge it is coupled with an attitude of cautious realism. What we know is knowledge about the world as it is; this simple idea in its turn is based on the assumption, first, that there is a world-as-it-is, and second, that it is knowable by methods within our grasp and control.

Critical theory

By pointing to alternative theoretical frameworks, alternative interpretations of allegedly objective data, and alternative ways of raising questions and getting answers – all these and other similar means cast doubt on the existing state of affairs, on our knowledge about it, and even doubt about the possibility of knowledge. The world is nothing but a construction – in some views, a mental construction, in other views, a social construction. But carried to an extreme of nihilistic relativism, this path may incapacitate travelers along it for action in the real world. Still a vigorous movement, doubts are arising within it: there is reason to believe that the work of mere criticism is losing some of its appeal (see for example various essays in Stam, Mos, Thorngate, & Kaplan 1993). Two titles in this volume express such doubts: "The fear of relativism in post-positivist psychology" (Paranjpe 1993) and "The limits of psychological critique" (Gergen 1993).

Visionary realism

As this is the path I am searching for, I describe it in hopeful terms. On the one hand there is realism – the belief that our experience of the world, both lay and scientific, tells us something, however approximate, about what the world is really like. Note the underlying assumption that there is a world and that our knowledge is about it.

On the other hand there is visionary hopefulness: since our realistic appraisal turns up serious faults in the way things are and serious gaps in our knowledge, a hopeful attitude required for a satisfying life demands a visionary outlook. With a realistic, critical attitude toward the world as it is, and toward our knowledge of it, we must do our best to imagine alternative paths to a better future. We entertain but go beyond imaginative, playful visions; we choose and invest seriously in alternatives we can really strive for. To be a visionary animal, as we humans inescapably are, requires hope. And hope requires a goal. Coleridge said some of this well:

> All Nature seems at work . . .
> And I the while, the sole unbusy thing,
> Nor honey make, nor pair, nor build, nor sing . . .
> Work without Hope draws nectar in a sieve.
> And Hope without an object cannot live.
> (Coleridge 1825)

The struggle to maintain this attitude of visionary realism requires movement back and forth between ideas founded on descriptions of reality (often unpleasant, as in the image of "factory windows") and ideas founded on the persistent hope for a better future.

Conclusion

I have dealt with two ways of considering a person's working life as a whole. First, there is the wide spectrum of motives to work, and not just the dichotomy between intrinsic and extrinsic motives currently in vogue. This spectrum of motives is socially useful because work must go on whether it is intrinsically motivated and attractive or repellent and extrinsically motivated.

Second, distinguishing between work and nonwork and calculating LDT provides a new way of looking at the historical evolution of work. Comparing the nineteenth, twentieth, and twenty-first centuries shows that changes in LDT have been effected by shortening of the work day and work week, increases in longevity, and lowering of the retirement age (indeed, for many, introducing the possibility of retirement). This combination of factors has led to a dramatic increase in LDT, and a further surge can be expected. Estimated LDT is about 47,000 hours for the nineteenth century, 140,000 hours for the twentieth century, and 235,000 hours for the twenty-first century.

Increasing LDT has major positive societal consequences. It ameliorates the conditions of people whose work is boring, dangerous, or unpleasant. Moreover, decreasing the total time individuals spend working can serve as a major way of reducing unemployment.

Increasing LDT also presents society with an array of problems that can be grouped together as *unoccupation*, that is, not knowing how to spend one's time. To be sure, formulating the problem in this way raises difficult questions about values, about education, and about social policy. They are questions that must be faced as the work and nonwork ethic evolves into the twenty-first century.

It should be emphasized that the somewhat rosy picture of the evolution of LDT that I have suggested will not apply to those sectors of the world population that we sometimes dismiss as "underdeveloped." Anyone with a sense of justice will wonder whether they might not better be described as "overexploited."

At present the world is still so burdened by urgent problems affecting the prospects for human survival that consideration of social and economic policy is mainly focused on the minimizing of pain. The time may soon come when we can and must turn our attention more fully to the problems of pleasure.

Epilogue: In the garden

I finished this essay on a Saturday night, pleased but vaguely dissatisfied with myself because I had not firmly grasped the nettles. I could accept the fact that I had not sketched a *path* to the future. But I had intended to describe a vision of that future, at least with regard to the deployment of LDT. And this I have not done.

In the newspaper Sunday morning two items caught my eye. The first was an editorial about the large-scale phasing out of jobs. The author quotes one executive as saying, "We need to shed jobs to meet customer flow." He cites a former executive, "It's very scary. American companies are really learning to do it smarter and that means with fewer people" (Herbert 1993).

The second item was a story about a garden in my neighborhood, a citizens' garden on land owned by New York City, 9,000 square feet hemmed in by apartment buildings on three sides and the street on the fourth. I went to see it at about 8 A.M. Sunday morning. The garden is truly a beautiful creation, and in the height of summer something to behold. In the center a grape arbor in the shape of a dome forms a cool space with a bench where one can sit. The dome gives the project its name: Development of Opportunities for Meaningful Education. In that small space there were curving paths, islands for growing edible vegetables, other islands for a glorious display of flowers. There was one person there, a woman watering the plants. We spoke at length. When we had warmed up enough, we introduced ourselves. She is Lynn Andrea Law, former lawyer, now a substitute teacher.

People who tend the garden or otherwise support the 15-year-old project include children in special education classes in various schools, neighborhood lawyers, businesspeople, the owners of the adjacent buildings, and teachers. They are unpaid volunteers with varying motives – protect anything green, teach children something they can appreciate and do, show off horticultural skills, neighborliness.

There will be hearings of the city's Planning Commission to determine the fate of the garden. There is a legitimate rival proposal to build 35 units of public housing on the site. There will be a struggle.[2]

This project, although more ambitious than most, is not an isolated case. All over this part of the city people grow flowers in public spaces. Often I meet people lugging pails of water. I spoke at length with one member of a group that had established a lily pond in a disused pool gone dry. They bring the water some distance, using a hose coming from an apartment house with a friendly staff. The pool is already stocked with a few goldfish, and more exciting fauna to come.

I do not tell this story to suggest that neighborhood improvement projects are the ultimate solution. But it is for the most part a pleasant path, and possibly one that will help to build human solidarity and create the necessary vision. Nor do I mean to say that a few dozen little gardens will solve the problem of unoccupation. But with a little imagination and a lot of effort, there are always projects to do; far more projects than people to do them.

When I was a boy I belonged to the Boy Scouts for a little while. In the Scout Handbook there was a page of sayings. I have always remembered the Athenian Boy's Oath: "To leave my city fairer than I found it."

Notes

1. While I corrected the manuscript for the printer there came to hand The Jobless Future: Sci-Tech and the Dogma of Work by Aronson and DiFazio (1994). This book develops a similar line of thought regarding time and vigor available for non-work. In another place Aronowitz (1992) has written that "the national economy simply no longer requires the vast army of labor that seeks wages and salaries."
2. Since this was written, the garden has been destroyed by bulldozing. For about a year there was nothing there but a fenced-in wasteland of weeds and mud. Now a box-like apartment building is going up. It too will be fenced in.

References

Amabile, T. M. (1983). *The social psychology of creativity*. New York: Springer-Verlag.

Aronowitz, S. (1992). *The politics of identity: Class, culture, social movements*. New York: Routledge.

Aronowitz, S., & DiFazio, W. (1994). *The jobless future: Sci-tech and the dogma of work*. Minneapolis: University of Minnesota Press.

Barnett, R. J. (1993). The end of jobs. *Harper's, 287*, 47–52.

Camus, A. (1942/1955). *The myth of Sisyphus*. New York: Vintage.

Colangelo, N., Assouline, S. G., Kerr, B., Huesman, R., & Johnson, D. (1993). *Mechanical inventiveness: A three phase study*. Ciba Foundation symposium on The Origins and Development of High Ability, 24–27 January 1993, London, England.

Coleridge, S. T. (1825). Work without hope. In I. A. Richards (Ed.), *The portable coleridge* (1950). New York: Viking.

Csikszentmihalyi, M. (1990). *Flow: The psychology of optimal experience*. New York: Harper & Row.

Douglass, F. (1845/1960). *Narrative of the life of Frederick Douglass*, B. Quarles (Ed.). Cambridge, MA: Harvard University Press.

Fischer, E. (1963). *The necessity of art: A Marxist approach*. Harmondsworth, UK: Penguin.

Gergen, K. J. (1993). Is there anything beyond the ideological critique of of individualism? In H. J. Stam, L. P. Moss, W. Thorngate, & B. Kaplan (Eds.), *Recent trends in theoretical psychology*, (Vol. 3, pp. 135–142). New York: Springer-Verlag.

Gombrich, E. (1950/1972). *The story of art*, 12th ed. London: Phaidon.

Gould, R. (1939). An experimental analysis of "level of aspiration." *Genetic Psychology Monographs, 21*, 1–116.

Gruber, H. E. (1976). Créativité et fonction constructive de la répétition. *Bulletin de psychologie de la Sorbonne, Numéro spécial pour le 80th anniversaire de Jean Piaget.*

Gruber, H. E. (1989). Creativity and human survival. In D. B. Wallace & H. E. Gruber, *Creative people at work: Twelve cognitive case studies*, pp. 278–287. New York: Oxford University Press.

Gruber, H. E. (1993a). Creativity in the moral domain: Ought implies can implies create. *Creativity Research Journal, 6*, 3–16

Gruber, H. E. (1993b). Toward a theory of social distress: Human destiny or social experiment gone wrong? In H. J. Stam, L. P. Mos, W. Thorngate, & B. Kaplan (Eds.), *Recent Trends in Theoretical Psychology* (Vol. 3, pp. 449–458). New York: Springer-Verlag.

Herbert, B. (1993). Looking for work. *New York Times*, August 8, p. E15.

Karsten, A. (1928). Psychische Sättigung. *Psychologische Forschung, 10*, 142–254 (reported in Lewin 1935).

Kwong, P. (1988). American sweatshops 1980s style: Chinese women garment workers. In G. M. Vroman, D. Burnham, & S. G. Gordon (Eds.), *Genes and gender: V, women at work: Socialization toward inequality*, pp. 81–92. New York: The Gordian Press.

Lewin, K. (1935). *A dynamic theory of personality.* New York: McGraw-Hill.

Lewin, K., Dembo, T., Festinger, L., & Sears, P. S. (1944). Level of Aspiration. In J. McV. Hunt (Ed.), *Personality and the behavior disorders*, pp. 333–378. New York: Ronald Press.

Marx, K. (1846/1939). *The German ideology.* New York: International.

Maslow, A. H. (1954). *Motivation and personality.* New York: Harper.

Orwell, G. (1933/1961). *Down and out in Paris and London.* New York: Harcourt Brace Jovanovich.

Paranjpe, A. C. (1993). The fear of relativism in post-positivist psychology. In H. J. Stam, L. P. Mos, W. Thorngate, & B. Kaplan (Eds.), *Recent trends in theoretical psychology* (Vol. 3, pp. 449–458). New York: Springer-Verlag.

Ryan, T. A. (1947). *Work and effort: The psychology of production.* New York: Ronald Press.

Schor, J. B. (1992). *The overworked American.* New York: Basic Books.

Sinclair, U. (1906/1965). *The jungle.* New York: Airmont.

Stam, H. J., Mos, L. P., Thorngate, W., & Kaplan, B. (Eds.). (1993). *Recent trends in theoretical psychology* (Vol. 3). New York: Springer-Verlag.

Sweetman, D. (1990). *Van Gogh, his life and his art.* New York: Crown.

Wolpert, L., & Richards, A. (1988). *A passion for science.* New York: Oxford University Press.

Index